GOING TO THE COUNTRYSIDE

CHINA UNDERSTANDINGS TODAY

Series Editors: Mary Gallagher and Xiaobing Tang

China Understandings Today is dedicated to the study of contemporary China and seeks to present the latest and most innovative scholarship in social sciences and the humanities to the academic community as well as the general public. The series is sponsored by the Lieberthal-Rogel Center for Chinese Studies at the University of Michigan.

Resisting Spirits: Drama Reform and Cultural Transformation in the People's Republic of China
  Maggie Greene

Going to the Countryside: The Rural in the Modern Chinese Cultural Imagination, 1915–1965
  Yu Zhang

GOING TO THE COUNTRYSIDE

The Rural in the Modern Chinese Cultural Imagination, 1915–1965

Yu Zhang

UNIVERSITY OF MICHIGAN PRESS
Ann Arbor

Copyright © 2020 by Yu Zhang
All rights reserved

For questions or permissions, please contact um.press.perms@umich.edu

Published in the United States of America by the
University of Michigan Press
Manufactured in the United States of America
Printed on acid-free paper
First published February 2020

A CIP catalog record for this book is available from the British Library.

Library of Congress Cataloging-in-Publication Data

Names: Zhang, Yu, 1979– author.
Title: Going to the countryside : the rural in the modern Chinese cultural imagination, 1915–1965 / Yu Zhang.
Description: Ann Arbor : University of Michigan Press, [2020] | Series: China understandings today | Includes bibliographical references and index.
Identifiers: LCCN 2019044418 (print) | LCCN 2019044419 (ebook) | ISBN 9780472074433 (hardcover ; alk. paper) | ISBN 9780472054435 (paper ; alk. paper) | ISBN 9780472126606 (e-book)
Subjects: LCSH: Urban-rural migration—Government policy—China—History—20th century. | China—Intellectual life—History—20th century.
Classification: LCC HB2114.A3 C44   2020 (print) | LCC HB2114.A3 (ebook) | DDC 307.2/60951—dc23
LC record available at https://lccn.loc.gov/2019044418
LC ebook record available at https://lccn.loc.gov/2019044419

Cover illustration: "On the Way to Yan'an," from *Good Companion* [*Liangyou*] 147 (February 1939). Image courtesy of the Shanghai Library.

for Bin Wang

Acknowledgments

The long years of writing this book have provided precious opportunities to experience intellectual excitements, to refresh my understandings of the world, to learn how to deal with difficulties and frustrations in writing and life, and to know many great scholars and friends. I owe a major debt of gratitude first to my teachers at Stanford. My deepest gratitude goes to Ban Wang for his intellectual generosity, patience, and magnanimity. I would also like to thank Russell Berman, Haiyan Lee, and Matthew Sommer for the intellectual stimulation they gave me that helped me to develop my own thinking during and after my graduate school years.

My teachers at the University of California, Santa Barbara—Ronald Egan, Michael Berry, and John Nathan—helped me to adjust with the transition from China to American academia during my first two years in the United States. I was most fortunate to have encountered Ronald Egan, and I feel most grateful for his warm and steadfast encouragement over the years and for his continuous mentorship later, after he started to teach at Stanford. I cherish the many good times with Susan Chan Egan, a dear friend whose wisdom and elegance have enlightened me on many aspects of life.

In the course of revision, I am most grateful to these three scholars and have benefited tremendously from their scholarship and comments: Xiaobing Tang offered most timely advice, which significantly enriched the development of this project; Jacob Eyferth read my dissertation and offered most helpful criticism and excellent suggestions; and Christine Ho has been a great source of constant inspiration to me and I thank her for carefully reading the manuscript and for her feedback and criticism. I would also like to thank the following scholars for their astute comments, rigorous questions, and helpful information on different parts of the book during different periods: Xiang Cai, Cheng Chang, J. P. Daughton, Xinyu Dong, Si-yen Fei, Paola Iovine, Quinn Javers, Rebecca Karl, Charles

Laughlin, Tiffany Lee, Mark Lewis, Yue Meng, Thomas Mullaney, Laikwan Pang, Ka Ming Wu, and Xueping Zhong.

I would also like to thank friends who have encouraged me during a challenging period of life. I feel most fortunate to have a friend like Philip Thai, whose friendship and generous support have sustained me in different stages of my academic life. I have learned so much from his scholarship and professionalism. I would also like to thank Calvin Hui, who opened up a new horizon to me and taught me how to treat the world gently. I am grateful to Helen Shin, who has led me to shape a positive view of life. Sincere gratitude also goes to Jessica Ka Yee Chan, Zhang Dewen, and Zhang Zizi at Virginia and Alexa Alice Joubin, Yu Min Claire Chen, and Liana Chen in Washington, DC. Thanks from the bottom of my heart to my classmates Li He and Ni Xiuping for spending much time accompanying me on field trips in the rural areas of Anhui and Zhejiang.

The book could not have been completed without fellowships and grants from several institutions. During the last two years of graduate school, my work was supported by the Chiang Ching Kuo Foundation Doctoral Fellowship, the Mabelle McLeod Lewis Memorial Fund for Grants in Aid of Scholarly Work, and the Stanford Freeman Spogli Institute China Studies Dissertation Grant. After graduation, a junior scholar grant from the Chiang Ching Kuo Foundation expedited the revision of the book. Thanks to a postdoctoral fellowship from the Society of Fellows in the Humanities at the University of Hong Kong, I was able to devote an entire year to writing and revising. I thank Derek Collins and Giorgio Biancorosso for an intellectually stimulating year at HKU and Angela Ki Che Leung for an enlightening lunch conversation that helped me reconsider some critical issues in my project. I am also grateful to the mutual support of the residential fellows, especially Robert Kramm for his thoughtful feedback on the introduction of the book.

The completion of the book coincided with the start of my career at Hong Kong Polytechnic University. I have the good fortune to work alongside supportive colleagues in the Department of Chinese Culture. In particular, I am full of gratitude to Xiaorong Han, who carefully read parts of the manuscript and offered valuable advice on my professional development. I cannot thank Brian Kai Hin Tsui enough for his generous sharing and help during this career transition. Besides, I would also like to express my gratitude to Dean Hung-lam Chu and other colleagues Lang Chen, Guangming Hu, Hsueh-Yi Lin, Mark Meulenbeld, Lu Pan, and Wicky Tse for their warmth and support that have made the department a great collegial academic environment. A special note of thanks goes to my teachers at Jilin University, Na Liu and Dong Yang. They inspired my early interest in literature and have never failed to be a source of encouragement and emotional support.

An earlier version of chapter 2 was published in *Modern Chinese Literature and Culture* 25, no. 1 (Spring 2013): 47–95, © 2013 by Foreign Language Publications. Chapter 6 is based on my previous essay, which appeared in *Twentieth-Century China* 42, no. 3 (October 2017): 255–73, © 2017 by John Hopkins University Press. I thank these two publishers for their permission to reuse the materials here, and I thank Kirk Denton and Zhao Ma for their excellent editorial comments.

Two anonymous reviewers for the University of Michigan Press have provided detailed feedback and constructive suggestions for further revision. Christopher Dreyer and Kevin Rennells of the University of Michigan Press have been insightful in helping me prepare the book. I gratefully acknowledge their help.

Finally, I wish to thank my parents and parents-in-law for their understanding and support over the years, and to thank the uncle and aunt who made California truly a home to me. Without my husband Bin Wang, I might never have been able to travel this far and pursue this career. He is my greatest good fortune, and I dedicate this book to him for twenty years of love and companionship and for the memories of growing up together as kindred spirits. The arrival of our son, Ankai, has brought so much joy to my heart and made me understand that the most enjoyable thing in the world is to see him growing up happily. Both of you are the sunshine of my life.

Contents

Introduction   1

Part I. The Rural as a Reflexive Vision of Chinese Enlightenment

ONE. How Far Are We Away from Home? Writings on Rural Hometowns and Homecomings in the Early Decades of the Twentieth Century   17

TWO. Creating the Rural Vernacular: Visual Imagination and Theatrical Performance in the Rural Reconstruction Movement in Ding County in the 1920s and 1930s   44

Part II. The Rural as a Constructive Vision of Chinese Revolution

THREE. Journeys to the Revolutionary Site: The Construct of Red China, Time Consciousness, and Patience, 1936–45   79

FOUR. Legitimizing Romance, Sentimentalizing the Law, and Romanticizing Labor: Valorizing Love-Law-Labor Conjunction in the Yan'an Revolutionary Culture of the 1940s   110

Part III. The Rural as an Industrial Vision of Chinese Socialism

FIVE. Creating a Rural Industrial Aesthetics: Socialist Homecoming and the Rural Modernization Project in Representational Forms in the 1950s and Early 1960s   147

SIX. Socialist Builders on the Rails and Road: Railway Travel, Industrialization, and Social Engineering in Chinese Socialist Films, 1949–65   182

Conclusion   208

Notes   213

Bibliography   259

Index   281

Digital materials related to this title can be found on the Fulcrum platform via the following citable URL: https://doi.org/10.3998/mpub.10142190

Introduction

This book focuses on the cultural practices and representations of "going to the countryside" as a distinctively modern experience in China between 1915 and 1965. This spatial move refers to intellectuals, reformers, revolutionaries, leftist journalists, and idealistic youth crossing the increasing gap between the city and the countryside. Far from simply a geographical move, this spatial crossing was intertwined with the larger discourses of enlightenment, revolution, and socialist industrialization, and is therefore crucial for understanding the relationship between the rural and the Chinese experience of modernity. "Going to the countryside" entailed new ways of looking at the world and ordinary people, brought about new experiences of space and time, initiated new means of human communication and interaction, generated new forms of cultural production, and ultimately created a new aesthetic, social, and political landscape. This spatial crossing reveals a fundamental epistemic shift resulting from the (re)discovery of the countryside in modern China.

In the past two decades, the field of modern Chinese literary and cultural studies has been dominated by studies of urban culture. This body of scholarship is part of the global trend of identifying modernity with urban development and assuming that modern life is essentially city life. Such studies discuss the role of cultural productions in shaping modern urban sensibilities, creating various forms of urban aesthetics, and participating in the urbanization process.[1] The "urban turn" in modern Chinese literary and cultural studies aimed to explore the diversities and complexities of the urban life to present Chinese urban modernity that has departed from "rural preoccupation," a scholarly trend that dominated the field of modern Chinese studies in the West before the 1980s.[2] "Rural preoccupation" refers to an image of China that has always been bound up with rural villages.[3] This book brings the rural back to the central concern of Chinese cultural studies but does not mean to reclaim that "rural preoccupation." Moreover, this book does not mean to challenge the historical symbiosis of the urban and the modern, or to propose a distinctive "rural modernity" among the "alternative modernities" in the words of Dilip Parameshwar Gaonkar.[4] The existing monographic scholarship on rural China is mainly concentrated in the fields of anthropology, history, and sociology that regard the countryside as a microcosm to observe and understand China's modern transformations in local societies. However, fantasies, aesthetics, representations, and imagination regarding the countryside as a constitutive part in the making of modern Chinese culture are largely missing from the present scholarly scene.[5]

The city and the country, as Raymond Williams suggests, are "changing historical realities, both in themselves and in their interrelations."[6] As two inseparable entities, the city and the country often coexist as various forms of juxtapositions throughout human history, and thus their connectivity is vital to our understanding of either side. Michel Foucault famously speaks of modern times as "the epoch of space," which he interprets as "the epoch of juxtaposition, the epoch of the near and far, of the side-by-side, of the dispersed." Human beings are living in the form of juxtaposition "when [their] experience of the world is less that of a long life developing through time than that of a network that connects points and intersects with its own skein."[7] Foucault therefore draws our attention to the importance of seeing the relations among sites; he also points out that renewed meanings are generated through the juxtaposition of different spaces because modernity is both a historical and a geographical-spatial project. However, to a large extent, these two types of important geographical entities—the city and the countryside—have remained as disparate scholarly subjects of inquiry in the current state of China studies. This book focuses on the idea of "crossing" the gap that separates the city from the countryside as a point of departure to explore various ways of establishing the linkage, interaction, and relationship of these two spaces. With the coming of modernity, for the first time in Chinese history both urban and rural people "crossed" the boundary, attempting to tackle the growing cultural, economic, political, and social divide and various types of shocks, which accordingly brought about strikingly new aesthetic and sensual experiences and new conceptual transformations. Through juxtaposing urban and rural spaces and emphasizing the movement from the city to the countryside, this study explores the new meanings of this spatial transition in the modern context.

As "an impressionable global newborn" in the twentieth century, the village stood as a site of plasticity and malleability to be socially engineered.[8] The rise of the nation-state was accompanied by the gradual attenuation of the individual's affective ties with his or her kinship world and local roots. The first half of twentieth-century Chinese history witnessed the invention of the peasantry as a collective national subject and as malleable historical figures subject to transformations and interpretations in relation to nationalist movements.[9] Modern Chinese intellectuals' growing attention to peasants led to their creation of a variety of discourses on the peasants.[10] Peasants were often described as figures of feudal backwardness that contrasted with Enlightenment discourse; as characters of innocence and ignorance in contrast to industrial, urban discourse; or as a unified collective revolutionary force pushing history forward. Simultaneously, rural space—once the locus of the gentry-scholar's self-representation and identity construction in imperial China—became a site that was empirically and representationally synonymous with the habitat and collective identity of the peasantry. The modernization process has further homogenized the villages into a space merely for agricultural production, and has turned villagers into peasants by erasing their other identities.[11] The countryside in this book refers to a much broader space that stages various historical actors far beyond the lifeworld of peasantry. The rediscovery of the rural in the modern age has generated new types of cultural productions and informed alternative cultural imaginations.[12]

Going to the Countryside explores the capacities of the category of the rural to (re)conceptualize the Chinese modern experience and demonstrates how these cultural productions and representations of the countryside in modern China have established a far richer semantic field of the rural. It demonstrates the ways the rural was re-experienced and reconceptualized in relation to China's modern imagination and cultural practice. Chinese modernity has been characterized by a dual process that created problems from the vast gap between the city and the countryside but simultaneously initiated constant efforts to cope with the gap personally, collectively, and institutionally. The process of "crossing" two distinct geographical spaces was often presented as continuous exploration of new modes of connectivity between these two imagined geographical entities. This book argues that this new body of cultural productions did not merely turn the rural into a constantly changing representational space; most importantly, the rural has been constructed as a distinct modern experiential and aesthetic realm characterized by revolutionary changes in human conceptions and sentiments, which were generated through the act of "crossing" these two spaces. The rural has been both a dense palimpsest on which various historical actors wrote and rewrote their agendas and an epistemological ground contesting the conceptions of enlightenment, revolution, and industrialization. The category of the rural opens up new possibilities to imagine alternative human subjectivities and experience. In this way, *Going to the Countryside* describes how various historical actors have reflected on the modern transformations outside the context of the city, how they attempted to remake rural culture, and simultaneously how their conceptions about the rural contributed to a renewed notion of national culture and identity. It also examines how the socialist state constructed the rural as a locus that staged new forms of experience and sensibilities in public discourses and propaganda culture to implement its social-engineering projects.

"Going to the Countryside" as Modern Experience in China

The sinologist F. W. Mote's oft-cited phrase "the urban-rural continuum" has been understood "as physical and as organizational realities, and as an aspect of Chinese psychology" that referred to the relatively smooth and free two-way geographical crossing between the city and the countryside without experiencing any forms of shock.[13] Though Mote's proposition that the rural components defined Chinese civilization has been controversial among historians, his formulation of a "continuum" is premised on the assumption of China as "an open society" and emphasizes the importance of the possibility of such social mobility as "the psychological fact" that could inspire ordinary people to pursue a better life.[14] Crucial to the urban-rural continuum was the mediating role played by the Chinese gentry-scholars in effecting a balance between ruler and peasantry, between the state and local society.[15] Throughout imperial Chinese history, the representations of the rural space and the act of going to the countryside were often closely associated with the literati's conscious construct of self-identity and their changing self-perceptions in relation to the state and the society. "Going to the countryside," often described as "returning to the gardens and fields" (*guitian*), was a figurative expression of one's resignation or retirement from an official post and return to a rural home, often indicating that the literati men pursued a reclusive life in the countryside.

The poetry of Six Dynasties recluse-poet Tao Yuanming (also known as Tao Qian, 365?–427) established a moral and emotional foundation for rural space in imperial China. However, scholars have discerned that Tao's poetic construct of "gardens and fields" (*tianyuan*) was often created through a selection of images and symbols and therefore worked as the literati's self-representation, whereas the farmers only functioned as part of the landscape in the farmstead poetry.[16] While the ideal of returning to the "gardens and fields" was held in high esteem throughout Chinese history, satirical accounts and social critiques of the ideal of "gardens and fields" as acts of hypocrisy and pretension were also simultaneously present in the premodern Chinese literature.[17] "Going to the countryside" in imperial China was also one of the duties of the literati-officials, such as "urging the farmers" (*quannong*) in the springtime as a highly political and ritualized activity for the empire-building project.[18] The rise of absentee landlordism in the late imperial period weakened the gentry's ties with the rural community; however, the gentry families still maintained agrarian connections through landholding in order to return to the countryside during a hard time and sustain the long-term prosperity of their clans.[19]

However, this centuries-old urban-rural continuum as "a symbiotic and sociable relationship" in China was suddenly disrupted in the late nineteenth century,[20] due to the worldwide capitalist and imperialist expansion, the abolition of the civil service examination in 1905, the collapse of the imperial political system in 1911, and the rise of Western-style higher-education institutions as well as rapid modern industrialization and technological development in the cities. Liang Shuming (1893–1988) regarded modern Chinese history as "a history of the disruption of the countryside" (*xiangcun pohuai shi*).[21] Liang's observation shifted attention from city-centered modernization and development to its severe social consequences in the countryside. The city and the countryside were accordingly produced and shaped as new spaces, each acquiring a distinct character.[22] Crossing the dividing line often involved experiencing different value systems, lifestyles, living conditions, and temporalities, and an artificially created hierarchy of the industrial, progressive center over the agrarian, underdeveloped periphery. The rural-urban distinctions started to constitute the individual's identity in the early 1900s, when villages were associated with the notion of backwardness.[23]

In early-twentieth-century China, "going to the countryside" was part of the global trend of "going to the people" movements that mainly responded to intense urban-based industrialization as well as to the urgency of cultivating a national consciousness in the nineteenth century.²⁴ Among various trends, the Russian *narodnik* (populist) movement in 1874–75 and in 1876–78 and the Japanese utopian New Village Movement (Atarashikimura), founded by Saneatsu Mushanokōji in 1918, were influential forces that shaped the thinking of the Chinese intelligentsia. The spatial move from the cities to the countryside stood out as a distinctly modern experience, and simultaneously gained new meanings. The Russian *narodnik* movement was driven by a search for an understanding of village society and peasantry in the interest of developing a national identity and shaping its citizenry. This movement was characterized as having proximity to the people, actively and deeply penetrating into village society in an effort to create a bridge between educated society and the *narod* (people). The central aspect of *narodnik* activities was "more than simple infatuation; they insisted on taking part in a life-and-blood experience among the people as essential to true knowledge and true communion."²⁵ The Japanese New Village Movement aimed to build a utopian-socialist community where people from a variety of backgrounds could live together in an egalitarian, nurturing environment based on mutual aid and shared manual labor. This movement also favored the peaceful resolution of conflicts rather than revolution.²⁶ The movement's aesthetic infatuation with anarchism made it appear impractical and thus less appealing to the younger generation.²⁷ Thus, "going to the countryside" movements in China were local instances of global phenomena: first-generation Chinese thinkers and practitioners who were interested in initiating movements and social trends of returning to the countryside emphasized national consciousness and acknowledged the value of manual labor through experiencing country life, reconnecting with rural people, and taking the village as a source of knowledge. Nonetheless, "going to the countryside" in modern China was far from an aesthetic retreat to nature; it was active social and political engagement by men of action rather than men of contemplation.

Published in *Ch'en pao* in February 1919, the essay "Youth and the Village" by Communist thinker Li Dazhao (1889–1927) was one of the earliest writings about going to the countryside in modern China. This essay was much influenced by both the Russian *narodniks* and the Japanese New Village Movement.²⁸ Li related "going to the countryside" (*dao minjian qu*) to the importance of creating an advanced, progressive "dynamic civilization" as opposed to the ancient, "static civilization." He called for young people to realize their dreams in rural areas to get the "stagnant race" of the Chinese on the move, and advocated human actions concerned with the vitality of life and the experience of mobility.²⁹ Li's essay reiterates the Russian radical populists' view, "proximity to the people," to encourage urban youth to undertake a life-and-blood experience among the people to gain knowledge and build connections with the rural masses. He emphasized the importance of empathy from urban youths to understand the peasants' lack of freedom, suffering, ignorance, and disadvantages, and urged them to meet the peasants as equals to forge ties of communion.³⁰

Zhou Zuoren (1885–1967) was widely known for his visit to the New Village in Japan in 1919. In his essay "The Spirit of the New Village" (*xincun de jingshen*), Zhou considered the New Village as symbolizing the creation of a life of dignity; and he explained that one must first fulfill the obligation of labor to gain the necessities for a healthy life. He emphasized the equal importance and the balance of manual labor and mental labor in creating a peaceful and harmonious society; the laborers and intellectual class could complement each other's lives and erase each other's anxieties. Though realizing the danger of completely prioritizing manual labor over mental labor, as Leo Tolstoy (1828–1910) did, Zhou valorized manual labor as an essential part of human life and as a mode that facilitates human communication and contributes to leveling social hierarchy. He contended that manual labor should be incorporated into the everyday life of the intellectual class. The ideas in both Li Dazhao's and Zhou Zuoren's writings were adapted into or responded to in the subsequent rise of various modes of going to the countryside.

"Going to the countryside" illustrates what John Fitzgerald refers to as "the politics of awakening," a mission undertaken by both reformers and revolutionaries in their travel to a distant land that often connected the awakening of the self, the people, the land, and ultimately China as a whole.³¹ As reformers, revolutionaries, and social science practitioners set off on expeditions to explore China's hinterland, the various trends of "going to the countryside" coincided with dramatic changes in the orientation of the Republican-era scholarly research methods, from bibliocentric studies to field research. The method is described by Thomas Mullaney as "the commitment to 'direct observation'—that is, the commitment to scholarship built upon a foundation of lengthy, unmediated, and sometimes grueling forays into the lived realities of everyday people."³² In the first half of the twentieth century, "going to the countryside" was closely bound up with the rise of political and social movements such as rural reconstruction and peasant revolution; the practice of new disciplines such as folklore studies, sociology, and geology; and the emergence of new genres such as native-soil fiction, social surveys, and reportage literature.

Existing scholarship has dealt with the epistemic shift in the emergence of new disciplines and genres that were associated with the act of going to the countryside. A shared concern is that the countryside has been regarded as a vast resource, and in public discourses, *minjian* (among the people) has often been metaphorically described as a cultural resource to be "mined" (*wajue*): folklorists collected ballads, songs, and tales, and socialist scientists and amateur social-survey writers gathered empirical facts, data, and information about local customs and history.[33] Leftist journalists' writings reconstructed the landscape of the Chinese wartime countryside as a battlefield that communicated new values through their "aesthetic experience."[34] Geologists established a new relationship with the vast remote land and connected patriotism and scientific investigation, and they bonded with fellow practitioners through the shared experience of gaining firsthand knowledge. The countryside was not only a locality with distinctive physiographic features but also an integrated part of the earth.[35] Painters in the socialist period went to the countryside and immersed themselves in country life as part of the institutionalized training and practice that combined physical labor and creative work.[36]

Going to the Countryside constructs a long historical arc of "going to the countryside" across the 1949 divide, but it does not aim to offer a comprehensive or encyclopedic history of going to the countryside in modern China.[37] Rather, this book investigates particularly telling cases of "going to the countryside" to illustrate how they intersected with the larger historical and social changes. *Going to the Countryside* starts with 1915, the founding year of the influential journal *New Youth* (*Xin Qingnian*), which symbolized the start of the May Fourth New Culture Movement and the Chinese enlightenment. One of the social consequences of May Fourth Enlightenment was a deepening of the cultural divide between the new urban-based intelligentsia and the folks in China's vast rural hinterland. The social elites' denigration of peasants was certainly not rare in imperial China, but what distinguishes the May Fourth discourse was the metonymic connection between the backwardness of the peasants and the backwardness of China as a nation. This book begins with the late 1910s and 1920s young generation from local gentry families, who went to the city to become aspiring nationals and cosmopolitans but still needed to reconnect with their rural home. It ends with the 1950s and 1960s, when the urban young generation were rallied by the social-engineering program to go to the countryside and frontier regions with a commitment to develop attachments to localities. The spatial crossing of "going to the countryside" was imbued with different meanings at different times and by different historical actors. This book demonstrates that "going to the countryside" has been an unbroken tradition and a continuous and historically contingent practice. Therefore, it contributes as a "prehistory" to the largest social-engineering program of the "up to the mountains, down to the villages" movement that culminated during the Cultural Revolution (1966–1976), when this spatial move was completely transformed from an individually and collectively voluntary spatial crossing to an enforced and also exhorted resettlement scheme.[38]

Approaching the Rural

In this book, the rural is not a uniform space. Rather, it serves as a shorthand expression for the relationships and life practices associated with underdeveloped areas,[39] such as villages, rural towns such as Yan'an, and the frontier regions. I approach the rural not merely as a geographic site, but also as an imaginary space, a discursive construct, a site of social engineering and cultural creation, a space for reworking local and international influences, and most importantly, as a representational space open to interdisciplinary inquiry across the fields of literature, film, history, and cultural studies. Sometimes "the city" and "the country" are geographically specified; at other times, they coexist and are juxtaposed as a pair of comparable (or contrasting) entities.

In English, the meaning of "rural" encompasses the locality and the life of peasants and country folk, including their occupations and culture. The rural is characteristic of country life as opposed to towns or cities.[40] In Chinese, the rural is associated with words such as *xiangtu* (native soil), *xiangcun* or *nongcun* (village), *nongren* (farmer), and *nongmin* (peasant). "*Xiangtu zhongguo*" (earthbound China) had been a globally circulated public discourse and image, which was coauthored and constructed by both the bilingual Chinese intelligentsia and Western intellectuals starting in the late nineteenth century; it was later reinforced in socialist China.[41] The image and discourse of rural China manifests the constant negotiation of the relationship between locality and universality in modern China. The local particularities have often been removed in representations, and the localities take on universal features that symbolize the nation.[42] For example, starting from the early twentieth century, the folklore movement drew from variegated local cultures to produce an organic, collective body of folk literature.[43] The images, signs, symbols, and sentiments about Chinese peasant life and the countryside were circulated in a global network of significance as discourses that often erased local particularities.[44]

Going to the Countryside transcends the conventional generic boundaries and deals with the changing imaginaries of the rural. It ranges from social-survey essay to modern fiction and reportage literature, from illustrations to theatrical performance and feature films, from official news essays to rural plays and storytelling, all of which have helped construct the rural space and informed the discourse of the countryside in modern China. Despite their differences and diversity, all these forms and media, with their public dimensions, have helped construct the rural as a new, distinct realm where people gained new conceptions and experiences. Simultaneously, new readers and audiences emerged as new modern subjects who developed interest in the countryside and rural life. It is true that literary, artistic, and cinematic representations are often at odds with the empirical reality portrayed by historians, anthropologists, and sociologists, but critics and scholars have noted the blurring of representation and reality as characteristic of the age of modernity, and proposed that history is, in fact, a history of representation because what constitutes culture is the production, circulation, and interpretation of representations.[45] My approach stresses the ways cultural productions have helped shape new human subjectivities and created affective and political communities through influencing people's understanding of the world. These cultural productions forged what we might call a "cultural imaginary"—a repository of images, ideas, and stories from which to construct new and modern visions and interpretations of the world.[46] Cross-generic readings form various juxtapositions through which canonical and noncanonical materials both defamiliarize and illuminate each other in a way that reveals new connections and significance.

This book covers the individual mode of sentimental homecoming, the reform mode of rural reconstruction, the revolutionary mode of journeys to the Yan'an Communist base, as well as the social-engineering, industrial mode of going to the countryside and frontier. The six chapters can be classified into two strands of "going to the countryside": returning to one's rural home with preexisting roots and reuniting with family members, former friends, and community elders; and going to the countryside as an unfamiliar and largely undeveloped or unexploited place to meet strangers, which eventually led to the formation of a new community built on affective relations and political commitments with a shared goal of nation- or state-building. The first two chapters discuss how "going to the countryside" in the forms of social investigation, homecoming, or rural reconstruction movements transformed the rural into a site to consider the encounter between the grand discourses of enlightenment and the concrete situations of the localities. **Chapter 1** examines a series of social-survey essays published in *New Youth* in the late 1910s and the representative texts of homecoming fiction written by new fiction writers in the early 1920s. The rural hometown became a representational and experiential space for these authors to acknowledge the coexistence of different values, lifestyles, and ways of human communication rather than diachronically opposing them as enlightened and benighted, progressive and backward. With its urban and cosmopolitan orientation, the emergent iconoclastic culture and disintegration of Confucian essentialism created great uncertainty about the present and the future alike, resulting in profound moral disorder, confusion, chaos, and social anarchy. These social-survey essays and this sentimental fiction endowed homecoming with a new meaning as a journey to cope with the "chaos" of the Republican period, and the rural simultaneously served as a self-reflexive (not merely "the other") space for enterprises of the May Fourth enlightenment. **Chapter 2** examines how the rural reconstruction movement facilitated by James Yen (1893–1990) and Xiong Foxi (1900–1965) in Ding County created a "rural vernacular" as a critical response to the vernacular movement of the May Fourth enlightenment. The "rural vernacular" took on popular cultural forms and aimed to convey the modern quotidian experience to the rural masses. Three initially urban-based, imported Western media—lantern slides, illustrated literacy primers for the peasants, and spoken drama—constituted a form of rural vernacular as a repository of images, ideas, and stories for the local peasants. These media were also employed as major pedagogical tools and transformative vehicles in the Ding County experiment to remake the village public into what I call "a space of attraction and empathy" that foregrounded a modern rural life and a rural community of citizens.

The Chinese revolution's pivotal spatial change from urban centers to rural areas in the late 1920s built the Maoist "utopic republic" in the revolutionary base of Yan'an (1936–47).[47] The mid-1930s was characterized by a dramatic discursive transition of the countryside from a site of "shame and backwardness" to a site of anticipation, strength, and resources.[48]

With its rich cultural repertoire providing a constructive vision of the Chinese revolution, northwest inland China gained national prominence and underwent a process of (re)signification and transformation. The following two chapters focus on how the intersection of the rural and the revolutionary constituted an aesthetic-political regime created in journalistic and literary representations of the journeys to the revolutionary base and the Maoist policy of going to the countryside.

Going to an inhospitable and poverty-stricken backwater town like Yan'an not only referred to embracing a sublime and heroic enterprise, it also meant experiencing revolution in its entirety by tolerating all its roughness and vulgarity. **Chapter 3** focuses on the subject about the aspiring youth's voluntary departure from urban centers for the inland town of Yan'an in the 1930s and early 1940s. By juxtaposing different genres and analyzing various representations of "going to Red China," this chapter highlights the intertwining of passion and patience in the ways urban revolutionaries and writers dealt with the paradoxical combination of radical politics and material impoverishment and of urban sensibilities and rural crudeness in the Yan'an period. **Chapter 4** turns to the way of "going to the countryside" dictated by the party as a deeper engagement with the people that emerged after Mao Zedong's (1893–1976) influential talks at the Yan'an Forum on Literature and Art in 1942. This chapter focuses on the stories adapted from real-life occurrences and engages with various revolutionary literary and art forms: short fiction, news essays, woodcut prints, rural plays, and oral storytelling. In the context of Yan'an, "going to the countryside" entailed crossing generic boundaries via a diverse set of media and forms, which in fact symbolized a unique way to communicate and transmit information and to create moral prescriptions based on the conjunction of law, love, and labor as a new mode of Communist governance. The new rural lifeworld was constructed as an aesthetic-political realm in which law, love, and labor were endowed with new meanings in their interrelations. This chapter also shows how revolutionary literature eventually transformed the recent, the ephemeral, and the obsolescent into the legendary, the memorable, and the everlasting.

Prior to 1949, "going to the countryside" often symbolized the way urban-bred elites were extending an "invitation card" to the rural masses, to invite them into the history, the nation, and the revolution.[49] During the early years of the People's Republic of China, however, journalistic, visual, and cinematic representations of this spatial crossing worked as an "invitation card" with alluring rural images to inspire urban-educated youth to go to the remote countryside and frontier areas. From a global perspective, in the 1950s and 1960s, representations of villages in fact mattered more than the empirical reality.[50] The city/country relationship in socialist China is characterized by the paradox of discursive equality and actual inequality as well as the discursive boundlessness of the countryside and the actual institutionalized hard boundary of the urban/rural divide. The standard conception of the rural often indicates that technology is absent. Yet the ambition to transform wastelands into industrialized zones characterized the Chinese collective mentality of the socialist period. The last two chapters discuss important elements of industrialization in the rural landscape. Focusing on the juxtaposition of "the rural" and "the industrial," these chapters address the representational and aesthetic images of the industrialized countryside that constituted the poetics of socialist industry and marked the uniqueness of China's national identity circulated at home and abroad during the Cold War period. "Going to the countryside" as a social-engineering project has been closely bound up with the development of industrial projects and modern transportation systems that enabled a dramatic reterritorialization of China to incorporate remote, isolated areas into its state space. The last two chapters examine how propaganda films sought to mobilize the state-initiated social-engineering program of "going to the countryside and frontiers" to overcome the urban-rural cleavage and articulated the socialist ideal of industrializing the countryside.

Chapter 5 focuses on the intersection of homecoming and the modern, state-led projects of industrializing the countryside in visual images and cinematic representation of the 1950s and early 1960s. This chapter showcases how such projects foregrounded the mass-based collective creativity that bridged the gap between mental labor and manual labor. What characterized socialist industrialization in its representational forms is the uncanny blending of play and labor, the artisanal and the industrial, and the handcrafted and the machine-made. Turning collective labor in the process of industrializing the countryside into a playful and artisanal experience in the socialist imagination reveals a fusion of the creativity and omnipotence of human labor and the affective components of the rural community. **Chapter 6** focuses on the representations of the idealistic youth in cities (particularly in Shanghai), who were transported by railway journey to participate in socialist industrialization in a series of 1950s and 1960s popular films. This chapter presents the frontier area as a new form of the rural defined by its remoteness and emptiness: a kind of remoteness that could be rapidly overcome through modern high-speed transportation, and a form of emptiness that emerged as the image of the construction site opened itself up as "a blank slate" to be painted with the Maoist "most beautiful words and most beautiful pictures,"[51] which in this context refers to creating the socialist industrial sublime on the empty wasteland in the frontier. The rural was constructed as a new experiential realm in which camaraderie, professional care, domestic warmth, and communitarian intimacy were mobilized into productive energy for the building of socialism. The story about China emerging as an industrializing country in the second half of the twentieth century has its global significance. Altogether, these two chapters highlight the formation of what I term the "rural industrial culture" that defines the identity of socialist China. In the broadly circulated images and cinematic representations, human emotional investment, thrilling creativity, artisanal labor, and utopian imaginings were incorporated into the construct of the socialist rural industrial culture and put a deep handprint onto the industrial enterprise.

Today's world is confronted with urgent issues such as urban overpopulation, global sustainability, and regional inequality as well as the alarming and uncertain future of agrarian societies.[52] Nonetheless, policymakers, writers, artists, and other social practitioners continued to initiate another round of "going to the countryside" often as a way to resist the developmentalism and urbanization and to explore possibilities of reconnecting with the rural areas, a spatial crossing that was imbued with similar and new significances, challenges, and dilemmas.

PART I

The Rural as a Reflexive Vision
of Chinese Enlightenment

CHAPTER 1

How Far Are We Away from Home?
Writings on Rural Hometowns and Homecomings in the Early Decades of the Twentieth Century

In the first decades of the twentieth century, more and more young people, many of whom were descendants of local gentry, left their rural homes to study in Western-style colleges and universities located in Beijing, Shanghai, and provincial capitals, eventually settling in urban centers.[1] Far from simply a physical or geographical move, "going to the city" was often discursively described as a journey to a land of hope and light motivated by these individuals' strong desire to become aspiring nationals and cosmopolitans.[2] This spatial crossing also simultaneously freed them from traditional familial obligations, allowing them to fully develop their potential, to experience the excitement of modern urban life and new professions, and to encounter like-minded friends, colleagues, romantic lovers, and self-chosen marriage partners. The rise of the nation-state as a new consciousness in modern China, with its goal to build a community of citizens, often resulted in the gradual attenuation of the individual's sentimental ties with his or her kinship and local roots. This critical spatial and cultural reorientation widened a profound social, political, and cultural gulf between the city and the countryside.[3] The social trend of "going to the cities" was simultaneously accompanied by the emergence of writings focusing on the rural hometown—social-survey essays and homecoming fiction from the late 1910s and early 1920s.

New Youth, an influential magazine widely read by liberal intellectuals and students in the late 1910s and early 1920s, initiated two often intertwined intellectual trends: cultural iconoclasm and social investigation. *New Youth* attacked Confucianism and its associated concepts, consequently affirming the individual's self-emancipation from patriarchal authority and supporting people's autonomy to choose their own marriage partners. *New Youth* also expressed an urgency about understanding China and its people, the majority of whom were represented as living in the countryside. This trend was accompanied by the emergence of a folklore movement and native-soil literature in the late 1910s. Intellectuals and writers turned their scholarly attention to China's rich varieties of local culture and the common people.[4] The call for literary revolution went hand in hand with the call for social investigation in rural China in *New Youth*. The linkage between these two seemingly distinct genres coincided with the similar trend in turn-of-the-century Europe, when sociology, like fiction, was also regarded as a form of representation that provided a view of social reality.[5] In the context of China, it is significant to rethink why social-survey essays and homecoming fiction as particular cultural practices both focused attention on the local experience in an age of cultural iconoclasm. Both of them claimed to take on an objective attitude toward the reality, but simultaneously blurred the line between objective rationality and emotional sensibilities.[6]

These urban writers of social surveys and homecoming fiction developed a distinct local consciousness, one in which the hometown was a living reality with a persistent past yet still contemporaneous with urban life. What existed in the hometown—the living family members and customs—still dominated the urban-sojourning young generation's minds. First-generation Chinese modern intellectuals and young students' rural experiences mainly originated in their hometowns in various localities across China. During the first decades of the twentieth century, the hometown often became an important representational and experiential space that brought forth a call for a deeper understanding of the society and the people. It also functioned as a space for intellectuals to critique the national character and to stage sentimental homecomings that formed the moral vision of the modern self. The hometown was a site that provided a source of raw materials for interdisciplinary productions, an enduring subject to be investigated, as well as a contested field for competing views and representations.[7] Then, what was the significance of taking a retrospective look at the rural, the hometown, and the local in the iconoclastic age?

During the May Fourth period, both conservatives and radicals found that the emergent iconoclastic culture and disintegration of Confucian essentialism created great uncertainty about the future and resulted in profound moral disorder, confusion, chaos, and social anarchy.[8] As far as ethics is concerned, the early years of the Republican period could be well characterized as an age of "chaos" resulting from the breakdown of the Confucian system.⁹ Mao Dun later reflected on this situation:

> The antitraditionalist feature in the early stage of May Fourth was very clear, but what kind of new culture should we build after opposing the old one? There was no definite answer to this question at the time. Some people attempted to answer the question, but no one's proposal could gain unanimous agreement and support. At the time, all the antitraditionalists were also not of the same social status; therefore, when it came to the question "What will the future look like?", people could not reach a consensus.¹⁰

The social and moral anarchy described by Mao Dun suggests that we should reconsider the significance of the social-survey essays and homecoming fiction as particular cultural practices in the iconoclastic period of the late 1910s and early 1920s. The connotations of individualism in the Chinese social context were full of confusion and contradictions from the outset, and Lydia Liu also reminds us that "those who lived through the period have told vastly different stories about the meaning of individualism to themselves and to one another."¹¹ This confusion and chaos were certainly not a particularly modern Chinese phenomenon. In *After Virtue: A Study in Moral Theory*, Alasdair MacIntyre presents his overarching concern with the similar modern predicament in the West: the age of modernity is characterized by pluralism, disparity, fragmentation, incoherence, contestation, and uncertainty as well as the disorder of contemporary moral thought. He points out that "morality is always to some degree tied to the socially local and particular and that the aspirations of the morality of modernity to a universality freed from all particularity is an illusion; and secondly there is no way to possess the virtues except as part of the tradition in which we inherit them and our understanding of them from a series of predecessors in which series heroic societies hold first place."¹² In light of this, this chapter examines the writings on the hometown from the perspective of "the socially local and the particular," the concrete circumstances and set of interconnected human relationships within which an individual performs his/her social role and takes the actions that are most appropriate and comprehensible.

The existing scholarship often discusses the Enlightenment discourse regarding the countryside from two perspectives: the nostalgia approach and the victimhood approach. Modern native-soil fiction writers living in the cities reconstructed their hometowns in writings with bittersweet memories of the past and mixed feelings toward the present. They often wrote about a village China of old customs, uncanny tales, and bizarre local practices that they knew from their childhood experience, and they constructed what David Der-wei Wang terms "imaginary nostalgia" toward the Chinese countryside. Wang describes the paradoxical position of modern authors who have deep-rooted concerns about their hometowns but are simultaneously uprooted from the rural region and so cannot know its actual reality. What obsessed these writers was a romanticized object of nostalgia or a fetishized view of what has disappeared.[13] Wang's well-known phrase "imaginary nostalgia" aptly captures a modern symptom, or a modern structure of feeling, that blends estrangement, melancholy, and a sense of rootlessness as well as nostalgia for the irretrievable past.

The other approach, victimhood, emphasizes the invention of rural China as the representational space of the old society; the peasantry as a culturally alien other and the passive, ignorant victims of oppression; and local customs as ugly, superstitious, and fundamentally useless.[14] Such a conception was often related to the self-empowerment of the political and cultural elites who assumed a superior, privileged position to enlighten the masses.[15] Therefore, the duality of the national versus the local was often perceived as a temporal difference and corresponded to the dichotomies of the present and the past, modernity and tradition, and progress versus stagnation.[16] This chapter calls attention to an alternative dimension and argues that the rural simultaneously served as a self-reflexive (not merely "the other") space to ruminate on the Enlightenment agenda during the May Fourth period. Homecoming gained a new meaning as a journey to cope with the "chaos" of the Republican period through observing "the socially local and the particular."

I. Writing Rural Home as Social Investigation

New Youth covers a diversity of writings, such as political essays, translations, poetry, fiction, and social-survey essays, serving as a forum for cross-genre conversations. The editors started a "social investigation" (*shehui diaocha*) column in March 1917 (vol. 4, issue 3) in the spirit of "knowing and understanding the other people." The column's introductory remarks, composed by a pioneer in Chinese sociology, Tao Lugong (aka

Tao Menghe, 1887–1960), began by declaring Tao's ambition to thoroughly investigate all aspects of rural society, including family life, rituals, and institutions.[17] With a rather eclectic view, Tao aimed to explore both the positives and negatives of Chinese society and accordingly look for methods of reform, to retain the good or remove the bad. Tao traced his change from writing a book about the whole of China's social scene to a realization that China was constituted of diverse localities, each of which had its own uniqueness and particularities. Still, he emphasized the importance of individuals looking beyond their own locality with an awareness that the places they lived were merely part of a much larger whole; he wanted to inform Chinese readers about the necessity of understanding other areas that they might have never visited. Tao believed that such a body of knowledge would help lower the barriers preventing mutual understanding to help urban readers to comprehend China as a whole. Because the majority of the Chinese people lived in rural areas and it was more urgent to deal with their problems rather than urban problems, he proposed that social investigation should start in the countryside. To Tao, investigating and understanding rural issues had to go beyond merely imposing urban assumptions on rural reality. Rather than treating rural society as a monolithic and homogeneous whole, Tao suggested that investigating local community required a strong value judgment to evaluate what would provide opportunities for the people to develop their potential, since the ultimate goal of the social investigation is to cure society of its ills.

Tao was deeply skeptical of traditional historiography, which in his view primarily celebrated emperors and literati-officials' benevolent governance in imperial China, whereas commoners' lives were described only in short, formulaic phrases. Tao was also disappointed in the local gazetteers (*fangzhi*), most of which also used formulaic phrases or only briefly mentioned local customs, institutions, and materials regarding social life. Tao's dismissal of traditional historiographies, such as the *Record of the Grand Historian* [*Shiji*] and local gazetteers, reflects the strong anti-traditionalism that characterized the May Fourth movement. Instead, he emphasized the importance of paying more attention to "life" (*shenghuo*), which he explained as the way of life of the masses rather than any individual life, and refers to the real situation (*zhenzhuang*) of the ordinary people's quotidian life. Tao's view of the life of the rural masses was pivotal in transforming the people as a discursive trope, as in the notion of "people as a base" (*minben*), into the real, living people discovered as subjective actors as China transitioned from a dynastic empire to a modern nation-state. Tao's emphasis on "life" was later exemplified in other survey writings about rural society and local life.

Immediately following Tao's introductory essay is a short essay titled "The Peasants in Zhenze" by Zhang Zuyin (1880–1942), who explored why the peasants there were living in severe poverty even though they worked diligently and had dexterous handicraft skills.[18] With a bottom-up perspective and an investigatory attitude, Zhang found that the peasants suffered from the deception and manipulation of the local landlords and loan sharks. Paying much attention to local particularities and regional inequalities, subsequent surveys published in *New Youth* are infused with the spirit of "learning and understanding" (*liaojie*), showing the actual conditions that fostered the local habits and customs, and demonstrating an emotional commitment to acquiring experiential knowledge through their own experience as locals, conversations with locals, and the medium of personal memory. In this manner, Tao followed the trend of sociological study that is based on individual village communities, turned away from grand historical generalization, and treated the local as the present, living social reality. The social-survey essays show that the authors viewed rural existence through both outsider and insider lenses; they presented the local hometown as a newly perceived social world. Despite their often uncertain outlook on social and cultural phenomena in the village, the social-survey writers saw the rationality, logic, and potential inherent in old customs, habits, and moralities in rural society and highlighted the vitality of the local people's ways of life. They did not attribute village social problems merely to the nature of rural society itself, but related them to the larger social, economic, and moral problems that accompanied China's transition to modernity.

It was not uncommon for researchers to take their rural birthplaces as the sites for fieldwork and social investigation.[19] Based on their own local experience, these survey writers played a social role and showed a public-spiritedness similar to those of the Confucian literati who were responsible for writing local histories in imperial China. What, then, was the significance of transforming a locality as the subject of the local gazetteer in imperial China to a locality in the social-survey essays as China was transitioning to a nation-state? The local gazetteer was produced via local initiatives and with a local orientation, and was closely related to elite families and their community ties. It therefore constituted an enduring native tradition with which to construct the identity of the local literati and provided material to explain local history.[20]

New Youth's social-survey essays restructured local social space by shifting the center of gravity to the concrete life of ordinary people, not elites, and offered descriptive rather than normative records, concerned with how things actually were rather than how people ought to act.[21] Modern social-survey writers were largely unconcerned with constructing the unique identity of a locality and instead focused on popular folk practices. They highlighted popular customs, including associations, folk religions, festivals, entertainments, weddings and funerals, public morality, and the rural people's daily experiences, including their professions, property, food, and clothing. To these authors, local customs are manifestations of local public life, social networks, and collective practices. Historian Tong Lam examines how the social-survey movement turned China into an epistemological ground and a laboratory for the political projects of nation- and state-building.[22] With a strong orientation toward nation-building and social transformation, these social surveys together constituted an aggregate social body and communicated to urban-based readers the empirical facts observed and collected as "the medium for discerning the truth about the human world."[23] Presented as a body of information and knowledge, the locality was circulated among the urban-based readers to invite their deeper understanding of the society and to imagine the nation as a congregated body of diverse localities rather than a homogeneous entity.

In May 1918, early in the new-culture movement, the editors of *New Youth* juxtaposed—unwittingly or not—Lu Xun's (1881–1936) "Diary of a Madman" with a social-survey essay titled "Social Investigation: the County of Cannei" by Ye Yuan (1889–1952) on his hometown.[24] The latter work was rarely mentioned in conjunction with the former, as the tremendous canonical status of Lu Xun's story overshadowed other writings published in that issue. Though these two texts were both representations of the hometown, they contained contrasting views. Lu Xun's allegorical "Diary of a Madman" is centered on the return of the narrator (a traditional literatus turned madman) to his hometown, sealed off from the outside world, a village that symbolizes China at large. The madman discovers in historical texts the cannibalistic core of Confucian virtue, which resonates with the May Fourth antitraditionalist slogan, "the established rituals and morality eat people" (*lijiao chiren*). But the story would lose its complexity if interpreted strictly in these terms, for its critique of Confucian morality and patriarchal family institutions involved a process of flattening a rich and complex Chinese history into a monolithic, homogenous whole—a history with the same gist on all of its pages.

Ye Yuan's essay is a recollection of life in his home county, the village of Cannei in southeastern Fujian Province. A graduate in economics from Peking University in 1917, Ye Yuan later became a well-known educator who served as the principal of Jimei school in Xia'men, Fujian Province, in 1920. The records of local institutions, rituals, customs, the people's lifestyle, and entertainment are written with a strong native-place sentiment. The author presented a sampling of personal memories and local history to describe his hometown. He did not completely adopt the affectively neutral prose style emblematic of social-survey writing, but applied a personal touch in rural-investigation writing that recalls Tong Lam's observation that sensibility and sentiment play a central role in producing social-scientific knowledge.[25] The beginning of the essay weaves the author's clan history with the history of his hometown. Taking much pride in Cannei, Ye wrote about his fellow villagers' diasporic life in Southeast Asia. He believed that their adventurous spirit, righteous and chivalrous character, and farming skills would enable them to establish a positive reputation for their hometown. In describing entertainment in his village, Ye initially regarded communal events as a form of superstition. While he recognized the strange and false components in annual performances, his detailed description of an annual temple opera event and the enthusiastic communal involvement is infused with sentimental personal memories. Although he mentions his reservations about the evil local custom of "collective violence between villages" (*xiedou*) in passing, much of his article is concerned with the well-being and self-sufficiency of the local people, who were described as leading a peaceful pastoral life.

In this particular issue of *New Youth*, the opposition between Lu Xun's cannibalistic view and Ye Yuan's paternalist conception of the Chinese family brought to the forefront the conflict between different values and principles, which coexisted from the very beginning of the May Fourth new-culture movement. In contrast to Lu Xun's tendency to essentialize and abstract the Confucian family institution in "Diary of a Madman" as cannibalism, Ye looked at the local particularities and praised the Chinese family as the fountainhead of the people's prosperity and the foundation of the country due to traditional notions of paternalism and reciprocity for the common good. In Ye's view, the family institution was intended to support and help the members of the community in times of need and to foster local consensus and mutual assistance. This "native-place sentiment" (*xiangqing*), the author proposed, is the affective foundation and a moral resource for the rural public. In a time when most authors writing new literature were very estranged from rural life, Ye Yuan's essay made the concrete life of the rural masses visible to national readers. Noticing the regional differences and inequalities in China, his rather eclectic view covered multiple aspects of learning the life in a rural community and described the local customs that connect, regulate, and nurture human relationships as constitutive parts of ordinary people's lives.

Two years later, under the name Mengzhen, Fu Sinian (1896–1950), the prominent Chinese educator and historian, wrote an essay titled "A Sketch of the Peasants' Situation in Part of Shandong Province" (January 1, 1920), based on personal observations of his hometown and neighboring areas in the northwest part of Shandong Province. In his essay, Fu challenged the view that all these rural areas were an undifferentiated, monolithic whole. He described the moral and affective world of the peasants and asserted that they have greater feelings of sympathy and shame than city people. Throughout the essay, Fu showed a well-connected village community: a village formed a big clan, and a family's relatives were considered the entire village's relatives; a family's friends were therefore the village's friends. And he emphasized a primitive, rural form of "equality": village members were equal—whether rich or poor, of high or low status—and had only age and generational differences. Echoing Ye Yuan's observation of paternalism in local society, this essay also highlighted that the village could maintain self-government and mutual assistance to build civil works projects, though Fu did see that such a public connected by an affective bond would lack power and foresight to develop larger public enterprises.

Similarly, in another article, "The Social Situation in Part of Shanxi Province," published in April 1920, the author, Xiao Cheng (?–19?), focused on the countryside where he had lived for a long time; to him, this day-to-day "familiarity with local life" became the vantage point from which to write about the local life world. He offered snapshots of the villagers' leisure time—five or six peasants sitting outdoors bathed in the sunshine, or in a shop gossiping about neighborhood occurrences and discussing traditional popular stories from novels such as *Journey to the West* and *Water Margin*. The author emphasized that the "sentiment and interest" contained in such chatting scenes were mainly situational and context-based, and could not be truly appreciated by outsiders; the local-based moral and ethical universe was formed through such daily personal conversations and storytelling. Xiao also described the relationship between landlords and long-term hired laborers as familial and personal, not depersonalized and contractual (which was characteristic of the absentee landlordism in late imperial China) or exploitative and oppressive (epitomizing class struggle in the Communist revolutionary discourse). The landlord treated hired laborers as family members; in return, the laborers showed their loyalty by working as diligently as they could. This mutual trust cemented an affective relationship between the members of different social statuses in rural society.

Social-survey essays made visible the multiple local customs and the collective life of rural society. In the same year, Ma Boyuan (1884–1939) published a social-survey essay titled "Local Customs in Hubei and Henan."[26] He acquired local knowledge and experienced the local world by traveling on foot, staying in a village, and sitting with local elders and chatting about their customs and situations. He situated local problems within a larger social framework, showing how local customs and morality were altered by the contingencies of far-off events in cities. Without imposing judgment, Ma brought to the forefront the dispute over public morality and the debate about which customs were good or bad. The controversy is presented in a dialogic manner between the author and the locals. Though Ma had reservations about the locals' judgments on these matters, he insisted on rendering their genuine voices and views. In their eyes, modern moral chaos resulted from the rise of the new military class and the vast power of money, which eroded traditional morals such as frugality, industry, honesty, and lawfulness. Instead, the present society valued qualities such as wastefulness, idleness, ambition, and adventurousness. These locals pointed out negative consequences and new fashions brought about by the diversification of society and the subsequent radical transformation of social values in the modern age. Although he referred to bad customs such as fortune-telling, geomancy, and foot-binding, Ma, like Ye Yuan, wrote positively of paternalistic organizations such as the Universal Well-being Association (*pulehui*) and the Old House Association (*laowuhui*), which united members of the community through principles of mutuality and equality, regardless of their social status.

Though both calls for the literary revolution and social investigation began in 1917, based on Mao Dun's later statistics, except for several stories written by Lu Xun and a few others, the majority of native-soil literature did not appear until after 1923.[27] After the Literary Studies Association (*wenxue yanjiu hui*) was founded in spring 1920, Mao Dun wrote a series of essays suggesting that real literature seeking to represent social life should focus on the darkness of the society. Native-soil literature, in Mao Dun's opinion, should use analytical methods to solve questions and pay attention to social problems out of love for the people who had been damaged and insulted.[28]

In the early 1920s, native-soil stories were written by mostly Beijing-based writers from various remote parts of China. Sharing the same goal as the social-survey essays, the new native-soil literature also attempted to represent the authenticity of social life, but the focus was on the darkness of society, ironically out of love for the oppressed.[29] From their vantage points in the cities, the authors mined their childhood memories of their rural homes, turning the familiar into the strange and the grotesque; geographical distance simultaneously produced subjective distance and disengagement from their hometowns. Though this body of literature covers multiple topics, the primary attention was on the peasants' ignorance and the ugly, cruel, and barbaric local customs that manipulated their fate. With a fuzzy boundary between fact and fiction, some native-soil stories bring local customs and bizarre folk practices into public visibility, such as women's victimization in various forms of marriage, feudal morality, superstition, and clan feuding; obsessive attention was given to how these local customs "persecuted" individuals.[30] Historian Qian Mu believes that Chinese culture is not bound to localities and customs: customs in China vary significantly by location, but the *li* ("the rites" or "propriety") are the same.[31] Such writings therefore completed a discursive substitution by equating local customs with Confucian rituals, and equating lower-class people's survival strategy with the repressive force of tradition. Rather than including multiple local customs and social practices, as local gazetteers and social-survey essays did, these stories often focused exclusively on one local custom, such as the "marriage in the underworld" (*minghun*), "using happiness to push off evil" (or "getting married when the patient is almost on the deathbed" [*chongxi*]), as well as child marriage (*tongyangxi*).[32] Other stories concerned cruel social practices such as wife-selling (*dianqi*), examples of violence and punishment such as the "fight between villages" (*xiedou*) and "burial by water" (*shuizang*), and obscure folk medical prescriptions such as using a bun steeped in human blood to cure tuberculosis.[33] Out of love for "the damaged and the insulted," these native-soil fiction writers paid attention to particular local customs, which they characterize as the "perpetrators" against individuals, and accordingly, these cruel customs became the evidence of the May Fourth slogan "man-eating ritual." By contrast, the social-survey essays published in *New Youth* in the late 1910s and early 1920s aimed to present a broader picture of various local customs, to show the concrete lives of the local people and local customs as a body of knowledge and information to national readers. Such representations follow Tao's emphasis on each locality being part of China as a larger whole and on its local particularities and diversities requiring a deeper understanding.

II. Sentimental Homecomings in the Iconoclastic Age

The gulf that separated the countryside from the city was instrumental in shaping modern homecoming narratives. This section turns to the stories about the homecoming experience as the individual narrator crosses the city/country divide. After the disintegration of the Confucian essentialism, this body of fiction created what Georg Lukacs refers to as "transcendental homelessness," a worldwide symptom brought about by modernity. The modern age witnessed the emergence of "the problematic individual," a lonely and confused person who experiences the loss of a harmonious, integrated, soulful connection with the world, feeling estranged from "a parental home" in the modern society of fragmentation.[34]

Chinese homecoming stories, most of which are written in the first person, are indeed the localized version of stories about "the problematic individual" as he or she faces the shifts of resources and opportunities to the cities and simultaneously straddles two divided and incommensurate spaces. In the Chinese context, "the problematic individual" was made visible through the emergence of a new authorial persona in modern fiction of the late 1910s and early 1920s, a time when the use of first-person narrative was most prevalent. Critics have found that the authority of the first-person narrative voice has often been reduced because the modern short story genre is open to various interpretative possibilities and allows for questions, indeterminacy, and nonclosure.[35] This reflected the inability of "the problematic individual" to grasp the wholeness of the world, mirroring the person's difficulty in reconciling his/her personal interiority with the outer social reality.

The theme of "the young man from the provinces" in nineteenth- and early-twentieth-century Western realist novels typically involved a protagonist's preoccupation with leading an individualistic life and achieving upward social mobility in metropolises such as Paris and London.[36] This mentality, however, was largely missing in fictional representations of the Chinese young men who left their rural hometowns for the cities, because their desire for individual upward social mobility was often subordinated to the urgent need for national survival. Moreover, unlike their Western counterparts, who often repudiated their provincial origins, young Chinese people from the countryside often tended to look back at their rural hometowns with complicated and mixed feelings of anxiety, melancholy, frustration, disillusionment, despondency, disappointment, alienation, and nostalgia. Homecoming becomes an excruciating psychological pain that at once obsesses and tortures the narrators, who often feel shame about their inability to "to return to one's hometown with honor" (*rong-gui guli*) and their unwillingness to agree to marriages arranged by their parents. Moreover, unlike their predecessors, the traditional gentry who were often the leaders of their respective communities in protecting local interests and promoting the collective welfare,[37] these modern individuals felt the inability to "return with glory" as a personal dilemma created by their being displaced in society and by the frustrations of unemployment and poverty in the city.

More often than not, native-soil fiction authors' attitudes could be quite ambivalent and ambiguous. Lu Xun's homecoming stories always deal with futile efforts at communication during the reencounter between the intellectual-narrator and the peasants.[38] "My Old Home" (1921) describes in sentimental, lyrical fashion the journey of an urban-educated eldest son of a traditional extended family back to his birthplace to take his mother and his niece away for good. After publication, "My Old Home" became popular among Chinese students in urban centers who identified with the narrator's life experience. Although the city was the locus for the early phase of nationalism, age-old native-place sentiments contributed significantly to its development as well, a fact that has been substantiated by historical studies.[39]

Previous studies of this modern classic emphasize the autobiographical mode of homecoming experience as a process of sublimating nostalgia and contributing to the formation of the modern subject, calling attention to the dynamic interplay between hope and despair in modern historical consciousness.[40] My reading of "My Old Home," however, not only shows the coexistence of different ways of communication but highlights "the socially local and the particular" as the most appropriate and comprehensible perspective, given the specific circumstances and the earnest lord-laborer relationship. The story showcases a concrete local context within which the local people perform their social roles and express themselves according to the appropriateness of their interpersonal human relationships. Lu Xun provides details about a world of communal life in the town and the seashore village back in his childhood years, such as the warm local hospitality that allowed thirsty passersby pick watermelons in the field, an act the locals would not consider "stealing." The story also shows the mild gentry paternalism in which the narrator's mother treats Runtu, the son of the former part-time laborer, as generously as she would treat a relative from afar. Despite class difference, the master and the servant were connected by a lasting and reciprocal relationship as a lifetime obligation that is at once patriarchal and affective. The interaction between Runtu and the narrator's family echoes Xiao Cheng's social-survey essay that describes the familial and personal lord-laborer relationship.

A much-discussed episode in the story is the narrator's poignant reunion with his childhood friend Runtu. At the moment of the reunion, neither can find the right language to express his complex and excited feelings until Runtu eventually breaks the silence and addresses the narrator as "Master"—a moment when "an invisible thick wall" rises between them. This episode of failed communication is often interpreted as an allegory about the limitations of the enlightenment project in communicating with the peasants and about the hierarchical relationship that dictates the world of adulthood in contrast to the equality and innocence of childhood. But the complexity and open-endedness of the story are manifested in the different communication modes and behavioral codes in village society, and in the limitations of language itself for expressing one's inner feelings. Fei Xiaotong observes that in face-to-face contact in rural society, nonverbal means of communication such as facial expressions and gestures can sometimes communicate better than language; in some instances, silence is even more effective in conveying meanings, and "language sometimes *distorts* actual meanings and emotions the very moment they are articulated through words."[41]

In the story, the limits to the use of language to convey human sentiment is complemented by a nonverbal gesture: the act of gift-giving. Attentiveness to details of peasant life characterizes this homecoming story. Runtu comes to visit the narrator from afar after a separation of more than twenty years. He brings some thoughtfully chosen farm produce as a gift and says humbly that "[i]n winter there is nothing worth bringing; but these few beans we dried ourselves, if you will excuse the liberty, sir."[42] The description of such interpersonal interactions grants this character of the lowest social class both dignity and sentimentality. Gift-giving is deeply embedded in the traditional rural-derived notion of *renqing* (human feeling) as "the notion of the necessity of reciprocity, obligation, and indebtedness in human relations."⁴³ Anthropologists Mayfair Yang and Yan Yunxiang both suggest a moderate emotional intensity in the notion of *renqing* but stress the moral and decorous character of social conduct and paths of emotional connections to strengthen human bonds.⁴⁴ Thoughtfully presenting his gifts, considering his family's poverty and the dullness of the season, Runtu adds a sentimental element to his relationship with the gentry family, mobilizing the affective components of human relations within the existing hierarchical system of social status. In the moral and affective universe of *renqing*, hierarchical order does not preclude emotional investment in human relations.

In the first half of the twentieth century, the Chinese intelligentsia had been preoccupied with a search for the language of the masses and an effective communicative mode to make modern and often abstract ideas accessible to them. However, conveying meaning (*dayi*) is not the same as expressing sentiment (*chuanqing*). "My Old Home" is not so much about recounting failed communication as about showing a locally more appropriate way of expressing sentiment in the rural society. On the surface, by depicting the intellectuals' face-to-face contact with the rural folk as part of a homecoming process, this story seems to dramatize a fault line in the process of nation formation, ideally perceived to be built on "deep, horizontal comradeship" but with actual inequality.⁴⁵ On a deeper level, this story draws readers to reflect on the difference between traditional hierarchy-marking etiquette and modern equality in the affective lord-laborer relationship; it reveals the potential limitation of the modern sense of equality in cementing the human ties between the urban-educated modern intellectual and the peasant.

The homecoming stories analyzed below were written when the modern individual emerged during a time of iconoclastic revolt against the Confucian patriarchy to transform the moral landscape and to strengthen and reinvigorate China in a period of national crisis. Historian Vera Schwarcz adopts the notion of different generations facing different situations to discuss May Fourth intellectuals.⁴⁶ The young May Fourth radicals faced the major issue of parental authority and arranged marriage, which were not the primary concerns of middle-aged cultural radicals such as Lu Xun's in his fiction until he addressed the social consequences of gaining individual freedom and fleeing the patriarchal family in "What Happens After Nora Leaves Home?" (1923) and his only love story, "Regret for the Past" (1925).

Writers in the following generation, such as Xu Qinwen (1897–1984),

Feng Yuanjun (1900–1974), and Yu Dafu (1896–1945), tackled from various perspectives the contradictions between self-realization and familial responsibilities—a tension often metaphorically represented as the gap between urban centers and rural homes. May Fourth enlightenment discourse affirmed individuals' sacred and inviolable right to determine the shape of their lives while downplaying obligation to the family. This right-gaining as a process of self-empowerment endowed the individual with a dual identity as victim and agent: victimhood resulted from the pressure of familial obligations that robbed individuals of opportunities to develop their potential, which therefore legitimized the individual's role as rebellious agent. Although the concept of the rights-based individual was oriented toward equality, independence, and freedom, it simultaneously entailed an undeniable elitism that empowered urban-educated and modern-thinking individuals. Despite its claims of all-inclusiveness and universality, the notion of the individual simultaneously enforced a social exclusion and created a group of depreciated social members, such as tyrannical parents, downtrodden peasants, and undesirable rural wives. Scholars have pointed out that such rights-based individuals have never been prevalent in the Chinese social context.[47] This view is further fine-tuned by the sentimental homecoming narratives analyzed below, which turn to the way modern individuals aimed to recuperate their familial bonds in the iconoclastic age.

Homecoming narratives resituate the individual within a set of preexisting human relationships and present him or her as an open and incomplete project in the formation of a modern self, an identity born out of living with many social and cultural conflicts. Simultaneously, in the transitional period, the individual becomes detached from the previous overarching values, wandering around in the city as what Charles Taylor terms the "disengaged self" and what Joseph Levenson refers to as the "rootless cosmopolitan."[48] The former is linked with a modern notion of freedom in which an individual can perform his or her own agency and dignity free from external interference or subordination to external authority, a freedom that tends to result in an atomistic existence.[49] Similarly, the latter well captures the tension between the global and the local after the individual is emancipated by severing previous kinship bonds but then has no mooring in the urban context.[50] Returning to one's rural home is therefore a journey from the world of strangers in urban centers to a society of kith and kin to reexperience familial bonds in the rural hometown. The living ties to family members and the local community proved essential in forging a modern identity.

Charles Taylor asserts that the idea of recognition played a vital role in the modern conception of identity for people to understand "who they are, [and] their fundamental defining characteristics as a human being."[51] He distinguishes two types of recognition. One occurs in the public sphere, in which a principle of universalism suggests the equal recognition of all citizens. The other occurs in "the intimate sphere," in which "we understand the formation of identity and the self as taking place in a continuing dialogue and struggle with significant others."[52] Though Taylor writes in the context of multiculturalism, his notion of twin forms of recognition is illuminating for our understanding of the early decades of twentieth-century China. The May Fourth generation severed their ties to family, tradition, and locality and aimed to gain equal recognition and dignity as citizens in a universalist and egalitarian sense when entering the national community. Nonetheless, the modern subject could never be complete without his or her agonizing, poignant reconnection to the family and entering a realm of particularistic bonds—one could never emancipate oneself fully from those whose affection and care influenced one early in life. This leads us to reexamine those homecoming stories to see how this reconnection occurred in the "intimate sphere" of one's rural home.

In March 1935, Lu Xun took the writer Xu Qinwen, who was both his student and fellow townsman, as an example to reflect on native-soil fiction. In the preface to a section about modern Chinese fiction in the *Compendium of Modern Chinese Literature*, Lu Xun underlined the dilemma facing native-soil writers: they had left their hometowns to live in "a strange place" (*yidi*), but looked back to "the father's garden"—a garden that no longer existed—to comfort themselves.[53] In an empathetic tone, Lu Xun wrote that "it would be more comfortable and self-consoling to recall the things that do not exist any more than those that exist but one cannot get close to."[54] Nonetheless, Xu Qinwen published his first anthology of stories, entitled *My Old Home* (Guxiang), in 1926, and it noted far more complicated feelings toward his hometown than simple obsession with his father's "disappeared garden." In the story "This Time's Leaving Home" (1922), Xu Qinwen focused on "those that exist but one cannot get close to," and utilized the same homecoming journey trope created by Lu Xun—returning home to leave it permanently. "This Time's Leaving Home," the first story in the collection, describes an urban-educated narrator's last day in his rural home as "the intimate sphere." The narrator, who is about to return to Beijing after a three-month visit, meticulously recounts every minute, emotionally charged detail of ordinary life prior to his departure, which not only reveals the narrator's reluctance to leave but leads him to prolong his stay.

The daughter of a clan of literati-officials, the narrator's mother has witnessed the lives of generations spanning from the imperial Qing dynasty to the modern Republican period. His mother's invocation of her father's leave-taking resonates emotionally in the narrator's heart, tying the narrator back to his long family history. In an age when patriarchal institutions were fiercely attacked, the mother's remembrance underscores the pedagogical function of the family institution described by Lionel Trilling: "traditionally the family has been a narrative institution: it was the past and it had a tale to tell of how things began, including the child himself; and it had counsel to give."[55] In other words, the family helps endow the individual with a historical identity and situates the narrator in the fabric of continuous social change. The amiable and loving mother is not only the focus of the story but is also placed at the center of the enduring patriarchal family structure. The narrator muses,

> Life has been changing all the time. The next moment I will not be the same as I am in this moment. In life once we part, we will part forever, because our life will not be the same when we meet again.... There is only one real mother in one's life. Even if I return to my hometown in ten years, my mother will still be readily recognized at the very first sight, which will be a comfort to me.[56]

Indeed, the narrator's mother, a caring figure, provides a perennial affective attachment and emotionally anchored space for the narrator, similar to what Prasenjit Duara calls the "regime of authenticity": the "always identifiable, unchanging subject of history" throughout the tumultuous progression of modern history.[57]

The affective image of the matriarch also simultaneously sentimentalizes the image of the patriarchal house that was demonized in the discourse of the late 1910s and 1920s. Indeed, the narrator's sentimental journey home is an acknowledgment of his own vulnerability and dependence on his beloved family. In particular, he cannot help doubting his decision to break the marriage contract arranged by his mother:

> She did not want me to take care of things a son should be responsible for, and I could not fulfill my duties as a son. She did not blame me, but I already felt deeply upset. When she seized the

stick [a stick for cooking] from me, surprisingly I started to doubt myself—it seems that I had made a mistake in breaking the engagement arranged by her. I would rather buy some cookies as breakfast on the road than have her get up early to cook for me, which will add to my depression.[58]

The narrator feels gratitude for his mother's unconditional love and nurturing, and also feels guilty about not being able to carry out his filial duty by agreeing to the arranged marriage. The iconoclastic attacks on filial piety during the May Fourth movement alienated the urban-educated from their elders and kinsmen at home. In this story, the narrator is deeply aware of the reciprocal bond between mother and son, and the interdependence of rights and obligations. Throughout Chinese history there had long been a tension between emphasizing filial piety as ritual obligations and highlighting it as affection and sentiment. The narrator regards filial piety not as a matter of ritual formality, of mandate and obedience, but as a feeling based on mutual care and indebtedness, and emphasizes acting out a new sense of filial sentiment through spontaneous and genuinely affectionate relations with his mother in the iconoclastic age. Charles Taylor suggests that one of the most significant transformations of modernity was the affirmation of the individual as the moral agent, and proposes that "most of us not only live with many goods but find that we have to rank them, and in some cases, this ranking makes one of them of supreme importance relative to the others."[59] To Taylor, the ethical choice is not a matter of making judgments about which is right or wrong, good or evil, but is a choice based on which principle or importance overrides the other. The narrator does not mean to confirm his leaving home as absolutely correct, but his decision is more appropriate and important than other options such as staying at home and agreeing to an arranged marriage. Xu's homecoming story is poignant and touching because the narrator-son recognizes the divergence of values and social norms between his mother's world and his own. He insists on breaking away from the arranged marriage while at the same time showing understanding of his mother's situation.

After bidding farewell to his mother, the narrator takes the ferry on his way back to the city. On the ferry, he eavesdrops on the townsfolk as they talk about his family affairs. Ignorant of the narrator's presence, the townsfolk lament that the narrator's mother has had to lead a solitary life since all her adult children have broken off their arranged marriage plans and left for the big cities to obtain higher education. None of her children, they think, has brought honor and wealth back to their family, as was expected in traditional society. These comments not only offer the narrator a better understanding of his mother's situation but also reveal his own dilemma as a member of the new intellectual class in a historical transitional period. The story ends with the narrator's arrival in Beijing, an "alien and faraway place" where cold and snobbish human interactions contrast with the maternal nurturing and familial intimacy of his rural home. No matter how much the narrator yearns for the embrace of an intimate community, he does not want to give up the freedom and opportunities offered by city life. Moreover, he soon must confront the distressing reality of unemployment. And yet, in spite of all these difficulties—even including the grim possibility of poverty and starvation—the narrator chooses to stay in the city rather than return to his hometown, even though he would be better off there. This is evidence of the tremendous impact the ideology of "going to the city" has on the modern individual: whereas it emancipates him or her from familial responsibilities and broadens his or her social horizons, it simultaneously severely restricts life options.

During the 1920s, marriage reform and freedom of personal choice in love were among the urban-educated elite's central concerns. The young generation of May Fourth rebels actively fought for self-fulfillment through resisting arranged marriage, which therefore deterred some from returning to their rural homes. In the stories of Feng Yuanjun, a prominent May Fourth woman writer, this dilemma is dramatized by an intense struggle between romantic love and filial sentiment, between the city and the rural hometown. Unlike the Confucian female exemplars of the late imperial Chinese novels, who voluntarily reconciles romantic sentiment with filial piety,[60] the female protagonists in Feng's fiction cannot subordinate either to the other, nor do they consider romantic love a decisive form of self-realization.

A number of Feng's contemporaries used the idea of free love as a weapon against patriarchal society, and Feng characterizes this trend in a series of short stories published in the 1920s, including "Separation," "After Separation," and "My Loving Mother." These stories deal with the same situation: a female protagonist, engaged to a local landlord's son by her mother, encounters in Beijing her true love, who is often already in an arranged marriage. She dreads returning to her rural home and at first attempts to escape from the arranged marriage, but at last gives up and accepts her fate. "Separation" ends with the protagonist waiting to be rescued by her lover after being secluded by her family, leaving the outcome open to surmise. She believes that "romantic love should satisfy every aspect of the individual's life,"[61] but she is also deeply aware of her possible blindness to other aspects of life and therefore engages in constant self-questioning. In the sequel, "After Separation," the female protagonist's tragic suicide is invoked by her cousin in a powerful declaration against arranged marriage; in "My Loving Mother," the female narrator and her mother achieve a final reconciliation. The various scenarios and changing narrative perspectives from story to story allow the author to imagine different approaches to the thorny issue of free love vis-à-vis arranged marriage.

Though the female protagonist in Feng's stories conceives of love as an absolute value and defies parental authority to the point of fleeing her gentry family, she also attempts to understand her mother's situation. "Love" is often rendered as *aiqing* (romantic love) in modern Chinese; however, to the narrator, "love" is not restricted to romantic love but includes maternal love. In "Separation," the female protagonist/narrator, Juanhua, tells how her life was destroyed by these contradictory loves and views herself as caught in a tragic dilemma: "For the sake of Mother's love, I cannot break away from the marriage contract with the Liu Family, and therefore I take much risk going back to visit my aging mother. For the sake of my lover, I would rather sacrifice my reputation in society and the joy of being with my family."[62] The narrator considers pursuing love not so much a bid for emancipation but a recognition of the *tragic* dimension and contradictory nature of life. This tragedy results from an ambitious mind trying to embrace all values at the expense of sacrificing the self. On a philosophical level, Feng Yuanjun's writings concern the conflicted loyalties and values structuring the modern world and confronting the modern individual. It is in this sense that the narrator characterizes herself "more as the agent rather than the victim of her tragedy," and in this way, Feng Yuanjun challenged the radical May Fourth male ideology of invoking romantic love as a weapon to combat patriarchal rule.[63]

Whereas Feng's early work, such as "Separation," reads like a monologue about the individual's interior struggle and persistence, her later story, "My Loving Mother," is an emotional odyssey that portrays the reconciliation of maternal love and romantic love. The story follows the narrator/protagonist's journey from Beijing to the province where her mother has just moved from the countryside. In the middle of the story, the protagonist's initial wrenching conflicts with her mother give way to a family reunion in which all share happiness and an intimate exchange of thoughts and ideas. The protagonist is astonished to find that, far from what she expected, her mother does not mean to pressure her into an arranged marriage. Rather, "what she felt most disappointed about in me is that I was not writing letters home, and not requesting money from her either,"[64] which the mother takes as evidence of her daughter's determination to cut herself off from the family. This detail shows that the living ties to family members—both economic and sentimental—are intertwined. Wang Lingzhen argues that Feng Yuanjun's writings articulated "an emotional, intersubjective relationship between mother and daughter," which suggests Feng's refusal to prioritize maternal love over romantic love and demonstrates the coexistence of different loves.[65]

In another of Feng's stories, "After My Mother Left," the narrator expresses her understanding of sentiment and righteousness: "Mothers treat their children at the cost of sacrifice, but how do children treat their mothers? With selfishness! With selfishness! Perhaps there are some occasions they also sacrifice a bit, but compared to their mothers' sacrifices, the ratio is simply one to one hundred."[66] Over the course of Feng's literary career, her protagonists shifted from family rebels to filial daughters who delight at being reunited with her mothers. The above analysis gives us insight into Lu Xun's keen observation of the "tender and sentimental feeling" (*chanmian feice zhiqing*) in Feng's work. Lu Xun interpreted it as ambivalence: "a resolution to launch a battle with tradition, but a fear of having a decisive battle with tradition."[67] As seen from the description of the mother, "fear" does not refer to the powerlessness of the modern woman but implies that she does not want to be caught in moral simplicity and blindness when traditional values were still powerfully organizing worldly relations.

Feng did not see herself as a celebrated, free-love-pursuing new woman, and instead reflected deeply on the social dilemmas caused by free love—particularly its devastating consequences for rural woman. "The chaste woman" (Zhenfu, 1926), a story written in the third person, deals with the tragic life of a rural woman who is cruelly abandoned by her husband and utterly forgotten by society. Under the pretext of free love, the urban-educated husband divorces her to marry a new woman. The disadvantaged rural wife lacks the opportunity to receive an urban, modern education, the precondition for becoming a new woman as well as an independent individual. The celebration of romantic love during the May Fourth period often resolves to transcend the social barriers of lineage, status, and class.⁶⁸ Ironically, this story reveals how the rural woman becomes a victim of the emancipatory ideology of the May Fourth culture due to her own status and class. In this way, Feng both identified with May Fourth iconoclasm and questioned its feasibility in social practice; she refused to adopt a simplistic view and astutely discerned many negative social consequences of emancipatory free love. Her stance is best illuminated by Martha C. Nussbaum's interpretation of maturity and adulthood: "knowledge of good, that is to say a value, in the world requires, we see, knowledge of evil, that is to say of the possibility of conflict, disorder, the contingent necessity of breaking or harming."⁶⁹ The pursuit of free love as an emancipatory enterprise eventually turned out to be cultural capital that could only be possessed by the new intellectual class, not socially disadvantaged members such as peasant women or rural wives.

Reading the stories discussed above as a coherent whole, we find that Feng raises a thoughtful question: who is the victim? May Fourth culture called for abandoning what Chen Duxiu (1879–1942) termed the "morality of slavery" to strengthen the young generation's resolve to leave their families and avoid becoming victims. However, Feng, representative of other contemporaries, leads us to see the flip side—for example, the affectionate yet conservative mother longing for the return of her daughter, as well as the miserable abandoned rural wife. Weren't they also social victims? How could they gain happiness and gratification in a rapidly changing world? As she realized that the privileges enjoyed by modern individuals might leave deep scars on other groups of people, Feng did not show a preference for any particular group, but drew attention to the tragic, self-contradictory dimension of modern life instead of claiming victory for the newly empowered.

From a male perspective, Yu Dafu resumed the discussion of the modern individual's act of negotiating the conflict between obligation and individual autonomy while directing our attention from the empowered, rights-claiming modern individual to the discursively disadvantaged rural wife. The journey home was also a major subject for the writer and poet Yu Dafu. In 1923, he published three pieces: "Returning Home" (*Huanxiang ji*), "A Supplement to Returning Home" (*Huanxiang houji*), and "Wisteria and Dodder" (*Niaoluoxing*). These stories are first-person narratives in a confessional manner, which often blurs the line between fiction and nonfiction. The first two pieces dwell on the lengthy journey of returning home, with less attention to the rural home itself. They function as a journey for the narrator to reflect on his personal frustrations; his insecurities; the desire for a peaceful, utopian life; his guilt about his inability to support his family; and his cynicism about contemporary politics.

"Wisteria and Dodder" is written for "an unhappy woman," which in this particular context refers to the narrator's rural wife. The Japan-educated narrator, a morally sensitive, pathological, pessimistic, and intellectual protagonist, embarks on a journey to his hometown, first from Japan and later from the metropolis of Shanghai. While still studying in Japan, the narrator succumbed to pressure from his mother and his rural hometown's tenacious customs, and he returned home to marry "a woman whom he must love but whom he cannot love." His rural wife's defining characteristic is "submissiveness," which refers to several qualities: an education in traditional womanhood and corresponding lack of modern education; growing up in a poor and isolated village; lacking urban fashion sense and femininity; and, usually, having bound feet.

At the outset of the story, the narrator stays in his urban apartment while his wife and son return to their rural hometown. He imagines them on the train and speculates, in an epistolary-confessionalist mode, about his wife's feelings toward him. In this act of empathetic identification, he alternately addresses his rural wife as "you," "the woman I have to love," and sometimes "the woman I love most," reflecting his ambivalent feelings.

> Sitting inside the train, you must be recalling the vile treatment you received from me while we lived together. Alas, my woman, the woman I have to love, please don't shed your tears on the train. Despite all the petty insults, tyranny, and abuse I subjected you to, deep inside I harbor sincere sympathy and love for you. I endured all the agony, suffering, and insult from society; who else can I voice all my complaints to if not to you? Alas, the woman I love most, you would forgive me if you understand my secrete feelings that I could not tell anyone.[70]

Afterward he imagines his wife watching a group of young people joyously frolicking in a meadow through the train window:

> Will that make you all the more embittered against me? It is understandable if you abhor me! If you detest me and hate me to the extreme, or even pray that I will die soon, that would make me feel

better. But that won't happen, and I know you can't. You are utterly incapable of it, for once you started to abhor me, you would instantly forgive me. Alas, when I think of your beautiful tender heart, I cannot tolerate or forgive myself.[71]

In this inner monologue, the narrator extends empathetic feeling across the fault line between the urban-educated male intellectual and the illiterate rural woman. The husband's pity for his wife is also closely associated with his perception of his own life. After eventually returning to his motherland from Japan, the narrator has to confront his sense of total uselessness and insignificance, and the lack of economic means to pursue individual freedom when society does not appreciate his talent and abilities. With a great sense of social frustration, the narrator, the self-titled "superfluous man," goes back to his rural hometown. His feeling of pity toward his wife is particularly intriguing in that he sees himself in her image. The narrator's identification with his rural wife seems to resemble the long-standing tradition in classical Chinese literature of taking romantic heterosexual love (such as the husband-wife relationship) to symbolize a ruler-subject relationship, a tradition in which the poetic narrator often takes on an androgynous identity.[72] In the modern context, the rural wife's submissiveness to and dependence on the husband mirrors the husband's powerlessness under village customs and in modern society. However, the narrator's identification does not effeminize him, but initiates his strong self-criticism: "I myself am a cowardly victim of society, but at home I am a tyrant, and at home toward you I gave vent to all the mistreatment, bullying and insult I received from the society."[73] This statement reveals how the modern individual, after severing his ties with patriarchal institutions, could still reproduce in his own relationships the same form of tyranny that he is strongly against. This self-criticism is an insight into how the patriarchal structure is often deposited in the deepest layer of human consciousness. Michael Egan discerns the tendency in most of Yu's stories to emphasize "the basic absurdity of his self-image."[74] In fact, underneath this "absurd self-image" is an autobiographical self who manages to confront profound moral confusions and transform his sense of victimhood into a tragic journey, similar to that described by Feng Yuanjun, of battling with contradictory forces. But ironically, his empathy toward his wife does not result in any real action that can change the status quo or improve her life.

In the face of unemployment, the narrator feels ashamed at accepting aid from his mother and his high-minded brother because of his sense of independence. In his economic distress, the narrator thinks of leading a peaceful hermit life in the countryside, but he soon gives up this idea, for it seems to be an escape from the ups and downs of modern life. The narrator equates returning to the countryside with "social downgrading" (*lunluo*, or socially downward mobility). If drinking and wandering like a vagabond in the city can be aesthetically interpreted as decadent, then returning to the countryside is a denial of any possibility for self-fulfillment. This echoes Xu Qinwen's resolve not to return home even if it meant starving to death. It seems that individual fulfillment and success can be only achieved outside the space of one's rural hometown. The imperative in Yu's story is that returning to one's hometown and living a simple and peaceful life is not an enterprise that the modern individual should pursue.

The May Fourth enlightenment's attack on the patriarchal family has presented an overarching narrative that in fact shows what Anthony Giddens emphasizes as the "disembeddedness" of social relations being lifted out of the particularities of contexts of presence; accordingly, "returning to the rural home" was meant to demonstrate the "situatedness" of the concrete local relationship.[75] This chapter focuses on the living present, the contemporaneous, the situated, the concrete, and the embedded. Customs and interpersonal relations, the "socially local and particular," were the central concern of social-survey essays and homecoming fiction. These writings direct readers to observe the local particularities and regional inequalities integral to the national imagination as well as the human connections and contradictions in values and modes of communication brought about by the culture of modernity. If the journey toward national community had to be achieved by severing local ties, then how could the newly formed nation establish itself in its own historical and cultural soil? It is in this sense that the process of nation-building was simultaneously accompanied by the urgency to understand "the socially local and particular."

With the shared theme of the lived experience of the rural world, the juxtaposition of social-survey essays and homecoming fiction as two parallel processes demonstrates how the hometown was opened as a representational and experiential space for knowledge production and emotional engagement. In the social-survey essays, the writers staged the hometown as a site through which they could produce a form of knowledge about rural society and its customs out of their own lived experience and investigation. Often written in a critical spirit to distinguish between good local customs and bad ones, social surveys confirmed the positive aspects that supported rural public life through indigenous notions such as paternalism, reciprocity, mutual aid, and the affective lord-laborer relationship, as well as folk entertainments such as storytelling and opera. Similarly, in homecoming fiction, the writers revealed the concrete ways in which human relationships work through their interactions with marginalized rural or provincial residents: downtrodden, impoverished peasants; stubborn, conservative matriarchs of the local gentry; and earthy, undesirable rural wives. Together these writings offer a critical prism through which to understand how these authors overcame moral simplicity and acknowledged the coexistence of different values, lifestyles, and ways of human communication rather than diachronically opposing them into sets of the enlightened and the benighted, the progressive and the backward.

CHAPTER 2

Creating the Rural Vernacular
Visual Imagination and Theatrical Performance in the Rural Reconstruction Movement in Ding County in the 1920s and 1930s

In 1929, James Yen (aka Yan Yangchu) and a group of like-minded intellectuals—"holders of old imperial degrees, professors of national universities, a college president and former member of the National Assembly, and a number of Ph.D.'s and M.D.'s from leading American universities"—left their prestigious positions and comfortable residences in the city of Beijing and moved to the villages of Ding County (Ding xian), in Hebei Province.[1] The event was summed up as "Ph.D.'s Back to the Village," and it caused a huge sensation at the time, involving "the most magnificent exodus of the intelligentsia into the country that had taken place in Chinese history to date."[2] Having observed the huge city/country cleavage during this journey, Yen compared the spatial distance between Beijing and Ding County to "a chronological one involving several centuries."[3] This journey opened a new and historically influential chapter in the "going to the people" movement in modern China—the rural reconstruction movement in Ding County in the late 1920s and 1930s. Unlike many of their prominent intellectual peers who were ensconced in urban universities, Yen and his followers left their comfortable scholarly lives, choosing instead to live in and research China's rural areas. It was no accident that Yen's move from the city to the country coincided with research trends of the day, which were shifting from bibliocentric research to on-site social investigation. That was a period when modern intellectuals needed to take time to understand peasants and country life, rather than settling for superficial impressions and assumptions. Emphasizing the importance of fieldwork, Yen treated the villages of Ding County as a social laboratory,[4] in which he initiated a series of social and cultural reforms, such as literacy campaigns and hygiene movements. The laboratory of Ding County would then serve as a training center for future practitioners and as a model that could be adopted by other parts of the country. In fact, Ding County drew international attention due to the American sociologist Sidney Gamble's (1890–1968) works, which became known as examples of social surveys and quantitative information.[5] At Yen's invitation, the playwright Xiong Foxi came to Ding County in 1932, committing himself to the "experiment of theatrical popularization" (*xiju dazhonghua shiyan*) and directing the drama department of the rural reconstruction movement until 1937. The theatrical performances, which incorporated involvement by peasant audiences, were celebrated as "a miracle in the evolution of new Chinese theatre" and a "dramatic liberation movement."[6]

From its beginning, "going to the people" as an intellectual, cultural, and social practice was criticized for its limited scope within the academic circle and for not reaching out to the majority of people, particularly those living in the remote countryside.[7] This chapter focuses on the extraordinary, imaginative experiments facilitated by James Yen, Xiong Foxi, and their colleagues in Ding County, with a goal of rejuvenating the nation through providing education to transform the everyday life of the peasants.[8] Yen and Xiong explored the possibility of bringing modern life to the rural area through the Ding County experiment and sought an effective mode of "going to the people." This chapter does not offer comprehensive intellectual biographies of James Yen and Xiong Foxi, nor does it engage in an empirical study of the movement's social impact on the peasant society of Ding County. The existing scholarship has provided detailed historical accounts of the rural reconstruction movement and its attempt to construct a rural vision of modern life. Charles W. Hayford situates the intersection of James Yen's biography and rural reconstruction in China's modern historical transformation and the China-America relationship, discussing the effort of educated Chinese to uplift the peasants.[9] Kate Merkel-Hess argues that the rural reconstruction reformers attempted to initiate the self-transformation and self-discipline of the peasants through education, envisioning a form of modernity and a new China grounded in the countryside by taking a "less violent, more participatory," "persuasive and educating" approach different from rural revolution.[10] Most efforts to (re)construct a kind of rural modernity through social experimentation in the countryside were either short-lived or failed.[11] This chapter takes the rural reconstruction at Ding County as a representative case to discuss the reform mode of going to the countryside and to conceptualize the Chinese modern outside the context of the city. However, this chapter highlights the visual and theatrical practices that constituted what I describe as a new form of *rural vernacular*, performed to achieve Yen's goal of building substantial connections between rural education and the everyday lives of the peasants.[12] These practices worked as a critical response to the May Fourth vernacular movement, exploring new types of human communication and interaction with the peasants and creating new forms of cultural productions to transform their everyday lives.

The May Fourth vernacular movement advocated for a "living literature" (*huo wenxue*), aiming to replace the status of classical Chinese written in literature and historiography with a modern vernacular. With its democratic aspirations, the movement played a crucial role in shifting cultural elites' attention to folk literature and the lives of common people. Nevertheless, the emergent vernacular language of this period was highly westernized in terms of syntax and the use of terms translated from foreign languages. As many critics, such as Shu-mei Shih, convincingly argue, this tendency toward westernization built up a "linguistic capital" accessible and available only to those trained in the new educational system or abroad, which undercut its democratic potential. In fact, the heavily Europeanized and Japanized vernacular was so distanced from the language spoken by the masses that it mainly functioned as the new intellectual elites' "will to power."[13] Far from being accessible to those in rural areas, the May Fourth vernacular created a new social hierarchy, even as it intended to sabotage such hierarchies.

This chapter focuses specifically on how Yen and his followers repudiated the linguistic capital that characterized the May Fourth enlightenment and how they created a series of cultural productions which I call the "rural vernacular," to develop a pedagogic community of attractions and empathy that aimed to train peasants how to act as modern citizens. In her discussion of the cinematic vernacular in the context of Republican urban mass culture, Zhen Zhang goes beyond the linguistic domain of a literary revolution practiced by the May Fourth intellectuals, extending the concept of vernacular to the larger realm of popular culture that encompasses different media and cultural forms in the city.[14] The modern vernacular has shifted from an intellectual discourse to the collective sensory experience embedded in everyday life, or as Zhang describes, "the vernacular here is configured as a cultural (linguistic, visual, sensory, and material) 'processor' that blends foreign and local, premodern and modern, high and low, cinematic and other cultural ingredients to create a domestic product with cosmopolitan appeal."[15] Drawing on Zhang's definition of the cinematic vernacular, I shift the historical location from the city-based to the village-based vernacular culture facilitated by rural reconstruction, and bring up the notion of the rural vernacular manifested in a cluster of modern media and cultural forms, including the written, the visual, and the performative, which contributed to creating a pedagogic, participatory community. The rural vernacular in this particular historical context functioned as a critical response to the elitist orientation underlying the May Fourth vernacular movement and attempted to reconnect with the rural masses, helping to bring the modern experience grounded in the concrete, everyday rural life to the rural masses. There is no denying that the Ding County experiment was an enlightenment project, but whereas previous enlightenment thinkers such as Liang Qichao had emphasized the goal of "rejuvenating the people" (*xinmin*), Yen aimed to show "how to do it."[16] The former indicated *what* core qualities the new citizens should possess, whereas the latter explored *how* to cultivate them. The Ding County experiment attempted to transform the villages into what I would characterize as "a space of attraction and empathy," in which the peasants were active participants in communal affairs and compassionate people with strong feelings of fellowship.

Specifically, the realm of rural vernacular in this context encompasses three initially urban-based, Western-imported media and performance forms—lantern slides, illustrated primers, and spoken drama—which were media and cultural forms employed as major pedagogical tools and transformative vehicles to remake public life in the villages. Together, these cultural forms created "a space of attraction and empathy" that staged a modern rural life and made joining modern public life and the nation an exhilarating experience that *attracted* the community of peasant citizens. Rather than engaging in an empirical study of the peasants' reactions to this movement, I focus on how literacy, visual images, and theatrical performances sought to forge a rural vernacular—a repository of images, ideas, and stories from which peasants could potentially construct new and modern visions and interpretations of the world.

At the same time, the Ding County experiment's citizenship training marked a new way of conceiving of the peasants. Due to the Enlightenment discourse and the rise of the city in the early decades of the twentieth century, the portrayal of peasants often relied, paradoxically, on two contradictory images: on the one hand, enlightened intellectuals regarded peasants as apathetic, obtuse, and passive, an impediment to China's pursuit of modernity, and irredeemable; on the other hand, the country folks were romanticized and imagined as simple, sentimental, innocent figures opposed to urban corruption and complexity.[17] Chinese peasants are often identified as having four prominent characteristics: ignorance, innocence, impoverishment, and powerfulness.[18] In practice, the Ding County experiment aimed to transform peasants into "scholar-farmers" who were active, capable, and compassionate members of their village and national communities, constantly *learning, thinking*, and *feeling*. Furthermore, Yen and Xiong adopted a new rhetoric of "us" that emphasized the interconnections among people and between rural localities and the wider world. This rhetoric rewrote the previous relationship between the enlightener "I" and the to-be-enlightened "other," fostered new kinds of communal ties inside rural society, and situated the village in a web of relations with the nation and the world. The village therefore became an emotionally charged space of collective unity centered on "our" matters, "our" community, and "our" nation.

In this chapter, I first discuss Yen's notion of the "scholar-farmer" and Ding County's literacy education program as powerful democratic statements against the historical and social circumstances of the time. I then address how visual materials were used to teach literacy, to cultivate a modern and a public consciousness, and to reconstruct rural life spaces to create "attractions." Last, I discuss three rural plays by Xiong Foxi, with special attention to the participatory style of their theatrical performances. The peasant audience's involvement in the performances, I demonstrate, promoted an aesthetic experience of modern public life in rural society, in which emotion and sympathy played a vital role.

I. The "Scholar-Farmer": "Intelligent and Progressive Citizens" in the Literacy Campaign in Ding County

Born into a traditional gentry-scholar's family, James Yen was first educated in classical Chinese learning and later received a Western education at Yale and Princeton. After returning to China from the United States in 1920, Yen enthusiastically devoted himself to the mass-education movement. Yen's educational background and his strong connections with American missionaries and academies often led to a misunderstanding of his experiment as westernized with the material aid from America.[19] In fact, Yen's experiment, like those conducted by his contemporaries Tao Xingzhi (1891–1946) and Liang Shuming, was also locally anchored. The movement started in major cities and then spread to rural areas in the late 1920s, when Yen and his followers realized that "educating the rural commoners is the most important way to resurrect and construct the nation."[20] Conceived as an integral part of Sun Yat-sen's "period of tutelage," the movement aimed to "eliminate illiteracy and make new citizens for China," suggesting that literacy was closely associated with "citizenship education." Scholars now often attribute the difference between context-based and context-free ways of thinking to the difference between oral modes and written modes of thought.[21] Freed from the particular, situational framework of local culture, literacy can help transform people's consciousness and inspire their active imagination of the nation beyond the local.

Throughout the world, literacy had long been restricted to a relatively small proportion of the population, separating the elite from the great majority of people. Scholars point out that cultural elites were interested in maintaining the gap between literate culture and oral culture, not in reducing it—thus exaggerating rather than addressing the inequality of the classes.[22] On a discursive level, the civil-service examination in imperial China was open to people from all social strata; however, Benjamin Elman points out that in reality, the "[u]nequal social distribution of linguistic and cultural resources" meant that the gentry family monopolized the necessary educational resources for their descendants to pass the exam.[23]

Yen's most important talks on rural reconstruction were first written in English, and later translated into Chinese. Aiming to change the *status quo* and reform Chinese society from the bottom, Yen proposed the notion of the "scholar-farmer" in a talk delivered in English in 1929:

> But the ability to read and write has been traditionally regarded as the special possession of the scholar class, just as medical knowledge is the special possession of the doctor. . . . The farmer, the artisan, the merchant, take it for granted that people of their class should not read. They look upon their illiteracy not as a shame or a disgrace but as a natural part of their life. . . . Under the republican regime, we believe, every Chinese man, woman and child should learn to read. "Scholar" and "farmer" should no longer stand in separate categories. We perceive a new union—the "scholar-farmer" developed in the "people's school," a school not for "common" people but for "equal" people, as the Chinese idiom has it. We have

no such term as "common" people. Ping, which we have adopted as our national watchword, stands for equality—equality of man, equality of opportunity.²⁴

In this lecture, Yen suggests that the mass education program should make education available to all, with literacy understood as a universal right, in order to break down the existing social hierarchy and achieve the goal of producing "scholar-farmers." Though Yen has been known for his comments on the peasants' characteristics as "ignorance, poverty, weakness, and selfishness" (*yu, qiong, ruo, si*), the notion of "scholar-farmer" also indicates Yen's acute awareness of their "potential intellectual and productive power."²⁵ Revealing the artificial line differentiating social strata, Yen emphasized that inequality was not an inborn attribute but an artificial creation of ideology. In traditional China, even gentry and peasants living in the same geographical locale were conceptually operating in different linguistic and cultural universes; therefore, Yen attempted to remove the obstacles that separate them so as to situate both in the same discursive space. Yen demystified what Gellner calls, in a different context, "the aura of inevitability, permanence and naturalness" associated with the ascribed differences of intelligence underlying the social distinction between literati and peasants.²⁶ Using the concept of "scholar-farmer," Yen intended to show the illiterate peasants that their intelligence was equal to that of others; their recognized skill as intensive farmers was one piece of evidence among many others.²⁷ To Yen, intelligence is not a marker of generic qualities that characterize social status, but an ability that needs to be trained and developed. The sociologist Fei Xiaotong points out that considering country people "stupid" in fact confuses knowledge and intelligence; illiteracy in the countryside resulted not from people's lack of intelligence but from the way rural society operated.²⁸ Yen did not want to bestow a particular identity on peasants, but rather to make "scholar" a universal identity available to all citizens. The ultimate goal was not merely to enable the illiterate to read, but to cultivate "intelligent and progressive citizens of the Chinese Republic."²⁹ The nation would thus be built on a solid intellectual foundation of a community of citizen-scholars, who were actively *learning* and *thinking* as they participated in communal and national affairs.

In Yen's view, the May Fourth New Culture Movement was restricted to a small circle of intellectuals: it did not have any impact on the lives of the commoners, not to mention that it failed to emancipate them from the oppression they had suffered.³⁰ Therefore, Yen's advocacy of literacy as a form of rural vernacular was a critical response to the linguistic capital and the new hierarchy emerging from the vernacular movement and the "going to the people" movement of the May Fourth period. The irony underlying the May Fourth vernacular movement is that modern society was constructed on a new form of inequality. In his thought-provoking work *The Ignorant Schoolmaster* (1991), the French thinker Jacques Rancière questions the logic of this particular model of emancipation driven by the goal of progress because it would lead to "stultification" of the people. He argues that developing "people's education" in a modern society often indicates "a working allegory of the way that inequality is reproduced by 'making visible' equality"; inequality, he says, "has a way of asserting itself through equality."[31] Rancière, therefore, proposes that equality should not be considered the ultimate goal; rather, the assumption underlying the educational process should be that people of all backgrounds are equal, because "the obstacle stopping the abilities of the ignorant one is not his or her ignorance, but the consent to inequality."[32] It is fitting to apply Rancière's observation to the May Fourth vernacular movement, when this "invisible inequality" was made visible in what Andrew Jones refers to as "a form of pedagogy through which the enlightened are entrusted with the elevation of the as-yet underdeveloped" in modern China.[33] Yen, of course, did not go as far as Mao, who sought to repudiate the teacher-pupil dichotomy altogether.[34] Nonetheless, he broke with the May Fourth paradigm and proposed a new rural vernacular distinct from the May Fourth modern vernacular. The notion of the scholar-farmer was thus employed as a democratic critique of unequal social conditions that the May Fourth failed to address. With this concept of scholar-farmer, "literacy capital"—defined by Joan Judge as "varying levels of reading knowledge that provided differing degrees of access to history, prestige, wealth, and power"—could be distributed to broader social strata to promote a democratic readership.[35]

Yen once pointed out that the Chinese have contracted three kinds of metaphorical illness caused by illiteracy: blindness, deafness, and dumbness: "the majority of the citizens could not read books or newspapers, so weren't they blind? They had little knowledge of the social reality, so weren't they deaf? In a society like this, who could speak? Most of them were *silent* too. Weren't they dumb?"[36] The three sicknesses caused the silence of the rural masses. This description evokes Gayatri Spivak's classic question regarding whether the subaltern could speak. Illness or the "sick man" was a prevalent metaphor for China's failure in the international arena since the beginning of the twentieth century.[37] Reformists and revolutionaries offered various solutions. Yen was no exception. He and his colleagues considered themselves able to cure the disease and adopted the metaphor of a doctor that recalls Lu Xun's story. After experiencing a national humiliation in Japan, Lu Xun decided to give up his original plan to become a doctor and produce literature to cure the spiritual flaws of the Chinese people rather than their bodily illnesses. Unlike Lu Xun's categorizing sickness into the dichotomy of the physical versus the spiritual, the body versus the mind, however, Yen considered sickness simply an indicator of the lack of indispensable technological equipment, namely, a failure to use "writing as a technology," in the words of Walter Ong. As a "technology," it is "not mere exterior aids but also interior transformations of consciousness."[38] Ong contends that years of learning and practicing writing as a technological skill help cultivate a person's intellectual capacity. Departing from those who were skeptical of the curability of the illness, Yen believed that the "illness" of illiteracy could be cured within four months if the peasants could acquire the "technology" through methodical teaching and practice.[39] Thus Yen envisioned a future of the nation in which the subaltern indeed could see, listen, and speak, but first needed to be technologically equipped and patiently trained and cultivated.

Yen's interest in literacy education dates back to his experience of teaching Chinese coolies in France during World War I, an experience that put him in close contact with Chinese laborers from peasant societies—an unlikely opportunity for the son of a gentry family in China.[40] In her 1945 interview with Yen, Pearl Buck recorded his recollection of the teaching experience in France:

> As he wrote down for them the messages which they wanted to send to their families, he came to see that though these men were illiterate they were *not really ignorant*. They thought *shrewdly* and *profoundly*, they understood, with a sort of practical common sense, the things they saw around them in France, they had *lively humor* and *warm hearts*. They were *industrious* and *courageous*. There in France this young Chinese intellectual began to be proud of these countrymen of his, whom he had never known before. He began to feel a stir in his soul. These men, he told himself, were worth teaching.[41]

Yen developed a strong identification with these peasants-turned-coolies: "'*I was one of them*,' he said frankly, . . . 'I myself didn't know *our* own people until I was in France, thrown into their midst there because of my five thousand coolies and men of labor. For the first time I began to see something of the bitterness and the distress of the people.'"[42] Yen broke down the dichotomy between self and other that often underlies enlightenment thinkers' conception of the people, and used instead the rhetoric of "us"—this rhetoric would come to dominate the rural reconstruction movement in Ding County. Yen identified with the Chinese coolies and placed peasants on the same footing as intellectuals. This attitude seems consistent with Rancière's proposal that equality is the point of departure rather than the ultimate goal. Yen had an empathetic understanding of the overall situation of rural China—its poverty, disease, and misgovernment—and of his peasant compatriots—their sufferings, virtues, and potentialities. Before he and his colleagues went to Ding County, Yen cautioned them against "assuming a patronizing attitude toward the people"[43] and urged them not to form their own circle in the Ding County. For Yen, citizenship training had a dual goal: it not only aimed to educate the illiterate, but also valued "educating the educated."[44] Because of this attitude, Buck considered Yen "an awakened intellectual,"[45] a phrase that evokes the rhetoric of "us": the ones who needed awakening were not only the masses, but also the social elite. Historian John Fitzgerald points to the centrality of the metaphor of "awakening" in the dramatic transformation of Chinese consciousness and politics in modern times.[46] But this idea of "awakening" was predicated on the belief that the social elites were the ones waking up the masses and saving China. By "awakened intellectual," Buck meant that Yen changed the way of viewing the common people and that he had come to identify himself as one of them. It is this feeling of identification and the effort of merging with village life that characterize the teaching of Yen and his colleagues. In his words, "I was part of them," and rural reconstruction should be "our" matter instead of simply theirs.

II. Lantern Slide and Illustrated Primer: The Visual Imaginary of the "Attraction" of Rural Life

Yen characterized his pedagogy as "visual education" to teach peasants literacy,[47] and visuality in his project mainly took two forms, lantern slides and illustrations, both intended to bridge visual literacy and verbal literacy and to conflate oral and written forms. The dynamic combination of images and texts created vividness and an aesthetic immediacy for viewers. Current studies on visuality in China generally focus on its function in urban consumer culture.[48] In this section, I demonstrate how visuality operated in a nonconsumer space such as the village, and how it played an important role in making a new public culture that differed fundamentally from the previous clan- and kinship-based communal life of rural society.

Slideshows were imported to China in the mid-nineteenth century, and offered the village people a view of the world beyond their locality.[49] In the early 1920s, this modern visual medium was discursively associated with a shocking incident described by Lu Xun in his "Preface to Outcry" (*Nahan zixu*). Shown at the end of one of Lu Xun's classes during his medical studies in Japan at the beginning of the twentieth century, the slide revealed a crowd of Chinese peasants, his fellow countrymen, watching an execution of another Chinese man. Lu Xun instantly related the apathy of the spectators toward the beheaded Chinese man and their ignorance of their common national belonging to the weakness of China. Influenced by this slide incident, Lu Xun vehemently critiqued the failings of the Chinese national character, particularly its lack of sympathy and fellow feeling.[50] In Rey Chow's interpretation, moreover, the slide incident was also a traumatic encounter with modern media, what she calls "technologized visuality."[51] Yen, by contrast, sought to turn this modern medium into an effective and attractive instrument to teach literacy and to forge a pedagogical community.[52] Emphasizing the impact of visual media and images on the student-spectator, Yen invoked the idea of *attraction* to incite the interest of the rural masses: "the word on the lantern slide was enlarged which could exert a big influence on students, for 85% of the knowledge people receive is from human eyes."[53] Using lantern slides as a teaching tool coincided with the tendency in avant-garde art and film of the early decades of the twentieth century in the West, echoing, for example, Sergei Eisenstein's invocation of the terms "attraction" and the "sensual or psychological impact" of the "exhibitional confrontation."[54] This direct stimulation and immediacy of the slide invited visual curiosity and elicited students' attention and participation. Projecting the word onto a screen also transformed abstract written words into accessible visual images, thus creating a realm of rural vernacular that could enhance the visual attributes inherent in the pictograms and ideograms that constitute the Chinese writing system. The impact of "technologized visuality" on audiences recalls Walter Benjamin's description of the revolutionary changes wrought on the human perception by cultural technologies such as film in his celebrated essay "The Work of Art in the Age of Mechanical Reproduction." Benjamin contends that modern visual media (such as cinema) tend to dispel any "aura" of art, thus allowing it to function as a potential instrument in the emancipation of the masses.[55] The use of lantern slides in Ding County dispelled the sacred "aura" of the Chinese writing system, once the monopoly of the literati class, and brought it to an audience of "scholar-farmers" as part of a shared intellectual possession.

"A community of feeling" and "a sense of fellowship" are ideas that figure prominently in Yen's educational project.[56] "Technologized visuality" and collective spectatorship in the midst of screening played a role in facilitating a modern sensory consciousness, in inspiring a collective spirit, and in forming a new communal culture. Because peasants had the habit of chatting whenever they gathered together, teaching by lantern slides helped inculcate in the rural students the modern manner of staying quiet in a public space.[57] Critical thinkers have cautioned against replacing oral forms with written forms, believing that this could result in the disintegration of communal culture and lead to the alienation of the individual.[58] The lantern slides, however, allowed rural audiences to share a visual experience and to read a "textbook" as "our book." Hence this restructured reading space and mode of reception through "technologized visuality" constituted a public space and a realm of rural vernacular, and simultaneously offered a solution to the alienation associated with modern life and modern technology. This idealized social setting did not replace the old structure of rural communal culture with solitary, private reading (which might result in an inward-turning tendency), but established an intersubjective and cooperative group.

With the goal of fitting into the social life of the village, Yen planned to build "lantern slide schools" (*huandeng xuexiao*) in the existing public spaces of the village society such as temples and ancestral halls, which had been used for teaching, ancestor worship, and communal rituals.[59] These school communities emerged from the voluntary interests of the villagers and were significantly different from the ritualized gatherings that normally filled these village spaces. Central to these communities was a new kind of teacher-student relationship, one that was far more egalitarian than the deferential master-disciple hierarchy. Yen adopted the principle of the "guiding student" (*daosheng*) in the hope of cultivating a learning atmosphere among fellow scholars.[60] The guiding students were selected by their classmates from among the brightest students in the class, and they acted as assistants to the teacher. With great self-respect and a sense of responsibility, the guiding students would teach their families or a class in the neighborhood after going home, and thus became the democratically selected communal leaders who shared knowledge with other members.⁶¹ This arrangement extended a learning atmosphere from the school into the community as a whole. In this sense, the rural reconstruction movement could ultimately become, as Yen expected, an indigenous project that was "self-operated, self-supported and self-propagated."⁶²

Most important for Yen was to relate literacy to the peasants' everyday lives and to provide a tool for improvement.⁶³ Illustrated primers were broadly used to teach urban illiterate people during the early 1920s.⁶⁴ *The Farmer's A Thousand Character Primer* (Nongmin qianzi ke) is from the series *The Thousand Character Primer* published by the Association for Promoting Chinese Mass Education (Zhonghua pingmin jiaoyu cujinhui), which was founded in 1923 with the goal of rescuing the nation and reforming society.⁶⁵ The illustrated primers were printed using lithographical techniques, first introduced by Western missionaries in 1826 yet not broadly used in China until 1876.⁶⁶ *The Farmer's A Thousand Character Primer* resembles the previous primers in many aspects but was adapted to the rural context with a selection of Chinese characters most frequently used in the peasants' everyday life.⁶⁷ It was constantly revised based on previous and ongoing teaching experience and readers' responses. The four volumes of the primer taught literacy and knowledge related to everyday life, social behavior, professions, hygiene, citizenship, agriculture, and science; they introduced motivational stories to encourage learning, particularly about the descendants of a poor family achieving success through learning. Every lesson comprised three parts: illustration, text, and new words.

Illustrations had long been used as a pedagogical tool to teach the illiterate masses various ritualistic, religious, and moral practices in imperial China.⁶⁸ Laikwan Pang suggests that unlike premodern illustrations, which normally followed cultural conventions and did not offer new information, modern print culture was characterized by a "realist desire," to "reach and comprehend the new modern reality, so that these pictures retain a subjective dimension."⁶⁹ Modern illustrations demonstrated that "the visual was the primary conveyer of information, and it emphasized and visualized change, the novel, and the particular."⁷⁰ The illustrated rural primers used in Yen's literacy campaign played a role in visualizing the written words for pedagogical purposes, but they also gained a certain degree of autonomy and were not merely subordinate to the words. The words and images worked together to produce mutual illumination. Consequently, the words could be applied in everyday use when peasant students encountered the referenced images in reality. The illustrations did not challenge deep-rooted values of rural society, such as filial piety and respect for learning and teachers. Nonetheless, the illustrations, which appeared on the right page of the primer, revealed a "realist desire" to capture changing reality—the actual and the idealized, the residual and the emerging—and conveyed messages far more complicated than the literal meanings of the words on the left side. Contemporary scholars tend to see modernity more as a transformation in human experience and perception than a clearly defined historical period.[71] This new configuration of experience in the Ding County experiment took the form of a rural vernacular, which suggested a new quotidian folklife that was not drastically torn or divided from the preexisting social fabric of the village.

By incorporating learning and reading into quotidian rural life, Yen attempted to abolish the labor division on which the antagonism between village and city was built and to cultivate a well-rounded new figure, the scholar-farmer, as the main actor of *The Farmer's A Thousand Character Primer*. Yen cautioned that rural reconstruction should avoid the danger of "raising the level of consumption without raising the level of production."[72] This illustrated primer envisioned a form of modern life that could be developed within the current economic conditions of the local community and could be enjoyed by the peasants living in their own village. The illustrations situated rural society in a broader web of relations and transformed the rural into a space where the villagers could reach out to build connections with both the nation and the world. Most of the illustrations in the textbook were visual representations of human relationships and group work, resisting the tendency to reproduce the atomized, solitary modern individual freed from social ties—an image that often dominates depictions of modern urban life. Some illustrations in the primer manifest Yen's ideas about preserving traditional values and adapting them into the modern world.

One of the main goals was to instruct peasants in various kinds of practical writing, such as couplets, postcards, letters, invitation cards, loan receipts, title deeds, invoices, and posters, making them aware that writing is part of everyday communication, and some lesson texts in fact serve as templates. All these forms of writing simultaneously constructed a contract- and trust-based society that was endorsed by written documents.[73] With a strong awareness of the need to "arouse the interest" of students and using detailed, thoughtful pedagogy, the literacy instructors were encouraged to adopt a visual education that started with illustrations in the classroom. This would generate questions and answers related to the text, and then they could teach how to write and read the words and conclude with reading the texts.

Kate Merkel-Hess has provided a detailed discussion of literacy and citizenship training and of how these primers constituted a rural vision of modernity.[74] However, my reading of the primer and its illustrations underscores how they attempted to reconstruct the living spaces of the peasants, such as the agricultural field, the rural home, and the school as well as the village at large. Reconstructing these social spaces involves inscribing the rural vernacular onto the quotidian spaces, and the ideas related to modernity were not abstract anymore but sensory and perceptual experiences of everyday life. What most visibly distinguishes *The Farmer's A Thousand Character Primer* is its reconstruction of the agricultural field as a new space related to the redefinition of the peasant identity as "scholar-farmer." The field is not only a space for collective labor but also a site for learning literacy, reading newspapers, and experimenting with new methods to improve the agricultural yield. Lesson 1 (Vol. 1) starts with a peasant who is deeply engrossed in reading the literacy primer while carrying a hoe and walking in the field. The text on the left side simply introduces an individual defined by name and age, while the illustration speaks more about a peasant's self-characterization as a scholar-farmer and highlights the "engrossed" peasant figure, who reflects the kind of "attraction" conveyed by the primer reading. Lesson 21 (Vol. 4) further describes the image of the "scholar-farmer" "engrossed" in the classroom, a collective of peasants who are young, dressed in clean clothes, dignified, modest, hardworking, conscientious, diligent, and persistent. The peasants' attitude of being "engrossed" seems no different in the agricultural field than in the classroom.

Some illustrations in the primer depict the important role that print culture should play in a modernized rural community, recalling Benedict Anderson's ideas on the role of print culture in forging an imagined national community.[75] Lesson 1 (Vol. 3) features two peasants sitting under a tree in the field; they are absorbed in reading a newspaper as an important channel to learn domestic and global news. In this visual representation, the national and the global have already penetrated the local field. Interestingly, the text on the left indicates that traveling beyond the village and reading newspapers are two important ways to learn, so that reading the newspaper can be a kind of mind travel. The picture presents an imaginary scene of the agricultural field where villagers can learn about a larger China and a wider world. Moreover, the primer provides a simple definition of peasant (*nongmin*): a person who tills the land (*zhongtian de ren*).[76] Simple as it is, the sentence has been freed of any pejorative meaning when peasants were often associated with backwardness in the enlightenment discourse. Lesson 8 (Vol. 4) describes the physical and mental divide of the peasantry, who toil physically but mentally are carefree and at liberty. Lesson 19 (Vol. 4) suggests that the identity of the peasant should be based on their skill-defined profession, similar to the skills merchants and workers use to make a living. All such descriptions take a neutral tone and show respect toward farming as a profession.

Domestic life is also one of the main subjects in *The Farmer's A Thousand Character Primer*, and the domestic space, both inside and outside the cottage, also acquires new meanings. The domestic space is redefined as a learning environment for both parents and children, a harmonious gathering place for family (mainly in the courtyard), and as a space to perform personal hygiene. For example, Lesson 3 (Vol. 1) features parents and siblings spending leisure time together in the courtyard. The domestic space is portrayed as a comfortable place to live, with gardens growing a variety of flowers and vegetables. In Lesson 4 (Vol. 1), although the text on the left simply indicates the gender and age composition of the family, the geometrical design of the family dining scene located in the courtyard in the illustration describes its structure: the parents are placed in a prominent position in the middle, and they are surrounded by the younger generation. The composition of the picture grants the father both authority and reverence; he is holding a bowl and has a serious facial expression, while the illustration also highlights the nurturing mother, who is feeding the youngest son. The primer suggests that filial piety remained one of the core moral values regulating human relationships, despite the fact that May Fourth intellectuals had fiercely attacked it as a key component of the oppressive patriarchal social system. For example, through writing a postcard, a son expresses his respect for and affection toward his father working in Peking; another son specially purchases an expensive mooncake as a rare gift for his mother.[77] These illustrations do not imply a simple continuation of traditional social hierarchies. Instead, they suggest both human affection and familial order, which, in Yen's words, represents an attempt to "conserve the sound and healthy customs and traditions of the past."[78]

Moreover, the domestic space fosters a learning environment. In Lesson 13 (Vol. 1), the image on the right shows a girl sitting at a desk with two young boys, deeply absorbed in reading the primer; the text on the left explains that the two younger siblings are inspired by their elder brother, who as their "teacher" leads them to study after returning home from school. The illustration also brings a visible gender dimension into the imaginary of modern rural life, in which female literacy was an important part of Yen's educational project; two-thirds of the students in the literacy campaign were young women and girls. Moreover, the domestic learning environment also calls for educated parents: an illustration (Lesson 45, Vol. 4) features parents and their little son and daughter sitting around the table teaching and studying, for "parents should receive education themselves in order to serve as good models for their children if they want their children to receive a good education."[79] The domestic space is also infused with a vision of "hygienic modernity" located in everyday life, in which the peasants reform their previous living habits—brushing teeth, washing hands and face, taking baths, washing clothes and quilts, cleaning the room, and cultivating good dietary habits—which directly shape the domestic space and strengthen the body.[80] Most important, "hygiene" here does not refer to an imported concept that often worked to distinguish the civilized from the barbarian, the city from the countryside. Rather, it is presented as a comfortable and pleasant experience brought to everyday rural life and later internalized in the habits of the peasants.

Not merely an institution aiming at teaching literacy, the school space also plays a key role in connecting the national and the local. The symbols of the nation are manifested in various images such as the national map, the photo of the founding father Sun Yat-sen, and the ritualistic act of celebrating the national holiday. The illustration in Lesson 2 (Vol. 2) shows China's national map that instills in the peasants an abstract sense of the entirety of the nation, whereas the text emphasizes the dual identity of the peasant-reader defined by both nationality and native place. The text for the National Holiday (Lesson 19, Vol. 2) suggests that the visibility of the national flag symbolizes the presence of the nation in the locality, and that the villagers are no different from the Chinese living overseas, as all of them simultaneously salute the national flag.

The primer does not represent the rural poverty and devastation prevalent in China in the 1920s and 1930s; as a textbook for peasants, it clearly tries to shape the peasants' good perceptions about themselves and to raise their self-respect by constructing two images of a utopian village: the traditional poeticized "peach-blossom-spring life" village (Lesson 5, Vol. 1) and the modernized model village (Lessons 23 and 24, Vol. 4). For the first kind, the illustration often includes lyrical images, as of ancient architecture such as pavilions; in the text on the left, familiar lyrical poetry brings the aesthetics of "gardens and fields" poetry to the rural space constructed with a selection of poetic symbols. The primer incorporates into its imaginary landscape an idyllic rural life, giving viewers a heartwarming glimpse of the countryside that was undergoing disruption and suffering. These pictures of pastoral life do not so much beautify the countryside with unrealistic images as grant a sense of dignity to rural residents and promote the "attraction" of village life. The primer illustrates a charming rural home that comprises pavilions, flower beds, and trees, and a rural life characterized by the deliciousness of fruits and the fragrance of flowers.[81]

For the second kind, the end of the primer includes three lessons (Lessons 22, 23, and 24, Vol. 4) describing the modernized model village named Equal People Village. The village features a landscape of modern institutions and facilities, such as kindergartens, schools at various levels and for multiple functions, a newspaper-reading room, a lecture hall, a literacy-learning place, a public sports playground, museums, hospitals, and a hygiene association. Based on the text on the left, it models the premodern rural society regulated by the village contracts, one that practices a degree of self-governance and hosts public organizations and associations.

Taking the village as a spatial and social location from which to envision Chinese modernity and the nation-state was not new. For example, a late Qing novel, *The Roar of the Lion* (Shizi hou, 1904–1905), by the noted revolutionary author Chen Tianhua (1875–1905), portrays a Civil Rights Village, located in the southwest of Zhoushan Island, Zhejiang Province. Depicted as a land of utopia and a prototype of civilization, the village features a landscape of modern westernized institutions and is characterized as embodying the spirit of democracy and freedom in stark contrast to the darkness, backwardness, and suffocation that characterized the last decade of the Qing Empire. Unlike the Civil Rights Village as a space free of and in contrast to Qing rule, however, Equal People Village is characterized as a microcosm of the nation under the rule of the nationalist government and reflects the Confucian ideal of "improving oneself, managing the family, governing the states, and bringing justice and virtue to the world" (*xiushen, qijia, zhiguo, pingtianxia*). The model village deploys the logic of extension, which means that the exemplariness grounded in an individual's self-cultivation can be extended to the family, to the village and county, and finally to the nation.[82] Kate Merkel-Hess notes that the rural modern "adopted the markers of urban modernity,"[83] and the makeup of the model village to a large extent transfers some urban attractions to the countryside, such as parks, libraries, kindergartens, and gymnasiums. This way, *The Farmer's A Thousand Character Primer* rewrites the relationship between the city and the countryside not in terms of dichotomies, for the countryside also enjoys convenience, good education, and entertainment, originally from the city. The neat, orderly arrangement of the buildings in the bird's-eye-view illustration also foregrounds the rural attractions: a peaceful, forested village equipped with all the modern conveniences, entertainment, and educational resources. While nation formation usually emphasizes mass migration from the country to the city, Yen's locally anchored rural reconstruction explored possibilities for peasants to improve their economic and social welfare while remaining in rural areas.

III. The Peasant Theater: Performing Empathy in the Public

The acquisition of political consciousness among the peasantry was one of the revolutionary issues of modern intellectual and political thought in modern China and beyond. Elites of various political stripes sought to enlighten the peasantry so that they could become a political force, whether for nation-building or revolution. For its part, the rural reconstruction movement in Ding County strove to cultivate "intelligent and progressive citizens of the Chinese Republic."[84] The movement promoted a different relationship between the intellectual and the rural audience. Xiong Foxi suggested that the intellectuals in the movement should not act as "preachers" (*chuandao shi*), but as *actors* (*xizi*): "though having the principle of uplifting the consciousness of the peasants, we will try our utmost to use artifice and theatrical skills and make the ideas implicit and tacit."[85] Xiong highlighted the *performative* aspect of the rural reconstruction movement and the intellectual's identity as a public *actor*. The rural reconstruction participants' social role was not to explain the new ideas, but to perform them. In modern China, the idea of the intellectual as a public actor was different from the widely accepted image of the May Fourth intellectual, an ideal of individual authenticity as well as eccentric and idiosyncratic personality, as represented in literary works such as *School Master Ni Huanzhi* (Ni Huanzhi, 1928) by Ye Shengtao (1894–1988).

In this novel, the protagonist's experience of reaching out to the masses ironically becomes a journey of self-fulfillment and personal development. This May Fourth personality cult was in fact the intrusion of the private, personal realm of experience into the public, impersonal realm, and the tendency to judge public figures as personalities and worship them as charismatic figures. By contrast, Xiong did not view the intellectual as a unique individual or preacher, but rather as an actor whose virtuosity in the "theatrical performance" could make the experience of modern politics for the rural masses an *attractive* show.[86]

What Xiong Foxi emphasized was a kind of emotional education as integral to this type of citizenship training in his theatrical practice during the movement. The established scholarship on affect now echoes Xiong's approach: many scholars have convincingly argued that feeling is not opposed to rationality, but is in fact part of value judgment.[87] Martha Nussbaum, for instance, proposes the idea of "rational compassion," contending that appropriate compassion is a constitutive part of good citizenship.[88] She then suggests that "an education for compassion" would help to "cultivate the ability to imagine the experiences of others and to participate in their suffering."[89] Arguing against the Enlightenment dualism of reason and emotion and Jürgen Habermas's ideal of a bourgeoisie public as a realm of rational engagement, both Haiyan Lee and Eugenia Lean demonstrate the importance of sentiment in constituting a modern public in China in the first half of the twentieth-century.[90] Indeed, the central importance of emotion in the Ding County experiment's citizenship training marked a new way of conceiving of the peasants.

After arriving at Ding County in 1932, the theater director and educator Xiong Foxi began to write rural plays and to create a unique peasant theater. He launched a kind of emotional education and transformed the village into an outdoor theater in which the peasants were both actors and spectators. Xiong's success in fusing the folk tradition with Western theatrical techniques has been discussed in detail by contemporary drama scholars.[91] Here, I focus on the role of emotion in theatrical performance in creating a space of attraction and empathy in which the peasants could gain a strong sense of participation and solidarity in communal affairs. I argue that the peasant audience's voluntary involvement in theatrical performances made the public and the nation an aesthetic experience through which it could exercise its membership and shape a collective subjectivity. Here aesthetics mainly refers to perception and sensation, rather than techniques and tastes accessible only to the highly educated.

The use of opera as a tool of education and entertainment for the masses has a long history in traditional China. Nonetheless, according to James Yen in his preface to Xiong's book *The Experiment of Theatrical Popularization* (Xiju dazhonghua zhi shiyan, 1937), using drama as an educational tool in the rural reconstruction movement fundamentally differed from traditional opera's function of "indoctrination" (*jiaohua*).[92] Due to a series of social and cultural changes in the early twentieth century, the idea of education gained new implications, emphasizing both democratic inclusiveness and political consciousness. Xiong also pointed out a few major points that characterized the modern idea of education. First, the active exploration of social issues and the organization of social activities displaced the philological and textual scholarship of the past. Second, students were not only the recipients of education, but also active participants in social movements. Third, education emphasized the fashioning of the new subject and new life.[93] This modern, politically charged idea of education suggested that the strength of the nation hinged on a broad base of intellectually and politically trained minds that could be forged through the socializing practices and aestheticizing effect of theaters and schoolrooms. The theatrical performance as an artistic and social project resembles what Friedrich Schiller considered the "aesthetic education of man," which sketches out "an aesthetic utopia that attributes to art a virtually social-revolutionary role."[94] As I will discuss below, the theatrical performance/education was promoted as a unifying force and entailed a form of communication that created a realm of rural vernacular and encouraged intersubjective relationships between people, shaping a politics firmly rooted in a refashioned local culture.

Prior to the rural reconstruction movement, the most popular theatrical forms in Ding County were *yangge* (a form of folk dance), *daxi* (big plays, such as Peking opera), and street entertainment.[95] Rather than reform local opera, Xiong insisted on staging Western-imported spoken drama for his theatrical experiment because content and form were inseparable and interdependent. In Xiong's case, the introduction of spoken drama to the rural world was itself a demonstration of a modern mode of communication. Nevertheless, the major forms of spoken drama in China at that time, the civilized play and student drama (*xuesheng ju*), both popular in big cities, were inadequate to build substantial connections with the real lives of peasants. Xiong therefore explored how to make the form of spoken drama accessible and enjoyable to peasants, through a process of what he called "theatrical rustication" (*xijunongminhua*).[96]

In imperial China, popular religion was closely tied to the village community; there was no strict functional division between religion and theater, or between ritual and opera, which constituted "a single ritual-operatic performance complex," in the words of David Johnson.[97] Theatrical performance provided the primary images—heroic and marvelous figures drawn from history and fantasy—for a Chinese peasant's religious universe and offered the symbolic and intellectual materials out of which peasants constructed their ideas about the human world. The new rural plays in the Ding County experiment made an unprecedented move by replacing the dramatic popular characters that dominated *daxi* with ordinary peasants. The theatrical experiment launched an aesthetic revolution that shifted the focus from great heroes and grand events to the lives of the anonymous. Although *yangge* performed day-to-day events, it mainly concerned the themes of filial piety, romantic love, and folk customs and the forms of comedy and courtroom drama.[98] In the theatrical experiment, by contrast, "the farmer has been able to see himself in such plays as 'The Handicaps of the Illiterate Farmer,' 'The Light of the Common People'— which is the Mass Education movement, and 'The Princely Man,'" which represented new experiences for the rural masses.[99] The peasant theater staged real-life matters such as bridge-building and tax collection as "our" matters, giving the peasants a sense of the exploitation they were suffering and locating the symptoms of an era and a society in the minute details of ordinary life.

Xiong was particularly impressed by a few incidents that demonstrated to him the impact these rural plays had on the peasants' everyday lives. After the play *The Butcher* (Tuhu) toured in some villages, the name of the hooligan character, Butcher Kong, lingered on the villagers' lips and became a nickname for the scoundrels they met with in real life.[100] In another case, after watching the rehearsal of the play *Cross the River* (Guodu), a peasant from a nearby village was shocked by the similarity between what was performed on stage and what had recently happened in his village—it seemed as if an ordinary village matter had been instantly performed on the stage.[101] These incidents revealed the blurring boundary between the theatrical stage and the stage of everyday life. Life bore a striking resemblance to art: real life was experienced as a performance at the same time that the performance became increasingly lifelike. Xiong's experiment repudiated the principle of *l'art pour l'art*, imagining literary creation not as a subjective experience of the individual author, but as a kind of work in progress in which art could become part of a larger advancement of social progress and changing social relations.[102]

In the beginning, rural-reconstruction-movement participants worked as actors in these rural plays. Gradually, however, the peasants became intrigued by this new kind of drama and voluntarily took over the stage and performed the plays for themselves.[103] This defies the stereotype of the conservative peasant unwilling to accept new forms and sticking with the old, habitual ways of thinking. Moreover, the peasants bore a dual identity as both the objects of the pedagogy and the subjects/actors on their own stage; in this way, spoken drama gained popular support and took root in the rural society. Xiong emphasized the peasant audience's reception and appreciation of the plays, rather than the "objective" quality of the scripts.[104] Dispensing with preconceived conceptions about rural society, Xiong and his colleagues actively engaged in personal observation and investigation. They always discussed their scripts with the local peasants after they finished the first drafts, and would then incorporate the peasants' opinions and sometimes significantly change the scripts.[105] The revision process involved the peasants as part of a collective authorship.

The peasant reaction and participation thus greatly affected Xiong's dramaturgy and performative principles. As in Bertolt Brecht's epic theater, in which every spectator is enabled to participate, Xiong stressed audience involvement. But unlike epic theater, whose art aimed to produce astonishment rather than empathy and to stress rational judgment instead of emotional involvement, Xiong's rural plays aimed to construct a theater of sympathy and to cultivate a compassionate spectator-citizen.[106] The key to the tremendous success of the rural plays was that Xiong did not intend to create a detached viewing experience for the peasant audience: the content of the play was not about "him" or "them," but about "our matters."[107]

In what follows, I discuss three plays written by Xiong, paying special attention to how their theatrical performance evoked empathetic responses from the peasant audience, granted peasants the power to define social justice, and eventually instilled a participatory consciousness in the peasants' daily lives. These three plays reflect an evolution in how Xiong developed his model of theatrical performance. Notably, each play foregrounds a major emotion, which was echoed by the audience during its performance: *anger* in *The Butcher*, *compassion* in *Driven to Revolt* (Bishang Liangshan), and the *collective passion* of human unity in *Cross the River*. These plays are signposts of an emotional trajectory, developing from the individual's voluntary feelings to collectively shared sentiments. The emotions and sentiments in the plays constituted an exploration of social justice in the realm of theater.

Produced in 1932, *The Butcher* instantly claimed a broad and devoted peasant audience due to the closeness of its subject matter to rural reality. The driving force in the plot development is public anger against a social injustice emerging from a personal grudge, the kind of conflict that is common in rural areas. The play begins with a dramatic demonstration of anger by two peasant brothers who are fighting over dividing the family property. However, this family conflict is taken advantage of by a usurious butcher, Kong, an outsider to the family who tricks the two brothers into a fierce fight to gain profits for himself. Kong pretends to seek an acceptable solution for them, manipulating the illiterate brothers into signing a contract that cedes their house to him. Not able to read the contract, the brothers become victims of their illiteracy. The play advocates for literacy as an effective weapon that peasants can use to protect their property. Instigated by Butcher Kong and driven by their fury, the two brothers decide to resort to a lawsuit to solve this family conflict. Up to this moment, these peasant brothers' anger has mainly taken the form of a personal grudge against Kong. At the very end of the play, Kong's scheme is foiled, and the two brothers come to realize how deeply he deceived them. What was the most dramatic about this play was the audience reaction at the end of the play: a peasant could not help standing up from the audience and shouting to the stage with anger.[108] As a spectator who could understand both sides of the issue, the young peasant's improvisational reaction was a voluntary display of inner emotion as well as a rational judgment.

Xiong was surprised and impressed by the audience reaction, because he had not designed a black-hearted butcher with the intention of irritating the audience. The audience participation therefore transformed what was a personal grudge in the play into a conscious public intervention—an intervention made through a public display of indignation in the theater. The audience member's interruption of the play showed strong emotional involvement, which differs from the Brechtian ideal of compelling the viewer to assume a critical distance from the dramatic events unfolding on stage. The philosopher Richard Solomon points to an intimate connection between emotion and justice, contending that "a sense of justice is first of all a matter of emotions, to be cultivated from our natural inclinations of fellow feeling and molded into a durable state of character."[109] The peasant's outburst during the performance was acceptable because the expression of anger was associated with a real social injustice. It showed his willingness to experience and engage with the world instead of sitting back passively as an outsider. The performance offered him an opportunity to air righteous anger and gave the subaltern a chance to express his judgment of social injustice in a theater-based moral community. Finally, the anger of the peasant victims in both the play and the peasant audience were legitimized by the play's ending; the drama ends with the spreading news that about 2,000 people had reported to the local court the many crimes committed by Butcher Kong. Xiong was open to three possible endings to the script: first, the two brothers beat Butcher Kong to death; second, Butcher Kong's property is confiscated and the peasants organize their own association; and third, Butcher Kong is handed over to a just government for punishment. In the end, Xiong chose the third scenario because he wanted to avoid showing mob violence on stage, while still appealing to the regulating force of a benevolent government.[110] Moreover, this ending also manifests the new definition of law and the promotion of its application to civil society, both by taking account of ordinary people's concern with property rights and by giving weight to the law's defense of individual economic rights.

The great popularity of *The Butcher* and the audience's voluntary involvement inspired Xiong to add more theatrical elements to other plays that could encourage audience participation. In 1934, the peasant theater staged *Driven to Revolt*, which was also titled *Wang Si* or *An Ox* (Niu). The play recalls the traditional vernacular novel, *Water Margin*, in which outlaws are portrayed as a group of heroes. In the rural play, a peasant named Wang Si, a filial son, caring husband, and obedient villager, is beleaguered by high rent from the landlord and by heavy taxes from the local government. Despite their suffering, the impoverished rural family shows strong sympathy toward their plow ox, who has served them well for fifteen years. Xiong adopted the notion of universal humanity to emphasize that the play was not associated with any real-life political camps. Driven by an instinct to survive and saddened by his mother's death, Wang Si is unknowingly led by his cousin into a circle of outlaws. On realizing the nature of the group, Wang Si resolutely leaves them and returns home. Unfortunately, he discovers that Landlord Peng has seized his wife. Later, local policemen wrongly accuse Wang Si of being an outlaw; he is arrested and put in prison.

The play was originally supposed to conclude with Wang Si shouting grievances and yelling for help as he is arrested. However, Xiong changed the dramatic ending because he felt the original might encourage peasants to become outlaws, which was certainly not what his theatrical education sought.[111] Xiong added a courtroom trial scene that broke the fourth wall and allowed the audience to directly speak to the stage. When Wang Si refuses to admit any wrongdoing, the magistrate decides to torture him to confess. At this point in the drama, an audience member spontaneously stood up and spoke for Wang Si, and the courtroom on stage was extended to the entire theatrical space, with the audience becoming both witnesses of the trial and actors within the play. Feeling the unfairness of the trial, the audience shouted to the stage "Wang Si is wronged!" and "He is a good person." A strong tension gripped the theater, as the audience instinctively felt that they were sitting in the court of the local government instead of a theater. Eventually the magistrate agreed with their request and Wang Si was granted bail, after which some members of the audience walked onto the stage to support Wang Si. The fictional court case on stage was thus solved through the intervention of the real audience.[112] Wang Si—whose benevolent humanity is highlighted in the play—confronts a tragic fate, which evoked the sympathy of the rural audience. The new ending shifted the play's focus on a peasant's outcry against his tragic fate to the audience's demonstration of sympathy in the public space of the theater. The dramatic courtroom trial highlighted the presence of a public audience who sympathized with Wang Si on a deeply emotional level, who transformed into a collective body of informed, critical judges, and who felt empowered to change legal proceedings. The entire theater could be characterized as a highly performative and emotionally invested public space.

Eugenia Lean draws attention to the shared function of theater and courtroom in 1930s China: the theater could provide a public space to stage real-life matters that could not be discussed in the public media under state control,[113] and the courtroom could become "a forum for spectacle, melodrama, and public debate" that offered opportunities for a mass audience to voice opinions and to stage "public sympathy" (*tongqing*) to influence the court's final decision.[114] Lean sees that the intertwining of emotion and mass culture paved the way for the emergence of a sentiment-based public sphere and the rise of participatory politics. She also stresses that a public could be defined not only in terms of the act of "seeing" but also in terms of "feeling" and "sympathizing."[115]

Through the enabling forces of "feeling" and "sympathizing," the peasant audiences for Ding County rural plays could actively participate in their communal affairs, rather than passively observing as outsiders. In the performance of *Driven to Revolt*, the judge was forced to reconsider Wang Si's legal case because of the public's sympathy for him, and he showed judicial compassion by granting the wronged peasant judicial exemption. The sympathy of ordinary peasants gained new social implications in the rural reconstruction movement. The question of who had the right or power to define justice was a central concern in modern society. In this theatrical performance, the peasant audience exercised their power to change the situation, and their public display of sympathy became a motivating force for advancing social change and creating a public for themselves. The audience exercised their emotional and moral judgment, which helped to build fellow feeling and collective unity (even though this had the potential to lead to mob violence). This way, the peasants could act as citizens who were able *to feel, to think, and to judge*, which contributed to the formation of a compassionate political subjectivity. In light of Martha Nussbaum's proposal for "an education for compassionate citizenship," this theatrical performance also demonstrates that compassion, even in the form of spontaneous reaction, was gained through artistic experience as a medium for the proper training and cultivation of human empathy in order to enrich human life and understanding.[116]

The plot design and performance style of *Driven to Revolt* was fundamentally different from later theatrical performances in communist Yan'an. Indeed, one of the popular plays during the Yan'an Peking Opera movement was also titled *Driven to Revolt* (1943). Adapted from *Water Margin*, this Peking opera version of *Driven to Revolt* was a historical drama performed in a traditional theatrical style. As such, it was strikingly different from the new form and new messages that characterized the theatrical experiment in Ding County. Whereas the former was concerned with dramatic revolutionary change, calling the peasants to take power to subvert the current system, the latter showcased the reformist ideal of rule of law and grassroots legal practice, emphasizing both the conscience of the community and the elasticity of the legal system.

Cross the River (1935) was widely regarded as the highest achievement among the theater experiments in Ding County. The play featured the rural masses' public passions that culminated in an outdoor theatrical performance in which every peasant audience member was actively involved. This play also incorporated music and singing, which were key components of traditional forms of theater. Taken together, these elements show the dramatist's combination of the traditions of both China and the West. Unlike the peasant protagonists in the plays discussed earlier, the hero in *Cross the River* is a college graduate, Zhang Guoben, who refuses to pursue a meaningless life of social climbing in the city; instead, he resolutely leaves the city and returns to his hometown, Zhang Village. According to Xiong, the character of Guoben was idealized and far from realistic; the rural reconstruction practitioners hoped to use this character to encourage young students to see rural reconstruction of their hometowns as a viable career option.[117]

In the play, a wide river separates Zhang Village from the county seat, causing great inconvenience to generations of villagers. The scoundrel ferry owner Hu monopolizes river crossings, from which he reaps exorbitant profits. A group of peasants, led by Zhang Guoben, decide to build a bridge for themselves. Regarding the bridge as a monument to the "interests of the masses" that would change the lives of the villagers,[118] Zhang organizes the peasants to break ground on the bridge, a symbol in the play suggesting both that the foundation of the nation is locally anchored and that the village is connected to the outside world. The peasants enthusiastically and courageously devote themselves to constructing the bridge, donating money and labor. Singing loudly and working strenuously, the peasants form a sublime scene of collective labor in which singing and action fuse into a public passion of "harmony, strength, and grandeur."[119] The peasants chant repeatedly, "How can one person's strength be enough? [. . .] only the strength of the group can make it."[120] The lyrics reinforce the increased strength the individual gains when he or she merges with the collective body of the community.

Fearing the loss of his monopoly, the malicious Hu manages to sabotage construction, and in the process a peasant boatman falls to his death. The police investigate the death, and Hu is eventually sent to prison. The ending of this play also went through different versions; the playwright finally settled on using the law to punish Hu and allowing the peasants to serve as witnesses to the case.[121] As with *Driven to Revolt*, the practitioners in the rural reconstruction movement felt a strong need to distinguish between the peasants' potential mob-like behavior and the act of appealing to the law for social justice.

This play ends on a triumphant note when Hu is seized and taken away by the police. Afterward, Zhang calls for the local peasants to actively participate in this communal enterprise:

> "As I said, it is *our responsibility* to build this bridge! Each new participant will add more strength. The more people involved, the greater the strength will be! This bridge seems like the soul of China, and can stand for the spirit of our nation! Xiao Li, Zhao San, Wu Mao, Shen Ba, come on, let us come *together*, work *together*, toil *together* and sweat *together*! Let us build a great foundation, from which everything new will be born!"[122]

Recasting the image of the nation in terms of concrete local matters—such as the building of a bridge—shows the nation not as something remote or abstract, but as legible and transparent, immediate and tangible in the peasants' daily lives. By calling peasants to participate in the construction of the bridge, Zhang, the elite intellectual, invites "the masses into history; and the invitation-card . . . [is] written in a language they understood," as Benedict Anderson puts it for a different context. Anderson goes on to ask "why the invitation came to seem so *attractive* and why such different alliances were able to issue it."[123] In my earlier discussion, I have shown that the "technologized visuality" and the theatrical performance constituted a form of rural vernacular that made the public a space of attraction and empathy for the peasants. *Cross the River* goes further to explore the way to win the hearts and minds of the rural crowd. What underlies the idea of construction is not only nation-building, but the fashioning of subjectivity through a collective experience; the latter is reminiscent of Xiong's association of education with construction. The play also foregrounds a shift in power from the local hooligan to a union of local peasants, bridge builders, and ferry workers, intimating that the nation has become an enabling force and a rallying call for the masses.

This new performance principle aimed to dissolve the boundaries between actors and spectacle and to blur reality and representation. It created a pleasure that was centered on the ability of audience members to move into the show and that gave them power to command the spectacle. Xiong's colleague, Yang Cunbin, described this theatrical inclusiveness and the power that comes with unity:

> In terms of audience, many individuals are grouped into a unity. Under the same goal, hundreds of thousands of audience members

are crying and laughing together, thinking together as well as feeling touched together. There is absolutely no trace of the individual either on or off the stage, only the spirit of the group. The intellects and sentiments of hundreds of thousands of people are fused into an organic unity and a force. During the process the masses are organized unconsciously and involuntarily, therefore having the greatest effect. Consequently, only drama can play such a concrete role in organizing the masses.[124]

To convert the masses into national citizens and new political subjects, the play suggests, there must be pleasure and exhilaration in the participation. This audience participation highlights the fusion of the intellects and sentiments of the masses in their aesthetic experience of forming the collective sensorium and communal unity, a process of creating a "space of attraction and empathy." Both viewing and acting could shape this collective identity, which paved the way for shaping a sense of esprit de corps and for cultivating the emotional education that was necessary, according to Xiong, for citizenship training. The performance created a shared experience that united both the actors and spectators as active members of the community and played a vital role in cultivating a participatory mentality. The Chinese people had long been accused of behaving like "a heap of sand," lacking any unity to resist outside aggression. Xiong's theatrical experiment demonstrated how to invoke their feelings, how to make them feel the strength of forming a collective, and, ultimately, how they could transcend various boundaries restricting their horizons. What was occurring onstage was a part of their everyday lives, and the villagers could also identify with the nation in a most visceral, immediate, and concrete manner. It was an "aesthetic practice," which Jacque Rancière would regard as "ways of doing and making" and "configurations of experience that create new modes of sense perception and induce novel forms of political subjectivity."[125] Audience involvement in the theater was to include the peasants in the aesthetic-political field of the nation and create a sense of shared experience through which people could begin to imagine themselves as part of a modern, public culture.

Dipesh Chakrabarty leads us to consider the nature of political modernity as peasants emerge in the modern sphere of politics and need to confront the unequal development within a nation. He evokes the metaphor of the "waiting room" to discuss whether or not peasants need to go through formal education and undergo a period of preparation and waiting before being entitled as citizens and full participants in the political life of the nation.[126] In the Ding County context, the reformers aimed to empower the peasants and instruct them through theatrical performance. The theatrical experiments in Ding County demonstrate that the object of the pedagogy could at the same time be a constantly changing subject and that the pedagogical process itself could create a space of "attraction and empathy" involving the agency and cooperation of the object of the pedagogy. By conceiving of the peasants as both the subjects and the objects of rural reconstruction, the theatrical experimentation envisioned the peasants as both actors and spectators—the peasant audience could be *attracted* into the national performance, thus becoming emotionally involved actors in the construction of the national spectacle. In Xiong Foxi's dramas, pedagogy and performance converge into a single process; learning and performing work hand in hand to forge political subjectivities that are not determined by pre-established goals.

Xiong found that the indoor theater could not fully serve the peasants' mushrooming passion for theatrical performance, particularly because the fourth wall cut off fluid interaction between the actors and the audience in the indoor space. The first permanent outdoor experimental theater designed and built for the performance of spoken drama was located in the remote village East Buluogang.[127] The outdoor stage was in fact designed to show respect to peasants' habitual way of watching traditional Chinese opera outdoors. The outdoor stage was simple and cheap to build.[128] In the outdoor theater, the stage and seats were connected by stairs, and the stage was therefore *not the other* world.[129] Moreover, the outdoor theaters in Ding County were multifunctional centers of political and cultural activities; they presented a series of peasant-centered dramas, facilitated a new collective life, and in this way intermixed the stage and public life.[130] They were not only used as spaces for theatrical performance, but as public forums for discussing communal issues, as centers for educational and cultural activities, and as training grounds for mass political participation. In these public spaces, the "masses" could shift from an abstract concept to a concrete collective through a communal sharing of sentiment.

With growing national and international attention to the countryside since the late 1920s, and driven by a strong awareness of the need to understand the people, the liberal reformers' social practices in Ding County experimented with an effective and affective communicative mode. The key idea that runs through this entire chapter is the creation and practice of a communicative mode as a legible and accessible rural vernacular, one that encompassed lantern slides, illustrated primers, and spoken drama. All these forms of cultural production and modern media in Ding County—the written, the visual, and the performative—constituted this rural vernacular. This is a kind of vernacular culture not only pushed the May Fourth vernacular to go deeper toward the rural people, it went beyond the linguistic domain of literacy education itself. This process featured a new collective sensorial experience that reconnected with the rural masses and facilitated new forms of human communication and interaction, along with a pedagogic community of "attraction and empathy." In this way, the rural vernacular combined the urban and the local, the premodern and modern, as well as the scholarly and the farmerly, often blurring the dividing lines between them to produce an equalizing and democratic training experience. I use the idea of the rural vernacular to characterize the Ding County experiment to emphasize its new configuration of human experience and perception and its grounding the modern as a newly accessible quotidian experience for the local peasants. Yen's experiments in the rural reconstruction movement in Ding County offer a fresh perspective from which to reconsider how the rural provides a self-reflexive instance of the enlightenment discourse, which was taking shape as rural culture was remade through its dialogue with the enlightenment and the nation.

Kate Merkel-Hess's study showcases how the approach of rural reconstruction reformers differed from radical revolution in the Chinese countryside.[131] Questions have often been raised about its impact on Communist cultural activities in the revolutionary base, Yan'an. It is true that Mao Zedong participated in Yen's 1923 literacy campaign in the city of Changsha, and in 1929 urged the party workers to use *The People's 1000-Character Literacy Primer* as a model to teach literacy in revolutionary areas. The cultural strategies used in Yen's rural reform movement later inspired the cultural policy in Yan'an, which used popular culture to reach and remold broader peasant audiences.[132] According to Charles Hayford, many of the educational techniques developed in Ding County were later adopted in Yan'an. Nonetheless, from the outset, Yen's liberal reform and Mao's radical revolution were very different.[133] Both Mao and Yen saw the peasants as the source of power for the emergence of a new China. Nonetheless, the former's elevation of the peasants revealed a tendency to reify their peasant identity as a defining characteristic of their class. The latter, on the other hand, intended to cultivate a community of "scholar-farmers" and make "scholar" a shared identity available to all social strata, and to erase the artificial line that separated peasants from the culturally and socially advantaged classes.[134]

In the 1920s and 1930s, rural reconstruction had become a global and transnational trend, and the village served as a space for expert reform.[135] Yen's experiment was inspiring to many of his contemporaries.[136] In the winter of 1933, the American journalist Edgar Snow (1905–1972) visited the rural reconstruction movement in Ding County. Inspired by the experiments being undertaken, Snow published two essays: "Awakening the Masses in China" in the daily newspaper the *New York Herald Tribune* and "How Rural China Is Being Remade" in the magazine *China Weekly Review*. In the first essay, Snow described the Ding County movement in effusive language as "some of the most dramatic and what may prove to be the most important work in 'life reconstruction' going on anywhere outside Soviet Russia," and went on to suggest that it could create a model to transform the peasants into new citizens. In Snow's view, the significance of the Ding County movement had gone beyond a local event and gained relevance to the world, for "anything which is destined to reshape the whole content of life for those millions is profoundly important to the world."[137] In the second essay, Snow described Ding County as an emblematic unit of a larger China and pointed to the primary reasons for China's backwardness—the people's ignorance, poverty, and disease, and a lack of public consciousness. He considered the Ding County experiment "the only scientific attempt yet made to evolve the kind of social order necessary if China is to survive as nation."[138] Hopeful about the potential of these experiments to change the lives of millions of Chinese peasants, Snow admired Yen's ambitious plan to turn Ding County into "the center for training mass education leaders for all of China," including the Communists.[139] However, at the end of his essay, he considered the harsh realities and expressed doubt that the local power brokers who monopolized the economy and politics would be willing to support Yen's experiment,[140] and concluded the essay with the thought that revolution was the only means by which the Chinese people could be emancipated, which inspired him to embark on a revolutionary journey of going to the countryside.[141]

PART II

The Rural as a Constructive Vision
of Chinese Revolution

CHAPTER 3

Journeys to the Revolutionary Site
The Construct of Red China, Time Consciousness, and Patience, 1936–45

The Communist revolution's pivotal spatial transition from urban centers to rural areas in the late 1920s after its disastrous defeat in the big cities, along with the breakout of the Anti-Japanese War (1937–1945), signaled the emergence of a new perception of the Chinese countryside and the peasantry. In the apt words of Brantly Womack, it turned the political periphery into the political center.[1] This spatial transition therefore turns the rural into the important site to imagine and envision radical revolutionary politics. The rural space underwent a transformation from the locus of the backwater areas to the revolutionary center associated with a hopeful future that represented another China. The revolutionary base not only competed with the rule of the Nationalist Party but identified itself as part of the global antifascist movement.

In June 1936, the American journalist Edgar Snow (1905–1972) left the imperial capital of Beiping, broke through the Nationalist Party's blockade, and embarked on a journey to Bao'an,[2] the first headquarters of the Chinese Communist Party's Central Committee and the Chinese Soviet Government during the Anti-Japanese War in northwest China. Snow's revolutionary expedition represents a journey of "going to the countryside" in two ways: it is the story of an American who traveled from his developed industrial home country to a predominantly agrarian China, then set out from Chinese metropolises such as Shanghai and Beijing, where he initially stayed, to the northwest rural hinterland. To Snow, this journey aimed to go beyond "the Forbidden City, a place of wonder and enchantment," to discover "the China of breaking toil, starvation, revolution, and foreign invasion."[3] His experience of staying with the Communists for a total of about six months was recorded in the publication of *Red*

Star Over China (*Red Star* hereafter, 1937) in English.⁴ The book was subsequently translated into Chinese under the title *Xixing manji* (*Journey to the West*); it sold tens of thousands of copies and turned China's northwest rural hinterland into a space of sensation and attraction.⁵ Its publication and tremendous popularity in China and abroad, in the words of John K. Fairbank, was "in itself an event in modern Chinese history,"⁶ for this journalist's work significantly influenced international and national perceptions of the Chinese revolution and subsequently shaped the course of modern Chinese history and remapped the Chinese political landscape.

Coinciding with Japan's invasion, *Red Star* inspired thousands of young students and intellectuals to make a pilgrimage to Yan'an in the hope of rescuing China. In a photo-text titled "On the Way to Yan'an" (Qu Yan'an tuzhong) in the Shanghai-based influential monthly periodical *The Good Companion* (*Liangyou*) in February 1939, a photo caption reads, "Every day, thousands of youth, from every corner of the country, come to Yan'an, either joining the army or attending the school. Some of them ride on donkeys, some ride bicycles, and some come on foot. These young people who pursue the light regardless of all the hardship will become China's future masters."⁷ In the public discourse, Yan'an, once a bleak border town with a small population, had become the Mecca for an exciting, adventurous life as well as a shared domain that bound people both geographically and politically.⁸

However, going to Yan'an not merely referred to embracing a sublime and heroic enterprise. It meant experiencing revolution in all its roughness and vulgarity; facing a harsh and sometimes depressing reality, tedious work, strenuous labor, trials and tribulations, and technological "regression"; and subordinating the individual mind to the revolutionary discipline. Among the enthusiastic young people were prominent leftist writers such as Chen Xuezhao (1906–1991), Ding Ling (1904–1986), and Fang Ji (1919–1998), each of whom wrote about life experience in Yan'an in a way rather different from Snow's *Red Star*.

Current studies on the political culture of Yan'an during its revolutionary period are mainly concentrated in the fields of history and political science. With its multivalent and often contradictory facets, Yan'an was situated in the "incongruity between socioeconomic liberation, on the one hand, and political-intellectual repression on the other."⁹ Yan'an symbolizes an indigenous and creative approach to poverty, inequality, and stagnation that represented the anticolonial struggle against imperialism.¹⁰ Yan'an also stands for a political "discourse community" and "symbolic capital" that constructed its own unique forms of truth, belief, and coded narrative.[11] Moreover, as the place of origin of the Rectification Campaign, Yan'an was also the site of violent and cruel power struggles among the top party leaders surrounding Mao.[12] An undeniable fact about its revolutionary culture was the struggle regarding the strong tensions and contradictions "between town and country, prosperous and poor, dynamic and stagnant."[13] This chapter takes the perspective of "the revolutionary journeys to Red China" to deal with these tensions as they are revealed in the writings at the time. This chapter does not aim to provide a comprehensive study of the rich body of literature and arts produced during the Yan'an period.[14] Instead it focuses on a sequence of representative journalistic and literary writings regarding how urban revolutionaries and writers deal with the paradoxical combinations of radical politics and material impoverishment, and of urban sensibilities and rural crudeness. More importantly, by juxtaposing different genres and analyzing various representations of "going to Red China," this chapter situates the revolutionary center in the midst of a series of tensions—between the epic and the prosaic, between grand history and disturbing everyday details, between the discursively progressive and the materially primitive, and between international inclusion and local division. Yan'an represents the revolution's strange mixture of affection and cruelty, sublimity and roughness. The rural is not a backdrop against which revolution unfolds; instead, it is deployed as a crucial spatial and social form in which to envision a modern type of emancipatory politics that demands both passion and patience.

Through the juxtaposition of the rural and the revolutionary in the journalistic and literary representations of the journey to Yan'an, I explore how the rural underwent a signifying process, acquired revolutionary significance, and took on a universal, global meaning. I first examine the construct of the revolutionary site in Snow's *Red Star* as "documentary expression" that dictates a sentimental way of looking at the poor and the ordinary. The intersection of the rural and the revolutionary constituted an aesthetic-political regime that encompassed vaudeville-style theatrical performance, nonalienated rural industrialization, and collective heroic personalities, all of which turned Yan'an into a symbolic space comprehensible to the rest of China and the world. I then turn to discuss time consciousness in Yan'an, exploring how radical revolutionary politics, with its goal of linear historical progress, is paradoxically measured by the agrarian rhythm of peasant life. Then I read Chen Xuezhao's journalistic writing about the quotidian details of her life in Yan'an in comparison with

Snow's *Red Star*. Lastly, I discuss the emergence of patience as a discourse in the writings about Yan'an, with a particular focus on the story "In the Hospital" by Ding Ling and the story "The Power of the Loom" by Fang Ji.

I. Constructing a Red China in Edgar Snow's Red Star Over China

Edgar Snow's *Red Star Over China*, which brought Red China to global visibility, should be situated in an international context. It coincided with the revalorization of the image of Chinese peasants in 1930s America, when the rural figure symbolized idealized subjectivity in the American left-wing political agenda.[15] The great success of Pearl Buck's *The Good Earth* in 1930s America reveals that both Chinese peasants and the Chinese rural society were universally appealing subjects. The image of the Chinese countryside did not seem strange to American readers during a period of mass rural migration from the Midwest and Southwest to California in the 1930s. *Red Star Over China* was the earliest and most influential of all the writings about Red China by Western observers and correspondents, and it played a key role in shaping the narrative about the Chinese revolution in the 1930s and 1940s.[16]

At the beginning of *Red Star*, writing in the emotional and powerful language, Edgar Snow celebrated himself as the first journalist to break through the nine-year news blockade since the first Chinese soviet was established, generating public visibility for the Communist movement at the time. *Red Star* comprises Snow's personal travelogue, his interviews with and short biographies of the Communist leaders, and an account of the Red Army's legendary Long March (October 1934–October 1936).[17] Commonly regarded as a liberal humanist rather than a communist, Snow claimed that he kept a distance from politics to maintain his journalistic objectivity, striving to answer questions about Red China "with confidence, accuracy, and facts based on personal investigation."[18] Nonetheless, *Red Star* reads like a sentimental tale. Trained at Columbia University's School of Journalism in 1927, Snow was much informed by the "documentary expression" that characterized the radical journalism of America and Europe in the 1930s and early 1940s.[19] *Red Star* should be categorized as "documentary nonfiction of the thirties," which is "writing that records the experience of common people, often in their own words; or first-hand reportage that tries to convey the texture of actuality as well as the facts."[20] As "a radically democratic genre,"[21] the "documentary" communicated a reality that was "not objective, but thoroughly personal,"[22] and introduced important "ways of looking at the poor, the damaged, the inconspicuous, and the ordinary."[23] On the one hand, this form emphasized the credibility and vividness that representations of actual facts can convey to readers,[24] and therefore entailed an activist agenda that functioned "to right wrongs, to promote social action," and attempted to "influence its audience's intellect and feelings."[25] On the other hand, "the documentary" looked at the world "from the common man's point of view," dignifying, ennobling, sentimentalizing, yet simultaneously simplifying those who were deprived, powerless, overlooked, unheard, and forgotten and transforming the marginalized into the remarkable.[26] The "credibility" and the "vividness" of actuality are created by "the primacy of feeling," which means "emotion counted more than fact."[27] This explains why Snow's account of the Chinese Communist revolution touched the hearts of so many readers and helped shape the course of modern Chinese history. It also represents the kind of wartime reportage that Charles Laughlin refers to as "the aesthetics of historical experience,"[28] which emphasizes the artistic qualities in the leftist journalism and proletarian literature of many nations, affirming the role of subjective experience in the presentation of current events.[29] Not simply an engaged traveler, Snow also adopted the reporting technique of "participant-observation," much valued in "documentary expression," reiterating and reinforcing the ideal of "nonfalsifiability" as well as the importance of "lived, firsthand experience" gained among the people.[30] Snow's pursuit of factual objectivity infused with emotional effusiveness underlies his conviction about the "nonfalsifiability" of the Communist revolution; he repeatedly emphasized his firsthand experience and eyewitness account to make the revolution a credible, vivid occurrence to the outside world. Nonetheless, "participant-observation" also runs the risk of creating "biased communication,"[31] which will lead to reducing and distorting reality because of emotionalism.[32]

Since 1927, the Communist Party had been confronted with the most devastating frustration since its establishment; furthermore, its revolutionary base lacked the industrial capability and sufficient material resources to sustain long-term fighting. Therefore, Snow was driven by the questions in the first chapter of *Red Star* and sought to explore the "inexorable force" that drove the Red Army soldiers to endure hundreds of battles, blockade, salt shortages, famine, disease, epidemic, and finally the Long March to fight "so long, so fiercely, so courageously, . . . [and] so invincibly" in an area lacking industrial utilities, money, and modern technologies.³³ Snow's encounter with the Chinese Communist Party was described by John Fairbank as representing a historical moment of "the powerful appeal which the Chinese Communist movement was still in the process of developing."³⁴ He was excited about his entry into "a stone fortress," the almost inaccessible territory of the "Celestial Reds" who were "fighting in the very heart of the most populous nation on earth."³⁵ And the iconic collective image of the soldiers fighting bravely had already taken on a planetary dimension. He used expressions such as "powerful appeal" and "inexorable force" and depictions of "incredibly stubborn warriors" to represent the Communists, turning the rural into a space dominated by a dynamic, vibrant force that would spread across China and beyond, rather than a static utopia. In what follows, I analyze how Snow actively developed ways to look at the poor and the ordinary through journeying in northwest China, attending theatrical performances, and conversing with the Communist leaders, especially Mao.

On his way to Bao'an, Snow stopped in Xi'an, the region where Chang'an (the ancient national capital) was located. At the end of the Tang dynasty the area started to decline and never recovered, which subsequently shaped the public discourse of "its decline."³⁶ Prior to the publication of *Red Star*, Fan Changjiang (1909–1970), one of the most influential Chinese journalists of the time, had already drawn public attention to the social and political crisis in the relatively unknown territories of the northwest with his book *The Northwest Corner of China* (Zhongguo de xibeijiao, 1936). Recounting firsthand social investigation during his long and hazardous journey, he highlighted both the richness of the history, geography, customs, and classical poetry regarding this area as well as the peasants' poverty, local corruption and exploitation, political and economic chaos, and the imminent Japanese invasion.³⁷ In a way similar to Fan Changjiang's writing about the geographical landscape, Snow also connected the historical past and the present politics, considering northwest China (one of the poorest parts of China) "the original confines of the birthplace of China" rather than a region that symbolizes decline.³⁸ In the early 1930s, the leftist journalists had reconstructed the landscape of the Chinese wartime countryside as a heroic battlefield for the nation's struggle for liberation.³⁹ The peasants are portrayed as part of the landscape in their writings, which "communicate the emergence of new values and a new form of community among soldiers and peasants."⁴⁰ With their commitment to concrete historical and social experience, the reporters transmitted the truth and their perception of actual events as a way to explore "the aesthetics of historical experience."[41] Snow's perception of the landscape blends the "actual" and the "imaginable," and his empirical observation of the geography of this area soon gives way to an imagined description of the rural landscape. What strikes Snow most is not the previous glory of the Han-Tang era, but his imaginings regarding "the rich and colorful pageant of [the Han-Tang] people."[42] Snow seems to celebrate the same locality that witnessed the convergence of both the ancient folk myth of rural China and the Communist movement's effort to make a new China. He encountered a young Communist, Deng Fa (who would escort Snow to the revolutionary base), and stood with him on a hill. As he imagined the resurgence of the great Han people who ruled a united and then progressive China, Snow was deeply immersed in the emotional impact of the landscape, and he engaged in a "documentary expression" way of looking at reality in which "emotion counted more than facts."[43] Snow's emotional reaction led him to envision the Red Army as the legitimate descendants of the Sons of Han, and to prophesize the final victory of the Chinese Communists. Moreover, the barren land of northwest China has always been endowed with rich colors and shapes, which evoke imaginings and poetic connections. He wrote about the land in the sunshine as being like "a magnificent sea of purpled hilltops with dark velvety folds running down" and "the pleats on a mandarin skirt";[44] the loess land has a kind of surreal beauty that combines the fantastic and the frightening.[45]

Contrary to the timid Chinese peasants Snow met elsewhere, the young peasant he ran into on his way to the red capital was good-looking, healthy, self-assured, and most important, unafraid and joyful.[46] By emphasizing the high spirits of these subalterns, *Red Star* creates a revolutionary space dominated by highly positive emotions such as happiness and optimism and simultaneously excludes negative emotions such as sadness, pessimism, ambivalence, hesitation, and anxiety. Regarding happiness as the capability to feel positive about one's existence, Snow was amazed that the Red Army soldiers were able to balance their personal tragedies and their spontaneous happiness, and therefore formed a cohesive military group of boundless spontaneous energy.[47]

In a chapter about Red Theater, in a sentimental and excited tone, Snow recorded his involvement with this big event in the town on a weekend. Attending the theatrical performance as a "participant-observer," Snow viewed the performance as a visual presentation and a sensual experience of democracy, witnessing the common folk—students, muleteers, workers, soldiers, carpenters, and villagers—all sitting on the riverside grass. What deeply impressed him is that the Red Army officers, sitting among and scattered throughout the crowd, receive no special treatment. No tickets or dress code were needed, and no spatial hierarchy divided the ordinary people and the leaders. The layout of the Red Theater as an open-air stage also displayed the spirit of openness and all-inclusiveness of a public social space as well as a natural environment, in which humans and animals such as goats grazing nearby were present simultaneously. The aesthetic represented by the Red Theater was not "subtlety and refinement," but a combination of propaganda and primitiveness that could still draw the full attention of the audience.[48] Situated in the specific context of the time, Snow highlights that the propaganda was simultaneously "the poignant truth" and the living reality in the eyes of the rural audience.[49]

Snow regarded the three-hour performance that combined "playlets, dancing, singing, and pantomime" in the Red Theater as vaudeville, a variety entertainment performance most popular from the 1880s to 1910s in America.[50] Before it was adapted into a profit-making business by entrepreneurs, vaudeville represented a democratic form of American popular culture: no-cost, organic, "something akin to folk dancing on the village green,"[51] open and accessible to all classes and age groups.[52] The performance was an enjoyable and diverse presentation that engaged the audience's close attention from beginning to end. Vaudeville's popularity and democratic nature lay in its "intoxicating sensation" and "spectacle within an atmosphere of levity and community."[53] Similar to its American counterpart, the Chinese version was characterized by use of primitive props, "its robust vitality, its sparkling humor, and a sort of participation between actors and audience," and important comic relief in which "bursts of laughter alternated with oaths of disgust and hatred for the Japanese."[54] Its vaudeville-type "democracy" highlighted its grassroots origin as well as the spectacle of an ideal incarnation of human community—a democratic new world that staged "the reign of the people."[55]

The performance in the Red Theater exposed the brutality and inhumanity of the Japanese invaders, calling the audience to action and stirring their disgust and hatred toward the foreign enemy. The vaudeville performance was a thrilling experience that stimulated human senses and worked to connect the people across all social classes and ages; it was simultaneously a form of antifascist democracy because it portrayed the revolution and inspired opposition to the Japanese invasion. As Richard Jean So has observed, the idea of democracy did not refer to an ideology or position during the interwar years of the 1930s and 1940s. Instead, the idea of democracy functioned as an "open form" with historical flexibility and "stood for whatever was not fascism."[56] According to Snow, the democratic nature of the theatrical performance lay in its "robust vitality" and the Communist-peasant bond emerging from the audience's engagement, the actor-spectator interaction, and shared emotional reactions. Snow described the notion of "democracy" as having a collective emotional resonance in the audience that cemented the ties of the common folk to the Communists.[57] Snow's description recalls Xiong Foxi's avant-garde theatrical experiments in Ding County in that the performing troupes adopted the ongoing events as the subject of their plays and emphasized actor-spectator interaction and the audience's emotional involvement. The theatrical performances in both Ding County and Bao'an were mainly intended as citizenship training through emotional education.

Before his journey, Snow was much driven by the question "how was it possible to speak of 'communism' or 'socialism' in China, where over 80 percent of the population was still agrarian, where industrialism was still in infant garments—if not infant paralysis?"[58] While traveling in the northwest, Snow encountered the "industrial center"—a town called Wuqi, and he was much amazed by the emergence of factories, machines, and busy industrial productions in a timeless, unchanging landscape with cave dwellings, animals as transport, and rape oil as lighting fuel.[59] What characterized the rural industry was the fusion of "the pastoral," "the primitive" and "the industrial." What was revealed to the readers was the self-sufficient nature of the handicraft- and home-based revolutionary industry as the revolutionary base was cut off from most economic connections and support. This was a survival strategy during the war that would later characterize socialist industrial production.[60]

What Snow described is not merely industrial production but what I would characterize as a form of industrial life that includes education and skill training (before working in the factories), athletic activities, studying literacy and reading, and entertainment such as watching plays. Exploitation, highly intense labor, severe injury, terrible living condition, and interpersonal cruelty often characterized the lives of workers in the factories of the metropolis of Shanghai,[61] and mirrored capitalist industrialization in nineteenth- and early twentieth-century America and Europe. Despite the primitive living conditions and scarce materials, Snow's description of the border region industries stresses their nonalienated nature and highlights industrial life as a healthy communal life. These workers watched performances, attended political gatherings, read newspapers, studied literacy, and participated in sports activities, all of which opened up a new world to them. Moreover, enjoying fresh air in the mountains, freedom, respect, and hope characterized the nonalienated, self-sufficient industrial culture of the rural hinterland. With their self-perceived identity as revolutionaries, the workers did not labor to accumulate capital, but for a higher cause and solemn goal: national salvation. This industrial culture played an important role in turning primitive living conditions into a communal life of dignity and vitality, and in balancing the Party's urgent wartime needs, the hours of intense work, and the healthy development of humanity as well as human gratification.

Red Star was imbued with Snow's strong awareness that people were making history, for in his preface to the Chinese translation in 1938, he poignantly emphasized the collective authorship of the book through the medium of his writing and recording; the Chinese revolutionary youths themselves created these living stories, which constituted history. The making of the book, in Snow's metaphorical expression, features the connection between martial actions and literary writing. In Snow's view, this is not merely the biography of the Chinese revolution, but the autobiography or the self-expression of the Chinese revolutionary youth.[62] In the preface to the Chinese version of *Red Star* (1938), Snow defines the book as *an oral history* and *an interview*, with subjects ranging from Communist leaders to common soldiers, farmers, workers, and intellectuals.[63] The interviews and biographies, however, still concentrate on Communist leaders such as Mao Zedong (1893–1976), Zhu De (1886–1976), Lin Biao (1907–1971), Zhou Enlai (1898–1976), He Long (1896–1969), and Peng Dehuai (1898–1974), all of whom seem to have had similar adventurous, rebellious, and courageous personalities. In Snow's view, these leaders, including Mao, were underprivileged members of society, egalitarian promoters of the welfare of the Chinese people, and steadfast opponents of Japanese imperialist expansion. Their personal histories all follow a similar pattern: the accounts start with their birthplaces and their personal growth, which demonstrate their strong desire to establish social justice with sympathy toward the oppressed and the poor, and finally merge their personal history into the linear development of the Chinese revolution. All these similar accounts foreground the collective heroic personalities inscribed on the rural hinterland.

The chapter titled "Soviet Strong Man," Snow's interview with Mao, exemplifies the process of turning a real-life person into a personality: Snow portrays Mao not only as "a gaunt, rather Lincolnesque figure"[64] but also as a Chinese peasant figure who embodies both "the heroic and the quotidian," as seen in his remarkable leadership and personal charm.[65] Snow writes poignantly about Mao's self-identification as a popular folk figure and a valiant outlaw, his participation in agricultural labor, and his charming character that combines a rustic, natural simplicity with a sense of humor, incisive wit, and worldly sophistication. Mao's appeal to the West lies in the fact that he represents a Chinese subaltern who is able to speak for himself through "direct quotations of a first-person testimony" in the context of "a growing but unfocused U.S. stake in Asian nationalism."[66] Snow translated Mao's stories about his experience of building local sovereignty into a proverbial tale of "robbing from the rich and giving to the poor," "a modern morality play of good against evil that transcended its immediate Chinese setting."[67] Pearl Buck emphasized the moral component in the narrative, comparing the book to both a "Robin Hood" novel and the classical Chinese novel *Water Margin*.[68] Hayden White discusses how the process of "emplotment" works in historical narratives, as the facts contained in the chronicle are encoded to form a specific kind of plot structure: "a historical narrative is not only a *reproduction* of the events reported on it, but also *a complex of symbols* which gives us directions for finding an *icon* of the structure of those events in our literary tradition."[69] Mao's narrative also gradually "passes out of the category of 'personal history'" as he transitions from a young rebel and skeptic to a member of a collective communist movement.[70] In carefully carving out a charismatic personality for Mao, Snow's record grants a human face, or a biography, to the nonhuman, teleological linear revolutionary history.

According to his biographer, Snow had acquired "a limited but serviceable competence in the (Chinese) language,"[71] and Mao spoke Chinese with a heavy Hunanese accent. The interview is based on intimate discussion, revision, correction, and proofreading that involved not only Snow and Mao, but also his Chinese interpreter Wu Liangping, who translated Snow's notes into Chinese for Mao to correct and afterward rendered the result back into English to guarantee the accuracy of the translation.[72] Snow used the word "conspirators" to describe this group: the process of interaction involved Snow's English and limited Chinese, Wu's modern vernacular Chinese and English, and Mao's local dialect; the production went through a few circles of dissemination, and the information was gathered in the context of mutual interaction. This reveals not so much the precision of literal translation as the process of imbuing the spirit of a local regime with a universal meaning—linguistic negotiation as part of the universalizing of modernity aiming to reduce the difference between the local and the universal.[73]

After Snow returned from the Communist base area, his interviews with Mao and the photos taken during the trip were published in both Chinese and Western newspapers and magazines, and thus Mao was introduced to the Western world.[74] Snow's essays were also immediately translated into Chinese and circulated widely among the Chinese beyond the revolutionary base. For example, the November 14, 1936, issue of the Shanghai-based *China Weekly Review* features a photo essay of Mao standing before the cave dwelling at Bao'an. There is no doubt that Mao was keenly aware that he was posing for both the camera and the world outside his revolutionary base. Mao's photo in Bao'an reinforced the vividness and credibility of Snow's writing as an eyewitness account. His enthusiastic descriptions of Mao are woven through this essay as an accompanying text, which seems to insert itself as a long "caption" for Mao's visual image. Much of this "caption" focuses on Mao's attitude toward Japanese imperialism.[75] Assuming the role of spokesman for the Chinese people, Mao asserted that the major problem of imperialism would be solved if Japan was defeated and driven out of China, and he called for the formation of both a National United Front and a World Anti-Japanese United Front. The feedback loop between the photo and this long "caption"-essay represents the production of the meaning of Mao's local regime as part of an antifascist movement that had global circulation; it generated universal meaning beyond the local circumstances that gave rise to it. The revolutionary base did not gain national and global visibility until Edgar Snow's legendary visit. Due to the wide distribution of writings and images about Yan'an through modern media and print culture, the process of making Red China into a heroic narrative was part of the global circulation of ideas, sentiments, and images through intimate encounters and dialogues between the American and the Chinese; it conveyed such elements as the primacy of feeling in the "documentary expression," vaudeville- and antifascist-type democracy, the collective heroic personalities, and the idealized spirit of nonalienated industrialism. His poignant accounts of heroism in Red China circulated rapidly among a broader audience, contributing to a kind of sentiment-in-flux, especially in national circuits, which made local, everyday elements fabulous and legendary. In Snow's *Red Star*, going to Red China was a journey of making the locality a perceptible body of "the other China" to be sensed immediately by readers both within and beyond China.[76]

Initially wondering whether he could even outline the history of Red

China, which was then only fragmentarily recorded, Snow finally wove a conceivable and comprehensive story out of a miscellaneous collection of unprocessed facts based on his travels, interviews, and investigations. Although readers were prone to trust Snow's objectivity, he did not simply translate "what has happened" into prose; rather, he turned remote, unfamiliar events into a coherent, culturally encoded narrative with meaning and values. In retrospect, we see that Snow's reportage not only provided "a 'scoop' of perishable news," it served more as "many facts of durable history."[77] This process showcases what Hayden White refers to as the isomorphic relationship between historical texts and literary artifacts. In Snow's narrative, the discourse of decline regarding northwest China has been transformed into the "powerful appeal" of the unity of the people and the "inexorable force" of the Red Army, finally integrating a collective heroic personality into the Communist telling of history. *Red Star*'s reality effect remade the Chinese rural hinterland and elevated northwest China to broad public visibility.

II. Time Consciousness in Yan'an

What I have discussed is that Snow's *Red Star* has turned a local regime into a rural space with global meanings and antifascist political aspirations. Part II focuses on time consciousness in Yan'an to see how this red capital had to adapt its local rhythm as it strove to catch up with the world and integrate itself into the global system. In writings about and photos of Yan'an during this period, leftist writers, artists, and intellectuals collectively shaped a public discourse of "the other China" that echoed *Red Star*. Due to the political division created by the Nationalist/Communist confrontation, China was no longer a unified nation across its vast, diverse geographical space. At the beginning of *Red Star*, Snow wrote of his excitement about leaving Beijing, which was secluded from the rest of China and its toil, starvation, revolution, and foreign invasion. He described his exciting adventure to Red China as "a journey of exploration into *a land hundreds of years and hundreds of miles* removed from the *medieval* splendors of the Forbidden City."[78] The temporal and physical distancing here seems to situate Beijing back in ancient times while simultaneously placing Red China in the present and the modern. Writing retrospectively about the huge impact of *Red Star* at the time, the American historian Owen Lattimore said that "it revealed the outlines of things until then unseen or only dimly guessed at. This was not propaganda. It was description. *There was another China*."[79] Similarly, the eminent musician Xian Xinghai (1904–1945) wrote in the March 4, 1938, entry of his journal, "I am afraid that I will be gradually left behind and will not make progress. China now has been divided into two worlds: one is sinking to the point of degeneration and corruption, whereas the other is ascending toward the bright and hopeful place. Yan'an is where the new China originates and flourishes."[80]

The collective discursive construct of "another China," or "the other China" was premised on the intertwining of modernity and revolution on a global level, because revolution connotes a brand-new beginning and a new stage in the course of history.[81] The expression "another China" describes a new cycle in Chinese history by aligning Chinese revolution with a new consciousness of time. This notion of "the other China" also situates Yan'an within a global context. The American journalist Anna Louise Strong recalled that the attraction of a town such as Yan'an that lacked material comforts and modern utilities lay in the fact that it provided opportunities to meet people with a broad vision of the world and to become close to people who were making a world.[82] A quick survey of the front pages of *Liberation Daily* (*Jiefang ribao*), the official newspaper of the Communist Party in Yan'an, shows that the Communists steadily looked beyond the narrow confines of their guerrilla base in the rural hinterland. They related themselves to other antifascist forces in the world and situated themselves in a global framework,[83] or, as Joseph Levenson observed, they were "nationalist and internationalist at the same time."[84]

Since the May Fourth period, China's entrance into the global system had been accompanied by a growing consciousness of time as a "measurable entity" by universal standards: "the Darwinian time of linear development, the Hegelian time of world history, and modern Western calendrical time."[85] With its use of the Western calendar and its strong awareness of pursuing historical progress, the revolutionary base of Yan'an certainly located itself within this global system and universal time and repudiated the traditional cyclical time (which was regarded as repetitive and stagnant). The measurable quality of linear temporality was emphasized by the modern virtue of punctuality made possible by the broad use of clocks and watches. In his discussion of the social functions of time for orientation and regulation, the German sociologist Norbert Elias argues that a heightened sense of punctuality is experienced as an internally compelling experience, and timing activities can serve to coordinate and synchronize what people do. This disciplining process was simultaneously a civilizing process.[86] Taking the giant clock above the Maritime Customs House in Shanghai as an example, Wen-hsin Yeh suggests that the clock's precise measurement of time symbolized the virtue of punctuality, and its synchronizing capacity therefore structured the temporal frame of everyday life and the emerging capitalist global order of which Shanghai was part. The disciplinary function and precise measurement of the clock also indicate its use in an urban and modern context as opposed to a rural and premodern one.[87] In fact, the "universal diffusion of pocket watches" as symbolic of modern life cultivated a sense of calculability and exactness that related business transactions to human relations.[88]

However, Yan'an's temporal progressiveness as a form of new beginning was not due to the accurate measurement of time and the broad use of the modern mechanical clock and watch.[89] Its local time was measured by the sundial, a big, crude, roughly approximate device that tells the time of the day according to the position of the sun in that particular place, and therefore cannot measure time chronometrically.[90] How, then, did agrarian time structure the rhythm of the revolution and set the pace of the revolutionary community, which aspired to strengthen China as an equal partner in the antifascist camp? Chen Xuezhao, a woman writer and journalist whose work is analyzed below, complained in *A Visit to Yan'an* that the local people often missed various meetings or had to wait around before a lecture started because there was no sense of standard time.[91] This lack of a sense of punctuality thus produced a common social experience of *waiting*. As Chen pointed out, it was difficult to have everyone arrive on time for meetings and lectures, so usually a two-hour meeting took about four hours, with the other two hours spent waiting. Such long waits often exhausted the attendees and caused complaints and conflicts.[92] The act of *waiting* became an illustrative moment of the difficulty of synchronizing human action and the asynchronous nature of time in Yan'an. Zhu Hongzhao suggests that everyday life in Yan'an and its lack of punctuality reveal a predominant collective consciousness: time was not considered an individual's private property, and thus its use was dictated by the revolutionary collective.[93] Yan'an's aspirations for national self-determination and its pursuit of wealth and power as well as a global consciousness were paced by the agrarian time. In discussing the emergence of modern times in the increasingly interconnected globalizing world of the nineteenth century, Vanessa Ogle argues that "(t)ime, or the absence thereof, thus became a measure for comparing different levels of evolution, historical development, and positionality on a global scale."⁹⁴ What is paradoxical about the ongoing grand revolutionary enterprise is that on the one hand, it radically pointed toward the promise of a Communist utopian future; on the other hand, it also took on the extremely slow speed of the agricultural and local rhythm, the boredom of everyday life, the huge waste of individuals' time, as well as the frustration of frequently waiting in a small hinterland town.

Yan'an did not appeal to temporal precision to unify its community; instead, it relied on constructing a unified revolutionary identity and a discourse community.⁹⁵ Although the administrative departments and ordinary people followed the national calendar, Yan'an did not represented "the other China" as a community of simultaneity based on the conception of empty and homogenous "clock" time put forth by Benedict Anderson. Instead, it replaced the time discipline of modern capitalism and metropolitan life with revolutionary discipline as an absolute priority and an organizing instrument of authority. If clocks serve people as a way to orient and regulate their behavior in relation to each other in the urban context, the revolutionary discipline works to enable individual self-restraint and external social compulsion in the rural hinterland.

III. Living a Local Life in Yan'an in Chen Xuezhao's A Visit to Yan'an

The time consciousness in Yan'an reveals a composite of universality and particularity, globality and locality in the revolutionary culture. In *Red Star*, the locality has been turned into an aesthetic-political realm with universal meanings. Part III diverts attention to the quotidian details of everyday life and the revolutionary site of Yan'an as a locality via a comparative reading of Snow's *Red Star* and Chen Xuezhao's *A Visit to Yan'an*. Xiaobing Tang has insightfully pointed out that "the dialectic movement of the heroic and the quotidian constitutes an inescapable condition of secular modernity" as seen in the passion for a utopian future and longing for a fulfilling life.⁹⁶ In August 1938, inspired by Snow's *Red Star* and following the path taken by many of her contemporaries, Chen Xuezhao, who had recently returned from France, made the difficult journey from Chongqing to Yan'an. Both Snow and Chen were avid global travelers, and their trips to Red China should be treated as integral parts of their cosmopolitan travels. But the contrasts between Snow's and Chen's narrative of Red China are striking partially due to their different intended audiences, for

Chen was mainly writing for the Chinese readers and Snow for a bilingual readership. Chen published a collection of essays under the title *A Visit to Yan'an* (Yanan fangwen ji) in 1940. The three years separating Snow's *Red Star* from Chen's essays made a dramatic difference in the portrayals of the journey to Yan'an. The social reality can be grasped through the details of particular cases; how to look and how to feel become important elements of the portrayal. Even prior to her arrival at Yan'an, Chen already had a complicated sense of the place as mixing bitter material conditions and spiritual excitement, and the closer she got, the more lackluster and impoverished the conditions became. Yet for all the desolation, poverty, and sparse population, Chen expressed a deep patriotism: "I still love it, and I am deeply in love with it, because this is our motherland."[97] Traveling over long distances enabled her to link her national consciousness with the particular land she was traversing and gained her a visceral relationship with her motherland—a concrete feeling that combined both exhilaration and hardship. During her ten-month stay, Chen visited primary schools and the Anti-Japanese Military and Political University (*kang da*), chatted with local people, interviewed Communist leaders and cadres, met other intellectuals and writers, sauntered on the streets and country roads, and rested in the cave dwellings.[98] But she maintained her own individual viewpoint and considered her visit to Yan'an a continuation of her trip to Europe, and wrote that France's Marseille and Yan'an shared an atmosphere of freedom and democracy: "On the streets of Yan'an, one could speak and laugh freely, the topics could range from state affairs to private matters, and one could talk about whatever he/she liked and speak loudly."[99]

Nonetheless, the heroism and progressive historical consciousness in Snow's narrative give way to fragmentary and ambivalent thoughts in Chen's notes, which cover the prosaic, intimate, and everyday details of her visit. *Red Star* resembles what Ban Wang describes as the socialist realistic novel, which "features a mythical and epic structure in which dream and history, individual and collective become one."[100] Chen's writing about Yan'an resembles the reportage literature, especially in its commitment to concrete experience and its resistance to being absorbed into propaganda machines to "critique the shortcomings of the socialist order it helped bring into being."[101] Although her travelogue was by no means a departure from the dominant grand narrative of history and revolution, her perspective as a woman allowed the audience to see many of the mundane facets of Yan'an that were completely ignored or obscured in Snow's writings. Her writing comprises miscellaneous opinions, perceptions, and thoughts about what she saw. Neither Snow nor Chen was insensitive to the details of everyday life, but their ways of dealing with such details are distinctive.

Snow was also curious about all the quotidian aspects of the Red Army, such as dress, eating, play, love, and work. However, in his epic narrative, the details are manifestations of externalized feelings and are compatible parts of the coherent historical totality, sustained by a belief in the unitary nature of multitudinous everyday details. For example, during his trip, Snow encountered an impoverished "red peasant" who insisted on killing one of her half-dozen chickens for him so that Snow would spread the good reputation of the reds to the outer world.[102] When Snow casually and impolitely called the teenager-red-army-soldiers "Hey" (Wei), they resisted by ignoring Snow and insisted that he should call them "comrades," which showed the equality principle of the comradeship that bound the Communist community.[103] Moreover, Snow also noticed Mao's enjoying his favorite food, red pepper, and even relating the symbolic meaning of the pepper to the revolutionaries.[104] His descriptions of both the peasant and the official in their everyday simplicity constituted a coherent narrative about a group of low socioeconomic standing in society, and their everyday doings become expressive actions infused with historical significance.

However, Chen's numerous details remain disjointed, rambling, and random. She writes in a self-deprecating manner, turning attention to "insignificant" quotidian matters. Describing herself as "a person who has no consciousness of partisanship" and "a wild person who knows no principles of organization,"[105] Chen writes this way:

> But, what can I write? Those great words should be reserved for great people to say and to write. I am only an ordinary person, an ordinary woman, and can only write a few sentences, a few sentences about those trivial, insignificant matters, such as our daily necessities like fuel, rice, cooking oil, and salt.[106]

In a chapter titled "Chat about Yan'an," Chen continues,

> How can I describe the life in Yan'an? Maybe only poems with beauty and sublimity can capture and convey its very spirit. But my writing is too clumsy, so I can only leave my dream for those Yan'an poets to realize. I am not able to straighten my clothes and sit properly to tell the story. My dear faraway friends, let me chat with

you in a casual way—talk with you a little about this today, and a little about that tomorrow, very unsystematic and subjective, but all these are simply my own life.[107]

Unlike Snow's writing, which embodies a masculine aggressiveness in its assumption of an objective and totalized narrative and its emphasis on the "powerful appeal" and "inexorable force," Chen's writing is marked by her gendered authorial voice, directed to an intimate circle of friends, and combines her modesty with a detailed attention to her subjective experience. Her "chatty" way of writing about Yan'an readily reminds us of the similar sensibility described by the Shanghai female writer Eileen Chang (1920–1995) in her essay collection *Floating Words* (Liuyan). Chang refuses to write a grand narrative, and her fascination with the illuminating moments that emerge from the seemingly irrelevant leads us to better understand Chen's feeling of being unable to capture Yan'an as a coherent totality. What is impressive about Chen's writing is the fact that she does not romanticize the poor or the experience of poverty, but has to confront the realities of poverty, squalor, barbarism, and hardship in this rural town. The early days at Yan'an seem to have been difficult, as living, eating, and shopping became extremely inconvenient. Chen grew accustomed to walking long distances on foot, because there were no buses or cars.[108] Though speaking in a cheerful tone, she was also disappointed at many aspects of life in Yan'an: a neighbor making noise at night, friction among the young people from different parts of the country,[109] and the indolence, selfishness, and cunning of the local people.[110] In addition, the bureaucratic administration was neither efficient nor scientific. Most strikingly, no matter how much she sets her mind to "eating bitterness," Chen from time to time complains about the sanitary conditions, particularly the public toilets in Yan'an, which were an example of the matters of daily life that diverted her attention from grand national affairs.[111] The local residents had no knowledge of modern hygiene and contracted various contagious diseases, resulting in a low population.[112] All these ordinary matters become visible "details" scattered throughout Chen's writing and can enable a rethinking of the grand history of revolution. Rey Chow defines details as "the sensuous, trivial, and superfluous textual presences that exist in an ambiguous relation with some larger 'vision' such as reform and revolution, which seeks to subordinate them but which is displaced by their surprising returns."[113] In the same way, all those details in Chen's writing disturb and disrupt the flow of a coherent experience in Yan'an as part of an inspiring revolutionary narrative. However, when Chen complains about the discomforts of daily life, she often immediately and consciously reverses this line of thought with a strong effort at self-persuasion: "Once leaving, I will recall it. I truly like the atmosphere of the life in Yan'an."[114] Nonetheless, *A Visit to Yan'an* still brings to public attention what was only briefly mentioned in Snow's legend—the necessities related to living and eating—as uneasy quotidian details that often interrupted the transcendence of revolution.[115]

IV. *The Importance of Being Patient*

Revolution has often been associated with collective passion, as evidenced in Snow's *Red Star*; however, Chen's writing diverted our attention to the quotidian life details underlying the revolution. Revolution has long been regarded as a highly emotionally charged collective enterprise and individual pursuit. Michael Dutton highlights passions such as anger, fear, and desire that often characterized the emotional intensity of revolution.[116] However, Part IV calls attention to the emergence of patience as an alternative form of revolutionary passion in its response to the material backwardness and the frustrating human relationships that existed within the affective revolutionary community bound by a strong political commitment. In this part, I take Ding Ling's short story "In the Hospital" and Fang Ji's "The Power of the Loom" as two examples to further discuss the emergence of patience as a discourse and a psychological technique. It copes with the great gap between the heroic and the quotidian, between the city and the countryside, the divergence that often plagued the urban intellectuals and writers in Yan'an.

The prominent leftist writer Ding Ling escaped from the Nationalist political prison and reached the Communist base of Bao'an in October 1936. She was warmly received by the Communist leaders.[117] Similar to other cultural leftists in Yan'an, Ding Ling portrayed her early days in Yan'an in a lyrical tone that conveys "brightness," as in the poem "Yan'an in July" (1937), in which she described the town as a place that combines pastoral peace, agricultural abundance, enthusiastic gatherings, devoted reading, and learning, all in a cosmopolitan atmosphere. In a 1939 essay, "How I Came to Shanbei," that recalls her journey to Bao'an, Ding Ling recounted exciting conversations about classical Chinese poetry and Western romanticism, and described comfortable and intimate domesticity with her fellows, as well as adventures such as riding horseback and encountering a legendary guerrilla warrior. However, her excited tone gives way to slight discontent by the end of the essay: after about three years her memory of north Shaanxi has faded and her feelings are now very rough, completely different from her mood in the early days.[118] This change indicates that the great enthusiasm of the early war period has already given way to "confusion and disillusionment."[119] In the story "When I Was in the Xia Village" and an essay, "My Reflections on March 8," Ding Ling departed from the formulaic, lyrical mode of expression about Yan'an and took up a prosaic way of writing about the complexity, bewilderment, and disappointment of her experience with Yan'an and revolution. Frustration regarding the "disturbing side" of the revolution is manifested most clearly in her story "In the Hospital" (1940). Among all the stories Ding Ling wrote during this period, it most clearly represents the strenuous urban-to-rural transition facing many intellectuals and urban youth. The rural town of Yan'an had gradually grown into a cosmopolitan space because of the arrival of experts, college students, and aspiring young people from all corners of the country, including many overseas Chinese and foreign visitors. Their active participation in public life turned this revolutionary base into a mosaic of the urban, the rural, the revolutionary, and the global. The revolutionary journey, then, does not simply end with Yan'an as the final destination, but demands a deeper and deeper immersion in the rural life. Revolution is often thought of as a form of "hotness" characterized by passionate and sublime emotions, excitement, and a form of "brightness" as represented in composite of images in the lyrical poetry celebrating Yan'an. However, "In the Hospital" leads readers to experience the "cold temperature" of revolution in a way similar to experiencing the bone-chilling "coldness" in the winter of northwestern China as well as the "dimness" of the faint, pale yellow lamplight inside the dark cave dwelling and the twilight outside in the border region.

Previous studies have taken the story as a sign of Ding Ling's difficult "transition from May Fourth Chinese feminism to Party communism" through "reinvent[ing] herself as a political writer" and "resolv[ing] certain tensions in her own past."[120] The metaphor of illness and the dysfunctional institution of the hospital reveal all the symptoms and negatives of the revolutionary system itself, which ironically forces a "cure" for the once-healthy individual through subordinating herself to the revolutionary discipline.[121] My reading of the story, however, not only focuses on the story's critical vision of the revolution, but highlights the concrete experience of revolution as a form of work in the countryside and the emergence of patience as both a discourse and a daily practice. Patience often works as a psychological technique to handle the emotions of the often-frustrated revolutionary agent in the rural space. In the face of the disappointing socioeconomic environment and human relationships in the rural area of the revolutionary base, the story suggests that the politics of patience is a vital part of the revolutionary passion and is an important professional quality to exercise the Yan'an policy of "closeness to the masses."

I analyze two forms of patience, embodied by the surgeon Zheng Peng's virtuosity and the suggestions from the mysterious, anonymous crippled person, respectively. The former displays patience as professional calmness, competence, immersive attention, and seriousness, and the latter refers to patience as a people skill for dealing with the ways of the world. These two characters each represent a solution to the disappointing social-economic environment of rural life and frustrating interpersonal relationships. However, since both characters are focalized through Lu Ping's eyes, the characterization of them is also inseparable from Lu Ping's own mentality.

The story starts with an omniscient narrative voice, moving in and out of the female protagonist Lu Ping's consciousness. In the beginning, Lu Ping is walking from afar into the framework of a dreary, bleak rural landscape—a stark contrast to the "light" of the revolution. The narrative often adopts a third-person limited point of view through Lu Ping's perspective and consciousness. While looking around, she masks her disappointment at the surroundings but still "deliberately wears a pleased expression." The dissonance between Lu Ping's internal feelings and external expression shows the contrast between her attempt to cross the psychological boundary about revolution as an ideal and as a concrete and often disheartening reality. After graduating from a school of obstetrics in Shanghai and working in a battlefield hospital, she moves to Yan'an, first studying at Resistance University, and is later sent to the rural hospital in the border region due to the "needs of the Party." This itinerary is characterized as a journey from metropolitan life and a modern educational institution to the rural revolutionary space, which is not only underdeveloped, as Edgar Snow described, but also a lifeworld with conditions similar to those of animals. The educated professional Lu Ping is relegated to the role of a female body, which in the eyes of the rural women shares the animal function of childbearing. The hospital is devoid of both financial and human resources. When Lu Ping worked in the battlefield hospital, she cared for the wounded soldiers with deep affection. In this rural hospital, from time to time she imagines herself going to the front as a surgeon, "rushing through the forest of guns and the rain of bullets," fantasizing that she is a woman soldier able to engage in a heroic, immediate social intervention rather than working as a midwife in a rural hospital.[122] If Lu Xun's early dream of becoming an itinerant army doctor involved a degree of freedom similar to that of a freelance writer, then Lu Ping's work is disciplined under both the strict control of the Party and the surveillance of the hospital as a bureaucratic institution. "Going to the countryside" in the revolutionary context of Yan'an seems to equate medical work, vocation, and contributing to revolution based on the needs of the Party. This story about revolution has no passionate components such as romance (as in the urban stories of "revolution plus love") and martyrdom; Lu Ping's experience compels readers to turn from this romanticized notion of revolution and longing for heroic behavior to the quotidian reality when revolution "enters the everyday as 'work'"—often tedious and irritating work.[123] Snow's "documentary" writing offers an ennobling view of the rural folk and the poor; in contrast, "In the Hospital" does not sentimentalize the poor; rather, the author exposes all the ugliness caused by poverty and backwardness in a way similar to the episodes of the cunning and cruelty of the masses in Chen's *A Visit to Yan'an*. The narrator is struck by the rural people's brutal insensibility to the jarring, horrendous material conditions. The story reveals the full ugliness resulting from poverty: it injures not only the body but the soul—as seen in the ugliness of the human faces, their lack of any refined feelings, and their indifference and ignorance as well as their curses.

Disappointed by the squalor and the unsanitary conditions, Lu Ping is obsessed with applying modern standards of hygiene and cleanliness in the rural hospital (whose staff actually look down on the notion of hygiene). She constantly washes the patients' quilts and clothing, sterilizes instruments, and organizes everything for easy use. She also tries to transform the hospital into a nurturing place, requesting picture books, magazines, and newspapers for the patients, and organizes events such as an informal social discussion group and a small recreational meeting in the hope of offering spiritual nourishment. Lu Ping considers the awareness of hygiene "a kind of habitual moral sense," a modern notion that the hygienic or material condition is fundamental not only to medical work but to the development of humanity, because poverty and squalor can seriously injure the capabilities of thinking, feeling, and desiring.[124] In fact, the Yan'an period also witnessed the broad propagation of the notion of hygiene: on November 24, 1941, *Liberation Daily* started a new column, "Hygiene" (*weisheng*), and regularly introduced information about sanitary reform and disease control. The modern valuation of hygiene, cleanliness, and sterilization seems to counter Mao's "Talks on Literature and Art in the Yan'an Forum," in which he recalls his own transformation in feeling from a college student to a true revolutionary, from one class to another. Joining the revolution and living among workers, peasants, and soldiers led Mao to see the intellectual as physically clean yet spiritually unclean and the peasants as physically filthy yet spiritually clean.[125] Mao's emphasis on the transformation of the individual entails their crossing the urban/rural divide drawn by the notion of hygiene. Embracing the rural and inculcating awareness of hygiene therefore symbolized the two sides of the Communist modernizing agenda.

With genuine admiration for her doctor friend Zheng Peng's professional expertise, Lu Ping comes to observe his surgery to save a patient's life. Lu Ping therefore witnesses Zheng Peng's attitude at work that dramatically contrasts with her own high emotion. The lengthy description highlights Zheng Peng's great patience, endurance, and calmness, as well as his dexterous professional expertise. Zheng Peng clearly differentiates between leisure time and work time, between private space and workplace. With his silence and seriousness, the operating room has been turned into a grand room of religious ceremony. Moreover, Zheng Peng also has an emotional investment in the medical instruments he uses: "the delicate metal instrument had a harsh cold shine, but to him they were familiar and dear." In the workplace, his power of professionalism becomes infectious and inspirational to the people surrounding him. The description of Zheng Peng's work emphasizes its meticulousness, as he tries to find a single piece of shrapnel that is about the size of a grain of rice, hidden deeply inside the patient's body, and he needs to pluck it out with the tiniest forceps. In comparison with "a strange sense of exhilaration and weakness" that finally controls Lu Ping, Zheng Peng's self-control is demonstrated in his long hours of enduring concentration and the stable emotion that sustains his energy and reinforces his concentration, particularly when the low temperature and smoke in the room have already made other assistants pass out. "That afternoon his [Zheng Peng's] head had been as dizzy as hers, but he had somehow kept control and finished the operation. Then he had gone to a deserted, snow-covered slope and had sat there for an hour while his head cleared."[126] All these details constitute the defining features of patience, as seen in Zheng Peng's superb skill in his work, his commitment, his devotion, and most importantly, his mastery of emotions as an important technique in professionalism.

The story reaches its climax when Lu Ping almost passes out while assisting Zheng Peng in the surgery. As Lu Ping watches, she seems to experience the scalpel cutting and operating on her through the process of synesthesia. The blood flows out of her body as if all her complicated, repressed feelings are pouring out.[127] Afterward, what she has experienced in the hospital—misunderstandings, accusations, and rumors—builds up to a crushing traumatic breakdown. A sentimental revolutionary with a love of literature, Lu Ping from time to time dreams of the gentleness and comfort of maternal love and her southern hometown. However, drawing strength from the darker side of the enlightenment, revolution has been inseparable from passions such as anger, fear, and desire.[128] Lu Ping experiences the rural world with fear, confusion, apprehension, and despondency, enduring spiteful gossip and rumors; she is seriously troubled by the question, "The revolution is for all mankind. Why, then, are even the closest comrades so lacking in love?"[129] Because of this contradiction, Lu Ping suffers from nervous exhaustion and wonders whether she is wavering in her support for the revolution. The confusion that saddens Lu Ping was echoed in Wang Shiwei's 1942 essay "The Wild Lily," which similarly depicts the frustrating relationship—the hypocrisy and selfishness, the lack of sympathy and love— among the comrades who initially came to Yan'an embracing revolution with a sacrificial spirit.[130]

With great enthusiasm, Lu Ping is "forever talking, arguing, or reiterating the unreasonable things that she had seen each day."[131] Her revolutionary passion sometimes takes the form of high emotions in everyday practice—such as excessive zeal, anxieties, anger, fear, dissatisfactions—various forms of impatience that cause restlessness and the subsequent sickness in both her physical body and her mental state. Such descriptions seem to be part of the youth culture in Yan'an; Wang Shiwei describes the young people complaining and boldly and loudly voicing their dissatisfactions and anger as they pursue "love and hotness" as well as "warmth and beauty" in Yan'an.[132] With a perceptive, gentle heart and compassion, Lu Ping is frustrated by all the crudeness and toughness that characterize the political life she has wholeheartedly embraced. In a state of utter confusion about revolution, Lu Ping starts to criticize everything to promote self-righteousness—"Every day she thought about how she should assail the others and bring them down. She believed firmly that truth was on her side."¹³³ Her intense emotion is moderated by the language of patience at the end of the story when she encounters a malaria patient with no feet, a mysterious, unidentified soldier who "seems to be detached from his own situation" and who plays a pivotal role in directing her to change her thinking about politics. Lu Ping's work experience in the rural hospital is simultaneously an emotional journey of "understanding the ways of the world." The mysterious handicapped man says to Lu Ping,

> "Yes, they are all unsatisfactory, but who can take their places? I tell you that their superiors are no different. Your knowledge is greater than theirs! You are more able to assume responsibilities than they are. However, oil, salt, firewood, and rice have to be obtained from somewhere. Can you make them? The work style must be changed, but is it so easy? You are a good person. You have a fine character. I could see it in your face the moment you came in. But you don't have an *overall strategy*. You're too young. *Don't be impatient*! GO SLOWLY."¹³⁴

The mysterious figure speaks in an understanding, persuasive tone to caution Lu Ping against moral simplicity, leading her to understand the division of labor and the complexities and contingencies that characterize interpersonal relationships and define the way of the world. The man calls attention to the diversified social composition of the revolutionary group; Lu Ping also needs to realize that the value system she is working within comes from a culturally sophisticated world, different from the hospital. Therefore, the man encourages Lu Ping to be patient—"Don't be impatient! Go slowly."—and to employ strategies that create potential for change instead of exercising a black-and-white moral judgment. The man speaks about the potential of the peasant class for making sound value judgments as well as the intellectuals for building better networks of communication with the peasants to achieve a more incisive and complete view of reality and morality. He tells Lu Ping that it will take a long time to achieve the ultimate goal of revolution, and that it will be achieved through patient education and gradual improvement. She should not feel frustrated by a small fragment of society—"don't just look to a few people," which at once reveals the problematic of focalization in the story world and indicates the narrative's self-reflexivity on the use of focalization in the story.¹³⁵

After experiencing a period of painful mental struggle and frustration, Lu Ping recovers and seeks a new life, which is described as "passing through numerous tempering fires" and "matur[ing] amidst hardship."[136] The character Lu Ping, with all her aspirations and frustrations, demonstrates both excruciating inner struggle and active external social intervention. This character exemplifies "the problematic of the self" that was often caught up in what Kirk Denton describes as the opposing discourses of romantic individualism and revolutionary collectivism, and "between desires to explore and assert the psychic reality of individuals and to join selflessly with the inexorable movement of Nation and History."[137] Patience here works as an important skill for the self to deal with the external world through self-adjustment and self-control. Revolution is equally about learning the way of the world and gaining a concrete experience of its paradoxical mixture of affection and cruelty, the sublime and the messy, international inclusiveness and local exclusion. Ding Ling's "In the Hospital" also works as an allegory beyond the revolutionary context, exploring how human beings moderate impatience and intolerance and finally cultivate maturity and patience in a challenging and often disappointing environment. The story was written when the Party's rectification campaign was getting under way, which formally occurred in 1942. It marked a major watershed in the development of Chinese communism, when any critical voice would be completely denied and excluded from the revolutionary realm, as seen most clearly in the literary dissident Wang Shiwei (1906–47) arrest and eventual execution after the publication of "Wild Lily."[138] Ding Ling was later severely criticized for the way she looked at reality, for the events in "In the Hospital" were brought into focus mainly through Lu Ping's point of view.[139] The reality represented in "In the Hospital" was criticized for being merely "partial, temporary, and particular" rather than "the more authentic reality."[140] However, Lu Ping's self-reflexivity at the end already implies a subtle transition toward the revolutionary agency demanded by the Party.

A brief survey reveals the prevalence of the discourse of patience in both the Party's and the intellectuals' writings around the time. As Mao said at the Yan'an Forum before the start of the Rectification Campaign, the revolutionaries had to "make up minds to undergo a long and even painful process of tempering," a *gradual* process that requires gaining familiarity with the masses through living and learning with them, which would lead to the final change in feelings from one class to another.[141] In another essay, "The United Front of the Cultural Work" (1944), Mao continued to indicate the necessity of patience in getting close to the rural masses: "[i]t often happens that objectively the masses need a certain change, but subjectively they are not yet conscious of the need, not yet willing or determined to make the change. In such cases, we should wait patiently. We should not make the change until, through our work, most of the masses have become conscious of the need and are willing and determined to carry it out."[142] In a short essay titled "On Love and Patience among Comrades" (*Lun tongzhi zhi ai yu nai*, 1942), the leftist writer Xiao Jun (1907–88) described many dissatisfactions among the revolutionaries about their work, relationships, the environment, and even the revolution itself. He points out the presence of the "Satan components" in the revolutionary team, which, he felt, worked as trials to test the people's will.[143] Xiao Jun persuaded himself as well as his comrades to overcome the threatening Satan moments and work through the ordeal. He proposed the idea of *nai* to reconcile various contradictions in the revolutionary team, and offered two explanations: *nai* refers to capability (*nengnai*) and *patience*. Patience means persuading, educating, and understanding as the means to build ties among comrades. Xiao Jun discerned the complementary relationship between the notions of "love" and "patience," for only with genuine love can one have true patience, and vice versa;[144] and being able to be patient is also a capability that a revolutionary needs to cultivate in himself. Mao's language of "patience" suggests the gradual process of human transformation, dictated by the revolutionary disciplining force under the guise of persuasion, whereas Ding Ling and Xiao Jun's writings about patience indicate the urban intellectuals' self-awareness and self-persuasion in their devotion to revolution in the face of the political reality of trials and tribulations.

The surgeon Zheng Peng's virtuosity and calmness, which defines patience itself as a skill/technique in "In the Hospital," were also qualities that were much needed in Yan'an Big Production Movement. In the May 20 and 21, 1945, editions of *Liberation Daily*, the writer Fang Ji published in two installments a story titled "The Power of the Loom" (*fangche de liliang*). The story shows that exercising patience not only programmed the urban intellectuals into a state of unified thought and labor during the Rectification Campaign but also created a human-tool conjunction that increased the efficiency of production and promoted a harmonious state of mind. "The Power of the Loom" illustrates the urban intellectuals' participation in handicraft production using primitive weaving technology to interlink labor, thought reform, and skill (or technique). The blockade cut off the border region from imports of machinery, and the industries in the revolutionary base were all manual handicrafts, as there was no electric power. Efficiency and proficiency could only be achieved through patience. The central question raised by the story is how to confront and deal with technological "regression" in a rural space discursively associated with historical "progress" brought about by revolutionary upheaval. On an allegorical level, this story reveals that the skill (or technique) of weaving cloth symbolizes a technique of disciplinary power internalized as a way of life in the commitment to communism.

The protagonist, Shen Ping, is a college graduate from Shanghai trained in electrical engineering. At the beginning of the story, Shen feels frustrated and angry at himself after finding that "managing a loom is way more difficult than installing an electric generator." After he is unable to weave even one thread during an entire morning sitting in front of this primitive wooden loom, Shen's enthusiasm for labor cools and he blames the loom and the cotton, and ultimately considers such a mode of production a backward waste of time. Though driven by a strong incentive to produce a certain length of cloth for a weaving competition, Shen Ping expresses his confusion: "I really don't know what exactly skill/technique (*jishu*) is." Little Yu, his female comrade who is lauded for her high efficiency and productive energy, addresses Shen's question emphatically: "To you, skill means *patience*!" Shen longs to reach the level of Little Yu, whose weaving generates the harmonious sound of the loom, which, Shen understands, embodies all the secrets of skill. In the context of the organizational production in the border region that highlights self-sufficiency and self-reliance, patience helped to initiate human ingenuity and "devising new techniques that required little or no capital to meet the needs of production"[145] in order to achieve "a human-tool continuum," a harmony that could boost productivity and efficiency.[146]

What makes the characterization of the protagonist particularly intriguing is that Shen takes production seriously as part of revolutionary enterprise, and his involvement in the Rectification Campaign is voluntary—and he is devoted and efficient, even though he has little experience in manual labor. Shen starts to realize that the loom is not simply a vehicle for him to experience labor but also an ordinary tool for him to seriously study technique and reach the production goal. Patience is manifested as a highly disciplined regular life, involving day-to-day quiet labor as well as getting to work early and leaving work late. Shen keeps improving, understanding his merits and demerits and what he should overcome and study further. But most importantly, great patience and perseverance lead to a state that links labor and thought reform: a naturally growing affection toward the initially untamed "loom." The weaving skill Shen finally masters is also a political technique of programming the inner self into a harmonious state with the outer surroundings, which generates a new feeling that fuses excitement and composure and enables him to concentrate his mind and improve efficiency in production. Shen finally wins the weaving contest for both the quality and the quantity of his product. What Edgar Snow celebrates as the nonalienated rural industrial culture in the border region manifests itself in the context of the story as a human-tool conjunction. The intimate feeling between the human and the loom forms a totality and creates a primitive human-tool conjunction that features a dynamic malleability of the human. The story ends with Shen finally hearing the sound of his own loom merging into the chorus of looms operated by other people and pleasant music also flowing from his own heart: the *unison* of the experience breaks down the division between the private self and public engagement, which works to maximize productivity.

These revolutionary journeys also represented experiencing "technological regression": from fast and convenient public transportation to walking on foot on country roads, and from clocks with precise time measurement to primitive time-keeping by sundials. It was also a journey from a modern medical school to a rural hospital with no sense of modern hygiene, and from high-speed mechanical and technological production to much slower weaving on wooden looms. Revolution has long been regarded as a highly emotionally charged collective enterprise and individual pursuit, with passion sustaining the long endurance of sacrifices, difficulties, frustrations, and terror. This chapter calls attention to the importance of patience as a daily practice in revolutionary work: professional calmness and composure, tolerance of other people's limitations and faults, as well as persistence in developing competence and efficiency in using hand-operated devices. Patience is a language constantly spoken by Mao and the revolutionaries in the forms of persuasion and self-persuasion. All these forms of patience entailed in the urban-to-rural transition reveal an alternative manifestation of revolutionary passion, perseverance, and endurance.

Ci Jiwei indicates that with its heightened consciousness of the future as the locus of meaning and purpose, utopianism in Chinese revolution often emphasizes both speediness and high emotions such as excitement. Therefore utopianism in the Chinese revolution often "threatened to undermine traditional patience and endurance, which had been so instrumental in maintaining the social fabric under circumstances of poverty and deprivation" after the establishment of the People's Republic of China.[147] My reading of these two stories in Yan'an shows that the revolutionary culture in Yan'an was a form of utopianism, but it associated patience with radical revolutionary politics. Patience takes on the role of a technique for handling emotions, such as professional calmness and composure, an understanding of entangled human relations and the way of the world, tolerance of other people's limitations and faults, as well as persistence in developing competence and efficiency in using hand-operated devices. My discovery of patience, on the one hand, shows an alternative way in which revolutionary passion manifests itself, and on the other hand, it distinguished the Yan'an period from the following frantic socialist period when patience was not a virtue anymore.

The conjunction of the rural and the revolutionary signaled a new way of looking at rural poverty and quotidian life through these revolutionary journeys. Although the discourses of patience in the writings of Ding Ling, Xiao Jun, Fang Ji, and Mao deal with different aspects of their political concerns, they nonetheless converged in their awareness that revolution did not take the form only of violent struggle and war. More often, revolution was manifested as an exercise of patience to release an individual's energy and potential—no matter whether it was caused by material underdevelopment, lack of a sense of punctuality, or the revolutionary urgency to rectify human minds and raise productivity.

CHAPTER 4

Legitimizing Romance, Sentimentalizing the Law, and Romanticizing Labor

Valorizing Love-Law-Labor Conjunction in the Yan'an Revolutionary Culture of the 1940s

In chapter 3, I discussed the movement of "going to the countryside" from the perspective of how Western journalists and Chinese urban writers and intellectuals coped with the huge difference they experienced between the city and the countryside. This chapter turns to another mode of "going to the countryside," a deeper engagement with the countryside that was exhorted after Mao's influential talks at the Yan'an Forum on Literature and Art in 1942. Mao's Yan'an talks symbolized the formation of a distinctive cultural policy in the Shaan-Gan-Ning border region, the major area ruled by the Chinese Communist Party (CCP) during the Anti-Japanese War (1937–1945).[1] In his talks, Mao repeatedly emphasized the need for literature and art to "serve the masses," which reinforced the revolution's intimate social engagement with rural people and the Party's aspiration to transform society from the bottom up. These practices of "going to the countryside" represented Mao's policy of leadership characterized as "flexible closeness to the masses and maximum effective mobilization of the people."[2] In addition to the dominant goal of "reaching a wider audience" (*puji*), Mao pointed out the importance of "raising standards" (*tigao*)— elevating the people's mind-sets—as complementary to the process of reaching a wider audience. The idea of "raising standards" was closely associated with the Communist revolution's goal of building a new rural culture in the inhospitable and poverty-stricken backwater town of Yan'an, which was crucial to the Communist regime at a time when the Party was recovering from the formidable defeat they suffered before and during the Long March (1934–36). Hung Chang-tai observes that the popular culture had taken on "new tasks and meanings" during wartime China and notes the "'ruralization' of Chinese culture" during wartime China, which means that the rise of a popular propaganda culture "caused the rapid fading of the urban, elitist character of Chinese culture and shifted the nation's attention to the countryside."[3] Meanwhile, scholars have also noted a paradox of the Chinese revolution: it must maintain its vision of radical social transformation and at the same time sufficiently adjust to the norms of conventional social behavior and the ethical principles of rural society.[4] Nonetheless, this transition did not simply turn attention to the countryside; more importantly, as the rural with its rich cultural repertoire helped constitute the Chinese revolution, it simultaneously underwent a process of "raising standards" and was (re)signified and transformed during the Yan'an period.

This chapter approaches the revolutionary mode of "going to the countryside" through examining two cases of party-sponsored cultural productions for the rural people: the peasant writer Zhao Shuli's (1906–1970) story "The Marriage of Little Erhei" (1943) and the making of Ma Xiwu–Liu Qiao stories (1943–1945). The former is a broadly circulated story that arose from the author's personal social investigation of a real-life legal case; the latter are fictional adaptations of one of the best-known marriage disputes in the border region. Moreover, together, these two cases embody the most typical cultural forms adopted in the border region and exemplify the multimedia regime of governance that was projected into various types of media: short stories, reports in official newspapers, woodblock prints, local opera, and rural storytelling. Recent studies of revolutionary and socialist culture have turned away from the previous emphasis on the manipulative and maneuvering nature of the political propaganda as a top-down instrument of imposition. They instead feature a renewed understanding of the function of propaganda culture as a strategy for the wartime survival of the Communists and have examined its flexibility and effectiveness in persuading and mobilizing the country people and in maximizing revolutionary inclusiveness, and have confirmed the centrality of the cultural performance in shaping politics.[5] This chapter analyzes how these cultural productions showed that village life in the border region was transformed into culturally encoded narratives; it also examines the vision of a remade countryside that was created in popular literature. Both cases are legal-based stories adapted from real-life occurrences, and suggest a sequence of cultural productions that made the village into a new rural lifeworld, and turned current affairs and daily news into forms of fictionality. In particular, I wish to highlight how revolutionary literature eventually transformed the recent, the ephemeral, and the obsolescent into the legendary, the memorable, and the everlasting. This process echoes Edgar Snow's reportage, which aimed to transform "perishable news" into "durable history."[6]

This chapter pays special attention to how the notions of love, law, and labor were endowed with new meanings in their interrelations and in their construct of a new village culture. Historians such as Xiaoping Cong have contributed detailed studies of marriage regulations and the wartime judicial system in 1940s Yan'an.[7] Focusing on the notion of the "self-determination" (*zizhu*) of marriage, Cong's work turns scholarly attention away from a top-down party policy about marriage regulation and women's emancipation and takes a close look at local women's own subjectivities, autonomy, and actual practice.[8] Rather than offering an empirical study of the same subject, my discussion of law here refers to what Louis Althusser terms the legal "ideological state apparatus" as a system of representations that express "the imaginary relationship of individuals to their real conditions of existence."[9] Moreover, romance/family narrative and national narrative have often been presented and compared as an analogy. The *love-law conjunction* also coordinates the rationality of law with the sentimentality of love; moreover, it showcases the fact that the representation of legal empowerment of the rural people is first and foremost a sentimental affair. Importantly, the *labor-love conjunction* in the rural context that simultaneously emerged from the revolutionary narrative in the 1940s is a deviation from the *"revolution plus love"* narrative found in leftist urban stories. Romantic love was not merely legitimized by law; it was justified by the romantic couple's devotion to labor and contribution to productivity in the revolutionary base area. The new rural lifeworld was constructed as an aesthetic-political realm in which law, love, and labor had been bound up with each other. This chapter highlights the emergence of the *love-law* and *love-law-labor* conjunction that underlay the revolutionary imaginary of the new rural lifeworld. These cultural narratives as didactic messages served as moral prescriptions that underlay the construct of a new rural culture in support of revolutionary governance during this period.

In this chapter, I first discuss the resignification of *love-law conjunction* in the rural romance, Zhao Shuli's "The Marriage of Little Erhei," through a comparative reading with Zhang Ailing's (1920–1995) urban legends written in the same year. I then turn to discuss the entangled relationship of human sentiment and law in the newspaper essays covering the

Ma Xiwu Way of Adjudicating Cases. Then I focus on the construct of a new rural lifeworld during the process of the fictional adaptation of the legal case into Ma Xiwu–Liu Qiao stories. The construct of a new rural lifeworld went hand in hand with the party's call for a new communicative style for rural people, which presents a utopian village soundscape in which the rural folks were murmuring, chatting, and gossiping, and the officials were attentively listening, explaining, and persuading. Finally, I examine how Han Qixiang's storytelling contributed to embedding party ideology in the local society.

I. The Love-Law Conjunction in Zhao Shuli's "The Marriage of Little Erhei": Resignifying the Language of Law

Under the influence of Mao's Yan'an talks, Zhao Shuli, "the first bona fide 'peasant writer'" in modern Chinese literary history, published his first masterpiece in 1943, "The Marriage of Little Erhei" ("Xiao Erhei jiehun"), set in the Shaan-Gan-Ning border region.[10] The material for Zhao's story came from his investigation of a 1942 lawsuit.[11] This story soon gained enormous popularity in the Shaan-Gan-Ning border region. It was praised for being "written out of *investigation* among the masses" in response to Mao's Yan'an talks advocating "going to the countryside."[12] However, at the conclusion of the lawsuit, two rural lovers failed to claim their rights to independent marriage arrangements, and one of them was beaten to death. The tragic real-life situation that Zhao investigated differs dramatically from the ultimate triumph of the lovers in his fiction. Turning a tragic real-life event into upbeat, comic fiction exemplifies the spirit of Mao's Yan'an talks, which urged revolutionary writers to look at "the bright side" rather than the dark side of reality and to apply "positive thinking" to construct optimistic mentalities.[13] This adaptation of reality into fiction shows that "the bright side" was not discovered. Rather, it was actively constructed through what Mao advocated as the author's "creative labor" in his Yan'an talks, an effort that involves both social investigation and fictional writing. This story has been regarded as a typical piece of Party propaganda. Accordingly, Zhao was considered to be a from-top-to-bottom spokesman of the Party apparatus. However, this does not contradict Zhao's self-perceived identity as a peasant writer who was able to look at village society from a bottom-to-the-top perspective and to express the village people's aspirations.[14]

On the one hand, the story discloses the moral chaos, corruption, and abuse of power in the village dominated by vicious village bullies usurping power and by morally reprehensible, backward parents. All of these factors led to a lack of communal unity in the village. On the other hand, it also tells of the emergence of a new rural world in which the two rural lovers, the most beautiful young woman and the handsomest young man in the village, Xiaoqin and little Erhei, bravely confront the intimidations and schemes of village bullies such as the Jinwang Brothers, and resolutely overcome pressures and interventions from their superstitious, stubborn parents, and are finally married and recognized as "the first good couple in the village."

According to Hung Chang-tai, the Communists were well aware of the great power of language in initiating social change and shaping a new political reality and social order.[15] The deployment of *fa* by the rural lovers in Zhao's 1943 story was a precursor to the establishment of the marriage law in the early years of the PRC. Zhao Shuli's story was closely related to the CCP's implementation of its policy of "self-willing/self-determined" marriage (*hunyin zizhu*) in the Shan-Gan-Ning border region during the 1940s. Xiaoping Cong's study suggests that this new principle was incorporated into the revised marriage regulations and worked to empower the local women and disrupt the patriarchal system in its legal practice.[16] There is a long tradition in Chinese history of using popular narratives to teach legal knowledge to the ordinary people. In keeping with this tradition, Zhao's story was circulated in the border region like a guidebook about how to use the law to legitimate an individual's right to choose his or her own marriage partner. Nonetheless, this chapter does not offer an empirical study of the marriage law reflected in this story. Rather, it approaches the literary representation of law as a symbolic moment that aimed to "elevate" rural reality. This means that the emergence of law (*fa*) functioned as a new language that brought a new experience to local audiences and provided a vision of a new rural reality. I focus on the entangled relationship between law and sentiment to discuss how a new rural lifeworld was created as part of the revolutionary culture.

The young couple's daring pursuit of love recalls the romantic stories produced in 1920s China, the once-popular literary form comprising typical components such as tyrannical parents, rebellious young lovers, elopement, and life-and-death struggles. "The Marriage of Little Erhei" is a radical rewriting in a rural setting of largely urban-based romances of the

1920s. In this rewriting, the rural lovers' pursuit of love is not only justified by their genuine feelings but also legitimized by the law. Eloping from home like May Fourth romantic adventurers is merely a makeshift strategy; the ultimate goal is to achieve happiness, stability, and communal recognition in order to lead a happy life. To the rural couple, love is not so much a pursuit of companionship as a way to resist malicious powers. It is a process of struggle in which the individual exercises his or her new freedom after being entitled to use law. Their language of love is a kind of "language of politics," which they use to reassure each other and to strengthen their minds for resistance, because "as long as the man and the woman are willing to get married, they can go to the district office and register. No one can interfere."[17] When threatened by village bullies, little Erhei speaks loudly, "We did not violate the law!" He takes up the language of *fa* (law) to defend their freedom to choose their marriage partners. Their marriage is finally legitimized when they are sent to the district office of the border region government.

In his influential *Chinese Characteristics* (1894), Arthur H. Smith writes that he was impressed by the Chinese people's admirable quality of "innate respect for law."[18] However, this recognition of the Chinese as "by nature and education a law-abiding people" in fact indicates the imperial Chinese law's discursive linkage with punishment and reveals that the defense of individual rights had to be subordinated to the penal concern of the law.[19] Importantly, in this story, little Erhei asserts that he is not "violating the law" (*fanfa*), which seems to exemplify the "law-abiding" quality of the Chinese people observed by Smith. However, a closer look reveals that the language of *fa* does not refer to punishment but in fact functions as the "weapon of the weak" (James C. Scott's words), which little Erhei takes up as an expedient and powerful weapon to defend himself when being trapped and imprisoned. The rural lovebirds' freedom to choose their marriage partner is finally legitimized when they are sent to the district office of the border region government. The penetrating impact of the marriage law in the early years of the PRC has been discussed by the historian Neil Diamant. While some scholars have been skeptical of the efficacy of the marriage law, Diamant argues that the use of new language helped members of the most oppressed social strata claim individual rights, because "rights once granted are not easily taken away or forgotten, and that language once learned, even among illiterates, could become part of a repertoire of skills used, individually or collectively, as a weapon."[20] In the story, rural folks are presented as speaking, not a language of blood and tears to express bitterness, but a language of love and law to express themselves assertively and persistently.

In his Yan'an talks, Mao emphasized physiology (*mianmao*) in the revolutionary writers' representations of new characters. Zhao Shuli noted that the new physiognomy related outer appearance to the moral character of the new citizens. "The first good couple of the village," are smart and physically appealing, and appear distinct from their feudal-thinking parents. Their marriage is not celebrated merely as a transitional communal event designed to reform their parents' minds through a process of legal education and practice; more importantly, it provides a motivational moment for the villagers to fight against the village bullies, the Jinwang Brothers. The rural masses finally gather in the public space of the village temple to exercise their newly gained freedom and rights. The Jinwang Brothers, who were in fact traitors during the Japanese invasion, are severely punished—a process of cleansing the village community of its alien elements and dividing "friend and enemy" in the new republic.

A comparative reading with two novellas by the urban writer Zhang Ailing (aka Eileen Chang, 1920–1995) clarifies the significance of *fa* as a brand new language in Zhao's story, and the particular importance of the *love-law* conjunction in Zhao's story. The novellas were published in the same year as Zhao's story, 1943. Zhang, a woman of aristocratic upbringing and metropolitan life experience, made her literary debut with the publication of two novellas, both set in Shanghai— *Love in a Fallen City* (Qingcheng zhi lian) and *The Golden Cangue* (Jinsuo ji). These works became instant successes and subsequently established her literary reputation in Japanese-occupied Shanghai. Zhang and Zhao's family and educational backgrounds, life trajectories, and living environments were quite different, but both of their writings concerned the young generation's pursuit of love, parental (or family) intervention, and self-centered mother, all of which are presented differently in urban bourgeoisie and rural revolutionary contexts.

An illuminating conversation between the female divorcee Bai Liusu and her natal family occurs in the beginning of Zhang's delicate urban romance *Love in a Fallen City*, suggesting how law and human sentiment are perceived in an extended family in an urban setting. After learning of the death of Liusu's ex-husband, her third brother, who has used up the properties she brought back after divorce, attempts to force her back into widowhood. In this way, her family hopes that Liusu can make a living for herself by serving as the keeper of the shrine. Refusing to return as a widowed woman, Liusu defends herself by appealing to the notion of law. While Liusu uses the notion of law to defend her rights and identity as a woman independent of her ex-husband's family, her elder brother invokes "heavenly principles and human customs as well as the three cardinal guides and five constant virtues" to refute her, undermining the sovereignty of law in modern times. Legal code (*fa*), ritual propriety (*li*), and human feeling (*qing*) had long been interrelated in legal administration in imperial China.[21] This conversation between Liusu and the third brother reveals the huge gap between the declared intent of the legal code and the de facto regulation of social customs.[22] The conversation between Liusu and her brother also ironically tells of the weakness and unreliability of the law when it is invoked to protect the individual's property and status in a period of social anarchy and chaos—a period when various standards, rules, rituals, and conventions could be deployed to serve personal and political interests. It is true that Liusu also speaks of law to defend herself, but the strength of ritual and kinship relations remains tenacious in Zhang's metropolis. In contrast, in little Erhei's village, the rural couple is empowered to speak the language of *fa* (law) to fight against various antagonistic forces and patriarchal customs and to finally legitimize their romance. Further, by reasserting the rule of rite over that of law, Liusu's extended family is shown to still be a patriarchal institution that makes women dependent on and subordinate to family authorities, rather than providing shelter for a divorced woman.

To battle her cruel family, Liusu embarks on an adventurous, circuitous, yet enthralling journey, marrying herself out to a rich urban dandy returning from abroad, Fan Liuyuan. Liusu and Liuyuan's romantic journey leads readers on a tour of the material culture of urban modernity. The locations of their romantic rendezvous include cinemas and dancing halls in Shanghai as well as grand hotels and luxurious restaurants in Hong Kong. Liusu's experience of metropolitan attractions is a tour of the visually sumptuous material aspects imported from the West rather than the "spiritual" aspects of Western civilization.[23] Whether in Shanghai or Hong Kong, to Liusu the city is a world crowded with "an endless number of strangers," all of whom are indifferent to each other and remain locked in their own private little worlds. The modern street as the "background" of the story plays barely any role as a public space that could have an impact on Liusu's life. Indeed, the process of Liusu's leaving her old-style extended family to create her own nuclear modern family (by eventually and successfully marrying Liuyuan) is a journey that reveals a woman's distress, helplessness, frustration, insecurity, and calculation in the clutches of a patriarchal society—the predicament that confronts a woman who needs to sustain a decent life through signing a marriage contract.

Likewise, in Zhang's *The Golden Cangue*, the image of the patriarchal institution looms large as the pitiless mother Qiqiao suffers from her husband's family's manipulation. Qiqiao recalls the dissolute mother Third Fairy in Zhao's "The Marriage of Little Erhei," who wants to sabotage her daughter's engagement to little Erhei. The resulting trauma leads her to deliberately destroy her own daughter Chang'an's pursuit of love. The story does not follow the linear, modern progression of time; instead, its cyclical course of time suggests the inescapable fatalism facing these female victims. Though she recognizes her mother's interference, Chang'an still passively accepts her fate, eventually withdrawing to a "space without light" to end the romance she desires. She witnesses her own tragedy, one in which she has no power to change. The patriarchal household in the story becomes a historically entrenched institution, which is not merely the creation of men, but an all-pervasive consciousness deeply built into all the constructs of the existing culture. In this way, in Zhang's fictional world, human history manifests itself as a cyclical repetition characterized by the endless production and reproduction of perpetrators and victims. A ubiquitous presence in Zhang's fictional world is the powerful image of the patriarchal house, which overtakes and re-feudalizes the modern city, where hundreds of thousands of helpless, lonely individuals live.

Zhang's protagonists, whether in Shanghai or Hong Kong, are deeply immersed in their private worlds as they walk along the modern streets or linger in what are conventionally considered to be public spheres such as coffee shops and cinemas. In contrast, Zhao's hero and heroine, though living in the primitive village, emerge as active, powerful agents of communal life. Zhang's urban female characters are still living in a world characterized by an authoritarian family system and the subjugation of women; however, Zhao's rural lovers bravely resist parental intervention, defending their right to choose their own marriage partners by appealing to the new idea of law. It would be overly simplistic to arrive at a conclusion that discursively favors the countryside and denigrates the city by comparing Zhang Ailing's grim urban allegories with Zhao Shuli's joyous village romance. Nonetheless, my comparative reading of their representations shows how a primitive village is associated with modern values through reinterpreting law as an empowering everyday language for the folk. Unlike Zhang Ailing's metropolis, Zhao's village departs from the modern world of Western-style streets, coffee shops, restaurants, dance halls, electricity, telephones, and automobiles. The contextual change from Zhang's to Zhao's fiction, however, is aptly characterized as a transition from the once-sophisticated, Westernized metropolitan culture to a primitive inland village. It is a change from Zhang's "world of strangers" on the urban streets to Zhao's "community of acquaintances" whose histories, anecdotes, personalities, and reputations are widely known in the village society. It is also a move from a world in which romantic lovers speak the "language of sexual relations" to a village where a rural couple speaks the "language of politics" and from a world of ruins and desolation (resulting from the war) to a world of resistance and triumph; it is move from the imminent destruction of a once-prosperous civilization to the epoch-making construction of a new social space.[24]

Revolutionary literature such as Zhao's writings worked differently from other types of writing, such as Zhang Ailing's urban literature and other realist works. Nonetheless, a reading of Zhao Shuli's "The Marriage of Little Erhei" in light of Zhang Ailing's fictional world leads us to see how revolutionary literature represented an aspiration to enable social practices and initiate social changes to establish its political legitimacy. Franco Moretti states that "the literary description is never a replica of something else, but rather a way of building and conveying a meaning, and establishing a classification of high and low, beautiful and ugly, old and new and so on."[25] In Mao's Yan'an talks, the notion of elevation embodied in the making of revolutionary literature and art is also a process of turning the natural, crude, but simultaneously vital, rich, and fundamentally raw materials of people's everyday lives into a concentrated, intense, typical, ideal, and more universal form of life; in other words, it imagines a type of literature and art that would go beyond the actuality of mundane life.[26] Mao emphasizes the creativity of "cultural workers" (*wenhua gongzuozhe*) as the medium to facilitate this transformative process. I consider the fact that establishing the "bright side" in Zhao's "The Marriage of Little Erhei" does not mirror real-life occurrences. Rather, it manifests the author's use of his "creative labor" to deploy the new meaning of law to imagine a new rural lifeworld; the love-law conjunction in the fictional construct of a new village showcases how the language of law is deployed to legitimize rural romance and lays a foundation for the formation of a new village community.

II. The Love-Law Conjunction in the Official Newspaper Space: The Ma Xiwu Way of Adjudicating Cases and the Emergence of a New Communication Style

The theme of the love-law conjunction in Zhao Shuli's "The Marriage of Little Erhei" persisted as a continued theme in other writings and performance culture. The following section turns to the love-law dynamic in the newspaper space and the Ma Xiwu Way of Adjudicating Cases. In 1943, Ma Xiwu (1899–1962), the newly appointed commissioner of the East Gansu region, often went down to the villages to conduct in-depth investigations and launch impromptu on-the-spot trials. Having successfully resolved some thorny legal cases, Ma was promoted as the model Communist judge. He was known to ordinary people in the border region as "clear-sky Ma" (*Ma Qingtian*), and his way of dealing with legal cases was named as "Ma Xiwu Way of Adjudicating Cases" (*Ma Xiwu shenpan fangshi*). It represented the temporary wartime trial system and way of administering civil and judicial matters in the region.[27] On March 13, 1944, the front page of the *Liberation Daily*, one of the most politically authoritative newspapers in Yan'an, ran the headline "Comrade Ma Xiwu's Way of Adjudicating Cases." This essay, written by a journalist in hard-news style, presents Ma Xiwu as a capable model party official and foregrounds as an exemplary case a marriage dispute Ma successfully handled in the border region. The *New China Daily* (*Xinhua ribao*), based in Chongqing, covered this legal case twice, on October 22, 1944, and April 11, 1945.[28] The journalistic essays and a woodblock print published in *Liberation Daily* reveals the self-representation of the state in its official discourses propagating exemplary cases and erecting models. Most important, the legal case was used to showcase the emergence of the new communicative style between the party officials and the masses: "explaining and persuading" (*jieshi shuofu*).

The marriage dispute concerns the conflicts of two families across more than a decade. Feng Yangui, a villager in Huachi County, Gansu Province, once made an engagement agreement for his daughter Feng Peng with another villager, Zhang Jincai, for his son Zhang Bai'er. Feng tricked his daughter into renouncing the engagement in the name of "freedom of marriage" and secretly arranged to marry her to another *unidentified person* in the neighboring village at a much higher price. The news essay on the *Liberation Daily* reads like a forensic document detailing Feng's exact sale price for his daughter. Later, the daughter ran into the son Bai'er *at a social banquet*, fell in love with him, and became determined to marry him. Learning the truth, Zhang broke into Feng's house with some villagers to "seize the bride." However, the rural couple's marriage was soon revoked after Feng filed a lawsuit. Soon after, Ma Xiwu arrived in Huachi County. After investigating, consulting, and chatting with the local cadres, the villagers, and Feng Peng herself, he launched a mass public trial in the village, seeking opinions from the peasant audience. The legal case was eventually corrected: the two fathers were both punished, and the marriage of the young couple was legitimized and approved before the public.

The second half of the news essay published on *Liberation Daily* lists three key points related to "Comrade Ma Xiwu's Way of Adjudicating Cases": in-depth investigation (*shenru diaocha*), conciliation (*tiaojie*), and "explaining and persuading" (*jieshi shuofu*), as well as "informal discussion" (*zuotan*). Social investigation as direct observation to understand society began in the late 1910s. This approach was later developed as a mode of communicating with the masses, a new mode of knowledge production and a new mode of governance for nation- and state-building.[29] Specifically, "investigation" encouraged Party cadres to go to the countryside to become familiar with particular circumstances and to build close contacts with the rural masses and not rely primarily on legal codes. "Conciliation" relied on the approach of "explaining and persuading" to solve civil conflicts among the masses; this approach treasured the opinions of the masses and had the ultimate goal of "reaching the minds and hearts of the people" (*zhuazhu renxin*). Key to the Yan'an mass line, this approach was in fact not simply a form of legislation, but indicated the emergence of *new ways of communication and human interaction*. "Informal discussion" represented a nongovernmental (or "among the people," *minjian*) way of settling disputes as well as informality and flexibility regarding time and locations, as opposed to the courtroom sitting (*zuotang*). In this legal case, Feng Peng ran into Judge Ma on a country road and filed legislation under a tree. These officials would deal with pending legal cases immediately. They would strike up conversations with people and file legislation at any time, whether it was the morning or evening; they would also seek justice on the country road, under a tree, on the top of a mountain, or beside a river.[30] The largely expanded temporal-spatial realm—"any time and any place"—constituted the realm of the folk.

"Explaining and persuading" had been broadly promoted as a new communication style in the Shaan-Gan-Ning border region. It highlights how officials spoke with the people and solved conflicts without threaten-

Fig. 1. Woodblock print *Ma Xiwu Mediating a Marriage Dispute Case* authored by Gu Yuan. It was initially published in the *Liberation Daily* (October 9, 1944).

ing or intimidating them.³¹ This is a communication manner that requires great patience toward the people and demands an understanding of both human sentiment and principles (*qingli*),³² which was helpful in reaching the ultimate goal of harmonizing communities and boosting agricultural productivity.³³ Moreover, "gossiping and chatting" (*shuoxianhua*) was also treated as a resource for officials to receive information and useful materials from the people.³⁴

On October 9, 1944, Gu Yuan (1919–1996), the best-known woodcut artist during the Yan'an period, published a print titled *Ma Xiwu Mediating a Marriage Dispute Case* in the *Liberation Daily* (fig. 1). Known for his romanticized portrayal of the countryside under the rule of the communist party,³⁵ Gu Yuan depicts the moment when the disputes were settled and the people in the public trial, gathered in a family courtyard, were feeling gratified that the trial had ended fairly.³⁶ Compositionally, the print has spatial clarity and maps a set of social relations: the horizontal format indicates that Ma is merged with the people, though he occupies the central position and is dressed differently from the villagers. This print highlights the party's authority-establishing moment in the local society through solving conflicts among the people and maintaining local governance. Spatial positioning and clothing highlight the visibility and central authority of the party official among the people. Standing between the rural couple and their fathers, the paternalistic Judge Ma intervenes in the local family relationship and protects the couple as he persuades their parents. He simultaneously separates the rural couple from their law-violating fathers, who seem to be intimidated by Ma. Due to the ambiguous facial expression of the characters in the print, I will not offer a speculative interpretation of the villagers. Xiaoping Cong suggests that the print did not show antagonism between the punished and the victors; rather, it emphasizes the representation of "a state-created public site" in which local voices could be incorporated into the judicial process.[37] The print visualizes a horizontally arranged community and dramatizes a moment of communal discussion through the grouping of the figures, the gestures of people's arms, the individual poses, and the diverse facial expressions of the peasants. Equally interesting is the formation of the rural public in the visual space—a relatively comfortable place for the people to chat and share opinions with each other. The woodblock print captures a dynamic moment of the public in the countryside. Unlike technology-generated dramatic changes in urban soundscape, the new rural soundscape relied on the emergence of new peasant subjectivities, whose gossiping and chatting are legitimized as forms of public speech and symbolize their existential condition. The "informality" that characterizes the rural masses gathering, chatting, and discussing matters in the family courtyard simultaneously presents a community of acquaintances as the basis of the village public.

The second news essay in 1945 provides a much more detailed account of the marriage dispute, under the title "A 'Seizing the Bride' Case" (*Yijian qianghun an*). It continues what was shown in the *Liberation Daily*, portraying Ma Xiwu as a human embodiment of the regime's legal apparatus and a collective persona, the capable Communist judge. The country-road meeting is further highlighted as a vivid account of Ma Xiwu's encounter with justice-seeking Feng Peng during Ma's official tour of Huachi County in the beginning of the news essay titled "A Case of 'Seizing the Bride'" published on *New China Daily* in 1945.[38] The writing about this episode underscores the *visibility* and *recognizability* of political officials among the country folk on an everyday occasion: when they meet on the country road, Feng Peng cannot help shouting, "It is you! Commissioner Ma! I have been looking for you!"[39] The country road functions as a public space, not only open and available to all, but also foregrounded and politicized as a horizontal site to allow officials and the people to have face-to-face contact and communication.

This essay's next section, "The People's Public Trial," describes how Ma invites the masses to speak about their views of the marriage dispute, and the formal public trial becomes another forum for them to speak their minds (*fabiao yijian*). This public gathering encompasses people of different ages and genders and highlights the transition from disagreement to consensus, a process concluded by a speech given by a labor hero.[40] An example of the "journalism of conviction" during the revolutionary period, the party newspaper functioned as a great engine of transformation from "tradition" to Communist-style "modernity," transforming the murmuring of the country folk's gossip into expressions of public opinion, loose talk into coherent statements. This journalistic essay reveals a political idealism that balances law, sentiment, and custom:

> The custom in the Border Region is that the people do not always have to write an indictment, and that there is no charge for filing a lawsuit. If observing government functionaries being negligent of duty or violating the law, the people have the right to lodge an accusation, adopting any form they want whenever and wherever they like. The common people are not necessarily able to memorize articles of law, and not everyone necessarily knows of the existence of such articles, but everyone *has a visceral feeling of* one point: there are no officials in the Border Region, only public servants (*gongjiaren*), and these public servants are required to serve the people.[41]

This paragraph shows that there was allegedly no need for the people to file a written document or know the articles of the legal code. But if the people could not understand the abstract language of the legal code, how could they use the law to defend themselves? By stressing how the rural masses would have a "visceral feeling," the above statement reveals the transformation of Party policies and legal codes from a written, abstract form to an experiential, perceptive form. This shift demanded the translation of abstract language into popular narratives that the country folk could feel deeply and thus follow. Law in this context was not abstract knowledge or formal language; rather, it was fleshed out as a perceptible experience open to the country folk.

III. The Making of Liu Qiao Stories: Reinventing New Characters and Revalorizing the Love-Labor Conjunction

Mao's talks indicate a revolutionary aspiration to create a prototype of a village-based cultural universe that would not be divided by the worlds of literacy and illiteracy and that traversed different media—books, newspapers, plays, operas, drawings, paintings, music, and song.[42] The rural staged the formation of a united cultural line (*wenhua tongyi zhanxian*): all these genres and media, old and new, provided the technical means to represent the new category of the rural.[43] The formation of a multimedia and cross-generic regime of governance as a united cultural line connects the printed, the theatrical, the visual, the oral, and the aural to effectively relate the revolutionary regime to the concerns of local society. Moreover, this cross-generic process of transmitting information as a significant feature of the Party's cultural policy of "going to the countryside" to some extent reflected the urgent need to broadcast and communicate, and thus convey ideas or political agendas to a broader audience and overcome class and spatial hierarchies. Specifically, this chapter shows that the transmission of information through different media mirrors the spirit of "explaining and persuading," a new communication style adopted by official cadres when they spoke with the masses.

The 1943 local marriage dispute generated wide publicity and captured the interest of elite writers, folk storytellers, and film directors, who carefully adapted it into popular cultural productions.[44] If Zhao Shuli's story "The Marriage of Little Erhei" was a dramatic departure from tragic real-life occurrence, then this legal case already contained all the positive elements desired and much needed by the Party. As such, we can see that the Ma Xiwu–Liu Qiao stories were based on a successful legal reconciliation and a happy ending in a real-life situation. This partially explains why this marriage dispute was broadly publicized in the border area. The metamorphosis of the legal case shows how elite and folk authors used their "creative labor" to imagine the details left out of the news reports, and how they added affective, sensuous components as well as quotidian details to the raw materials of current events.[45] Unlike modern novels, which often represent the particular experiences of particular individuals, such as Zhang Ailing's *Love in a Fallen City*, the theatrical performance and storytelling in Yan'an often functioned to turn particulars into universals (or typical characters). The female intellectual author Yuan Jing (1914–1990), noted as one of the authors of the popular novel *The New Legend of Heroes and Heroines*, first wrote a Qin local opera, *Liu Qiao Seeking Justice* (Liu Qiao Gaozhuang), based on the news story, staging it in Yan'an in the summer of 1945. Afterward, a Communist cadre retold the story of the play to Han Qixiang, an illiterate, impoverished, and blind male storyteller, who was considered one of the most celebrated folk artists in the border region.[46] Following the structure and content of Yuan's play, Han soon produced a Shaanxi-style story, *Liu Qiao's Reunion* (*Liuqiao Tuanyuan*, 1946). This chapter traces the evolution and circulation of the Liu Qiao stories through different media—official newspapers, woodblock prints, local opera, and rural storytelling. The circulation and development of the story mirrored the vertical movement of "going to the countryside," which shows that the new idea of law trickled down from official statements and was translated into popular narratives accessible to the rural people to legitimize the rule of the Party. The circulation of the Liu Qiao stories through different modes of media and communication constituted the multimedia regime of governance. Xiaoping Cong's study was devoted to a close discussion of the adaptations of the legal case in cultural representations from the perspectives of the interaction between state discourse (newspaper reports) and local communities as well as the construct of modern womanhood in relation to the post-May-Fourth generation.[47] My discussion, however, turns to the resignification and revalorization of law, labor, and love in the fictional narrative that sees the creation of the labor hero (i.e., the pair of "man tilling, woman weaving") and the agricultural field as the rendezvous of romantic love.

These stories turn real rural couples in legal cases into fictional characters that represented the socialist new person, Xiaoqin and little Erhei, and Liu Qiao and Zhao Zhu, in popular literary forms. Prasenjit Duara refers to this process as "the making/remaking of the people," because the folk "must embody some abiding worth, but [are] in need of urgent renovation to serve as the basis of the modern nation."[48] This adaptation of the marriage dispute shares many similarities with the reinvention of the new image of the Chinese folk as a reservoir of emotional authenticity in the 1920s folklore movement[49] and as representing "a global discursive history that has always served the purpose of state building and reification of national identities."[50] Undoubtedly, the production of Liu Qiao stories and the elite-peasant collective authorship is part of what the Chinese critic Li Tuo describes as the "revolutionary popular culture," a term that refers to the party-state's creation of popular culture based on socialist doctrine in the name of the people.[51] Popular culture in the Yan'an period was in fact built on a legacy developed in the late Qing and May Fourth period, which sought to "redefine the nation in terms of the 'people,' to carry out mass education, and to uplift the people through culture sponsored from above."[52] Nonetheless, the May Fourth folklore movement and 1920s native-soil fiction have been noted for often producing "the folk" as the temporal-spatial Other of modernity or as a figure of timelessness. What distinguished the cultural productions in Yan'an was that although the "new person" took on the image of the peasants, it in fact embodied a collective image of new citizens with a new physiognomy, who represent the new people, *not simply the peasants*.

Moreover, the adaptation of Liu Qiao–Ma Xiwu stories served as a narrative nexus that connected the important ongoing policies in Yan'an. It brought together not only the new marriage law and the new form of village governance (*xiangcun zhili moshi*), but also the women's weaving movement (*fufang yundong*), mutual aid and collective labor, the new-style family (*xinshi jiating*), the establishment of labor hero system (*laodong yingxiong zhidu*), the reformation of idlers (*erliuzi*), and wartime village-based democracy (*minzhu*). All these party policies were in fact driven by the ultimate goal of maximizing wartime productivity, mobilization, and popularization that were so well illustrated by the creation of the new village in the narrative representations.

Benedict Anderson has famously argued that the newspaper as the cultural form of print capitalism effectively created a sense of simultaneity that underlies the temporal structure of the national community; nonetheless, he also observes the ephemeral popularity and obsolescence of the newspaper as a "one-day bestseller."[53] Yet Anderson does not further discuss whether the ritualistic act of newspaper-reading included or precluded illiterate country folks from imagining the larger national community. The change in genre from news report to story, from printed words to living speech, was also a change in modes of communication, perception, and experience. In other words, the newspaper report was what Walter Benjamin observed as "journalistic information" or "happening per se," which isolated information from experience due to its freshness and brevity.[54] Notably, the retelling of the legal case featured a shift in focus from the prominent exemplar of a Communist official in the Party newspaper to a courageous rural woman, and it took the form of a popular narrative, as seen in the change in title from "The Ma Xiwu Way of Adjudicating Cases" to "Liu Qiao Seeking Justice" and "Liu Qiao's Reunion." This parallels the spatial transition from a bird's-eye view of officialdom to an on-the-ground view of country folk—in other words, from the totalizing eye of Party policy to the people's concrete, skillful everyday life. Thus, making the Liu Qiao story out of news reports also aimed to turn the fortuitousness, discontinuity, and segmentation of recent events into long-lasting memories. The making of the Ma Xiwu–Liu Qiao stories therefore demonstrates another mode of national imagination: the transformation of short-lived news into memorable popular narratives, such as spoken drama and storytelling, which helped to create lasting memories and deeper imprints in the hearts and minds of the people in the border region. Yuan's and Han's cultural productions illustrated how abstract principles and fragmentary episodes in the Party-controlled newspapers were transformed into coherent narratives through local cultural media.

Following the same story line as the legal case, Yuan Jing not only created new characters in the play *Liu Qiao Seeking Justice*, but also rigidly categorized them as a way to establish what Franco Merreti argued about "establishing right and wrong, beauty and ugliness" in the previous discussion.[55] Han Qixiang adopted the same cast of characters, though his work differed in some textual details. In the fictional representations, all the actors in the legal case are given new names except the party official, Ma Xiwu. Doing so suggests that the Party is the only real-life character. The renaming of the characters reveals the quasifictional nature of the people, who are at once particular and universal, real and fictional. The unidentified merchant to whom Feng Peng was betrothed in the journalistic essay is shaped into a disreputable, unsightly, and handicapped landlord named Wang Shouchang (a new character), a process in which an enemy or ugliness is created out of anonymity. Simultaneously, as a new character who did not even exist in the legal case, the landlord Wang Shouchang as an invented enemy is at once a parasite to be attacked and a phantasmic character deployed to show conflict and division. Like "the first good couple in the village" in the story "The Marriage of Little Erhei," these adaptations repeat the process of creating a *physiognomy* for the new people of the revolutionary regime. Like the rural couple in Zhao Shuli's "The Marriage of Little Erhei," Liu Qiao and Zhao Zhu's romantic love is a continuation of May Fourth free love that was central to its narrative of emancipating the individual from the shackles of patriarchal institutions: marriage was seen as a genuine emotional bond, and the individual had the right to choose his or her partner. Liu Qiao was instantly attracted to the handsome, strong, and intelligent labor hero and production team leader Zhao Zhu. Although Liu Qiao and Zhao Zhu were originally engaged through their parents, their love is legitimized and celebrated only when they meet as two strangers, attracted to each other's beauty and falling in love spontaneously and naturally. It is an immediate sensual attraction that bonds them together. But simultaneously, the rural couple's reunion also conforms to the local convention of engagement contracts. Arranged marriage as a foundational institution in fact worked as a de facto law in traditional agricultural society, a regulation that the people felt obliged to conform to and that had been enacted through social pressure.⁵⁶ In this case, Liu Qiao and Zhao Zhu's marriage is legitimized not only by the authenticity of the couple's feeling (the internal law of the heart), but also by its abiding by the local contract (the external contractual relationship) and the Party's marriage regulations. What is noticeable is the making of the new village lifeworld through presenting a series of new symbolic figures and images: the labor hero, the weaving woman, and the agricultural field—the imagery of "man tilling, woman weaving"—all of which contribute to the resignification and revalorization of labor and love.

Labor Hero

The male protagonist Zhao Zhu is depicted as a labor hero, the leader of the "labor-exchange team" (*biangong dui*) in the village. The Yan'an period issued the honorary title of "labor hero" to commend those who had great accomplishments in agricultural production. For example, the peasant Wu Manyou (1893–1959) was established as an unprecedented role model of a labor hero who gained broad communal respect. Wu was praised for industriousness, versatility in multiple engagements, great management skills in the rural economy, and doing a good job of organizing and planning agricultural production.⁵⁷ Driven by the urgent need for economic independence through promoting the "Big Production Movement," the Shaan-Gan-Ning border region enabled the rural masses to gain a sense of individual dignity and achievement, rather than merely paying heavy taxes. As a Chinese journalist observed, the huge success of the labor-hero system increased labor efficiency and created a miracle of high productivity unimaginable under the whip of forced labor in Yan'an.⁵⁸

The establishment of labor-hero system was contingent on the new notion of labor. In everyday speech and in daily practice, hard manual labor was regarded as suffering (*shouku*), a kind of toil that produced no sense of happiness or enjoyment. The new notion of labor underwent a radical transformation, highlighting what labor meant to the self and the nation: labor not only brought ample food and clothing to the individual and the family; it also contributed to victory in the Anti-Japanese War and national emancipation. Accordingly, labor should be regarded as a source of pleasure and dignity.⁵⁹ Turning ordinary laborers into heroes comparable to military and political heroes presents a self-awakening moment, encouraging ordinary laborers, as emancipated persons (*jiefangle de ren*), to rethink the significance and the purpose of their labor. Simultaneously, an attack on idlers (*erliuzi*) accompanied the establishment of the labor-hero system.

The Liu Qiao stories give an aesthetic dimension to the image of the labor hero: Zhao Zhu, represented as handsome, is not only a charming labor hero but also a highly respected figure in the village community. The labor hero is robust, strong, and fresh, in contrast to the ugly, old, nasty idlers (*erliuzi*, particularly as applied to the images of landlords and matchmakers). Categorizing physical appearance on a beauty/ugliness divide should not be taken at face value; rather, it shows a perceptive judgment of looking and seeing based on outer appearance. Fei Xiaotong draws our attention to the importance of physiognomy in legal judgments in rural society: in imperial China, when administering a sentence in the *yamen* (government office), the county magistrate often "uses his insights into *physiognomy* to decide which person—by virtue of being ugly, slyer, or otherwise more repulsive—must be the perpetrator of the moral injustice."[60] In this way, the aesthetic construct of the labor hero already related his physiognomy with his inner quality.

Weaving Woman

In the dramatic narrative, the identity of Feng Peng in the legal case was turned into the weaving woman Liu Qiao. Before the revolution, the local women had never woven fabrics until the border region government initiated the Women's Weaving Movement (*fufang yundong*) in 1938. The movement developed gradually as handlooms and cotton were prepared and women's enthusiasm for weaving was aroused. With its goal of supplying cloth, "weaving" was endowed with great significance at the time: women could contribute to the family economy, raise their own social status, and gain respect from their husbands. Moreover, weaving helped changed the "physiognomy" of the local people, because the village people started to wear new clothes and pants and looked neat and dignified after village women learned weaving.[61] This way, the idyllic scene of "man tilling, woman weaving" was not really a local convention of labor division in the border region, but an *invented tradition* to mobilize the local people to serve the urgent wartime need to produce clothes and fabrics.

"Man Tilling, Woman Weaving"

In the traditional Chinese cultural universe, the images of "man tilling, woman weaving" often symbolize the close ties between the state and agriculture and represent the intertwined relationship between the social ideals of farming and political order.[62] The invented local tradition was naturalized by the villagers' description of Liu Qiao and Zhao Zhu as an ideal couple:

> Act 9
>
> Villager Shuan: "Zhao Zhu is really a good laborer, and Liu Qiao is noted for her weaving skills."
> Villager Suo: "The tilling man and weaving woman make a good couple, just like *the Cowherd and the Weaving Maid*."[63]

Later in the public trial:

> Act 11
>
> Arbiter: "Zhao Zhu and Liu Qiao are in love with each other, so of course they should get married. The tilling man and weaving woman are working hard, and they make *a fine citizen couple* in the Border Region."[64]

The beginning of Han's storytelling also unfolds likes this:

> "Our border region is a good place, where men till the soil, women weave, and everyone is busy.
> "Having ample food and ample clothes, the people lead a fine life; with the government implementing democratic ways, the mood here is excellent....
> "I wrote a new book to tell about *the new type of person* emerging; everything I say is authentic, and my words contain no lies."[65]

This turns a contemporary romance into the centuries-long ideal of a happy, productive family with a labor division based on traditional gender norms. The social scene of weaving and tilling that sustained the ordinary life also symbolizes the good marriage of an affectionate couple and the good citizens in the border region. The new rural culture in these representations is characterized as a new "everydayness" in which the living energies of labor and love, private desire and social responsibility converge. Symbolizing a romantic utopia of domestic and state harmony, "man tilling and woman weaving" is reminiscent of the ancient political ideal of harmony between farmer and ruler. In this context, this phrase has undergone a resignifying process and has been granted new aesthetic, social, and political meanings. The social scene of "tilling man and weaving woman" is not represented as a private productive unit, but rather channels the peasants' private feelings into energy for productivity to contribute to the strength of the regime, a process that transformed the self-interest of the rural masses into the public good as the higher consciousness of revolution. The connections between family and state, between romance and nation-building, have already been discussed by scholars. Doris Sommer points out the importance of the language of love in the domestic sphere in the nation-building novels, and raises the notion of "national romance" as "an erotics of politics to show how the variety of social ideals inscribed in the novels are all ostensibly grounded in the 'natural' romance that legitimates the nation-family through love."[66] Both "The Marriage of Little Erhei" and the Ma Xiwu–Liu Qiao stories exemplify a form of "national romance" and "an erotics of politics" that intertwines personal sentiment and national destiny, love and productivity, domestic affairs and public issues, by incorporating rural romance into the revolutionary culture.

The Agricultural Field

In the legal case, the rural couple first encountered each other and fell in love at a social banquet. However, what is strikingly different in the fictional adaptations is that the social banquet is replaced by the agricultural field as the rendezvous for their "love at the first sight" romantic encounter and mutual erotic attraction. The previous urban "romance plus love" narrative is often enacted in urban public spaces frequently associated with consumer culture.[67] However, with the changing notion of labor in the border region, the emergence of the agricultural field incorporates the dimension of labor into the love-law conjunction: romantic love was legitimized only when it was associated with labor during the revolutionary period. In the eyes of the rural people, the rural lovers are "a good match" (*pei*), and their union is an organic form conforming to the law of nature: "if Liu Qiao marries Wang Shouchang, it would be a fresh flower stuck into cow dung," while the match between Zhao Zhu and Liu Qiao seems like "a gold doll paired with a silver doll, and a gourd paired with a pumpkin, so nothing could be better!"[68] Anthropological studies have shown that romantic love in Chinese village life is usually not expressed through words but through the nonverbal action of labor.[69] To some extent, labor works as an expressive form of love and love as an energetic form of labor in the rural lifeworld. The hardworking couple reveals that the ability to work effectively and well would certainly qualify them as "a good match" in the eyes of the villagers, and functions as the important quality to evaluate the love relationship. The romance staged on the agricultural field shows how labor and love, energy and sentiment are intertwined.

IV. The Emergence of the New Village Soundscape: Chatting, Gossiping, and Listening

In the story "The Marriage of Little Erhei," speaking the language of "law" works as the "weapon of the weak" to legitimize romantic love, and anticipates the formation of a new village culture. Law in the Liu Qiao story symbolizes the mode of village governance. The legal adjudication in the Yan'an period favored "explaining and persuading" as well as conciliation (*tiaojie*),[70] all of which relied on communication and interaction such as chatting, gossiping, and public meetings (*qunzhong hui*) with the goal of making contact with the people.[71] Moreover, the often-frightening, serious courtroom listening was replaced by another form of listening, an interactive, communicative act between Communist officials and peasants in quotidian life spaces such as peasants' cave dwellings and agricultural fields. Xiaobing Tang describes people talking boldly, fluently, and loudly in public, and simultaneously singing excitingly and passionately, which constituted a sublime sonic culture in the town of Yan'an.[72] "Going to the countryside" brought a different sonic experience and helped created a new village soundscape that highlighted chatting, listening, and gossiping in fictional representations.

The preceding chapters discussed different modes of social investigation using direct observation to understand the society, starting from the late 1910s. This approach was later developed as a communication mode with the masses, a new mode of knowledge production, and a new mode of governance for building the nation-state. Mao's revolutionary project further promoted social investigation that privileged direct experience as the source of knowledge, as specified in his article "Oppose Book Worship" (1930); an example is the "investigation meetings" (*diaochahui*) to interview local people (the political technique of "closeness to the people" as the "mass line" in the Yan'an period).[73] In Yuan's version, right after leaving the arbiter's office, Ma goes into the homes of the local people, chats with them, and listens to their opinions. Thus, local governance moves from the office of the government to the cave dwelling (*yaodong*) of the common people.

Act 9

At the villager Hu's home (a cave dwelling)

Commissioner Ma: "My purpose in coming here today is to get to the bottom of the cause and effect of this legal case. Let's have a chat."
Township head: "The common people all have eyes, and they absolutely understand the ins and outs of this. Commissioner, just listen to me!"
. . .
Villager Ma: . . . "Commissioner, just listen to me!"[74]

Ma *listens* to all the village talk and eyewitness accounts concerning the marriage dispute. He learns how Yangui managed to sell his daughter, how Liu Qiao and Zhao Zhu's father were deceived by Yangui, what Yangui's and Landlord Wang's reputations are, and the details of Wang's ugly features and Liu Qiao's and Zhao Zhu's "love at first sight." This scene of visiting the rural masses shows how the Communist cadres obtain "inside information" and create an ambience of intimacy through chatting and listening, and how they made the ordinary people the most reliable source of evidence and truth.[75] Gossip offers ways to understand people's intimate concerns about themselves and others. The cultural phenomenon of gossip is always associated with the nuances of human interaction. Scholars who study the positive virtues of gossip suggest that the social function of gossip is to "create ties of intimacy between those gossiping," and to "assert social values, not as static tradition but as learned and lived practices," and summarize public opinion, report behavior, and evaluate reputations. The actual content of gossip is often secondary to its role in "gaining membership in any group," and "gossip also serves to bring conformity with village values and objectives."[76] Tong Lam stresses that sensibilities and sentiments were indispensable to the production of social-scientific facts.[77] In a similar manner, yet from a different perspective, fictional representations reveal the use of the quotidian modes of interpersonal exchange between Party cadres and peasants during the investigation. Patient and attentive listening to local gossip and chatting with the country folk in their domestic spaces are also forms of affective expressions and sociality that the Party used to acquire evidence and gain membership in local society.

As mentioned above, Ma was known to ordinary people in the border region as "clear-sky Ma" (*Ma Qingtian*). As such, he embodies the fusion of two figures: an organic peasant intellectual who actively seeks engagement with the people, and Judge Bao, the preeminent embodiment of justice in the Chinese popular imagination. Judge Bao has been widely conceived not as the real minister and political critic in Chinese history, but as the courtroom judge of popular drama and fiction.[78] Ma's resemblance to Judge Bao embeds him in the previously existing "cultural nexus of power," a term coined by Prasenjit Duara.[79] Through discursively replacing Judge Bao by the widespread story of Judge Ma, the Ma Xiwu–Liu Qiao stories demonstrate how political power reached local society through symbolic and dynamic representations of the party regime in popular culture.

Ma's forensic investigation is a far cry from Judge Bao's use of supernatural power and interrogation to gather evidence and deduce facts from clues, and it bears no resemblance to the analytical reasoning of modern detective fiction. Instead, Ma's investigation stresses the act of *attentive listening* to the rural masses, for the Party believed that the judgment of the people were better than a single local official, and real justice resides in the conscience and public opinion of the people rather than in legal codes. Ma's nonverbal communication mode not only functions to collect information from the masses; it also conveys sentiment, as the act of "listening" (rather than courtroom listening) assumes the emotional authenticity of the people and reveals a form of affective attention to members of a disadvantaged group who were once silent in history. This process also turns the participants from strangers into

136 GOING TO THE COUNTRYSIDE

members or acquaintances of the community, a process that conveyed sentiment to win the hearts and minds of the people and to establish the Party's authority in the local society.

Later, in the public trial held in the courtyard of the county government, the rural masses reaffirm what they previously talked about in private and speak their minds loudly. The communal event very much stresses the all-inclusiveness of the rural masses in terms of gender and age. It illustrates Mao's emphasis on the "mass line" and revolutionary "campaign"-style justice that involved the masses in adjudication.

Act 11

The courtyard of the county government

Villager Li (toward the people): "This is our common people's matter...."
Arbiter: "Today we are having a great mass meeting, and anyone who wants to can speak his or her mind."
Villager Quan: "This marriage is really a good match, a good match!"...
Chorus: "A fair judgment! ... We *all* approve!"[80]

In Yuan Jing's version, the rural masses' newly formed sense of participation is shown as a strong desire to speak in public, and gossip is used to mobilize the local network. Gossip usually takes place backstage, out of public sight. The political scientist James Scott considers gossip a "hidden transcript" used by relatively powerless groups such as peasants as an everyday form of resistance, one that avoids direct, outright confrontations with superiors.[81] Whether gossip can be regarded as a form of public discourse for weaker political groups (such as women and peasants) remains a controversial subject. This is because gossip is usually performed privately as a form of communication among acquaintances rather than as a public exchange of opinions among strangers.[82] The transferring of private gossip into the public trial in the fictional representations represents a process of politicizing gossip in the revolutionary public space.[83] Nonetheless, the collective gathering in the above representations completely ignores the mob violence and brutal spectacles operated in the name of democracy that often occurred in public trials during the land reform movement in the border region.[84]

V. Han Qixiang's New Storytelling: A Transition from Newspaper Space to Folk Space

Storytelling has been very popular in the village communities in the Shaan-Gan-Ning border region. Unlike *yangge*, which was only performed during an annual season, storytelling as folk entertainment was regular and frequent and could reach the remotest villages and the broadest audience in the area. The coming of a well-known storyteller to a village was an occasion to gather the entire village community. The folk literature writer Lin Shan (1910–1984) addressed the tradition and new development of storytelling and discussed the great possibilities for reforming the minds of storytellers and their willingness to change. An important fact Lin discovered was the "voluntariness" of the storytellers: bathed in the new atmosphere of the border region, some storytellers independently created and circulated new storytelling about the revolution-related subjects even before the Party began reforming storytelling.[85] The storyteller Han Qixiang was regarded as the one who used the "most lively and most vivid language from the people"[86] and "who received most help, who [was] most progressive in his political understanding, and who [was] most creative and productive."[87]

Yuan Jing and Han Qixiang's elite-folk cooperation reveals the greatly reduced importance of originality in literary creation and of the copyright of the individual author. These two local adaptations, according to Gao Mingfu, were an ideal example of the mutual learning and illumination that benefited both elite and peasant authors, as highlighted in Mao's Yan'an talks.[88] Hung Chang-tai has questioned the elite-folk cooperation, and indicates that the party cadres in fact supervised the folk artists like Han and turned storytelling into propaganda work as a kind of "elevation."[89] Hung further points out "the uneasy tension between the storyteller's creativity and the Party organizer's political intrusion into his work" in Han's *Liu Qiao's Reunion*, and notes that the imposed political agenda still left room for the development of Han's individual style.[90] I want to further emphasize that the oral form of storytelling he used in his rendering of the Liu Qiao story is as important as how Han Qixiang's work was adapted from Yuan Jing's opera. Rather than using an abstract style, as in the news essay, the storytelling became Han's "communicable experience" that he bought from the town and passed on to those who were listening.

Therefore, mediated through Han's deft craftsmanship of adaptation, the legal case that was transmitted from newspaper space to folk space in fact underwent a process of transforming perishable information into a memorable tale with worldly views.[91]

In a ballad Han wrote, it is particularly noticeable that Han self-consciously told of storytelling that contained the idea of *xuanchuan* (propagandize) with a strong sense of performing a mission granted by the Party's official institutions.[92] *Xuanchuan* in this context has often been interpreted as the Party's political ideology. As such, it often bore connotations of manipulation and control. Richard Jean So has situated the term *xuanchuan* within the national and international context of the 1930s and 1940s, emphasizing its discursive flexibility and positive meaning as "mass communication" and "mass persuasion" during the interwar period.[93] Therefore, there was no clear differentiation between talking to a friend and disseminating a political message.[94] The operation of the notion of *xuanchuan* and literature often reveals the combination of mass communication/persuasion with affect and meaning. Undoubtedly Han Qixiang undertook the responsibility of *xuanchuan* of communicating with a largely illiterate rural population. This elevated a traditional storyteller into a cultural worker, "a prolific writer," and "a talent" for revolution. Han Qixiang worked as the agent that the CCP cultural policy aimed to use to "make wider contact with the masses in the context of their everyday lives" and to articulate propaganda "both temporally and geographically."[95] It is impossible to tell how much Han's mind had to be reformed and transformed to be fully converted into a Communist storyteller. But through storytelling, Han Qixiang also performed a form of *xuanchuan* that blurred the boundary between delivering political ideology and engaging in an intimate form of "chatting" as well as "explaining and persuading" with villagers.

Storytelling is not merely a particular local art form of the border region, but also a kind of oral culture before a live audience common to all preliterate folk societies. The paradox lies is the contrast between the evanescent nature of the fleeting sound itself and the long-lasting effect of the storytelling, which lingers in listeners' minds and was inscribed on the audience's hearts. With its empathetic and participatory nature, oral performance could include in a shared community the oral performer, the audience, and the characters.[96] The storytelling's closeness to the human lifeworld facilitated "assimilating the alien, objective world to the more immediate, familiar interaction of human beings."[97] The transfer of information from Yuan's spoken drama to Han's storytelling metaphorically shows the revolutionary regime's deeper penetration from towns and larger villages with concentrated populations to small villages with scattered residents. Carrying a few simple musical instruments and accompanied by a few party members, Han, like a medieval troubadour, toured through small villages and sang the familiar tale of "man tilling, woman weaving," showing how it could be part of the new lifestyle of new people.[98] Scholars have noted Chinese Communists' reliance on local acquaintances as a means of breaking into village society.[99] Han used the vocabulary of people's daily lives to tell his stories and constantly emphasized their "authenticity." As a well-known storyteller in the border region, he performed the role of the acquaintance, mediating between the state and the local society and introducing the Party to local villagers. Han Qixiang was known for his memory of many folktales, legends, and drama scripts. An aspect of the Party's education and reform entailed training Han's memory to absorb new ingredients from Party ideology.

Benedict Anderson has regarded a nation as an imagined community mainly as a horizontal site that connects strangers. The use of the different modes of communication we have discussed demonstrated a vertical movement in the process of building the revolutionary site as the precursor to future nation-state building. This sequence of communication not only shows how peasants in remote villages stayed informed about politics, but also how it constituted a multimedia regime of governance, transforming "perishable news" into "durable history" and memorable tales.

Historian Brian James DeMare has noted the complicated process of transforming revolutionary culture into the local context.[100] Though Han's version highlights some plots differently than Yuan, it shares a great deal with Yuan's drama, combining into his storytelling new ideas such as citizenship and the abolishment of venal marriage. These differences reveal how Han's creative style was drawn from his previous repertoire of knowledge and performance before he was converted to an official storyteller. Han's and Yuan's versions offer different perspectives on the same situation. For example, Han fantasizes about their resorting to collective violence to achieve justice, as well as reaffirming "good customs" in the village, such as the collective sentiment of conscience in the rural community and the daughter's filial piety. The process of turning recent news into storytelling is a process of turning clock time into timelessness and transforming the ephemeral and perishable into something long-lasting. Both Yuan and Han describe the broad public attention that the marriage dispute attracted. After the arbiter first decides to annul their marriage, many villagers institute appeals, requesting that the legal case be reconsidered. A close reading of these two texts reveals that Han accentuates the strong communal support and shows the power of the conscience of the rural society. In Han's version, when they learn that Liu Qiao was deceived by her father and therefore unknowingly betrothed to Landlord Wang, the young peasants in Zhao Zhu's team immediately "feel outraged by the injustice" (*baobuping*).[101] Later on, such gossip spreads in the community, helping to form a social network through which the peasants not only participate in communal affairs by consuming the information, but also assert their values and define communal moral standards out of their own conscience through the very act of "gossiping and debating between right and wrong" (*yilun*).[102] Zhao Zhu's father is outraged and decides to "seize the bride" Liu Qiao back. In Yuan's low-key handling of the event, Zhao Zhu's father only gathers a few friends to help, whereas in Han's version this "seizing the bride" activity, which is regarded as uncivil by the arbiter, receives widespread support from the entire community and even looks like a public demonstration:

> When people discern injustice, even heaven is thrown out of kilter. Heaven sends thunder and lightning to initiate redress. Trees everywhere emit sorrowful sounds. Old man Zhao is seething with anger, and rallies men together in front and behind. All families, big and large, are hotly debating the right and wrong of what has happened. Everyone is eager to go boldly to capture the bride. The team of laborers is assembled, just as if a general has activated his troops. . . . All the villagers, young and old, form in battle array. One carries a willow branch club, one holds a fireplace poker. Over here they shout, over there they answer. They run down the road as fast as the wind. Clouds turn black, hiding the moon, as heaven and earth shake, rushing out from their own village a sea of black heads. Over the hill and across the peak they rush. In no time at all they get to the Liu family door. Fully armed as they are, their martial power is great. Encircling the house on all sides, in row after row, in front and behind, packed so tight, no breath of air between them. Old man Zhao emerges in a towering rage, just like Zhang Fei overrunning an ancient city.[103]

This episode exemplifies that, far from acting as the tool of the Party, the peasant storyteller asserted his own narrative agency in adapting an elite cultural production and Party policy to a local framework.[104] The villagers' violent action is justified by the laws of heaven. Fusing fantasy and reality, Zhao Zhu's father acts as if he were a general gathering soldiers—a scene reminiscent of the traditional vernacular novel *Water Margin*. Making oral texts memorable relies on the skillful use of such traditional elements as abiding knowledge and experience in rural society and embodying law as a form of worldly wisdom and contractual agreements that regulate illiterate communities.[105] The present takes on a form of timelessness and resembles the familiar past. The act of "seizing the bride" is justified due to broad communal consensus and support. Although there is a hint of legal and bureaucratic anarchy in the description of "seizing the bride," this episode shows that justice is defined as the conscience of the rural community that often goes beyond law.

In Yuan's version, Ma does not directly receive letters from the rural masses who were disappointed at the arbiter's verdict. This legal case is referred to him by the village head. However, in Han's version, the villagers directly write to Ma to redress the injustice on behalf of Liu Qiao and Zhao Zhu. Yuan's description of the communal discussion of this marriage dispute still strictly follows the formal procedure of a legal trial. However, the public meeting in Han Qixiang's story becomes truly "informal." At the end of the meeting, Han Qixiang provides this description:

> Many people take to their feet and proclaim, "Their marriage is as perfect as the match of the Cowherd and the Weaving Maid. Why did the arbiter dissolve their union, making them cry and agonize? In our eyes it is clear that the government's action is wrong." . . .
> Commissioner Ma announces that "In our border region we are now implementing democratic ways. My friends, how do you think we should decide this particular case?" With that, all the people assembled there—those standing and those sitting, the men and the women, the young and the elderly—they all become arbiters.[106]

The "informality" that characterized the public trial suggests that the meeting becomes a forum in which the rural masses can voice opinions critical of ineffective local governance. The rural masses, who represent the conscience of the community in Han's storytelling, are fantasizing about a moment in which they can play the role of judges of their own affairs. Describing Judge Ma addressing the villagers as "my friends," Han's storytelling again indicates the form of *xuanchuan*, which often blurred the border between delivering a political message and chatting with a friend. The party also advocated the new-style family (*xinshi jiating*) that promoted democratic relationships within the family. A family with harmonious relationships would contribute to labor and economic growth in the border region. The relationship of "loving father and filial son" was still strongly promoted in the border region as part of the democratic relationship inside the family.[107] A comparative reading of these episodes leads to interesting observations in terms of both gender representations. As the titles reveal, Yuan Jing's opera stresses "seeking justice" (*gaozhuang*), whereas Han's storytelling emphasizes "reunion" (*tuanyuan*). Xiaoping Cong also discerns that the rebellious daughter in Yuan's play has shifted to the pitiful and passive daughter in Han's storytelling.[108] In Yuan's theatrical adaptation, Liu Qiao becomes more and more assertive and rebellious regarding parental authority, while at the end of Han's story, Liu Qiao still shows mercy toward her father and pleads for his punishment to be reduced. Therefore, "reunion" in Han's version refers not only to the ultimate union of the romantic lovers but also to the reconciliation between the filial daughter Liu Qiao and her father. The tension between the two representations of Liu Qiao lies in the contrast between the image of a rebellious new woman who resolutely repudiates her bond with her tyrannical father on the one hand (Yuan's play), and the image of a docile woman who maintains her affective ties with her father on the other (Han's story). Han's story ends with Liu Qiao's request that her father's punishment be reduced, which is approved by both Ma and the rural masses; thus, the voices critical of the local government in *Liu Qiao's Reunion* are soon reconciled, with the "reunion" embodied in the daughter's filial piety and her happy marriage.

From the foregoing discussion, it is clear that "going to the countryside" as the core of Yan'an cultural policy entails different modes of perception, communication, and information-transmission via a diverse set of media—short stories, news essays, woodcut prints, rural plays, and oral traditions. This chapter has shown that cultural productions were bound up with the social practice of "going to the countryside" initiated by Mao's Yan'an talks, and turned the rural into a multimedia space of revolutionary governance. The two stories, Zhao Shuli's "The Marriage of Little Erhei" and the legal-case-based Ma Xiwu–Liu Qiao stories, illustrate how the revolutionary culture mobilized the affective components in the local society to build a new rural culture and serve the revolutionary cause. The revolutionary culture in the countryside that connects labor, love, and law also shows the intersection between village governance and the ordinary life spaces. These two stories do not simply serve as guidebooks for the popularization of the new marriage regulation and Communist gender ideology. They highlight the representation of law in the realm of popular culture, and they showcase the entangled relations between human sentiment and law during the Party's effort to establish its political authority. In the wartime decade of the 1940s, these two cases provide intriguing examples for considering the importance of communication and the series of cultural forms that connects the written and the oral, urban forms and folk forms. Each cultural form represents a particular communicative mode, and the sequence of information transmission forms a communicative network. Moreover, the fictional adaptations of the Ma Xiwu–Liu Qiao stories feature the important role of rural gossip as a quotidian communicative style in the revolution to build an intimate community that often blurred the boundary between the domestic and the public, between strangers and acquaintances, and between the subaltern and the empowered.

Moreover, current scholarship focuses on "speaking bitterness" in the process of uniting the people by orchestrating the public expression of their feelings.[109] These two cases highlight the love-law combination and suggest that the language of love and law is used to shape revolutionary subjectivity. The law-love conjunction in both "The Marriage of Little Erhei" and Ma Xiwu–Liu Qiao stories also shows how the notions of love, law, and labor were revalorized and infused with new content under the spirit of Mao's talks, and how these notions demonstrated the making of new people in the revolutionary regime as legally disciplined (law), emotionally mobilized (love), and physically energetic (labor).

The new marriage regulations in the border region in the 1940s had been developed into the marriage law after the establishment of the People's Republic of China.[110] Based on both Yuan and Han's work, a Ping opera titled *Liu Qiao'er* was put on stage in 1950, and the opera film *Liu Qiao'er* was produced in 1956. Differing from some dogmatic cinematic representations of rural life at the time, *Liu Qiao'er* was widely enjoyed by both rural and urban audiences.[111] The Liu Qiao stories shed light on the process in which a local marriage was turned into the archetype of the national romance that inspired new generations of Chinese youth to pursue freedom of marriage in the 1940s and later after the founding of the PRC.[112] The production of the cinematic version of the Liu Qiao story further reveals the way the socialist state attempted to establish a new rural culture as a predominant part of the national culture with the founding of the People's Republic.[113]

PART III

The Rural as an Industrial Vision of Chinese Socialism

CHAPTER 5

Creating a Rural Industrial Aesthetics
Socialist Homecoming and the Rural Modernization Project in Representational Forms in the 1950s and Early 1960s

In June 1959, ten years after the establishment of the People's Republic, Mao Zedong returned to his hometown Shaoshan, a village in Hunan Province, after an absence of over thirty years. In a seven-character regulated verse titled "Return to Shaoshan," he wrote:

> I regret the passing, the dying, of the vague dream:
> My native orchards thirty-two years ago.
> Yet red banners roused the serfs, who seized three-pronged lances
> When the warlords raised whips in their black hands.
> We were brave and sacrifice was easy
> And we asked the sun, the moon, to alter the sky.
> Now I see a thousand waves of beans and rice and am happy.
> In the evening haze heroes are coming home.[1]

This homecoming journey offered Mao a chance to imagine the dramatic transformation of the environment of his hometown from a battlefield to a peaceful land of agricultural bounty. The peasants, who previously fought bravely as soldiers in a militarized landscape for the Chinese revolution, have become heroes who labor in the fields for socialist construction. The hometown depicted by Mao is less a concrete, particular locality than a symbolic form of the nation from which Mao could draw a blueprint. This poem resumes the Yan'an tradition of comparing labor to heroic behavior and sublime action. This was also a period when the memories of the pre-1949 military victories were not only translated into the ambition of conquering nature but helped build national confidence that with human willpower, anything is possible. Mao's poem echoed the socialist state's policy in the mid-1950s that called on peasant sons and daughters who had received education in secondary schools in the cities and towns to return to their rural homes instead of seeking city jobs. Homecoming in this era intersected with China's efforts to industrialize and modernize the countryside as well as increase agricultural production.

By the summer of 1955, despite rapid industrialization, China faced a series of problems, such as lagging agricultural productivity, urban unemployment, and rural underemployment. Mao Zedong's well-known message delivered in December 1955 that "the countryside is a broad universe, and one will achieve great accomplishments there" paradoxically fused the discursive boundlessness of the countryside and the actual institutionalized hard boundary of the urban/rural divide (due to the household registration system).[2] On March 22, 1957, Liu Shaoqi (1898–1969), then the vice president, gave a speech to middle-school students in Changsha, Hunan Province, urging them to go back to participate in agricultural production. Liu's speech, which was published as an editorial in *The People's Daily* on April 8, made it explicit that agricultural production would be the main career path for school graduates. Mainly dictated by the economic necessity at the time, "the return to the village" movement (*huixiang*) reached its peak in the spring of 1962.[3] Socialist discourse on homecoming is not merely a spatial crossing of the urban-rural chasm. The act of leaving the city and moving back to the rural home has been treated as a moral and ideological decision. Popular songs, visual images, films, and literature from this time also suggest that the aesthetic construct of the nation had taken on the image of the rural hometown, an ancient land now dominated by youthful energy. Homecoming is depicted as a journey in which the young generation is urged to imagine themselves transforming the natural world, eliminating poverty, and building modern infrastructure, at the same time experiencing a self-sufficient life and building a world based on collective political ideals, one in which personal gratification merges with collective happiness.

With its developmental urge, China sought to overcome its backwardness, but simultaneously presented to the world with a uniquely socialist version of industrial culture. The elimination of the distinction between the city and the countryside was largely contingent on making the village a desirable, aesthetically appealing place to live. Urban industrialization was undoubtedly the focus of the socialist state from its founding year, but paradoxically what was striking was that the socialist state consciously created a rural industrial aesthetics to construct its national self-image. The juxtaposition of "the rural" and "the industrial" discussed in this chapter does not specifically refer to the rural industrialization associated with the abortive "Great Leap Forward" campaign.[4] Instead, this chapter discusses how the effort to industrialize the village was represented in socialist cinema and visual culture.

Current studies of socialist culture have turned away from taking propaganda as mere political manipulation, instead emphasizing a process of negotiation that saw a socialist culture in the making and highlighting the accessible, enjoyable, inspirational, creative, and pedagogical characteristics of socialist art and literature, which played a pivotal role in shaping new socialist subjects.[5] Another trend of recent studies is to situate China's socialist literature and culture within international socialism and global media, discussing how China's propaganda culture was part of the network of globally circulated images and meanings.[6] In accord with the current trend of reevaluating socialist culture, this chapter emphasizes that industrializing the countryside was represented as a new experiential and aesthetic realm in the historical context of socialist capital accumulation and industrialization that demanded intensive human labor. If eliminating the distinction between mental labor and manual labor was one cf the core principles of Mao's thought, then the much-advocated mass-based collective creativity was imagined as bridging the gap between these two distinct forms of labor. Socialist creativity was manifested visibly in that socialist industry in its representational and aesthetic forms blurred the boundary between play and labor, the artisanal and the industrial, and the handcrafted and the machine-made. This chapter highlights the formation of the rural industrial culture in which collective labor is turned into a playful, artisanal experience. What is foregrounded in the cinematic representations erases the exploitative nature of manual labor from visibility to the audience and reveals a fusion of the creativity and omnipotence of human labor, illustrating the spirit of self-sufficiency and self-reliance in the global circulation of Chinese socialism of the day.

This chapter first discusses "returning to the rural home and industrializing the countryside" and the homecoming discourse that was integrated into the social engineering program. Then I turn to the socialist brand of creativity that was highlighted in the process of industrializing the countryside during a time when the socialist state relied much on ideological representations. Finally, I focus on two popular films, *The Young People in Our Village* (1959) and its sequel (1963), to illustrate the making of a rural industrial aesthetics instead of empirical studies of real social cases because the goal was to examine the operation of the socialist ideology. Specifically, I discuss the themes of "play as labor" and "artisanal as industrial" that underlay the rural industrializing projects. This chapter focuses on the films as instances of socialist works that sought to mobilize state-initiated homecoming to overcome the urban-rural cleavage, and to articulate the socialist ideal of industrialization with public works projects such as building canals and lighting systems. Postrevolutionary films showed a process of turning labor into play, love into energy, and forced productivity into lively inventiveness, a process of transformation essential to the socialist state's creating perceptions of labor. This chapter ends with a reflection on the construct of the industrialized countryside as socialist China's national self-image.

I. Industrializing the Countryside and Returning to the Rural Home in Discourses and Representations

Built into the party's call for young students to return to their rural homes as a social engineering program were the native-place sentiment and a new discourse regarding youth and village. Native-place sentiment was one of the moral languages spoken in the public media to cultivate in urban-educated young nationals a strong local consciousness and to urge them to return home. "Our young man" is an important global figure in the modern novel—characterized by his thinking about "the representative body, not the personal life"; he was a character who helped build a connection between an individual and the collective body of national readers.[7] This global figure was placed in local Chinese settings and frequently appears throughout twentieth-century Chinese literature and cultural history. In late 1910s and 1920s literature, sentimental, urban-educated young people, lonely and sometimes frustrated, often briefly return to their rural homes, but eventually they go back to the cities.[8] It was not until the socialist period that the image of "our young man," a figure who reconciled the national and the local and repoliticized traditional native-place sentiment, started to dominate the popular imagination. The combination of "youth" and "village" recalls Franco Moretti's assertion that youth is not a biological differentiation in traditional village society any more. Instead, the image of youth "achieves its symbolic centrality" in the culture of modernity due to youths' mobility and restlessness.[9] It is in this sense that the young people in socialist representations and discourses embrace "a bewitching and risky process full of great expectations."[10] As symbolic figures, "our young people" in the village relate the countryside to the liveliest, most energetic, vibrant, yet indeterminate component of modern culture. With young people playing a leading role, the hometown is no longer a place of timelessness but a site of constant change.

A 1955 homecoming film titled *The Story of the Summer* (Xiatian de gushi) echoed the theme of peasant sons and daughters who respond to the Communist Party's call to return home. It highlights the issue of how to assess the individual's "great promise" (*you chuxi*) and how to balance mental labor and manual labor. The protagonist, Jinsheng, the most promising junior high school student in his village, gives up the opportunity to study in high school and plays a leading role in agricultural production in his village. His dream is to take root in his hometown and build a mechanized farm in the future. Jinsheng asks a rhetorical question: "If everyone deals with big things, who will take care of small matters?" Cai Xiang points out the expected unity of "national affairs" (*guojia dashi*) and "small matters of daily life" (*shenghuo xiaoshi*) in socialist politics; the intent was to connect national affairs and daily life to give citizens a concrete sense of the nation and to bring previously marginalized, ordinary people into the sphere of politics through active participation.[11] In the mid-1950s context of state-initiated homecoming, however, socialist discourse about turning attention from national affairs to quotidian matters worked to convert aspiring internationalists and nationals into devoted locals. This discourse persuaded the young generation that the national was contained in the local and urged them to develop a passion for small things such as harvesting crops, collecting dung, and accounting for village production. *The Story of the Summer* denies the idea of being "the mighty and the haughty" (*renshangren*) as a form of upward social mobility, which in this context refers to meritocratic social differentiation resulting from having received higher education. The process of making "our young man" Jinsheng an exemplar reveals how political mobilization completely overtakes individual aspirations for upward mobility. The film ends with the male protagonist expressing his ideal of building a small, mechanized farm in a beautiful, pastoral, poetic landscape, a scene envisioned similarly in the 1958 poster discussed below.

The 1960s witnessed the mass propagation of real-life role models such as Xing Yanzi (1941–) and Dong Jiageng (1940–), an effort intended to inspire the young generation to start their careers in Chinese villages.

After graduating from junior high school, both went back to their rural homes instead of remaining in the city. In 1958, Xing Yanzi, a seventeen-year-old middle-school graduate, left the city of Tianjin, where most of her family lived and where her father worked as the head of a factory, and moved to the village of Sijiazhuang. Xing later recalled that she went to the countryside to spend time with her grandfather, who had raised her, rather than out of any lofty political consciousness. In Sijiazhuang, Xing first worked in the dining hall and later organized a team of local peasant women to work in farming, fishing, and weaving. Their endeavors helped the commune to overcome a difficult period. Xing's story was soon discovered by the media and in 1960 received broad coverage in major newspapers and broadcasts. Making Xing Yanzi into a public hero was a process of turning an individual's spontaneous personal filial sentiment toward a kinsman into an exemplar of the state-endorsed "ambition" of transforming the village. She was the cover person of the October 1960 issue of *China Pictorial* (*Renmin huabao*), and was advertised as a national hero. The production of the image of the national hero had been standardized: the heroic human figure was always magnified in a low-angle shot and thus looked strong, healthy, and happy with the light reflecting off her skin. Xing holds a scythe as if she were a wartime hero wielding weapons to defend the country. She is positioned against an expansive blue sky and gazes into the distance, determined to build the countryside. Her charisma is enhanced by her amiable facial expression, creating the picture of a national heroine who is at once inspirational and approachable, a combination of heroism and quotidian closeness. Together with the similar story of Dong Jiageng, the story of Xing Yanzi played an important role in promoting the subsequent nationwide "up to the mountains and down to the villages" movement. The promotion of Xing and Dong as moral paragons was one of the numerous official efforts to foster public and private morality by establishing a pantheon of role models in what Borge Bakken calls "the exemplary society."[12] Both Xing and Dong exemplified reconciliation of the perennial tension between individual ambition and the needs of the state. The nostalgias and frustrations of the homecoming journey, often mixed in May Fourth fiction, were replaced by a strong sense of fulfillment from participating in collective industrial and agricultural projects in the socialist discourse.

Abolishing the difference between the city and the countryside is the shared goal of Marxism and Maoism; however, Mao's dramatic reversal of the Marxian relationship of the city and the countryside repudiated the notion that the city is the central site for modernization and social transformation. Historian Maurice Meisner describes the rural vision in constructing Chinese socialism and a new form of "the countryside surrounding the cities" this way: "The Maoist aim was neither to 'ruralize' the city nor to 'urbanize' the countryside. It was, rather, to modernize the countryside. The cities were gradually to be absorbed into a modernized and communized rural milieu as society moved to the ultimate goal of abolishing the distinction between town and countryside."[13] The image of the rural revolutionary base before 1949 could be adapted in the postrevolutionary period into a new image of the modernized countryside that could represent and symbolize socialist China. It is true that "all efforts were concentrated on large-scale, modern, and predominantly urban industries" to serve the developmental urge in the post-revolutionary period.[14] However, what is most striking is that newly emerging visual images and films often combine "the rural" and "the industrial" in the new socialist setting and in the representations of labor, skill, and technology. These visual representations defined the rural industrial aesthetics that symbolized the national image of socialist China.

Mao's ideal of an industrialized utopian countryside is illustrated in a 1958 poster titled *The Prospect and Future of the Village* (*Nongcun yuanjing tu*) designed by Zhang Yuqing (fig. 2).[15] In 1955, the socialist state started to organize existing villages into large, state-imposed collectives and communes to replace the market and the household economy.

Reflecting socialism's orientation toward the future, the print highlights agricultural productivity and mechanization; China's agricultural transformation involves machines such as tractors, harvesters, and grinding machines.[16] Moreover, it imagines a form of *non-alienated industrial culture*: with the assistance of the machines, humans are freed from toil and pain, and collective labor gives them a chance to socialize while working with ease and enjoyment. It highlights the harmonious coexistence of the natural landscape, people, and machines in the industrialized village commune without alienation and estrangement. In the print, most of the figures are women; rural modernization was discursively constructed as an emancipatory project that situated rural young women in the public space of production as the equals of men; the heavy responsibilities of domestic labor entailed in women's traditional roles as wives, mothers, and daughters were rendered invisible in the picture. Women's labor was celebrated and utilized to boost the country's productivity, though when it came to women's emancipation during the revolutionary and postrevo-

Fig. 2. *The Prospect and Future of the Village* (Zhang Yuqing, 1958).

lutionary periods, the difference between official discourses and true historical experience was huge.¹⁷ The village commune is at once a beautiful and productive space, a paradoxical combination of the aesthetic and the instrumental. Underlying the rural peacefulness is well-managed nature, an environment that has already been tamed: in the background, natural scenery includes small hills with soft profiles and neatly trimmed trees. The poster portrays a small, self-sufficient, mechanized model village that features regularity, tidiness, simplification, and legibility; it therefore symbolizes what James Scott refers to as the "visual aesthetic of progress" that contrasts the modern and the primitive and showcases "the miniaturization of perfection."¹⁸

China Pictorial (*Renmin huabao*), an influential journal broadly circulated inside and outside China since 1946, published a series of essays regarding industrializing the countryside showing how building hydropower stations maximized the use of local resources and helped create a new local community. The small-scale hydropower stations were often built extremely quickly, in a spirit similar to that of the Great Leap Forward. Building the station was simultaneously depicted as a process of constructing an affective space connected to the local people's native-place sentiments and to their ideal of bringing a better life to their hometown. The small-scale hydropower station's multiple functions are emphasized, and similar to the 1958 poster, it constitutes at once an aesthetic space and a production unit.

A 1960 essay in *China Pictorial* described the building of twelve small-scale Shuanglong hydropower electric stations as a magical process of turning a barren mountain into one that contained "ten thousand treasures."¹⁹ The stations would bring about communal sharing and utilization of natural resources in all aspects of everyday life.²⁰ Another essay took the example of the Xi River in Lintong County, Shaanxi Province, highlighting how nature was being turned into a multifunctional space and an inexhaustible resource for human beings. The water is primarily used to irrigate the extensive agricultural fields and scenic area, and secondarily to cultivate fish and domestic poultry such as ducks. Moreover, the hydropower station on the river provides electricity for household use in the surrounding villages.²¹ The process of turning rivers and lakes into hydropower stations showcases the instrumental nature of modern technological thinking, but these hydropower stations simultaneously function as enchanting natural scenic spots for the people to relax and enjoy their leisure time. The visual images of the countryside published in *China Pictorial* during the socialist period were uniformly pastoral, peaceful, and romantic.²² From the ecocritical perspective, the combination of the instrumental and the pastoral seems paradoxical—the ongoing processes of industrial exploitation of nature and aesthetic appreciation of nature take place simultaneously. Underlying such an image was the dominant idea of nature as knowable, manageable, and predestined for use in the dominant human-centered modernity project; nature could be disciplined, regulated, and eventually conquered.²³

II. The Socialist Brand of Creativity in the Industrial Imagination

Throughout the revolutionary and postrevolutionary periods, Chinese socialists were highly aware of the Marxist economic prerequisites for establishing communism. Anxieties about the absence of such prerequisites often resulted in fantasies about fast-forwarding economic development. In the socialist discourse, the anti-imperialist solution of self-sufficiency and self-reliance relied on "the boundless creative power" of the rural masses. A glimpse at issues of *the People's Daily* (*Renmin ribao*) since 1946 shows that the socialist creativity was described as collective-based, grand (*weidade*), infinite (or unlimited) (*wuqiong wujin de, wuxian de*), and resourceful (*fengfude*). This socialist obsession with and exaggeration of the people's creativity intensified the ideological imperative of inspiring the people's creativity, energy, and capabilities that had been pushed since the beginning of the twentieth century.²⁴

Raymond Williams suggests that creativity, a characteristic of the modern age, refers to originality and innovation and is associated with productivity.[25] With its origin in the divine creation of the world, since the dawn of modernity the notion of creativity has undergone a secularizing and democratizing process to emphasize the human creative capacity.[26] In the modern West, the secularization of creative power manifested itself in the two human capacities of "artistic creativity and epistemological knowledge."[27] In the context of Western capitalism, creativity often takes productivity as its ultimate purpose and goal, and it drives all kinds of innovative efforts.[28] The emphasis on human creativity and human agency during the Cold War period was closely associated with the binary opposition between human and nature.[29] The relationship between human and nature in the twentieth century has been characterized as one of mastery and possession, based on the assumption that human capacity can transcend natural limitations. Accordingly, the human-nature relationship during the Cold War was translated into a friend-enemy relationship. Nature was considered to be predestined to be conquered and transformed by man.[30]

How was creativity conceptualized and practiced in the socialist historical context? Like capitalist creativity, socialist creativity was much driven by the ultimate goal of productivity. But just as science was always closely related to politics and modernization to revolution in socialist China, creativity was also bound up with politics and revolution.[31] The socialist brand of creativity had its roots in the Communist revolutionary enterprise. Historian Mark Selden describes "the creativity of the Chinese people" as the core of the "Yenan [Yan'an] Way" that came into being through the wartime practice:

> Viewed as an integrated program, the Yenan Way represents a distinctive approach to economic development, social transformation, and people's war. Its characteristic features included a heavy reliance on the creativity of the Chinese people, particularly the peasantry, and a faith in the ultimate triumph of man over nature, poverty, and exploitation. Unequivocally rejecting domination by an administrative or technical elite operating through a centralized bureaucracy, it emphasized popular participation, decentralization, and community power. Underlying this approach was a conception of human nature which held that men, all men, could transcend the limitations of class, experience, and ideology to act creatively in building a new China.[32]

The socialist creativity is closely related to Mao's idea of "the advantages of backwardness" as a response to the extreme resource scarcity, material constraints, war-exacerbated misery, and local stagnation of rural China. "The Yenan Way" is indeed an all-encompassing approach to building the connection between creativity and the countryside during the Chinese revolution. Therefore, "act[ing] creatively" stands as the most important characteristic that defines the socialist new person. Eventually, building a new China became a collective-based and community-involved creative project that invited the enthusiastic participation of the people and could release human potential and transcend any limitations.

Unlike the kind of creativity promoted in today's booming creative economy, socialist creativity is mainly a form of collective creativity, the collective capacities of the people that can only emerge from community-involved practice and production to make progress in the human-centered modernity project. Though individual geniuses were often promoted as role models, creativity was still considered the great resource possessed by the collective; individual creativity was merely part of the collective wisdom. Moreover, collective creativity functions in a way that dismisses and denies limitations on human life and promises that humans will stand unrivaled on the earth. Creativity is a critical resource to explore, develop, and utilize, offering an imaginative solution to technological backwardness. The ultimate goal was to release the creativity of the people and to construct a productive, creative subjectivity of Chinese socialism. Socialist creativity indeed functioned as the very agent that could abolish the difference between manual labor and mental labor and could integrate creative ideas into hard manual labor.

In revolutionary and postrevolutionary periods, the people's creativity was manifested in many realms, including literature and arts, revolution, industrial construction, and labor as well as technological innovation. As Richard King points out, "creative method" also dominated the period of the Great Leap Forward, in the sense that the utopia imagined and represented by the writers and artists was not a distorted or fabricated false reality but a manifestation of the creativity of both the cultural workers and the people.[33] While there has been much discussion of socialist morality and revolutionary virtues, the notion of creativity emphasizes how the revolutionary potential of the peasants and their power were manifested in the effort to construct socialism. Because creativity was regarded as the agent that could initiate a radical transformation of society and advance the progressive movement of history, it linked the extraordinary and the ordinary and anticipated the miracles emerging from quotidian life in the socialist context.

Scientific dissemination (*kexue puji*) was one of the ideological missions of the socialist state and dates back to the Yan'an period. It aimed to "convince Chinese people to discard their previous superstitious beliefs and embrace a scientific worldview consistent with the philosophical and political teachings of Marxism."[34] Socialist China made a great effort to expand education to a much wider section of the population, such as peasants and workers. Periodicals and primers on popular science were published and widely distributed, and many defined their target audience as those living in rural areas.[35] The socialist period also produced many scientific educational films, which aimed to promote new technologies, share people's experiences of taming nature, and introduce basic knowledge in the fields of natural and social sciences.[36]

Moreover, the popular magazines at the time encouraged readers to engage in "small inventions" (*xiao faming*). The magazine *Popular Science* (*Kexue dazhong*) started columns on such topics as "small crafts" (*xiao gongyi*, April 1951) and "laboratories for small inventions" (*xiao faming yanjiushi*, May 1951) aimed at teaching readers how to produce small, do-it-yourself products. These columns were intended to promote the spirit of self-reliance and self-sufficiency, crucial to the newly established state as it struggled to gain independence from imperialist invasions.[37] In a 1958 short animated film titled *Little Inventors* (Xiao faming jia, dir. Jin Xi), the animal students are inspired by their elephant teacher to invent a mechanical device to transport the students across hills. This invention of the conveyor belt helps the animal students avoid the long distance of the circuitous mountain road and "fly" directly to the school. "Racking one's brain and finding a solution" becomes one of the key ideas of primary-school education. This animated film translates a childhood playlike "small invention" into a large engineering project with a lively exhibition of human creativity.

In public media, socialist China promoted its goal of turning the countryside into industrialized areas through developing projects such as irrigation and electrification. The government built large-scale and medium-sized reservoirs and hydropower electric stations, which were regarded as important projects to industrialize the countryside. *China Pictorial* published a series of short essays and photos portraying the representational aesthetics of industrializing the countryside in socialist China and the connection between the rural and creativity. A 1959 essay titled "Advancing toward Irrigation" (*Xiang shuilihua yuejin*) published in *China Pictorial* explains that developing irrigation has been a nationwide project. From north to south and from west to east, many villages in different provinces started to cut through mountains, open roads, channel water to agricultural fields, and build irrigation projects.[38] The article illustrated an extended industrial landscape in which watercourses could be rechanneled and the topographic features of the villages and mountains could be carved and reshaped. Published on the tenth anniversary of the founding of the PRC, this essay celebrated the accomplishments of the socialist country with its decade of building irrigation projects that helped promote agricultural production and fight against drought.

The notion of *qiaogan* ("labor or work skillfully") vividly describes the integration of creative ideas into manual labor, an adaptation of Mao's notion of erasing the difference between mental labor and manual labor. In the essay "Advancing toward Irrigation," the idea of *qiaogan* describes how the people skillfully make tools and equipment that massively improves efficiency and productivity.[39] It gives an example of how *qiaogan* is a significant supplement to "working arduously" (*kugan*). *Qiaogan* mainly manifests itself in "small inventions" or technological renovations of tools to achieve partial or full mechanization.[40] A pulley invented for shipping earth made with indigenous technologies is twenty times as efficient and productive as the previous hand-operated cart. With its stress on high productivity and efficiency, *qiaogan* could lead to a shortcut from material scarcity to material prosperity.

The idea of *qiaogan* was also elaborated in a 1959 essay in *China Pictorial* on the peasant inventor (*nongmin famingjia*).[41] This essay features a peasant genius inventor named Zhang Guangyi as a role model; his story was covered by *The People's Daily*. He was praised as a capable person for renovating agricultural tools with the spirit of "having the courage to execute all creative ideas that come to his mind" (*ganxiang ganzuo*). Though he had only one year of education before the founding of the People's Republic, Zhang was able to fully develop his creative potential by renovating eighty-six kinds of agricultural tools, driven by both the urgent need for agricultural production and enthusiastic support from the party and the people. Zhang was recruited as a researcher in the Research Institute of Chinese Agricultural Science due to his achievements. His career trajectory from a local peasant amateur inventor to an expert who gained national recognition is an almost magical transition from the ordinary to the extraordinary, achieved through creativity.

III. Industry on the Playground in The Young People in Our Village: *Labor-as-Play*

The film industry in the socialist period after the founding of the PRC was a state-sponsored image-building program. Socialist cinema was undoubtedly one of the most effective vehicles for circulating socialist ideology and demonstrating the new image of socialist China both at home and abroad.[42] Matthew Johnson observes that films about rural transformation, model villages, and other subjects "all served to advertise Beijing's newfound strength to audiences at home and abroad."[43]

As the most powerful apparatus to build the socialist political culture, cinematic representations were part of the statecraft to design rural life from above and to construct a new socialist countryside in the early years of the PRC.[44] Among them were a 1959 masterpiece titled *The Young People in Our Village* and its 1963 sequel of the same title (both directed by Su Li), both of which represented the experience of returning to the rural home under socialism. They were produced and distributed by Changchun Film Studio. Within four months after the first episode of the film was released, it had been watched by nearly fifteen million people and appealed to both urban and rural audiences. A reader wrote to the magazine *Popular Movies* (*Dazhong dianying*) that the movie revealed "a time when legends can be created."[45] Many young people even modeled themselves on the protagonists and used their names to name their own work teams.[46] It was the film's huge success that led to the production of the sequel under the same name in 1963. That film is about building a hydropower station to electrify the village. According to the director Su Li, the two films in fact responded to the "Four Modernizations" in the countryside proposed by Mao. The 1958 film staged modernization of irrigation on the screenscape, and the 1963 one experimented with electrification modernization in the film.[47]

Both films are representative of socialist realism; the socialist representation of the industrialized countryside was simultaneously an aesthetic program and a practice of art and politics. As "the fundamental principle of the aesthetic conception of revolutionary politics," socialist realism emphasizes that the purpose of art is to mobilize the people and transform the world. This whole process is characterized by the immediacy of change, the vividness of lived reality, and the involvement of the broadest population of people. As a radical modernist aesthetic form, socialist realism was often associated with a utopian impulse, ideological rigidity, teleological development, and social uniformity.[48] Its claim to be a truthful representation of the reality is often complicated by contradictions: on the one hand, it was highly selective in representing reality and offered a form of officially sanctioned reality, while on the other hand it highlighted the pursuit of a higher order of sociohistorical truth. With both domestic and international audiences in mind, these films did not aim to faithfully document real life in the countryside, but rather served as a utopian discourse about a brand-new socialist world. Socialist films glossed over significant parts of reality—particularly the reality that millions of people died from famine and violence during the Great Leap Forward. However, following Yomi Braester's observation that the role of socialist cinema was "part of a larger *experiment* by the socialist state,"[49] this chapter suggests that it is not so much the fact that the cinematic representations were at odds with social reality but that the screenscape itself became an audiovisual space to experiment with utopian dreams of furnishing agrarian settings with modern industrial power.[50] The screenscape became a laboratory for exercising the collective creativity and experiments to bring irrigation and electricity to the rural areas.

In the 1959 film *The Young People in Our Village*, urban-educated middle-school students returned to their rural home, and together with other young people in the village, set out to cut through the mountains that separate their village from water resources, and to construct an irrigation canal to channel the water. Their hometown is barren, mountainous, and undergoing a severe drought. The villagers have to walk long distances to get water. It is true that the portrayal of country life is highly idealized; however, the film does not avoid severe problems such as the water shortage that plagued many areas of rural China, a national pathology that has been discursively related to backwardness and underdevelopment. The film revolves around the ambitious collaborative industrial project to channel water to the village from the Dragon Spring ten miles away. This project is initiated and carried out by "our young people," represented by Gao Zhanwu, a war hero who has recently returned to the village after leaving the military; Kong Shuzhen, a high-school graduate newly returned from the city; Cao Maolin, a local artisan and peasant; and other active young people who aspire to improve living conditions in the village and to transform it into a beautiful and fruitful dreamland. This echoes the utopian vision of the Yan'an spirit, which aimed to transform the remote, underdeveloped regions of China into spaces of material abundance. In the spirit of the Great Leap Forward that man could triumph over the most formidable material obstacles, the film highlights socialist, mass-based creativity, the power of manual labor, and romantic love in the context of the grand project of building a new socialist countryside.

The film incorporates a playful spirit into the entire process of industrializing the countryside. These young people leaving their village carrying their luggage to the Dragon Spring area look like they are leaving for summer camp and entering a play area. After arriving at the Dragon Spring, they stay in the Dragon King Temple; they are overjoyed by the abundance of fresh water and start to wash, drink, splash water on each other, and tease the statue of the Dragon King. Their laughter and mischief and the festive atmosphere blur the line between the military-style construction (which Zhanwu calls "an arduous combat task") and an exciting game. For these young people, it was exhilarating to socialize with other young members of the village away from the watchful gaze of parents, the village head, and other seniors. Building the irrigation canal transports the audience and performers out of the ordinary life of toil and boredom into a sphere of excitement and fun. The rural field is simultaneously an industrial workplace staging collective labor, a rendezvous for courtship of the young generation, and a playground for camping, hunting, entertaining, singing, dancing, and partying.

The following sequence depicts a group of young men climbing down from the mountaintop and starting to dig holes on the cliff. The war veteran and team leader Zhanwu supervises and issues commands on the construction site as if he is still an army platoon leader, initiating "Mao's War Against Nature" to transform the natural environment.[51] Afterward, Shuzhen immediately follows their example and goes down to join the young people. Zhanwu criticizes her rashness but is impressed by her bravery. Maolin explains that "while a little girl, she was like this, climbing onto the roof of the house and the tree. She was not scared of anything." Maolin's comments seem to suggest that cutting through mountains and channeling water is the same as the childhood play of climbing onto the roof and up the tree, which combines military seriousness with a frolicsome spirit. These playful moments create an intriguing confusion: is this a battlefield, an industrial construction site, or simply a playground? Why does the film represent the military-style enterprise of conquering nature as a form of play? How does the play elements function in a socialist setting?[52]

Both Zhen Zhang and Xinyu Dong in their studies of early Chinese cinema discuss people's fascination with mechanical gadgets in the increasingly technologized everyday life at the turn of the twentieth century. Zhen Zhang highlights the prevalence of *youxi* (play or playfulness) in both urban socialization and entertainment as "a mode of cognition involving sensuous, somatic, and tactile forms of perception; a noncoercive engagement with the other that opens the self to experience."[53] Xinyu Dong stresses the early Chinese cinema's fascination with the work-play dialectic, the playful elements, and the spirit of inventiveness.[54] This chapter chooses a different perspective, discussing the role of play in cinematic representations of socialist rural industrialization. In the film, the socialist young people enter the industrial-site-cum-playground as participants-players. The films lead the audience into a purely aesthetic experience of rural industrial construction as a world of miracles that goes beyond ordinary life. The industrial site is a space separated from their usual lives, a play community dominated by genuine freedom, superabundant energy, tension, light-heartedness, and carefree joyfulness.

Noting the union of play and culture, Dutch historian Johan Huizinga suggests that "the great archetypal activities of human society are all permeated with play from the start."[55] He defines play as "a free activity standing quite consciously outside 'ordinary' life as being 'not serious,' but at the same time absorbing the player intensely and utterly."[56] He highlights the formal characteristics of play as free and voluntary, full of fun and enjoyment, a kind of contest and performance before the public.[57] It is a special form of action or activity that allows participants to step out of the ordinary world "of toil and care, the calculation of advantage or the acquisition of useful goods."[58] Play has multiple social functions, such as releasing vital energy, supplying relaxation, and satisfying unfulfilled longings, among others.[59] Moreover, Huizinga suggests, "play lies outside the antithesis of wisdom and folly, and equally outside those of truth and falsehood, good and evil. Although it is a non-material activity, it has no moral function. The valuations of vice and virtue do not apply here."[60] Therefore, the play sphere should not be evaluated in terms of the yardsticks of ordinary life that are conditioned by the opposition between right and wrong, good and evil, and true and false. Huizinga also observes that what characterizes play is the spirit of "happy inspiration."[61] All of these positive qualities nurture "happy inspiration" and therefore inspire creative energy. As a positive emotion, playfulness is of low emotional intensity. It can still, however, produce human agency, inspire active thinking and creativity, and generate energy that connects the ordinary and the extraordinary, eventually enabling young people to cope with the challenge of material scarcity. Rather than being separated from work, play is always associated with the stimulating, the creative, the pleasant, and the energetic; play constitutes the important feature of socialist builders, who always appear to be lively (*shengdong*).⁶²

Throughout the film there is a visible tendency to conflate play and labor in rural industrialization: labor is not toil anymore, but brisk or vigorous bodily movement and action for amusement; simultaneously, collective labor is displayed as a collective performance. The film shows how human creativity and energy are channeled into playful collective manual labor. The Japanese literary critic Karatani Kojin points out that there was in fact no clear division between play and labor in preindustrial society, when experienced workers regarded labor as play. However, the rise of industrial capitalism reorganized modern society, and automation turned the working experience into mere labor.⁶³ Blurring the boundary between labor and play thus reveals the socialist aspiration to seek an alternative to the capitalist working experience. Another exemplary episode illustrates the smooth transition from indoor entertainment and play to outdoor labor for canal construction. When pouring rain causes a few house-size boulders to fall, blocking the flow of water, Zhanwu decides to hold an evening party to ease people's anxiety. The party reaches its climax when Zhanwu performs a Korean-style dance he learned in the military (fig. 3), which is followed by the chorus singing of all the young people directed by Shuzhen (fig. 4). The purpose of holding a party is "emotion-raising" (*tigao qingxu*), a key component used in the pre-1949 revolutionary struggle.⁶⁴ The scene of play—dancing, singing, laughing—is congruent with Jason McGrath's observation that Mao-era cinema was "much more fun than its reputation as mere propaganda would have us believe."⁶⁵ This "fun" quality that characterizes the socialist films helped to engender pleasure, energy, and creativity resulting from "play," which generates productive passion and counteracts the reality of hard labor. The party ends with passionate group singing led by Shuzhen. With the soundtrack still playing, the camera cuts to the next sequence, in which the young people labor on the mountain (fig. 5). The film editing forms a collage and constructs new meanings. The shift from play to labor underscores such linkages: dancing is a kinetic practice of socialization, and singing is an expression of one's inner voice and power, while labor becomes an expressive act of play, a form of "dancing and singing" as an experience of Promethean mastery and an active affective engagement with one's physical surroundings.

The smooth transition from the entertainment party to the construction site signals a perceptual change from the toil of physical labor to the village youth's experiencing "happy inspiration" through collective action,

Fig. 3. *The Young People in Our Village* (1959). The young people are dancing and singing at a party held for their entertainment (1:12:08).

Fig. 4. *The Young People in Our Village* (1959). The young people are dancing and singing in a party held for their entertainment (1:12:32).

Fig. 5. *The Young People in Our Village* (1959). The young people are digging on top of the mountain (1:12:46).

which celebrates the sublimity of their shared ideal of building a hometown of material abundance and prosperity. Collective labor fuses the state ideology of development with the development of human potential through play. Playfulness in the representational forms of socialist industrialization should be understood in relation to the labor-intensive nature of Chinese industrialization. The labor of the Chinese people was key to socialist industrialization in a state committed to rapid development. However, socialist labor in its representational forms has been shown as rather different from both the exploitative labor in capitalist factories and the slavelike labor recruited by dynastic empires.[66] Arif Dirlik contends that the spirit of self-reliance and delayed gratification depicted in scenes of collective labor in fact rendered invisible the fact that the socialist state exploited the people's labor.[67] Ci Jiwei describes the early years of socialist China featured "a people who were exhausted yet jubilant, a people worn down by war and poverty but newly energized by the meaning and hope that the cause of communism had restored to their lives."[68] I argue that through the medium of the play sphere, the film translates the coercive and exploitative feature of hard labor into the mobilizing structure of Chinese socialism. To remove poverty is to rid the people of exhaustion and have them regain their collective energy and excitement. Representing labor as play therefore incorporates energy, creativity, and dynamism into industrial construction. The construction site is accordingly represented not as a place that exhausts the working people, but as one that releases unlimited human capacity, actualizes human potential, and generates the people's energy and passion. Highlighted in this play-labor conjunction is the way the play impulse helps dilute the component of "coerciveness" and cancels out the repression and exploitation of labor; this allows the socialist audience to imagine a mode of aesthetics that can counteract, at the level of perception, the toil, hardship, and material scarcity of reality.

This particular shot of sculpting the mountain is also a performance of collective labor in nature. In the mountaintop shot, the use of artificial light turns the natural mountain into a very artificial setting. In the composition of the shot, the mountain takes center stage, and its size relative to the human figures creates visual effects such that the young people digging the mountain look as if they are carving an artwork. This "as if" very much speaks to the virtual nature of play and the isomorphism of play and labor. Collective productions characterized Mao-era culture in such realms as painting, sculpture, and architecture as well as literature, performance, and other art spheres.[69] Scholars have noted the power of representations of collective manual labor to transform both individuals and China's landscape, and to provide a site of unification to connect the people.[70] Influenced by the European labor movement in the nineteenth century, unskilled physical labor in China's revolutionary and socialist periods was considered not inferior but noble, fundamentally defining human beings. Labor was accordingly put "on equal terms with other activities like the administration, the arts, and skilled crafts" and "viewed as a pure expression of human culture."[71]

This long shot of the mountain (fig. 4) seems to blur the boundary between physical labor and skilled crafts, and makes the canal project seem more like sculpture, a work of art, than an engineering project. This film turns strenuous, often unskilled rural manual labor into dexterous artisanal labor through intimate, hands-on contact with natural materials. The long shot in *The Young People in Our Village* portrays an artisanal practice and a collective passion for work, showing that physical labor creates boundless possibilities, releasing youthful energy to create a work of art. This shot recalls one of Mao's favorite fables—"the foolish man removes the mountain"—which emphasizes the power of the collective and the spirit of being resolute, persevering, and self-reliant.[72] However, changing the water's course though human power amounts to changing the physiognomy of the surrounding mountains through artisanal labor. These robust socialist youths are in fact making a durable artifact that is being dug, carved, and shaped and that will withstand the passage of time. Their artisanal labor in the project of conquering nature demonstrates the "malleability" of localities as much as the malleability of the socialist subjects.[73]

As products of the aesthetic principle "synthesis of revolutionary realism and revolutionary romanticism" raised by Mao Zedong and Zhou Yang in 1958,[74] these films brought to light the link between the aesthetic and the productive simultaneously embodied in socialist creative labor and socialist rural industrialization. In this way, the aesthetic construct of the socialist village became a site to encourage villagers to transcend local restrictions, to imagine a better future, and to release their subjective potential to participate in reality in the making. It is to some extent similar to the notion of "elevation" raised in Mao's Yan'an talks as a principle of literary and artistic creation.

Like the Shaan-Gan-Ning border region during the wartime period, labor remained a constitutive part of the utopia of romantic love. The construction site in *The Young People in Our Village* also functions as a place for courtship and romantic love, which is a continuation and adaptation of the love-labor conjunction on the agricultural field in the Yan'an period, as discussed in chapter 4. In a 1959 essay published in *Popular Cinema* (*Dazhong dianying*), author Chen Mo describes the movie as "a symphony of labor, love, and revolutionary drive."[75] Chen suggests that the construction site is not merely a place for physical labor. Rather, the poetics of the film lie in interweaving the young people's enthusiasm for labor, ambition, friendship, love, and revolutionary vigor. The construction site becomes a social nexus that relates all these affective human relationships and also works as a medium for releasing human emotion and energy, rather than merely being a backdrop for the twin processes of conquering nature and cultivating human affection. The film features several young men—Zhanwu, Maolin, and Keming (another middle school graduate who has recently returned to the village)—all of whom fall in love with the same girl, Shuzhen. Building the irrigation canal parallels the young men's courtship of their shared object of affection. Zhanwu and Shuzhen fall in love at first sight, and most importantly, they share the dream of transforming their hometown. The prominent presence of romantic love in these films reveals that courting and erotic components were channeled into the collective passion of socialist construction and were recognized as an important source of productive energy.

At the beginning of the film, a description of the appeal of water to the villagers is followed by a country-road sequence in which Shuzhen strides proudly into the frame, singing happily and loudly in the valley. The young men standing on the mountaintop are instantly attracted to her, to the extent that they even forget to drink the precious water brought from afar.[76] Both the country road and the act of homecoming are placed in the foreground in the lyrical setting. In socialist films, the country road, the spatial connection between the town and the village, is always bathed in bright sunshine. Shuzhen's exuberant beauty and happy singing quench the thirst of the young men better than drinking water does. It would be too simplistic a reading to designate Shuzhen as what Laura Mulvey refers to as the object of the heterosexual male gaze operating in the contemporary culture of patriarchal dominance.[77] What matters in this segment is not whether Shuzhen is the object of the male gaze, but that the "erotic" component she embodies does not make her passive or inferior. Instead, her charisma is a stimulating force that energizes the young men who are "gazing" from the top of the hill. The foregrounding of the country road stages the public visibility of a charming woman and the romantic desire she arouses in the hearts of the young men. The motivating force of the young woman becomes even more visible during the mass gathering organized by Zhanwu to convince the villagers to construct the canal. Because many villagers feel uncertain or are unwilling to participate, Shuzhen stands up, requests that people participate in the canal building, and cuts off her braids to show her determination. This courageous behavior plays a tremendous role in inspiring the villagers, male and female, old and young, and she successfully enlists the strongest and most active young people in the village. The construction site is turned into a *playground* on which "our young people" are passionately loving, happily playing, and energetically working. The films blend seriousness and playfulness, eroticism and energy, in the construction of socialism, inviting the audience into a playful industrial dream world.

IV. A Handmade and Homemade Industry: The Industrial-as-Artisanal

Before the founding of the PRC, Mao had pointed out the importance of a transition from craftsmanship to machinery as the social basis for building a new democratic country.[78] Sigrid Schmalzer suggests that right after 1949, disseminating scientific information came to be considered highly significant "to enable laborers to grasp scientific production technology, to disseminate knowledge of natural science so as to eliminate superstitious thought, to publicize new inventions from the laboring classes in order to cultivate patriotic spirit, and to spread knowledge of health and hygiene in order to protect the people's health."[79] Schmalzer further suggests that though scientific dissemination was a top-down enterprise, there was no clearly marked boundary between "experts" and the masses.[80] One of the goals of the Great Leap Forward movement was to shape the new masses as "masters of science and technology" and to remove the differentiation of manual labor and mental labor.[81]

The Young People in Our Village and its sequel feature the young people's collective efforts to build an irrigation canal and an electric hydropower station, during which they display their creativity in making "small inventions" and incorporating artisanal components into the industrial project. Schmalzer points out the *tu/yang* (native and peasants/foreign and elite) binary in science during the socialist period.[82] It would be incorrect to define "small inventions" as a form of *tu* science, largely because it was based on universally accessible knowledge rather than local, indigenous skills. However, "small inventions" do embody the value of *tu* as "self-reliance, mass mobilization, practical application" through using local, readily obtained materials.[83] These representations of operating with "small inventions" figure prominently in both installments of the film. This chapter now turns to the aesthetic component of the industrial-as-artisanal, showing how the socialist brand of creativity bridges mental and manual labor, and also bridges the gap between meager material resources and grand infrastructure projects. The French poet Charles Baudelaire indicates that the industrial qualities of inventiveness, the naïveté of genius, and an adventurous imagination are associated with the rise of modernity, whereas the artisanal qualities of dexterity, adroitness, and craftsmanship are considered essentially premodern.[84] Interestingly, however, as a distinctive aesthetic feature in the cinematic representations of socialist rural industrialization, "the industrial-as-artisanal" blurs the boundary between the two sets of values.

In these two films, "small inventions" embody the people's creativity and take the form of rural craftsmanship, which blends into the imaginary of rural industrialization. These two films continue early cinema's fascination with craftsmanship and the idea of inventiveness.[85] Play and invention were not part of what Zhang Zhen describes as the "playful vernacular modernism" of the urban entertainment culture of 1920s Shanghai, but were integral to a state-initiated socialist program with an experimental spirit.[86] The years between the late 1950s and the early 1960s witnessed a series of tumultuous events: the tragic Great Leap Forward, the three years of the Great Famine from 1958 to 1960, as well as the deterioration of the relationship between China and the Soviet Union and the Soviets' subsequent withdrawal of experts who were supporting China's economic and technological development. *The Young People in Our Village* shows the craftsmanship used in small gadgets and carpentry in canal building; the 1963 sequel extends artisanship into the field of science and technology and depicts local artisans acting as modern engineers to build a hydroelectric power station.

Known affectionately by other villagers as a "master of seventy-three professions" (*qishisan hang*), the character Cao Maolin possesses many talents, including traditional skills such as farming, hunting, and artisanal abilities. This fictional figure also reminds us of the peasant inventor Zhang Guangyi, who had capabilities of *qiaogan* as discussed earlier. Foregrounded in the films and key to the experiment and solution-seeking is the ingenuity and resourceful mind of the rural artisan, whose work forms an interface between local agency and the grand project of industrialization, between the subjective fantasy of creative imagination and objective material forms of reality. In the first installment about canal building, during the process of exploding the hill Maolin has a creative idea: tie incense to a blasting fuse with a few matches to ignite the fuse without injury. The camera moves from a close-up of the simple invention to one of these gadgets hanging on the cliff; it then cuts to a long shot of the mountain being blown up. This transition from the small to the grand illustrates how small inventions could be used to manipulate nature and to facilitate larger social and historical changes, such as rural industrialization.

In the last stage of canal building, the female carpenter, Xiaocui, is asked to make a wooden mine cart. She selects Maolin to help her. The

Fig. 6. *The Young People in Our Village* (1959). Maolin and Xiaocui collaborate to make a mine cart to move mining debris (1:30:21).

next segment features their collaboration and recognition of each other's talent. Maolin and Xiaocui collaborate to make a mine cart by changing some of its parts, which wins the villagers' heartfelt praise for their talents (fig. 6). Romantic love grows out of their appreciation for each other's virtuosity and ingenuity in this cooperative venture. After finishing the mine cart, Maolin and Xiaocui use two mirrors to reflect light into the dark tunnel being built through the mountain (fig. 7). Unlike "the silent craftsmen of ancient and medieval China" described by Joseph Needham,[87] this craft-savvy couple is widely praised in their community, and elevated to the status of creative geniuses. Similar to preindustrial forms of artisanal products, these inventions blend the intimacy of the homemade with the industrial. The "do-it-yourself" nature of "small inventions" illustrates the popular belief that the true source of revolutionary creativity is "the people," the vast peasant masses. The concept of "small inventions" means that manual tasks also have a creative dimension and play a role in erasing the distinction between mental and manual labor in socialist discourse.

Creating a Rural Industrial Aesthetics   173

Fig. 7. *The Young People in Our Village* (1959). Maolin and Xiaocui use two mirrors to reflect light into the dark tunnel (1:30:43).

Simple, low-budget, small inventions also symbolized the virtues of self-sufficiency and self-reliance that defined the spirit of the socialist period.

The sequel can be regarded as a combination of feature film and science-education film, for it works as a guidebook for popular scientific literacy. For example, when Xiaocui asks Maolin why electricity is measured in different units, Maolin answers in terms that would be familiar to peasant, noting that scientific units are commensurate with other types of units, such as those for measuring cloth and weighing rice and salt. This group of young people in the village, motivated by the goal of building a hydropower station and educating the people in science, form an electrification training class, turning the village into a learning community. In the film, when the villagers remain skeptical about the benefits of building the power station, Maolin attempts to convince them of the efficiency of using electric machinery. He makes a miniature wooden model of a power-driven flour-milling machine, itself a work of art produced by a rural artisan (fig. 8). The flour-milling machine that appears

Fig. 8. *The Young People in Our Village* (1963). Maolin makes a miniature wooden model of a power-driven flour-milling machine (13:03).

Fig. 9. *The Young People in Our Village* (1963). The flour-milling machine that appears later in the film looks like an enlarged version of the wooden model (1:28:01).

later in the film looks like an enlarged version of the model (fig. 9). The shift exhibits the isomorphism of handicraft and machine, the artisanal and the industrial. Models are usually diminutive and relatively simple, but they invite the people to use their imaginations. The juxtaposition of these two shots, the machine and the model of the machine, creates the illusion that the industrial object is merely developed from Maolin's miniature and that the industrial machine is simply a larger version of the handcrafted artisanal object.

In the sequel, the young people plan to make their own wooden water turbine, because they are unable to buy an iron one. Eager to finish building the hydropower station, Maolin cooperates with the urban-educated Keming to make a temporary wooden water turbine by hand. The cooperation between rural craftsman and urban-educated youth exemplifies collective enterprise in rural industrialization. Translating a drawing issued by the party into a water turbine made by the locals is depicted with an overlapped dissolve and a quick superimposition, which creates the impression of the fast passage of time. Through the intimate touch of the rural people's hands, the water turbine in fact becomes a craftsman's "work of art." The making of the wooden water turbine is meant to show that an industrial object can also be an artisanal product. Walter Benjamin suggests that "the objective (and progressive) tendency of industrialism is to fuse art and technology, fantasy and function, meaningful symbol and useful tool, and that this fusion is, indeed, the very essence of socialist culture."[88]

On the surface, "small inventions" are part of the scientific popularization advocated by the state, and also suggest that rural industrialization is accomplished largely by local agents; industrialization at the village level emphasizes local initiatives and self-sufficiency. However, these "small inventions" differ in nature from local skills. The task of the young inventors is to create an approximation of advanced technology using local materials. However, one can observe that the film is based on a total "misunderstanding" of empirical science as well as craft knowledge and skills. An experienced craftsman like Maolin might have the skills to replicate a sophisticated turbine using wood, but it would not work in practice because a hydropower turbine must be made of metal and requires a scientific precision not demonstrated here.[89] Taking the paper industry in a county in Sichuan Province as an example, Jacob Eyferth explains that local skills are "embodied in the brains and bodies of practitioners, situated in natural and manmade environments, and distributed across groups of practitioners"; they involve family and neighbor relationships in the local community.[90] The "small inventions" represented in the films are in fact in accord with universal principles and basic scientific knowledge and are not embedded in the concrete aspects and social relationships of particular localities.

The use of these "small inventions" in the sequel presents socialist industrialization using a visual guidebook of rapid development in the village. Compared to local skills, which involve interlinked natural and man-made conditions, "small inventions" are a product of simplification and reductionism of real situations, and constitute the very signifying system that inscribes the message from the state onto rural society. James Scott pinpoints the pernicious reductionism that has accompanied the modernist state's "cult of efficiency"[91] and emphasizes "a powerful aesthetic dimension," which is "an abbreviated visual image of efficiency that is less a scientific proposition to be tested than a quasi-religious faith in a visual sign or representation of order."[92] The universal principle in the modern state is to dismiss local particularities, diversity, and constantly changing local conditions; therefore, "small inventions" *look* right—which does not mean they work or function well.[93] The cinematic construct of the rural dreamworld reorganizes the rural community to mobilize a new form of communal life favored by state policy. Central state engineering takes on what James Scott refers to as "a certain aesthetic, or a visual codification" of modern rural life and community life, and writes "the newest and most beautiful words" and paints "the newest and most beautiful pictures" on the rural landscape.[94]

The sequel also illustrates the aesthetic codification of modern rural life in its juxtaposition of romantic love and industrial machine. Romantic love and dating are described as "chasing play," in the words of the conservative but recently enlightened villager Kong Yinyang. In the festive atmosphere of a rural couple's wedding, Kong uses vivid language to describe romantic love: "when dating, the pair of lovers would find a place with hills and water: the female would smile, running ahead, while the male would run after her, chasing and chasing; eventually the man would catch up with her.... Free love is almost always like this." Kong's use of verbs such as "running" and "chasing" to describe the performance of romantic love on the agricultural field recalls the flow of electricity. Kong ponders the nature of electricity and of free love, and finds that both are characterized by stimulation and mobility, as a dynamic flow. Electricity becomes inextricably enmeshed in the everyday lives of the villagers.

Electrification, with its sometimes deplored mechanization and artificiality, does not destroy the communal peace and harmonious life of the village. The last segment of the film takes place during the autumn harvest and features a scene in which the movement of machinery smoothly transitions to the next shot, in which the romantic lovers gaze affectionately at each other from a distance. Montage editing creates a mixture of human sentiment and technology. The analogy between human emotion and technology suggests that the energy generated by emotion can be deployed in the cause of socialist construction. Comparing "electricity" to love shows that the machine and technology have been integrated into human interaction, not so much technological utopianism as "electrified" human love speeding up production and making possible technological acceleration to transform village life. The "electricity" between two lovers is transformed into something parallel to the technological acceleration of agricultural production. The film characterizes rural industrialization by the twin processes of industrializing and sentimentalizing it. The technological capacity to produce is intertwined with the human capacity to love and to dream. In creating a socialist utopian place called "our village," the film imagines the rural landscape as a technologically progressive and emotionally effusive place.

In *The Young People in Our Village* and its sequel, using primitive tools and rudimentary mathematical knowledge, the young people in the village construct both a canal and a hydropower station, both of which are the products of human hands—or large-scale rural handicrafts. The presence of the artisanal in socialist industrialization seems to suggest that rural industrialization is itself an artifact—a craft that blends intimacy, affection, and the self-sufficiency of the homemade and handmade into rural industrialization. Just as the miniature wooden model made by Maolin is compared to the much larger machine that appears later in the film, "our village" is a miniature compared to the grand entity of China. On the other hand, the use of the artisanal in an industrial project shows "the boundless creative power" of the rural masses and simultaneously creates a myth of the omnipotence of human creativity, the belief that the human hand can dominate nature and recreate the world. The poetics of socialist industrialization lies in the uncanny combination of the omnipotent and the affective, which underscores the politics of self-reliance and self-sufficiency in Chinese socialism.

"Our village" is in fact a dreamscape, a utopian realm that is at once "the good place" and "no place" mediated through play and invention.

The construction site is an educational playground and an experimental laboratory for hands-on approaches. This exaggeration of the peasants' creativity contributes to the dominant discourse about the self-sufficiency of peasants. The film and its sequel portrayed a socialist utopia in which industrial projects were imagined to be *handmade* and *homemade* enterprises; they depicted an intense enterprise of conquering nature as a series of playful events and small inventions characterized by artisanal ingenuity and creativity.

V. The Industrialized Countryside as Socialist China's National Self-image

This chapter weaves together homecoming, the socialist brand of collective creativity, and the aesthetic components of "labor-as-play" and "industrial-as-artisanal" in cinematic representations that formed a kind of rural industrial culture. These aesthetic components were an important part of nonalienated industrial culture, which seemed to resume the Yan'an industrial culture that Edgar Snow briefly described in *Red Star Over China*. Richard King uses the term "the romance of industry" to describe the euphoria of enthusiasm, labor, energy, and competition that generated enormous human power and aesthetic wonder in the industrialization of the Great Leap Forward.[95] My analysis of the poetics and aesthetics of rural industrialization emphasizes the revolutionary change in creating a new realm of human perception and experience through transforming repetitive, monotonous, and often painful manual labor into joyful creative play, and turning industrial coldness and hardness into artisanal warmth and malleability. The playful and artisanal aspects of industrial projects work as productive concepts to show the sophisticated mobilization of human energy and creativity articulated by the socialist ideology, inspiring boundless energy and creativity within the current restrictions of the primitive condition of intense manual labor.

Inside China, *The Young People in Our Village* created a dreamworld aimed at motivating urban young people to return to their villages to fulfill the developmental needs of the state and to embrace a new form of communal life. Based on the available record, *The Young People in Our Village* was also widely shown outside China.[96] Within China, the attractions and popularity of the films represented the official discourse that aimed to turn the rural subject into a shared culture widely enjoyed by both urban and rural audiences. Outside China, the aesthetic construct of a national village represented socialist China's public image-building that showed its unique rural identity. Such aesthetic constructs dramatically changed the previous discourse about rural China, which was discursively constructed by missionaries and sinologists to show the difference between China and the West.[97] The socialist cinematic representations of the locality were not about particularity or constructing local identity, but concerned national identity in a way that relieved the local of all its particularities. The hometown "our village" indeed functioned as a microcosm of socialist China, and accordingly, as the countryside took on new significance China became a larger version of the rural hometown. China's socialist ideology has gone through a process of self-orientalization, emphasizing the uniqueness of Chinese socialism to express its strength as a newly established nation-state.[98] This version of the industrialized countryside reflected a poetics of socialist industry and marked the uniqueness of China's national identity circulated at home and abroad during the Cold War period.

Mao's version of socialism and industrialization helped satisfy some members of the Western intelligentsia's imagination regarding socialist China.[99] Some Western intellectuals in the 1960s became acutely disenchanted with Western modernity. In the absence of reliable information, they were attracted by the images and fragmentary accounts of China, and drawn to a romanticized version of socialist China. As Richard Wolin describes, they wondered "whether the Chinese approach to industrialization might be a viable path to modernization, one that might circumvent the upsets and dislocations of the predominant Western models."[100] Historian Rhoads Murphey, one of the Western observers and scholars inspired by Maoism during the Cold War period, praised the creativity of the socialist conception of rural industrialization.[101] Disillusioned by Western industrialization, which is often characterized by grimy, dehumanizing, overcrowded cities, Murphey wrote, "many in the West cherish the hope that somehow the Chinese can produce a form of development which avoids the worst mistakes of the Western model and leads the way to a better world for all of us, as the Maoist vision indeed promises."[102] Representations from China gratified the antimodernist critics who were disenchanted with scientific rationality in the postindustrial world and turned to the order and virtues of a country with a much lower level of industrialization.

The rural feature of Chinese revolution and socialist industrialization had contributed to socialist China's ideological influence in the world.

The socialist utopia depicted in globally circulated images in the 1950s and 1960s represented China's state-sponsored soft power. Components such as play, artisanship, and romance were the "soft" dimensions incorporated into the hard power of socialist China. The socialist state built a metaphorical link between the village and China as a whole, and adopted the rhetoric of the self-sufficiency as China built a self-reliant economy free from the control of foreign capital and as the country struggled to survive antagonistic international politics. This sovereignty was a goal of socialist China as it reclaimed autonomy, gained historical agency, and built its unique rural identity. However, historian Jacob Eyferth questions the image of the self-sufficient and self-reliant village, pointing out that the socialist policy of enhancing rural self-sufficiency in fact turned villages into insular collectives, which "removed rural people from the web of mutual dependency and exchange of which they had been part."[103] While socialist China presented the world with a mild image of the industrialized countryside and an aesthetic construct of its national identity, it simultaneously engaged in an internal exploitation, extracting rural resources to fuel urban heavy industry. During the Cultural Revolution, "self-sufficiency" turned into what Arif Dirlik calls "an atavistic assertion of a revolutionary brand of nationalistic chauvinism."[104]

The celebration of rural industrialization staged in the socialist countryside in socialist cinematic representations was completely absent in films produced in the post-Mao period, even though rural subjects (*nongcun pian*) continued to be a major focus of filmmakers.[105] Barren land and water shortages—obstacles that China needed to overcome to enter modernity—were a continuous theme throughout the socialist and post-socialist periods.[106] The widely acclaimed 1986 film *Old Well* (*Laojing*) is an example. Like *The Young People in Our Village*, the film is set in a remote village where the villagers have been plagued by poverty and water shortages for generations. Digging wells and searching for water have cost many lives. The film reiterates the theme of homecoming and the search for water that aims to change the village life. Returned high-school graduates Wangquan and Qiaoying attempt to find water to fulfill the wishes of the village head. After several failed attempts and careful investigations, Wangquan and Qiaoying use modern hydraulic technology to locate the water resource (rather than relying on rural artisanship) and successfully dig a well that can provide for the daily needs of the village. Although both films depict barriers, frustrations, and final victory in the process of looking for water for a village, there are striking contrasts. Well-digging replaces the much more ambitious enterprise of cutting through a mountain and building a canal. Unlike the grand image of a canal, which represents vitality, connection, mobility, and effusive energy, the image of the "old well" suggests the underground, the hidden, the dark, the static, and the isolated.[107] The two episodes of *The Young People in Our Village* turned the grand enterprise of conquering nature into a display of young people's playful labor. Labor heroes in socialist literature and cinema always seem to have boundless energy and show no physical fatigue even though they do not have enough rest. In contrast, the process of digging a well is fraught with exhaustion, impatience, agitation, and the boredom of repetitive manual labor. Building an irrigation canal celebrates the power of the people to make new beginnings, whereas well digging is associated with numerous human injuries and death. It is the vulnerable and fragile human bodies, not the energized ones, that sustain this communal enterprise. Although the film *Old Well* still acknowledges human agency and the virtue of perseverance, the film (as seen in the episode of Wangquan and Qiaoying investigating the valley) highlights the mythic power and tenacity of nature and the smallness of the human being in the broad cosmos, visualizing the dramatic ideological reversal and huge disillusionment during the post-Mao period.

CHAPTER 6

Socialist Builders on the Rails and Road
Railway Travel, Industrialization, and Social Engineering in Chinese Socialist Films, 1949–65

In the opening shot of the 1957 Chinese film *The Nurse's Diary* (*Hushi riji*),[1] the camera sweeps through the campus of Shanghai Nursing School in the exuberant springtime: students are joyfully walking and sitting on the lawn, bathed in sunlight. This scene of youth is accompanied by the diegetic singing of the film's theme song, which celebrates "the train of our time" (*shidai de lieche*). It is performed by a group of female students on a dormitory balcony: "The train in our own time, rumbling; the youthful enthusiasm, overflowing from the compartment," they sing. After the introduction of the intertwined themes of youth, the railway, and mobility, the camera moves on to a group of female students who are enthusiastically discussing where the most desirable place is to start their new careers after graduation. The names of frontier provinces such as Xinjiang and Hainan, with their romantic and exotic associations, evoke great passion in the young students. After insisting that her only choice would be to remain in Shanghai, a girl sitting apart from the others is immediately ridiculed by her classmates for her lack of knowledge of the country beyond Shanghai and her lack of experience with railway travel. In this context, the collective romantic longing for railway travel reveals the young generation's obsession with the vitality of life and the experience of mobility, which would serve the state program of industrialization and socialist mobilization.

This episode highlights the great appeal of the railway travel and the frontier regions, and it well represents the early years of the PRC and the social engineering program that transferred young urbanites to underdeveloped frontier settlements and remote villages. The program started in the mid-1950s and reached its culmination during the Cultural Revolution (1966–1976). Before the official start of the "up to the mountains, down to the villages" movement in the late 1960s, socialist industrialization required the accumulation of human capital from universities and factories located in major cities such as Shanghai. In the 1950s and early 1960s, a series of films were produced in which modern transportation vehicles—trains and trucks—transferred idealistic youth from the cities, particularly Shanghai, to outlying places to participate in socialist industrialization. This chapter examines these films as inspirational works, integral to the state-initiated relocation program, that motivated many people to devote their youthful years to building socialism in underdeveloped areas. Going to underdeveloped areas was described as an adventurous journey for these aspiring urban young people, who imagined themselves transforming the natural world and the national landscape through advancing industrial development and accelerating historical progress in the 1950s and 1960s. Focusing on the relationship between utopian cinematic representations and social engineering, this chapter examines how the films sought to mobilize the state-initiated relocation program and to articulate the socialist ideal of industrialization.

What figures prominently in these mobilization films is the experience of railway travel and the construction site; they are closely intertwined as part of the larger industrialization and social engineering project, because the construction site symbolizes the destination and the ultimate purpose of the railway travel. Construction sites in these films are often represented as grand, remote, and empty spaces; these scenes made no references to specific locations or to the people who were native to these sites. This chapter continues to discuss the conjunction of the rural and the technological/industrial in the remote wasteland. It is true that the wasteland and the countryside are undeniably two distinct forms of rural area, and that after World War I, European and American modernist writers used the idea of the wasteland as a metaphor in their harsh critique of the acquisitiveness of the society.[2] Nonetheless, this chapter includes the wasteland as an analytical category of the rural, particularly the wasteland in the frontier region (most of which were rural areas), since socialist China was driven by a strong ambition to dramatically transform wasteland into productive rural space through radical modernization.[3] Metaphorically and figuratively, the rural represents the virgin land of remoteness and emptiness; with the use of fast-speed technology and modern transportation, the remoteness could rapidly be overcome, and the rural forms of emptiness would unfold like blank canvases to be painted with "the most beautiful pictures." This chapter focuses on urban youth's "going to the countryside" as a form of national mobilization and a social engineering project, and characterizes a new form of the rural in terms of remoteness, emptiness, and underdevelopment. The rural has often been regarded as a geographical-social-cultural complex that embodies premodern relationships, but the emergence of a remote, empty land in socialist films deserves special attention. It echoes Mao's widely known "poor and blank" thesis raised in 1958:

> Apart from their other characteristics, the outstanding thing about China's 600 million people is that they are "poor and blank." This may seem a bad thing, but in reality it is a good thing. Poverty gives rise to the desire for change, the desire for action, and the desire for revolution. On a blank sheet of paper free from any mark, the freshest and most beautiful characters can be written, the freshest and most beautiful pictures can be painted.[4]

Mao describes the peasant as "a blank sheet of paper" free of historical burdens and complexities. However, the metaphorical meaning of "a blank sheet of paper" as emptiness could be extended to refer to the broad, underdeveloped land. In this well-known quote, the use of superlative degree—"the freshest and most beautiful"—implies the desire of the socialist state to reach the most advanced level without undergoing step-by-step progress. Converting the land of emptiness and remoteness into thriving industrial areas is presented as a straightforward and immediate way to establish a socialist landscape in which humans are actively creating a new environment.

Railway travel opened up new geographical space for nation-building; the forward march of rail transportation not only reflects the modern cult of speed, it shows the socialist state's desire to penetrate into the remote areas of the country. This chapter further discusses the socialist state's fascination with exploring and conquering the wilderness of emptiness and remoteness, and incorporating uncharted spaces into the national landscape as part of its modernization project. It is not particular, specific localities that were discovered, however, but "disembedded" empty ground that could be opened to produce the socialist landscape.[5] Cinematic representations of the rural take on dual meanings: first, the discovery of remote regions of the homeland by the socialist builders shows how the national landscape was being awakened through the railway travel.[6] Second, the emptiness is also the site for a process of inscribing new meanings and a new code of social ethics on "the blank sheet of paper," which entails pursuing efficiency, recognizing the importance of on-site work, supporting an adventurous spirit, encouraging communitarian collaboration, and developing a strong sense of social responsibility. Social and collective meanings are being built on the previously empty land.

In its early years, the PRC confronted the urgent task of building modern industry in a backward country. The need for rapid industrialization was manifested in the ubiquitous presence of construction sites in both reality and fictional representations. The Chinese socialist nation itself was a "construction site" where people were mobilized and molded into socialist builders. In this chapter, however, the construction sites are mostly in the underdeveloped frontier region, which is at once an industrial site and a natural wilderness; it is often unidentified as an abstract empty space and a virgin land. Embodying the spirit of modern development, the construction site accessed by railway is a space that stages human-machine interaction, channels human affectivity into productive energy, and mediates the relationship between humans and the land. It works as a social nexus that connects people across their professional specializations and highlights their shared identity as socialist builders.

This chapter focuses on the human-machine dynamic in representations of railway travel and construction sites as elements of the industrial enterprise. The human-machine dynamic underlies industrialization, and it has been integral to understanding Chinese socialist modernity as well as modernity in general. Tina Mai Chen has discussed the human-machine continuum as central to remaking mass subjectivity in the articulation of socialism. Her study emphasizes human-machine interchangeability in creating a new revolutionary subject, in pushing the boundary of humanity and simultaneously rejecting dehumanized, alienated labor.[7] This chapter further analyzes the rejection of human alienation in Chinese socialist industrial culture, emphasizing the affective components that are integrated into the human-machine dynamic to mobilize popular energy, as seen in representations of railway travel and the construction site. I argue that the rural, an abstract spatial form of emptiness, remoteness, and underdevelopment, was constructed as a new aesthetic realm in which camaraderie, professional care, domestic warmth, and communitarian intimacy generate energy for building socialism. All these forms of affectivity were mobilized into productive energy to raise the efficiency of production. It is in this sense that socialist industrialization was a sentimental enterprise built into the mobilizational structure of socialist China. This chapter argues that railway travel and the construction site represent the poetics of socialist industrialization: an industrial enterprise that is at the same time an affective and technologized regime that stages both the grand enterprise of conquering nature and a quotidian, intimate human community. The audiovisual experience offered by ideological films often presented an exhilarating railway journey that quickly overcame the great distance between metropolises such as Shanghai and the remote frontiers, and a process in which strangers developed an intimate community on the construction site.

This chapter examines the representations of socialist industrialization in these films: *The Nurse's Diary, A Blade of Grass on the Kunlun Mountain* (*Kunlun shan shang yikecao*, 1962), and *The Young Generation* (*Nianqing de yidai*, 1965). These films showcase the peripheral yet organic part of Chinese socialism: a landscape of wilderness in *The Nurse's Diary*, of challenging and rugged mountains in *A Blade of Grass*, and of a mysterious distant place in *The Young Generation*. Though these films concern life in the border regions, the frontier is mainly portrayed as an empty space without ethnic minority residents.[8] Without dismissing or uncritically extolling these films, and using in-depth textual analysis in relation to the political context of the day, we can read them as creating a system of signification and new social experience that was part of Chinese political culture in the 1950s and 1960s.[9]

First I examine how in the early years of the PRC cinematic representations of railway travel helped facilitate the national imagination through blending human emotional engagement with revolution, the nation, and industrialization. Then I move to a detailed analysis of railway travel in *The Nurse's Diary*, which showcases the convergence of emotional excitement and technological movement—factors that contributed to the formation of the resonant (or voluntary) socialist subjects during the relocation process. The construction site in that film is the stage for showing how an empty wasteland of the frontier region is transformed into the socialist industrial utopia. Finally, I analyze the representations in *A Blade of Grass on the Kunlun Mountain* and *The Young Generation* of the geologists as socialist builders who are mentally and physically engaged in fieldwork. They experience a psychological conversion from initial hesitation to a final determination to "eat bitterness" (*chiku*) and "take root" (*zhagen*) as they establish a relationship with the land. The chapter concludes with a reflection on the changing social and cultural implications of the train in the post–Mao screenscape, in which the image of the railroad often functions as the object of the rural gaze.

I. Emotion in Motion: Representations of the Railway Travel in the Socialist Context

The railroad, one of the most important technological innovations of the nineteenth century, accelerated the industrialization and geographical expansion of Western countries. Railway travel created a new temporal and spatial consciousness, resulting in a new form of human perception. The German historian Wolfgang Schivelbusch argued that railways played a key role in reshaping national landscapes by blurring the boundaries between the city and the countryside, sweeping away local time and establishing standardized national time.[10] As agents of nation-building and symbols of speed, railway systems helped build geographical linkages and changed citizens' spatial perceptions, forming a unified nation as "geographical integration [solved] the problem of political integration."[11]

The Chinese railway network emerged during the self-strengthening movement (1861–1895) in the late Qing and took shape under the Nationalist government in the 1930s. After the establishment of the PRC, the Chinese government restored many parts of railway networks built in previous decades. Between 1953 and 1957, the main goal was to extend railways to remote areas and to the construction sites of mining bases and factories.[12] The railroads opened up China's vast underdeveloped and largely uncharted interior, facilitating socialist industrialization and promoting national unity.

The rapid, systematic development of national railway systems exemplifies the conjoining of socialist governance with technological infrastructure. The nationwide circulation of the newly produced films coincided with the construction of railroads that carried communications to the far corners of the country. As Paul Clark writes, "one film from a studio in Beijing or Changchun in several hundred copies can be seen in the same version by herders in the far northwest in Xinjiang, peasants in Sichuan, students and clerks in Shanghai, and fishermen in Hainan in the south."[13] The broad circulation of films enabled the experience of virtual travel of the country through cinema and thereby triggered the emergence of a new national spectatorship. Socialist cinema was simultaneously incorporated into the agenda of state-building, with the aim of permeating and exploring vast, underdeveloped areas and incorporating them into the national landscape.[14] By bringing these remote areas "closer" to a national audience, socialist cinema portrayed the vast national territory as a living, visible body in order to establish its sovereignty.

Films produced in China in the socialist period have long been dismissed as products of the state propaganda machine. In recent years, film scholars have eschewed dogmatic ideological analysis and aimed to "integrate Chinese cinema into a world history of the medium."[15] Through a focus on the global image of the railway, this chapter situates Chinese socialist cinematic representations back to the global context, in which railway travel as "an industrialized mode of transportation" and cinema as "an industrialized form of representation" naturally converged.[16] Cinematic representations of railway journeys have been approached as a simulacrum of travel: in long tracking shots that offer viewers a sense of mobility, cinema often leads the audience on a journey—an experience that has been aptly captured by Anne Friedberg's compound term "mobilized virtual gaze" and by Charles Musser's expression the "spectator as passenger convention."[17] Socialist representations portrayed the railway journey as virtual travel, linking nation-building with a sensual experience of the power of locomotion, of journeying through an industrializing landscape, and of shrinking temporal and spatial distance.

The film *Bridge* (*Qiao*), the first feature film produced by the Communist Party in 1949, is illustrative of cinematic representations of railway travel in the Chinese revolutionary and socialist context.[18] The film shows a group of workers who attempt to repair a railway bridge over the Sungari River so that the Communist army can cross during the civil war in northeast China. *Bridge* illustrates how the train works as a symbolic figure, relying not on discursive analysis or cognitive understanding but in use as a sensual image to evoke revolutionary passion in the masses and inspire them to action. The last segment of the film showcases the scene of the "train moving forward, passengers singing," which recurs in subsequent socialist representations of railway travel such as *The Nurse's Diary*. Industrialization and human emotion are visually fused in the ritualistic moment of the train passing over the repaired bridge. The combination of the lyrical expression (sentimentality) and the mechanical movement (sensation) in the film echoes Weihong Bao's suggestion that "the dual operation of sentimentality and sensation" in the early Chinese films and the cultivation of a new audience and a new national subject as "emotional being."[19]

Scenes of "taking the train" were prominent in post-1949 cinema and were represented in a variety of modes. Railroads were sometimes battlefields on which heroic Communist soldiers defended their country and defeated their enemies, as in *Railway Guerrilla* (*Tiedao youjidui*, 1956) and *Railway Bodyguards* (*Tiedao weishi*, 1960). In other films, such as *Lanlan and Dongdong* (*Lanlan yu dongdong*, 1958), *Train No. 12* (*Shi'erci lieche*, 1960), and *An Express Train* (*Tekuai lieche*, 1965), the train was the stage for "drama in the compartment,"[20] creating a collective space for people from all walks of life to form a cooperative, congenial, and affectionate socialist community. In *Magnolia Flower in Blossom* (*Malan huakai*, 1956), *The Shanghai Girl* (*Shanghai guniang*, 1957), *The Nurse's Diary*, and *The Young Generation*, railway journeys show the passion of idealistic youth who have left their urban homes for remote areas during an era of socialist construction. The train, in all these films, became a collective emotional space in which the act of "taking the train" embodies the citizens' physical and emotional engagement with revolution, nation, and industrialization. Railway travel became a new means of expressing technological, experiential, and ideological conditions, and it reflects the way the state reorganized national space and redistributed human resources. The kinetic sensation not only illustrates that individuals were part of a technological assemblage, it gives a form to socialist life, in which the passengers could be positioned both ideologically and geographically. In this sense, railway travel is a paradoxical combination of mobility, vitality, and action on the one hand, and rigid state regimentation and relocation of the population on the other. A paradox underlying the image of the railway as a "blend of romantic freedom with classic order"[21] in the socialist context can be reframed as blending romantic freedom with the ideological state apparatus.

II. Railway Travel in The Nurse's Diary: Making the Voluntary Socialist Subject

Produced and released during the relatively relaxed Hundred Flowers period (1956–1957), *The Nurse's Diary* centers on the story of Jian Suhua, a recent female graduate of the Nursing School of Shanghai, who leaves the city and plunges into socialist construction in a frontier area with her classmate, Tang Xiaofang. Their travel to the frontier and working and socializing with the workers on a construction site is depicted as a journey of adventure, self-fulfillment, enjoyment, and affection. Disregarding the hardship and sacrifice that leaving Shanghai might entail, Jian Suhua asserts her choice without hesitation: "I will obey the call of the organization, and I will go to the places in the motherland where I am most needed." This slogan, familiar to people living in the socialist period, represented the "calling from afar" structure that transformed the national urgency of developing underdeveloped areas into the socialist citizen's concrete awareness of "feeling needed." The entire nation was turned into a living, organic body, with the villages and frontier areas earnestly calling the young generation to participate in the enterprise of socialist rejuvenation. The film's narrative uses the act of journal-keeping to present the life trajectory of protagonist Jian Suhua from Shanghai to the frontier. Her "voluntariness" is expressed through both formal and informal, public and private acts: keeping a diary, expressing determination with her confidante late at night, and making a promise in front of the amiable, motherly school principal. The female protagonist's voluntary will is made even more evident when she insists on going to the frontier despite the school principal's offer of an opportunity to stay in Shanghai and continue a good life with her doctor fiancé. Jian Suhua's expression of her passion in the lyrical, private setting highlights how the "private self" that is poured out in her diary has been made into a public demonstration of her sincerity. This is a highly idealized social scene in which an individual's aspiration meshes with the needs of the new socialist state in the early phase of nation building in socialist China.

Jian Suhua bids farewell to her family in Shanghai and gets on the train to the remote frontier region with Tang Xiaofang, a journey that connects the metropolis of Shanghai with underdeveloped areas. Combining long shots, medium shots, and close-ups, *The Nurse's Diary* presents a sequence of railroad scenes that highlight the aesthetic appeal of this machine that makes mobility possible—the sensation of speed, the roar of the engine, and sweeping views of the landscape (fig. 10).[22] The cinematic device creates the illusion that the long distance between Shanghai and the border areas will soon be overcome by high speed, and the train's moving forward symbolizes what Paola Iovene refers to as "anticipation" as a consciousness of the future.[23] As the train "progresses," the young people in the compartment start to sing the theme song that celebrates their youth and idealism. In this context, the speed of the rumbling train—immediate, unmediated, and transitory—expresses and channels human emotions. This connec-

Fig. 10. *The Nurse's Diary* (1956). A sequence of shots depicting the railway journey, highlighting the aesthetic appeal of the machine that provides mobility (16:26).

Fig. 11. *The Nurse's Diary* (1956). A group of young people who share no past, only the current moment: "train moving forward, passengers singing."

tion associates ancient, inborn human emotion with advanced mechanical movement. A group of young people from all walks of life have gathered in the socialist compartment, making it into a new space of camaraderie. The image contrasts with that of the train compartment in Republican Chinese literature, which reflects the social perils of capitalist urban life among strangers.[24] Under socialism, in *The Nurse's Diary*, the compartment undergoes a resignifying process as a microcosm of the new society. Through collective singing about their passion to contribute to the socialist industrialization going on in the distance, a group of young people are quickly transformed from strangers into an intimate community, a group who shares no past, only the current moment of "train moving forward, passengers singing," and who foresee a collective future of building factories to create a sublime industrial landscape, a collective hope expressed in the lyric of the theme song (fig. 11).

Railway travel, accompanied by collective singing, links spatial crossing with the emotional experience of a musical melody. The singing of the passengers merges with the rhythm of the train engine and the rotating wheels, which not only illustrates the formation of the collective subjectivity but reveals an imbrication of a machine with perceptual and psychological impulses. The depiction of the perfect happy society certainly obscures the poor transportation conditions that often exhausted and frustrated travelers at the time. But the episode of happy singing in the compartment is not so much a false representation of society as a way to harness emotional excitement to generate cohesive popular energy in the triumphalist narrative of socialism. The Chinese revolutionary tradition was long characterized as using emotional energy and commitment to support the revolutionary cause.[25] The fusion of the train as an attractive technology with the emotional state of the people inside the train reinforces the intensity of human emotion and aestheticizes mechanical speed. In his study of the "acoustics of publicity," which describes the public's sonic experience, Brian Curried discusses the formation of the resonant subject and emphasizes that to be public also means to "have a resonance, to resonate, to reverberate."[26] With the camera moving between the inside and the outside of the train compartment, the alternation between "train moving forward, passengers singing," also seen in *Bridge*, creates a seemingly perfect ambience of resonance. This scene turns the train into an audiovisual icon, a new form of musical publicity as well as an interactive social sphere. The convergence of technology and sentiment provides an experience of idealized wholeness that was part of the soundtrack of the early socialist period and contributed to making the resonant (or voluntary) subjects demanded by the socialist government. Arif Dirlik has analyzed "two meanings of socialism": as an ideology of revolution with a utopian aspiration to create a just, egalitarian, and democratic society and as an ideology of modernization and national development with instrumental, parochial, and pragmatic goals.[27] *The Nurse's Diary* embodies these two meanings of socialism on screen as it reiterates the pattern of "train moving forward, passengers singing" that combines utopian aspirations and a pragmatic engineering project for industrial development.

III. The Construction Site in The Nurse's Diary: Reclaiming an Industrial and Affective Landscape

In the film, after getting off the train, Jian Suhua, Tang Xiaofang, and their fellow travelers take donkey-drawn carts to their destination. The camera shifts to a close-up of Jian and Tang snuggling and smiling on the cart, apparently looking forward to a new life in this area. Driven by both national calling and personal motives, they betray no outward expressions of disappointment or intimidation. The movement from Shanghai to the border areas is encoded as a change of transportation modes: from the mechanical to the donkey-drawn, from civilization to primitiveness. A long shot of the donkey carts slowly being led into the depths of the diegetic space leads to a view of a barren, empty, snow-covered wasteland.

This episode exhibits the conspicuous presence of the frontier-as-construction-site in the film. In its early years, the People's Republic confronted the urgent task of building modern industry in a backward country. The need for rapid industrialization was manifested in the ubiquitous presence of construction sites, in both reality and fictional representations.[28] The PRC was portrayed, both literally and figuratively, as an industrial and sentimental construction site that extended from cities to the countryside, from political centers to frontier areas. In this essay, the construction site specifically refers to the frontier region that stages the interaction between human, machine, and nature.

The image of the construction site has been a global symbol of the spirit of modern development, as represented in the last act of Goethe's *Faust*.[29] The emotionally intense life of construction takes on a radically new form: "no longer dreams and fantasies, or even theories, but concrete programs, operational plans for transforming earth and sea."[30] Brimming with boundless energy, the construction site is a focus of collective anxiety about being "underdeveloped" and a shared aspiration for rapid development—an ideology shared by both advanced capitalist and developing countries in the twentieth century.[31] The Faustian element, a preoccupation with wealth and power, first appeared in China in the writing of the late Qing literatus and translator Yan Fu, who brought Spencerian social Darwinism to China; Yan Fu described the critical difference between the West and China as a question not of matter but of *energy*. Accordingly, what was urgently needed in China were key values, such as "dynamism, purposive action, energy, assertiveness, and the realization of all potentialities."[32] These qualities remained fundamental to the consciousness of the Chinese intelligentsia throughout the twentieth century.[33] The construction site is a stage for this consciousness, and is accordingly represented not as a place that exhausts working people, but a site that reveals that human capacity is unlimited, and that actualizes human potential and generates the people's energy and passion.

The director Tao Jin (1916–1986) recounted his excitement on facing the wilderness in the border region of Inner Mongolia and envisioning its dramatic transformation into an industrialized landscape. Tao expresses in a lyrical language that "every inch of our film is genuinely recording the great 'poetic age.'"[34] To him, the building of socialist industry is a poetic enterprise, and it will happen with "marvelously fast speed"; an industrial scene is dominated by chimneys, rows of factories, and other buildings. The imminence of the transformation dramatically shortens the distance between the present and the utopian future. The fascination with the speed of the train echoes the rapid transformation of a wasteland into an industrial zone. In the film, on arriving at their destination,[35] Jian Suhua and Tang Xiaofang hastily ask the team leader, Gao Changping, about the location of "our" factory. Following Gao's pointing finger, a series of point-of-view shots present a vast, empty wasteland, accompanied by Gao's off-screen description of where different sections of the factory will be located. Paola Iovene points out the unreal qualities and anticipatory imagination of the construction site in the film.[36] Seeing confusion on their faces, Gao describes for the women an imaginary infrastructure of the future and optimistically encourages them to make roads and houses by hand. As industrial developers and socialist builders, Jian Suhua and Tang Xiaofang embrace the land on which they will construct their "dream factory" and transform the entire landscape—they see things as they are becoming and ought to be, rather than as they are (fig. 12).[37]

Fig. 12. *The Nurse's Diary* (1956). Jian Suhua and Tang Xiaofang embrace the land on which they will construct their "dream factory."

Fig. 13. *The Nurse's Diary* (1956). Jian Suhua's journey to the construction site.

Jian Suhua's travel from Shanghai to the underdeveloped northern frontier is a dramatic move from the expert system of a modern hospital to an open field. This geographical transition has always been associated with an epistemic shift in twentieth-century China. After her arrival at the frontier, she soon finds out that leaving the clinic to provide immediate care for the workers on site would not only be convenient to the workers, it would speed up construction by being more efficient. She makes a few proposals to the head of the clinic and takes the initiative to go to the construction site with a medical bag. The film features a long sequence of Jian's journey to the construction site. Her trip is viewed from a variety of perspectives (fig. 13). First, a tracking shot follows her walking in the wilderness toward the site, displaying her gentle yet passionate "socialist-realist gaze."[38] The gentle female gaze moderates the masculine violence associated with machines and the state apparatus that makes the construction possible. Jian takes a truck to the industrial zone.

Then the audience is treated to a panoramic view of the diegetic space, where various transportation and construction vehicles—cranes, trucks, giant excavators, and tractors—symbolize the building of the superstructure of the country. The view switches from her static perspective to a dynamic, panoramic view of people working, moving, building, communicating, and organizing on the construction site. Like many socialist films of the time, this film reveals an obsession with images of machines stirring the earth and paving the way. The images and sounds highlight how bodies, senses, and machines are closely intertwined, as China entered a new epoch marked by the integration of living, working, and dreaming spaces. Jian's gaze, which is in intimate contact with the frontier space, also works to fill the gap between the primitive and the civilized as she envisions a smooth, homogenous national territory.

Providing medical care on the construction site builds a direct, interactive relationship with the workers and serves the cult of efficiency in building socialism. In the course of performing her duties, Jian climbs to the top of the towering building to give a worker an injection. When she is finally lowered by crane to the ground, the workers are deeply impressed by her devotion and courage. The camera follows Jian's close involvement with the workers (moving from the ground to the top and then back again), which provides a panoramic view of the construction site and presents the site itself as a space of heart-warming human community. The film ends with the completion of the "dream factory" and the departure of Gao's construction team. Standing in the central square,

Jian and Gao appreciate the grandeur of the factory, which symbolizes the creation of a socialist space in which human feelings and natural materials are miraculously transfigured into permanent forms that take on a public existence. Speaking in militarized language, Gao expresses pride in their achievement of "driving away the wind-blown sand, the weeds, and the beasts, and eventually building a factory," and celebrates the conquest of nature and the establishment of socialist industrial utopia in what was previously unsettled wilderness.

IV. "Eating Bitterness" and "Taking Root": Establishing the Human-Land Relationship in 1960s China

The Nurse's Diary portrayed the mode of "calling from afar" as a form of mobilization and showed energetic collective labor on the construction site. The cinematic representations of the social engineering project of Shanghai youth going to the frontier in the 1960s was characterized by the individual's psychological transition from initial escapism and reluctance to a firm determination to "take root" in the frontier. This became a moment of enlightenment and sublimation in the ritualized action and political commitment of "taking the oath." This section examines two socialist films: *A Blade of Grass on the Kunlun Mountain* and *The Young Generation*, in both of which the representations of the machines of mobility—the truck and the train—highlight ideological imperatives that were largely invisible in *The Nurse's Diary* but became the main goals of socialist construction in the 1960s: "eating bitterness" and "taking root." In *A Blade of Grass*, the natural environment of the Kunlun Mountain not only works as an industrial mining base that needs to be explored, it mirrors the individual's psychological space demanding to be transformed. In *The Young Generation*, the main goal of "construction" is to cultivate revolutionary successors.

When the Soviet Union withdrew its technicians and economic assistance and halted scientific exchanges in the 1960s, China faced a pressing need to readjust its foreign and domestic policies. The Chinese socialist state was forced to rely on its own meager manufacturing skills and modest scientific base. Meanwhile, Mao warned against the possibility of switching from socialism to capitalism in China because of the global confrontation between the socialist and capitalist countries and the crisis in the Chinese socialist system. Recovering from the great famine after

1961, the socialist state underwent rapid economic recovery and industrial development; however, this led to a social quest for a better material life and simultaneously deepened the ever-growing gap between the city and the countryside, creating new forms of social inequality.[39] All this caused deep anxiety within socialism, which was followed by Mao's emphasis on the urgency of cultivating "revolutionary successors" to continue the revolutionary enterprise in 1964, as most clearly seen in the film *The Young Generation*.

In these two 1960s films, railway travel and the construction site are strongly related to the iconic figure of the geologist-cum-socialist-builder, for the protagonists in the two films are all geologists. As soon as the early decades of the twentieth century, training geologists had been connected with training a mentally and physically strong citizenry. The social experience of fieldwork was meant to instill values of nationalistic sacrifice and commitment as well as skills in scientific investigation.[40] However, in these two films, these geologists are represented less as individual scientists than as "revolutionary successors"[41] transported to frontier areas. Liu Shaoqi (1898–1969) took up a military metaphor to romanticize the profession of geologists as "guerrillas for the period of peaceful transformation"; thus, prospecting on the frontier was turned into a poeticized mission conveyed with lyrical exuberance.[42] A mass enthusiasm for geology enabled the newly founded PRC to exercise a form of internal colonization to develop its heavy industry by accumulating capital within its own territory. The elevated ideological status of geologists suggests that they represented the defining qualities required for the young generation. As both scientists and political subjects, geologists were expected to have multiple capabilities, trainings, and virtues. They were physically strong, enjoyed vigorous outdoor pursuits, made frequent expeditions, knew how to live in a harsh climate; and had firsthand knowledge of the remote, barren frontiers. They achieved unity with their peers through collective labor, and they displayed patriotism, willingness to sacrifice, and commitment in strenuous on-site work as they got in touch with the land.[43] Hard physical exercise was as important as scientific training. In particular, their direct engagement with the land for epistemological explorations would mobilize the youths who had been sent to the country, who were expected to have intimate contact with the countryside through manual labor. The iconic geologist reflects the socialist ideal of eliminating the difference between mental labor and manual labor and symbolizes the Marxian "all-around" individual engaged in a variety of labors and pursuits, breaking down occupational specializations and bridging scientific expertise and manual labor.

These two films explicitly show the hardship of living in the frontier regions, but experiencing such hardship was compulsory training for those who wanted to become revolutionary successors. Grace Yen Shen has highlighted the patriotic feelings that the geologists attached to fieldwork and the land, as captured by the lyrics of the 1941 Geological Society song, which describes and emphasizes the geological features of different regions of China.[44] What, then, made the patriotism of geologists in the socialist 1960s different from that of the Republican period? "The Song of the Prospecting Team" (Kantan duiyuan zhige) from *The Young Generation* gained great popularity after the film was released. Though its patriotism is also depicted as a way to explore rich mining resources for the motherland, a comparison with the 1941 lyrics shows that the 1965 song stresses molding a revolutionary subjectivity that embodies great enthusiasm and infinite hope and intellect in overcoming difficulties and fatigue in human interactions with a harsh natural environment.

In *A Blade of Grass*, the railway travel, which takes the young woman geologist-protagonist Li Wanli to the Kunlun Mountain, is merely a fleeting scene, signaling the young generation's passion for remote underdeveloped regions similar to that seen in *The Nurse's Diary*. However, trucks are the major transportation vehicle on the plateau, which indicates a different mentality than that in *The Nurse's Diary*. Though taking the train is still represented as an exciting journey in *The Young Generation*, the central focus of the film is the arduous, extensive process of persuading urban youth to take the train to the frontier, which is not only physical travel but a symbolic action similar to "taking the oath" to become revolutionary successors.

Adapted from a short story written by Wang Zongyuan (1919–1971) titled "Sister Hui" (Huisao), *A Blade of Grass* was one of the first socialist films to employ a female point of view and narrative voice.[45] It concerns a female graduate from the Geology Academy, Li Wanli, who decides to go to Kunlun Mountain, on the border between Xinjiang and Tibet, to participate in the national mining industry. Li Wanli was initially motivated by a magazine cover photo in which a beautifully dressed Tibetan girl stands happily on the green plateau; her fantasy about an exciting life on the plateau is completely shattered, however, once she encounters the ruthless natural environment after she arrives. In the beginning of the film, the long tracking shot of the truck moving on the plateau leads the audience to think how the young generation from other regions might deal with the remoteness and build ties with the land. From start to finish, the film-viewing experience becomes a journey that parallels Li Wanli's travels in the remote frontier region and her psychological trajectory. The human-land relationship is manifested clearly in the alternating views of the bleak, snow-covered mountainous landscape and the exhausted Shanghai woman, who in the accompanying voice-over expresses depression and homesickness at the prospect of working on the mountain. A close-up of the wheels of the truck suggests an arduous, seemingly endless journey—far from the fascination with the speed of railway travel and the exhilarating experience of the Shanghai youth taking the train in *The Nurse's Diary*.

The film divides the trip into two segments, with the arrival at a rest stop for long-distance drivers providing an emotional and psychological transition. Li Wanli meets a courageous and warm rural woman named Sister Hui, and enlightened by Hui's poignant story, she finally makes up her mind to "eat bitterness" and swears to "take root" on the mountain.[46] In the film, two important spaces constitute the socialist construction site. One is the natural environment of Kunlun Mountain; the other is the artificially built space of Sister Hui's Driver's Home. The former symbolizes the sublime and the frightening, whereas the latter signifies the quotidian, the comfortable, and the intimate. The mountain also represents man's desire to conquer nature, while the home provides a resting place for meeting people's biological and spiritual needs. The juxtaposition of these two places shows the coexistence and sometimes complementarity of these two sensibilities. And the mysterious, grand Kunlun Mountain and the small, cozy house together constitute the socialist industrial dreamworld. The film portrays the reorganization and restructuring of a large revolutionary family as a collective production unit, which comprises all the components of family life, including maternal love, homemade food, intimate chatting and caring, and sharing personal stories and feelings, all of which are part of the socialist industrial culture on the plateau. The construction site connects the sublime goal of socialist industrialization with the quotidian desire for comfort and warmth, and connects the socialist state's masculine will to conquer nature with the culture of maternal care and affection.

Sister Hui tells her husband's story of overcoming a difficult, precarious situation after observing the tenacity of Kunlun grass, deeply rooted on the Kunlun Mountain, which reminded him of Chairman's Mao's words encouraging the Communists to "be as faithful as pine and cypress trees, and as strong as poplars and willows to be able to survive wherever they will be planted." This suggests that the Kunlun grass—both as a discourse and an image—plays an important role in mediating the relationship between human and land. This moment illustrates the power of words, which enabled Hui's husband to "swear" to "take root" on the plateau. Li Wanli holds the grass in her hand, moved and enlightened by other drivers' touching stories about enduring hardship on the mountain, as told by Sister Hui (fig. 14). The story-sharing moments not only play an important role in transforming and reforming Li Wanli's mentality but also turn strangers like Li Wanli, Sister Hui, and the truck driver Liu into members of a big revolutionary family. The formation of these ties is accompanied by uplifting melodies and slogan-like inner monologues.[47] Elizabeth Perry observes that the Chinese Communist Party capitalized on the ambivalence and malleability of human feelings and strategically shaped them in their desired direction.[48] The next day, as if by magic, Li Wanli's emotion has been completely changed; she regains her energy and cheerfully restarts her journey by truck. She takes a fresh look at the mountain, which is now covered by shimmering snow and appears inspiring and cheerful in the morning sun—a view entirely different from its earlier gloomy appearance (fig. 15). In the socialist discourse, nature is often regarded as external to humans and as an enemy to be conquered. However, when human beings are compared to a blade of grass that "takes root" in the wilderness, it suggests a homology between humans and plants, and indicates that humans are indeed part of nature. This explains why Kunlun Mountain itself represents both the physical presence of nature and the psychological space of the human being. Through the convergence of personal growth and transforming nature, the practice of "eating bitterness" helps forge the dual identity of the geologist-cum-socialist-builder, as a scientist conducting fieldwork while enduring hardship and suffering, and as a revolutionary subject forged through the Foucauldian notion of "technologies of the self."[49]

Whereas *A Blade of Grass* juxtaposes individual growth and socialist building, the 1965 film *The Young Generation* is concerned exclusively with cultivating "revolutionary successors" as the single focus of "construction." Based on a popular dramatic work written by the playwright Chen Yun (1923–1999), the film revolves around two contrasting figures, geologists Xiao Jiye and Lin Yusheng. Unlike Xiao Jiye, who is devoted to the socialist construction on the frontier, Lin Yusheng pretends to be

Fig. 14. *A Blade of Grass on the Kunlun Mountain* (1962). An intimate chat inside the house.

Fig. 15. *A Blade of Grass on the Kunlun Mountain* (1962). The Kunlun Mountain.

sick and obtains a medical leave to return to Shanghai to lead a comfortable life. The central thread of the story focuses on Lin's psychological transition as he decides to "eat bitterness" and "take root" in the frontier settlement. On the one hand, going to the frontier and the countryside is tied to the pursuit of a higher happiness—not individual happiness, but the obligation-based happiness achieved through collective labor, exercising creativity, and creating a better future. On the other hand, what enables Lin Yusheng to be thoroughly enlightened is the moment when he finds the letter written by his birth parents—the revolutionary martyrs—right before they were executed by the Nationalists. Reading the letter is a sacred moment in which he is called to sacrifice himself for the sake of resuming the revolutionary enterprise. "Going to the frontier and the countryside" has already been a paradoxical combination of experiencing both happiness and sacrifice.[50]

Unlike the original stage play, which is set in a living room, the film resumes the fascination with "taking the train" in Chinese socialist cinema. It starts with a brief depiction of life in the border area and a panoramic view of the industrialized landscape through railway travel, and ends with the platform scene where the parents see their children off to take the train to the frontier. The farewell scene at the train station was a hallmark of the mid to late 1960s, when millions of young students took trains to border regions and remote farms. At the beginning, Xiao Jiye takes the train back to Shanghai to verify a newly discovered mineral resource. Through the window of his compartment on the train, he sees industrialization on a grand scale, as a sublime spectacle dominated by imposing factories and high chimneys. The advancing train is accompanied by soundtrack music full of power and grandeur, like a march that imitates the rhythm of the train's rumbling. Complementing the train on the screen, the music establishes the powerful emotional tenor of the industrial sublime and represents socialist industrialization as an emotionally effusive enterprise. The same musical theme recurring in the middle of the film shapes the audiovisual space of living and working in the industrial sublime.

The young people's dreams of embracing a sublime revolutionary enterprise are frequently expressed in ritualistic language. Everyday conversations in *A Blade of Grass* are still largely unaffected, but in *The Young Generation*, the spoken oaths permeate every aspect of daily life. The exaggerated manner of swearing political allegiance may arise at any moment in the middle of a conversation—in a family discussion, during a hospital visit, or at a moment of farewell on a train platform—turning everyday language into firm political determination.[51] The parents who wave to them from the train platforms in *The Nurse's Diary* and *A Blade of Grass* are mainly portrayed as caring mothers worried about the future of their daughters; none plays a role in the decision to go to the frontier provinces. *The Young Generation* ends with a platform scene in which a large group of Shanghai youths follow Xiao and take the train to the frontier region.[52] In *The Young Generation*, however, the parents perform as collective amplifiers transmitting Chairman Mao's exhortations to persuade their children to go to the frontier. They were the "revolutionary successors" described by Xiaobing Tang not as political rebels but as filial sons and daughters with submissive attitudes, loyally willing to comply with patriarchal authorities.[53] These parents are not as anxious or caring as those in *The Nurse's Diary* and *A Blade of Grass*, but are thrilled over their children's participation in socialist construction. They speak a ritualistic language exhorting their children to devote themselves to remote areas. The action of taking the train also takes on ritualistic meaning, functioning similar to the gesture of taking the oath. At the end of the film, the camera cuts to a shot of the roaring locomotive, followed by a shot of Lin Yusheng's younger sister, who is standing on the train and declaring her excitement about going to the remote area. These altruistic, innocent, socialist "children" of the 1960s, longing to "take root, germinate, bloom, and fructify" across the country, would eventually become fixtures in remote areas, like Li Wanli in *A Blade of Grass*.

Railway travel had been a prominent symbol throughout the years of the Cultural Revolution, as was seen in a widely circulated 1970 poster. The print epitomizes the moment when millions of young urbanites were being transferred to underdeveloped frontier settlements and remote villages by train. A famous slogan is written on the margin of the poster: "go to the villages, go to the frontiers, go to the places in the motherland where you are most needed."[54] The slogan transformed the urgent national need to construct underdeveloped areas into a socialist citizen's concrete perception of "feeling needed." The entire nation was turned into an organic body, with the villages and frontier areas earnestly calling the young generation to participate through the exciting experience of a railway journey. The two representatives of sent-down youth express effusive enthusiasm and happiness, feelings orchestrated by the Party and the state and merged into railway travel so that human emotions blend with the movement of the machine.

This chapter is a journey through the first seventeen years of the PRC, placing cinematic representations of urban youths' experiences of railway travel and working in the frontier regions in the larger context of the socialist political culture. With the locomotive as "the engine of progress" and "a promise of imminent utopia,"[55] the railroad symbolizes the national aspiration to develop from an agricultural to a predominantly industrial state in a country possessing only primitive systems of communication and transportation. The three films discussed in this chapter present a sweeping, panoramic view of the industrialized national landscape, giving the audience the illusion of moving through the world at different paces, either fast travel by railway across the urban-rural divide or an arduous truck trip on the plateau. The journey is at once virtual and real, and offers both spatial connection and temporal simultaneity, creating a sense that the remote periphery was readily reachable. The Chinese critic Cai Xiang discusses how the political technique of mobilization was internalized into the narrative structure of Chinese socialist literature.[56] Nowhere is this more visible than in the cinematic representations that translated mass political mobilization into the virtual movement of high-speed travel via modern transportations in the socialist period.

Both "taking the train" and working on the construction site epitomize what Xiaobing Tang refers to as the "lyrical age," when "the mundane" and "the ordinary" were poeticized and ascribed metaphysical, transcendental, and global significance.[57] "The lyrical age" emphasized the "immediacy" of collective participation in socialism, a popular sentiment engineered by the Althusserian ideological state apparatus (as the operation of modern technology).[58] This shaped the emotional structure of sentimentalized socialist industrialization. The PRC's social engineering program, as seen in its drive for development and its comprehensive planning of human settlement and production, often resulted in tension between the sweeping socialist state plan to distribute human resources and its citizens' concrete needs and aspirations. Turning human beings into resources to contribute to the strength of the state was instrumental. However, socialist cinema portrayed the relocation program as an emotionally charged journey involving the fusion of technology and emotion, putting on an ideological veneer to rehumanize the merely instrumental state apparatus and to contribute to the creation of a nonalienated industrial socialist culture. The fusion of emotion and motion gave flesh and blood to an industrial state machine, rallying all the bodily elements of individuals into a productive body politic of the nation-state.

The socialist ideals of breaking down occupational specialization and leveling social hierarchy were also integrated into representations of the construction site, where nurses, workers, geologists, housewives, and truck drivers constitute a forced community of strangers that eventually turns into a collegial and collaborative community with a shared identity as "socialist builders." The construction site becomes a social nexus for human relationships, and also works as a *medium* for releasing human emotion and energy. Socialist industrialization stages both a grand enterprise of conquering nature and a quotidian, heart-warming human community. Ban Wang in his analysis of revolutionary cinema emphasizes the aspect of sublimation in which sexual desire is rechanneled into revolutionary passion.[59] My reading of the films about socialist industrialization and construction shows how quotidian sentiments such as camaraderie, professional care, domestic warmth, and communitarian intimacy were all utilized to generate collective energy and serve productive efficiency.

In post-Mao literature and film, the railroad took on new cultural and political implications due to the dramatic ideological reversal after the Cultural Revolution.[60] In Lu Xinhua's (1954–) short story "The Scar" (1978), the returning train that takes the sent-down youth back to the city carries the exhausted passengers who dwell on personal and collective trauma, rather than focusing on a machine and a celebration of the socialist industrial sublime.[61] In the post-Mao period, cinematic representations of the railroad incorporated a new perspective of "taking a look at the train," a new perspective that also saw the disappearance of the construction site as part of railway travel in the diagetic space of the film. Rhapsodic 1950s and 1960s films celebrated the populist identity of the nation and the joy of bodily engagement with revolution, modernization, industrialization, and progressive history; those of the 1980s highlighted the act of "gazing" and the object of desire. How was the changing perception of the railway built into the radical transformation of sensual experience and discourse under different social conditions? The shift from "taking the train" to "taking a look at the train" suggests that the perception of modernity shifted from an integral and participatory experience to a spectacle of material embodiment. Groups of urban youth in compartments during the railway journey to "wherever the motherland needs us" in earlier films gives way to villagers' strong desire to "take a look" at the train.[62] These changes symbolize a transition in China's self-perceived identity, from an industrializing state in the early socialist period to a debilitated agricultural society in the 1980s—even though by then, China had achieved much more industrialization. In the films produced in the early 1980s, trains are usually portrayed as distant, mysterious objects in the eyes of tradition-bound village people. "Taking a look at the train" is an exciting event for the rural wife in the film *The Voice of the Village* (*Xiangyin*, 1983) and for the village young people who have recently survived the woes and wrongs of the Cultural Revolution in the film *A Love-Forsaken Corner* (*Bei aiqing yiwang de jiaolua*, 1981). Today, railroads continue to be vital connections between the city and the countryside, both in reality and in media, in films such as *Last Train Home* (2009). Independent documentary films also employed an innovative change in the focus of the camera. In earlier socialist films the camera was on the train and in a compartment, but in a documentary titled *Along the Railway* (*Tielu yanxian*, 2000), the camera movement leads the viewer to take a deeper, closer look at the lives of the bedraggled homeless people walking along the train tracks. It recalls Walter Benjamin's critique of the Marxian view of revolution as the "locomotive of world history." Benjamin is deeply skeptical of the discourse of progress, and suggests that "perhaps revolutions are the reaching of humanity traveling in this train for the emergency brake."[63] Once the brake is pulled, viewers divert their attention from monumental landmarks and industrial magnificence (such as the industrialized landscape in *The Young Generation*) to small, discarded, or overlooked objects along the railway, such as ruins and dust, as well as the fragile, disadvantaged people living on the margins of society. Today, railways are still the main form of mass transportation throughout China. Driving in high-speed modern vehicles, citizens in the post-Mao period have witnessed how the once "solid" socialist monumentality "melt[ed] into air." Still, socialist vestiges remain in various visible and invisible forms, as the railroad continues its journey to connect and separate.

Conclusion

This study discusses the geographical move of "going to the countryside" in modern China. The spatial crossing indicates an experience through which various historical actors—Chinese intellectuals, reformers, revolutionaries, leftist journalists, and aspiring youth—defined and contested the meanings of enlightenment, revolution, and socialist industrialization, and simultaneously navigated the growing cultural, economic, political, and social divides. The study moves from the early twentieth century to the eve of the official breakout of the Cultural Revolution, constructing a new narrative revolving around "going to the countryside" as a novel modern experience. This book shows that the spatial moves of going to the countryside must be understood as practices that mediated the universal and the particular, the abstract and the concrete, the national and the local, as well as the industrial and the artisanal. The rural was turned into an experiential site to contest and reconceptualize a set of globally circulated ideas, such as enlightenment, universal education, nationhood, citizenship, revolution, romantic love, law, labor, and science and technology. These modern notions underwent redefinition and acquired new meanings and significance in the rural contexts. Social-survey writers, novelists, rural reconstruction practitioners, leftist journalists and intellectuals, party cadres, cultural workers, folk artists, and socialist filmmakers brought together divergent views and representations of going to the countryside. The state-sponsored rustication program "up to the mountains, down to the village" (which started as early as 1955) culminated during the Cultural Revolution period when educated urban youth were exhorted to go to the countryside to participate in agricultural labor. After the Cultural Revolution was over, the Chinese countryside was often portrayed in association with youthful passion and nostalgia as well as traumatic memories of suffering, hardship, painful loss, anti-intellectualism, and huge disillusionment with Maoist politics.

The institutionalized urban-rural inequality during the Mao era has continued to influence the extraordinary urban-rural cleavage in post-Mao China.[1] China's urbanization process has been unprecedented in rapidity and scope since Deng Xiaoping's Reform and Opening. Starting from the mid-1980s, China has witnessed large-scale migration from rural to urban areas. The migrant workers as a source of cheap labor have contributed to China's fast-paced economic development and to the global capitalist expansion. In 2011, for the first time in Chinese history the urban population started to exceed the rural population, which is described as "a tremendous change that has never happened in the past thousand years" (*qiannian weiyou zhi dabianju*); that phrase was originally used to describe China's traumatic clash with the West at the end of the nineteenth century.[2] Whereas Chinese metropolises such as Beijing and Shanghai have consciously identified themselves with other global cities such as New York, London, Tokyo, and Singapore, the Chinese countryside has become a discursive site for scholars and social critics to problematize neoliberalism's overriding principles of development and competition and to disclose the huge sacrifices of rural migrant workers to make China's rise possible. Yan Hairong contends that the countryside has become "a field of death" where rural young people cannot construct a meaningful identity, and that "embedded in the post-Mao culture of modernity is an epistemic violence against the countryside that spectralizes the rural in both material and symbolic practices."[3] Wang Xiaoming in his investigation of a village located in the backland of Daliang Mountain in 2004 observes that capitalist urban transformation is not simply a place-based event, but in fact works as a powerful ideology that has a huge impact on people's minds, behavior, and life choices in the countryside.[4]

Nonetheless, the decades since 2000 have also witnessed constant efforts at both official and unofficial levels to initiate a return to the countryside. The Chinese government started its nationwide "socialist new countryside construction" movement in 2005; it also established urban-rural integration policies that aim to embed villages into "a nationwide urban network" to decrease the urban-rural distinction.[5] In 2014, in his talks at the Beijing Forum on Literature and Art, Chinese president Xi Jinping strongly urged writers, artists, and filmmakers to live among the people and gain experience in the countryside.[6] That same year, the government promoted the role model of "local worthies" (*xiangxian*) and advised educated citizens with rural roots to return to their hometowns to serve as teachers and exemplars and contribute to local communities.[7] In

2015, the government further raised the notion of "the innovation of the culture of local worthies" as part of the contemporary rural construction agenda. By 2017, vitalizing the countryside had become the national strategy, which was closely bound up with the goal of building an ecological civilization as an alternative to Western industrial civilization and developmentalism in party discourses.

Notwithstanding regional diversity in local history and culture, starting from the late 1990s, numerous accounts in scholarly works, popular magazines, documentary films, and on the web have borne witness to personal experiences of returning to the countryside. Scholars and social practitioners have constantly engaged in on-site research and investigations in the countryside, seeking solutions to the pressing social problems of "three rural issues" (*sannong*): peasants, rural society, and agriculture.[8] Such efforts have drawn public attention to the other face of China, which the country's rise built on its urban prosperity and rapid development has often obscured. Contemporary writers and journalists also have adopted homecoming narratives in their nonfiction writings that combine social investigation and personal memory. Focusing on their home villages, they lament the poverty, underdevelopment, corrupted morality, and desolation of the Chinese countryside as well as its disintegrating communities.[9] Nonetheless, in some parts of China, the countryside has been transformed into a manageable cultural resource for both education and entertainment, and such rural attractions have been incorporated into the contemporary cultural economy. For example, public-minded artists have explored ancient villages and launched locally based yet highly cosmopolitan art projects, collaborating with foreign artists, organizing art festivals and photography exhibitions, and renovating local architecture. Their own artistic experiments function as social critiques of excessive urbanization and as a kind of social practice that combines rural reconstruction with the cultural economy.[10] Moreover, some urbanites have identified themselves as new farmers and have gone to the countryside to develop "natural/organic agriculture" (*ziran nongye*) to produce green food and work for sustainable development.[11] During vacations and holidays, a popular form of tourism for urbanites is to travel to ancient villages and stay in farm guesthouses for a short period to experience country life. All of these types of travels to the rural areas have also turned the countryside into a site for reflecting on global capitalism and uneven development and for exploring alternatives to urban-centered modern life.[12]

In 2018, the Chinese government started to envision the blueprint of "strong agriculture, beautiful countryside, and rich peasants" as a goal to be achieved by 2050. State policy has started to give priority to agricultural development to "vitalize the countryside" (*zhenxing xiangcun*). Scholars optimistically suggest that today's China is changing from pursuing industrialization to the current promotion of ecological civilization, deindustrialization, and urban-rural integration. They consider such social change to be not only a fundamental emancipation from the illusion of developmentalism, but also a possible solution to the three rural problems (*sannong*).[13] As China self-consciously constructs its own subjectivity on the global stage, the state strategy of "vitalizing the countryside" and the national promotion of "ecological civilization" (*shengtai wenming*) are discursively bound up with China's pursuit of a different path and its construct of a new identity. Nonetheless, it remains uncertain whether China can really produce a new industrial culture alternative to developmentalism. Scholars have indicated that China has undergone a fundamental transition from "earthbound China" (*xiangtu zhongguo*) to "urban-rural China" (*chengxiang zhongguo*), which occurred at a point between 2003 and 2010. This is a new type of connection characterized by urban-rural interaction and integration and mutually dependent and complementary relations.[14] However, despite the official promotion, urban-rural integration still faces a series of social problems. The large population of migrant workers continued to be treated as second-class citizens and marginalized groups in the cities they are building; their urban-bred sons and daughters are not willing to go back to live in their rural hometowns but simultaneously cannot find their own places in the city. To the urban-educated who were originally from the rural areas, the countryside is the hometown to which they would never return, because what is most intolerable is the devastation of the moral corruption in the countryside rather than its poverty, backwardness, coarseness, and the pollution of the natural environment.[15] The writer Han Shaogong (1953–) could not help asking, "where is the touching native-place sentiment and homesickness"?[16] The image of "the beautiful countryside" as both national goal of rural construction and personal memory of the fading past continues to be ambiguous. With all these vitalizing efforts, will the traditional moral and ethical universe of village society be restored and rebuilt? What concrete kind of "beautiful village" should we envision? How should we reconsider the significance of the countryside and (re)conceptualize the meaning of the rural as contemporary China develops toward a postmodern, postindustrial society? More remains to be explored as we attempt to understand "going to the countryside" as a perennial human spatial and psychological transformation.

Notes

Introduction

1. For example, Alexander Des Forges, *Mediasphere Shanghai: The Aesthetics of Cultural Production* (Honolulu: University of Hawai'i Press, 2007); Leo Ou-fan Lee, *Shanghai Modern: The Flowering of a New Urban Culture in China, 1930–1945* (Cambridge, MA: Harvard University Press, 1999); Shu-mei Shih, *The Lure of the Modern: Writing Modernism in Semicolonial China, 1917–1937* (Berkeley: University of California Press, 2001); Wen-hsin Yeh, ed., *Becoming Chinese: Passages to Modernity and Beyond* (Berkeley: University of California Press, 2000); Wen-hsin Yeh, *Shanghai Splendor: A Cultural History, 1843–1949* (Berkeley: University of California Press, 2008); Yingjin Zhang, *The City in Modern Chinese Literature and Film: Configurations of Space, Time, and Gender* (Stanford: Stanford University Press, 1996); Zhen Zhang, *An Amorous History of the Silver Screen: Shanghai Cinema, 1896–1937* (Chicago: University of Chicago Press, 2005).

Two of the most recently published works on urban China are Robin Visser's *Cities Surround the Countryside: Urban Aesthetics in Postsocialist China* (Durham: Duke University Press, 2010), which focuses on the emergence of "postsocialist Chinese urban aesthetics" in a wide range of cultural productions when China fully embraced urbanization in the twenty-first century, and Yomi Braester's *Painting the City Red: Chinese Cinema and the Urban Contract* (Durham: Duke University Press, 2010), which highlights the interpenetration and interaction between urban transformation and visual media.

2. Leo Ou-fan Lee, *Shanghai Modern: The Flowering of a New Urban Culture in China, 1930–1945* (Cambridge, MA: Harvard University Press, 1999), xi.

3. Lee, *Shanghai Modern*, xi.

4. Dilip Parameshwar Gaonkar, ed., *Alternative Modernities* (Durham: Duke University Press, 2001).

5. The only exception is Yi-Tsi Mei Feuerwerker, *Ideology, Power, Text: Self-Representation and the Peasant "Other" in Modern Chinese Literature* (Stanford: Stanford University Press, 1998).

6. Raymond Williams, *The Country and the City* (New York: Oxford University Press, 1973), 289.

7. Michel Foucault, "Of Other Spaces," *Diacritics* 16 (Spring 1986): 22.

8. Nicole Sackley, "The Village as Cold War Site: Experts, Development, and the History of Rural Reconstruction," *Journal of Global History* 6, no. 3 (2011): 484, 503.

9. See Xiaorong Han, *The Chinese Discourses on the Peasant: 1900–1949* (Albany: State University of New York Press, 2005). For a discussion of the intellectual-peasant relationship as the binary positions of "subject and object" and "self and other," see Yi-Tsi Mei Feuerwerker, *Ideology, Power, Text: Self-Representation and the Peasant "Other" in Modern Chinese Literature* (Stanford: Stanford University Press, 1998).

10. Han, *Chinese Discourses*, 19–72.

11. See Henrietta Harrison, *The Man Awakened from Dreams: One Man's Life in a North China Village, 1857–1942* (Stanford: Stanford University Press, 2005), 166–68.

12. For a related discussion, see Hung Chang-tai, *War and Popular Culture: Resistance in Modern China, 1937–1945* (Berkeley: University of California Press, 1994).

13. Frederick W. Mote, "The Transformation of Nanking, 1350–1400," in *The City in Late Imperial China*, ed. G. William Skinner (Stanford: Stanford University Press, 1977), 101–53, 103.

14. For example, Si-yen Fei, *Negotiating Urban Space: Nanjing and Late Ming Urbanization* (Cambridge, MA: Harvard University Press, 2010); Mote, "Transformation of Nanking," 101–53, 103.

15. Fei Hsiao-tung, *China's Gentry: Essays in Rural-Urban Relations* (Chicago: University of Chicago Press, 1953).

16. See Stephen Owen, "The Self's Perfect Mirror: Poetry as Autobiography," in *The Vitality of the Lyric Voice: Shih Poetry from the Late Han to the T'ang*, ed. Shuen-fu Lin and Stephen Owen (Princeton: Princeton University Press, 1986), 71–101; Tian Xiaofei, *Tao Yuanming & Manuscript Culture: The Record of a Dusty Table* (Seattle: University of Washington Press, 2005).

17. For example, the eighteenth-century Chinese novel *The Scholars* [*Rulin waishi*], written by Wu Jingzi (1701–1754).

18. Tian, *Tao Yuanming*, 119–21.

19. Hilary J. Beattie, *Land and Lineage in China: A Study of T'ung-ch'eng County, Anhwei, in the Ming and Ch'ing Dynasties* (Cambridge: Cambridge University Press, 1979).

20. Arif Dirlik and Roxann Prazniak, "Introduction," in *Global Capitalism and the Future of Agrarian Society*, ed. Dirlik, Prazniak, and Alexander Woodside (London: Routledge, 2016), 6.

21. Shuming Liang, *The Collective Work of Liang Shuming* [*Liang Shuming Quanji*], vol. 5 (Jinan, China: Shandong renmin chubanshe, 1989), 349.

22. For a detailed description, see David Faure and Tao Tao Liu, "Introduction," in *Town and Country in China: Identity and Perception*, ed. David Faure and Tao Tao Liu (Oxford: Palgrave, 2002), 1–3.

23. Faure and Liu, "Introduction," 1.

24. For a discussion of "going to the people" as a universal phenomenon, see Han, *Chinese Discourses*, 11–12.

25. Cathy A. Frierson, *Peasant Icons: Representations of Rural People in Late Nineteenth-Century Russia* (Oxford: Oxford University Press, 1993), 39.

26. For details, see Susan Daruvala, *Zhou Zuoren and an Alternative Chinese Response to Modernity* (Cambridge, MA: Harvard University Asia Center, 2000), 50. Christopher T. Keaveney, *Beyond Brushtalk: Sino-Japanese Literary Exchange in the Interwar Period* (Hong Kong: Hong Kong University Press, 2009), 85.

27. Prasenjit Duara, "Local Worlds: The Poetics and Politics of the Native Place in Modern China," *South Atlantic Quarterly* 99, no. 1 (Winter 2000): 18–19. Charles Wishart Hayford, *To the People: James Yen and Village China* (New York: Columbia University Press, 1990), 55.

28. Li Dazhao, "Youth and the Village" [Qingnian yu nongcun], in *Li Dazhao Quanji* (Shijiazhuang Shi: Hebei jiao yu chubanshe, 1999), 565–68. Li later dismissed the New Village Movement as "too local and reclusive to form public opinion on the national scale needed to produce basic solutions. The village was not a source of power, but a recipient of uplift." See Hayford, *To the People*, 54.

29. Li Dazhao, "Stagnant Civilization and Dynamic Civilization" [Jing de wenming yu dong de wenming] and "Youth and the Village" [Qingnian yu nongcun], in *Li Dazhao Quanji*.

30. What underlay the empathetic understanding and identification was the centrality of sentiment that characterized "the relationship between the modern subject and the modern political community" in the early twentieth century, as Haiyan Lee argues; "the modern subject is first and foremost a sentimental subject," and "the modern nation is first and foremost a community of sympathy." See Haiyan Lee, *Revolution of the Heart: A Genealogy of Love in China, 1900–1950* (Stanford: Stanford University Press, 2007), 6–7.

31. See John Fitzgerald, *Awakening China: Politics, Culture, and Class in the Nationalist Revolution* (Stanford: Stanford University Press, 1996), 126–39.

32. Thomas Mullaney, *Coming to Terms with the Nation: Ethnic Classification in Modern China* (Berkeley: University of California Press, 2011), 96.

33. Chang-tai Hung, *Going to the People: Chinese Intellectuals and Folk Literature, 1918–1937* (Cambridge, MA: Harvard University Press, 1985). Tong Lam, *A Passion for Facts: Social Surveys and the Construction of the Chinese Nation-State, 1900–1949* (Berkeley: University of California Press, 2011).

34. Charles Laughlin, *Chinese Reportage: The Aesthetics of Historical Experience* (Durham: Duke University Press, 2002).

35. Grace Yen Shen, *Unearthing the Nation: Modern Geology and Nationalism in Republican China* (Chicago: University of Chicago Press, 2014).

36. Christine I. Ho, *Drawing from Life: Socialist Realism and Socialist Painting in the People's Republic of China* (forthcoming from University of California Press, 2020).

37. Within its limited space, this book does not cover other forms of rural reconstructions launched by the Kuomintang (KMT) government and warlords in the Republican period, the Communist land reforms and the intellectuals' reeducation through labor reform in the countryside (*xiafang*), and the KMT's land reforms in Taiwan. Moreover,

this study does not attempt to chart a teleological historical path or a linear progression toward the "up to the mountains, down to the villages" movement during the Cultural Revolution.

38. For a nuanced study of the city/country divide during the socialist period and its impact on ordinary people's interactions as they crossed the boundary during the socialist period, see Jeremy Brown, *City Versus Countryside in Mao's China: Negotiating the Divide* (New York: Cambridge University Press, 2012). For detailed discussions of "up to the mountains, down to the villages," see Thomas P. Bernstein, *Up to the Mountains and Down to the Villages: The Transfer of Youth from Urban to Rural China* (New Haven: Yale University Press, 1977). Michel Bonnin, *The Lost Generation: The Rustication of China's Educated Youth (1968–1980)* (Hong Kong: Chinese University Press, 2013).

39. My definition of the rural is drawn from Dipesh Chakrabarty's definition of the peasant, in *Provincializing Europe: Postcolonial Thought and Historical Difference* (Princeton: Princeton University Press, 2008), 11.

40. *The Oxford English Dictionary*, 2nd ed., prepared by J. A. Simpson and E. S. C. Weiner, vol. XIV (Oxford: Clarendon Press, 1989), 283–84. Also see Yingjin Zhang, *The City in Modern Chinese Literature and Film: Configurations of Space, Time, and Gender* (Stanford: Stanford University Press, 1996), 7–8. Zhang emphasizes the affective values associated with the word *xiang*.

41. To name a few examples, Arthur Smith, *Village Life in China: A Study in Sociology* (New York: F. H. Revell, 1899); Arthur Smith, *Chinese Characteristics* (New York: Revell, 1894); Xiaotong Fei, *From the Soil: The Foundations of Chinese Society*, trans. Gary G. Hamilton and Wang Zheng (Berkeley: University of California Press, 1992).

42. Fitzgerald, *Awakening China*, 71–72.

43. Hung, *Going to the People*.

44. In the view of Ding Fan, in the field of modern Chinese literature and culture, Chinese native-soil fiction (*xiangtu xiaoshuo*) is regarded as a subgenre under the category of modern vernacular fiction. "Native soil" as a universal theme of world literature not only underwent a continuous organic evolution but also established its unique aesthetic features, such as divinity (*shenxing*), diaspora (*liuyu*), and sadness (*beiqing*). To Ding, "local color" (*difang secai*) and "scenes of local customs" (*fengsu huamian*) are the most important components that characterize the native-soil fiction. See Ding Fan, *A History of Chinese Native Soil Fiction* [*Zhongguo xiangtu xiaoshuo shi*] (Beijing: Beijing University Press, 2007), 1–9.

45. For example, Vanessa Schwartz and Leo Charney, "Introduction," in *Cinema and the Invention of Modern Life*, ed. Leo Charney and Vanessa R. Schwartz (Berkeley: University of California Press, 1995), 7; Edward Said, *Culture and Imperialism* (New York: Vintage, 1993), 56; and Vanessa R. Schwartz, *Spectacular Realities: Early Mass Culture in Fin-de-Siècle Paris* (Berkeley: University of California Press, 1998), 4.

46. See Dilip Parameshwar Gaonkar, "Toward New Imaginaries: An Introduction," *Public Culture* 14, no. 1 (Winter 2002): 1–19. "Cultural imaginary" is a term that is adapted from "social imaginary," coined by Cornelius Castoriadis and later elaborated

by Charles Taylor "as an enabling but not fully explicable symbolic matrix within which a people imagine and act as world-making collective agents" (qtd. in Gaonkar, p. 1).

47. David Apter and Tony Saich, *Revolutionary Discourse in Mao's Republic* (Cambridge, MA: Harvard University Press, 1994).

48. Hayford, *To the People*, 111.

49. Benedict Anderson, *Imagined Communities: Reflections on the Origin and Spread of Nationalism* (London: Verso, 1983), 82.

50. Sackley, "The Village as Cold War Site."

51. This is my adaptation of Mao's phrase of the "advantage of backwardness." This thesis initially projected "the most beautiful picture" onto the "blank slate" of the peasants.

52. See Dirlik, Prazniak, and Woodside, eds., *Global Capitalism*.

Chapter 1

1. For details, see Yeh Wen-hsin, *The Alienated Academy: Culture and Politics in Republican China, 1919–1937* (Cambridge, MA: Council on East Asian Studies, Harvard University, 1990).

2. For example, see Ye Shengtao, *Ni Huanzhi* (Beijing: Renmin wenxue chubanshe, 1953).

3. For a detailed study of how the founding of modern educational institutions had alienated the urban educated from their native places and rural roots, see Yeh Wen-hsin, *The Alienated Academy*.

4. See Chang-tai Hung, *Going to the People: Chinese Intellectuals and Folk Literature, 1918–1937* (Cambridge, MA: Council on East Asian Studies, Harvard University, 1985), xi–xii.

5. Wolf Lepenies, *Between Literature and Science: The Rise of Sociology* (Cambridge: Cambridge University Press, 1988), 1. The Chinese writer Mao Dun also saw literature as a mode of social science to construct a new kind of objectivity. For details, see Ann Anagnost, *National Past-Times: Narrative, Representation, and Power in Modern China* (Durham: Duke University Press, 1997), 26–27.

6. This chapter does not aim to offer a comprehensive study of the history of social-survey essays in China, and only focuses on the essays about the rural hometown in relation to homecoming fiction. For a detailed discussion of the social-survey movement, see Tong Lam, *A Passion for Facts: Social Surveys and the Construction of the Chinese Nation-State, 1900–1949* (Berkeley: University of California Press, 2011).

7. For details, see Prasenjit Duara, "Local Worlds: The Poetics and Politics of the Native Place in Modern China," *South Atlantic Quarterly* 99, no. 1 (Winter 2000): 13. The idea of the native place was endowed with different meanings at different times and by different historical actors; it should be understood in relation to changing political and ideological contexts. See Bryna Goodman, *Native Place, City, and Nation: Regional*

Networks and Identities in Shanghai, 1853–1937 (Berkeley: University of California Press, 1995), 307–8.

8. Jiayan Yan, *Zhongguo xiandai xiaoshuo liupaishi* [A History of Schools of Chinese Fiction] (Beijing: Renmin wenxue chubanshe. 1989), 29–30. Lloyd E. Eastman describes the moral uncertainty at the time this way: "[M]any Chinese have felt that the jettisoning of Confucianism in the early twentieth century and the failure to replace it with any comparable form of moral training created an ethical vacuum." See Lloyd E. Eastman, *Family, Fields, and Ancestors: Constancy and Change in China's Social and Economic History, 1550–1949* (New York: Oxford University Press, 1988), 199.

9. John Fitzgerald, *Awakening China: Politics, Culture, and Class in the Nationalist Revolution* (Stanford: Stanford University Press, 1996), 70.

10. Mao Dun, "Xiaoshuo yiji daoyan" [Introduction to *The First Anthology of Modern Chinese Fiction*], in *Zhongguo xinwenxue daxi daoyanji, 1917–1927* [A Collection of Introductions to *The Compendium of Modern Chinese Literature*], ed. Liu Yunfeng (Tianjin: Tianjin renmin chubanshe, 2008), 54.

11. Lydia H. Liu, *Translingual Practice: Literature, National Culture, and Translated Modernity—China, 1900–1937* (Stanford: Stanford University Press, 1995), 78.

12. Alasdair MacIntyre, *After Virtue: A Study in Moral Theory* (Notre Dame, IN: University of Notre Dame Press, 1984), 126–27.

13. David Der-wei Wang, "Imaginary Nostalgia: Shen Congwen, Song Zelai, Mo Yan, and Li Yongping," In *From May Fourth to June Fourth: Fiction and Film in Twentieth-Century China*, ed. Ellen Widmer and David Der-wei Wang (Cambridge, MA: Harvard University Press, 1993), 107–32.

14. See Myron Cohen, "Cultural and Political Inventions in Modern China: The Case of the Chinese 'Peasant,'" *Daedalus* 122, no. 2, China in Transformation (Spring 1993): 151–55.

15. See Cohen, "Cultural and Political Inventions," 151–55.

16. Prasenjit Duara, "Local Worlds."

17. Tao Lugong, "Introductory Remark," *New Youth* 4, no. 3 (March 3, 1917): 221–24.

18. Zhang Zuyin, "The Peasants in Zhenze," *New Youth* 4, no. 3 (March 3, 1917): 224–28.

19. See Xiaorong Han, *The Chinese Discourses on the Peasant: 1900–1949* (New York: State University of New York Press, 2005), 129–31.

20. For a detailed discussion of the local gazetteer, see Peter K. Bol, "The Rise of Local History: History, Geography, and Culture in Southern Song and Yuan Wuzhou," *Harvard Journal of Asiatic Studies* 61, no. 1 (June 2001): 37–76.

21. R. David Arkush, *Fei Xiaotong and Sociology in Revolutionary China* (Cambridge, MA: Harvard University Press, 1981), 24–25.

22. Lam, *A Passion for Facts*, 5.

23. Lam, *A Passion for Facts*, 6.

24. Ye Yuan, "Social Investigation: The County of Cannei" [Shehui diaocha: Cannei xiang], *New Youth* 4, no. 5 (May 15, 1918): 441–45.

25. Lam, *A Passion for Facts*, 6–8.

26. Ma Boyuan, "The Local Custom in Hubei and Henan" [Hubei Henan di fengsu], *New Youth* 8, no. 1 (September 1, 1920): 1–11.

27. Mao Dun, "Introduction to *The First Anthology*," 60.

28. See Zheng Zhenduo, "Introduction to *The Anthology of Literary Debate*" [Wenxue lunzheng ji daoyan], in *Zhongguo xinwenxue daxi daoyan ji, 1917–1927*, 38. The distinction between native-soil fiction (*xiangtu xiaoshuo*) and rural fiction (*nongcun xiaoshuo*) lies in the fact that the latter did not appear until the 1930s. See Yu Ronghu, *The Changing Theories on the Chinese Native Soil Fiction* [Zhongguo xian dai xiang tu wen xue li lun liu bian lun] (Beijing: Zhongguo shehui kexue chuban she, 2011), 2–5, 35. Unlike *nongcun*, which denotes the place in a more impersonal sense, *xiangtu* takes on affective associations and therefore embodies strong personal connections.

29. As Marston Anderson argues, "many realist works operate on two levels, one of 'objective' social representation and one of self-conscious allegory." See Marston Anderson, *The Limits of Realism: Chinese Fiction in the Revolutionary Period* (Berkeley: University of California Press, 1990), 6–7.

30. Unlike the representations of the folks as cruel and cannibalistic, some native-soil stories portray them as preserving "a deep reservoir of emotions and humanity." See Haiyan Lee, "The Other Chinese: Romancing the Folk in May Fourth Native Soil Fiction," *Concentric: Literary and Cultural Studies* 33, no. 2 (2007): 31.

31. Jerry Dennerline, *Qian Mu and the World of Seven Mansions* (New Haven: Yale University Press, 1988), 8–9.

32. For example, *minghun* in the story "The Wedding of Juying" [Juying de chujia] by Wang Luyan (1902–1944); *chongxi* in "Candle Flame" [Zhuyan] by Tai Jingnong (1902–1990).

33. These local customs were described in these native-soil stories: *Dianqi* in "Earthworms" [Qiuyin men] and "The Wounded" [Fushang zhe] by Tai Jingnong and "The Gambler Jishun" by Xu Jie, *xiedou* in "Tragic Flog" [Canwu, 1924] by Xu Jie (1901–1993). An example of bizarre folk medical practice is in Lu Xun's "Medicine."

34. Georg Lukacs, *The Theory of the Novel: A Historical-Philosophical Essay on the Forms of Great Epic Literature* (Cambridge, MA: MIT Press, 1971), 48, 71.

35. Lydia H. Liu, "Narratives of Modern Selfhood: First-Person Fiction in May Fourth Literature," in *Politics, Ideology, and Literary Discourse in Modern China: Theoretical Interventions and Cultural Critique*, ed. Liu Kang and Xiaobing Tang (Durham: Duke University Press, 1993), 102–3; Henry Y. H. Zhao, *The Uneasy Narrator: Chinese Fiction from the Traditional to the Modern* (Oxford: Oxford University Press. 1995), 172.

36. For details, see A. K. Chanda, "The Young Man from the Provinces," *Comparative Literature* 33, no. 4 (Autumn 1981): 321–41.

37. See Chung-li Chang, *The Chinese Gentry: Studies on Their Role in Nineteenth-Century Chinese Society* (Seattle: University of Washington Press, 1955), 51.

38. For example, Lu Xun's other homecoming stories like "The New Year's Sacrifice" and "In the Tavern."

39. See Goodman, *Native Place, City, and Nation*.

40. Xiaobing Tang, *Chinese Modern: The Heroic and the Quotidian* (Durham: Duke University Press, 2000), 74–96. Ban Wang, *Illuminations from the Past: Trauma, Memory and History in Modern China* (Stanford: Stanford University Press, 2004), 51–57.

41. Fei Hsiao-t'ung, *From the Soil: The Foundations of Chinese Society. A Translation of Fei Xiaotong's* Xiangtu zhongguo, trans. Gary Hamilton and Wang Zheng (Berkeley: University of California Press, 1992), 51.

42. The original text is from Lu Xun, "My Old Home" [Guxiang], *Lu Xun Xuanji* [A Selection of Lu Xun's Work] (Beijing: Renmin wenxue chubanshe, 1959), 41–59. The translation is from *Selected Stories of Lu Hsun: The True Stories of Ah-Q and Other Stories*, trans. Gladys Yang and Yang Hsien-yi (Peking: Foreign Language Press, 1960), 61.

43. Mayfair Mei-hui Yang, *Gifts, Favors and Banquets: The Art of Social Relationships in China* (Ithaca: Cornell University Press, 1994), 122.

44. Yang, *Gifts, Favors and Banquets*, 122. Yan Yunxiang. *The Flow of Gifts: Reciprocity and Social Networks in a Chinese Village* (Stanford: Stanford University Press, 1996), 141–46.

45. Benedict Anderson, *Imagined Communities: Reflections on the Origin and Spread of Nationalism* (London: Verso, 1983), 7.

46. Vera Schwarcz, *The Chinese Enlightenment Intellectuals and the Legacy of the May Fourth Movement of 1919* (Berkeley: University of California Press, 1990).

47. For example, Xu Jilin, "The Origin of Individualism: A Study of the View about the Self in the May Fourth" [Geren zhuyi de qiyuan: Wusi shiqi de ziwoguan yanjiu], *Social Science in Tianjin* [Tianjin shehui kexue] 6 (2008): 113–24.

48. Joseph R. Levenson, "The Province, the Nation, and the World: The Problem of Chinese Identity," in *Approaches to Modern Chinese History*, ed. Albert Feuerweker, Rhoads Murphey, and Mary C. Wright (Berkeley: University of California Press, 1967), 268–88.

49. Charles Taylor, *Human Agency and Language: Philosophical Papers 1* (Cambridge: Cambridge University Press, 1985), 5.

50. Levenson, "The Province, the Nation, and the World," 273.

51. Charles Taylor, "The Politics of Recognition," in *Multiculturalism: Examining the Politics of Recognition*, ed. and introduced by Amy Gutmann (Princeton: Princeton University Press, 1994), 25.

52. Taylor, "Politics of Recognition," 37.

53. The phrase "a strange place," which refers to the cities, appears frequently in native-soil fiction and echoes the idea that urban migration was perceived as a sojourn rather than a permanent stay. See Goodman, *Native Place, City and Nation*, 5–6.

54. Lu Xun, "Xiaoshuo erji daoyan" [Introduction to *The Second Anthology of Fiction*], in *Zhongguo xinwenxue daxi daoyan ji, 1917–1927*, 86.

55. Lionel Trilling, *Sincerity and Authenticity* (Cambridge, MA: Harvard University Press, 1971), 139.

56. Xu Qinwen, *Guxiang* [My Hometown] (Shanghai: Beixin shuju, 1926), 9–10.

57. Prasenjit Duara, "The Regime of Authenticity: Timelessness, Gender, and National History in Modern China," *History and Theory* 37, no. 3 (Oct. 1998): 287.

58. Xu Qinwen, *Guxiang* [My Hometown] (Shanghai: Beixin shuju, 1926), 4–5.

59. Charles Taylor, *Sources of the Self: The Making of the Modern Identity* (Cambridge, MA: Harvard University Press, 1989), 62.

60. Lee Haiyan, *Revolution of the Heart: A Genealogy of Love in China, 1900–1950* (Stanford: Stanford University Press, 2007), 51–75.

61. Feng Yuanjun, "Separation" [Gejue], in *Feng Yuanjun xiaoshuo: Chunhen* [The Fiction of Feng Yuanjun: Spring Traces] (Shanghai: Shanghai guji chubanshe, 1997), 3.

62. Feng Yuanjun, "Separation," 9.

63. Jin Feng argues that Feng Yuanjun "did not accentuate the revolutionary significance" of the Chinese Nora's departure from the patriarchal family, but instead concentrated on "the acute agony her heroine experiences at the point of breaking away from the family." In Jin Feng, *The New Woman in Early Twentieth-Century Chinese Fiction* (West Lafayette, IN: Purdue University Press, 2004), 133–35.

64. Feng Yuanjun, "My Loving Mother" [Cimu], in *Feng Yuanjun xiaoshuo: Chunhen*, 34.

65. Wang Lingzhen, *Personal Matters: Women's Autobiographical Practice in Twentieth-Century China* (Stanford: Stanford University Press, 2004), 76–79.

66. Feng Yuanjun, "After My Mother Left" [Cimu zouhou], in *Feng Yuanjun xiaoshuo: Chunhen*, 60.

67. Lu Xun, "Xiaoshuo erji daoyan," in *Zhongguo xinwenxue daxi daoyan ji, 1917–1927*, 84.

68. For details, see Haiyan Lee, *Revolution of the Heart* (Stanford: Stanford University Press, 2007), 95–139.

69. Martha C. Nussbaum, *Love's Knowledge: Essays on Philosophy and Literature* (New York: Oxford University Press, 1990), 131.

70. Yu Dafu, "Wisteria and Dodder" [Niaoluo xing], in *The Collected Works of Yu Dafu* [*Yu Dafu wenji*, vol. 1, Fiction] (Hong Kong: Shenghuo, dushu, xinzhi sanlian shudian xianggang fendian and Huacheng chubanshe, 1982), 213–14.

71. Yu Dafu, "Wisteria and Dodder" [Niaoluo xing], 214.

72. See Geng Song, *The Fragile Scholar: Power and Masculinity in Chinese Culture.* (Hong Kong: Hong Kong University Press, 2004), 51–52.

73. Yu Dafu, "Wisteria and Dodder" [Niaoluo xing], 223.

74. Michael Egan, "Yu Dafu and the Transition to Modern Chinese Literature," in *Modern Chinese Literature in the May Fourth Era*, ed. Merle Goldman (Cambridge, MA: Harvard University Press, 1977), 312.

75. Anthony Giddens, *The Consequences of Modernity* (Cambridge, UK: Polity Press, 1990), 53.

Chapter 2

1. Pearl Buck, *Tell the People: Talks with James Yen about the Mass Education Movement* (New York: John Day Company, 1945), 58. For a detailed account of Ding County, see Li Jinghan, Dingxian shehui gaikuang diaocha [A Survey of Ding County Society] (Beiping: Zhongguo pingmin jiaoyu cujinhui), 1933; and Sidney David Gramble, *Ting Hsien: A North China Rural Community* (Stanford, CA: Stanford University Press), 1968.
2. Buck, *Tell the People*, 58.
3. James Yen, *Ting Hsien Experiment: 1930–1931* (Ting Hsien: Chinese National Association of the Mass Education Movements, 1931), 3.
4. According to Tong Lam, the metaphor of "social laboratory" refers to "an epistemological and geographic site that encouraged and allowed for experiments and innovations" in the Republican period. For details, see Tong Lam, *A Passion for Facts: Social Surveys and the Construction of the Chinese Nation State, 1900–1949* (Berkeley: University of California Press, 2011), 142–70.
5. Sidney D. Gamble. *Ting Hsien, a North China Rural Community* (New York: International Secretariat Institute of Pacific Relations, 1954; rep. Stanford University Press, 1968); Sidney D. Gamble, *Chinese Village Plays from the Ting Hsien Region (Yang Ke Hsüan): A Collection of Forty-Eight Chinese Rural Plays as Staged by Villagers from Ting Hsien in Northern China* (Amsterdam: APA–Philo Press, 1970).
6. Siyuan Liu, "A Mixed-Blooded Child, Neither Western nor Eastern: Sinicization of Western-Style Theatre in Rural China in the 1930s," *Asian Theatre Journal* 25, no. 2 (Fall): 273.
7. See Chang-tai Hung, *Going to the People: Chinese Intellectuals and Folk Literature, 1918–1937* (Cambridge, MA: Harvard University Press, 1985), 179.
8. Yan Yangchu, "Nongcun yundong de shiming" (The Mission of the Rural Movements), in *Yan Yangchu quanji* [The Anthology of Yan Yangchu], vol. 1, ed. Song Enrong (Changsha: Hunan jiaoyu, 1989), 293–304, 294, 297.
9. Charles W. Hayford, *To the People: James Yen and Village China* (New York: Columbia University Press, 1990).
10. Kate Merkel-Hess, *The Rural Modern: Reconstructing the Self and State in Republican China* (Chicago: University of Chicago Press, 2016); Kate Merkel-Hess, "Acting Out Reform: Theatre and Village in the Republican Rural Reconstruction Movement." *Twentieth-Century China* 37, no. 2 (2012): 161–80.
11. The Ding County experiment was abruptly halted by the Japanese invasion in 1937.
12. I use the concept of "rural vernacular" to highlight that the focus of the chapter is to examine the way how the Ding County experiment attempted to transmit knowledge and transform the minds of the local peasants rather than discuss the reception of the new ideas by the local peasants.
13. Shu-mei Shih, *The Lure of the Modern: Writing Modernism in Semicolonial China, 1917–1937* (Berkeley: University of California Press, 2001), 70–72.

14. Zhen Zhang, *An Amorous History of the Silver Screen: Shanghai Cinema, 1896–1937* (Chicago: University of Chicago Press, 2005), 1–41.

15. Zhang, *An Amorous History of the Silver Screen*, 30. For a discussion of the vernacular in Chinese urban culture, see Miriam Hansen, "Fallen Women, Rising Stars, New Horizons: Shanghai Silent Film as Vernacular Modernism," *Film Quarterly* 54, no. 1 (2000): 10–22.

16. Wu Xiangxiang, *Yan Yangchu zhuan—wei Quanqiu xiangcun gaizao fendou liushinian* [Biography of Yan Yangchu: Sixty Years' Rural Reform in the World] (Changsha: Yuelu shushe, 2001), 3.

17. The first image is discussed in Yi-tsi Mei Feuerwerker, *Ideology, Power, Text: Self-Representation and the Peasant "Other"* (Stanford: Stanford University Press, 1998). This image was also associated with the notion of "national character" and Lu Xun's critique of the peasant mentality. For details about national character and its literary representation, see Lydia Liu, *Translingual Practice: Literature, National Culture, and Translated Modernity—China, 1900–1937* (Stanford: Stanford University Press, 1995), 45–76. For discussions of the romanticized notion of the "folk," see Chang-tai Hung, *Going to the People*. Haiyan Lee, "Tears That Crumble the Great Wall: The Archeology of Feeling in the May Fourth Folklore Movement," *Journal of Asian Studies* 64, no. 1 (2005): 35–65; "The Other Chinese: Romancing the Folk in May Fourth Native Soil Fiction," *Concentric: Literary and Cultural Studies* 33, no. 2 (2007): 9–34.

18. Xiaorong Han, *The Chinese Discourses on the Peasant: 1900–1949* (Albany: State University of New York Press, 2005), 19–72.

19. Guy Alitto, *The Last Confucian: Liang Shu-ming and the Chinese Dilemma of Modernity* (Berkeley: University of California Press, 1986), 240.

20. In Wu Xiangxiang, *Yan Yangchu zhuan*, 58.

21. For example, Ernest Gellner, *Nations and Nationalism* (Ithaca: Cornell University Press, 1983), 12; Anthony Giddens, *The Giddens Reader*, ed. Philip Cassel (Stanford: Stanford University Press, 1993), 28; Jack Goody and Ian Watt, "The Consequences of Literacy," *Comparative Studies in Society and History* 5, no. 3 (1963): 306; and Walter J. Ong, *Orality and Literacy: The Technologizing of the Word* (London: Routledge, 1982), 49.

22. Goody and Watt, "The Consequences of Literacy," 314; Gellner, *Nations and Nationalism*, 10.

23. Benjamin A. Elman, "Political, Social, and Cultural Reproduction via Civil Service Examination in Late Imperial China," *Journal of Asian Studies* 50, no. 1 (1991): 17.

24. James Y. C. Yen, "China's New Scholar-Farmer," in *China's New Scholar-Farmer* (Yan Yangchu), *China's New Scholar-Farmer* (Ting Hsien: Chinese National Association of the Mass Education Movement, 1929), 10–11. For the Chinese version, Yan Yangchu, "You wenhua de zhongguo xinnongmin," in *Yan Yangchu quanji* [The Anthology of Yan Yangchu], vol. 1, ed. Song Enrong (Changsha: Hunan jiaoyu, 1989), 141–60, 146–47. Yen intentionally chooses the word "farmer" over "peasant," because the former indicates an association with citizenship whereas the latter implies a group that is passive, helpless, and unenlightened. For a detailed discussion of the transformation from farmer to

peasant, see Myron L. Cohen, "Cultural and Political Inventions in Modern China: The Case of the Chinese 'Peasant,'" *Daedaus* 122, no. 2 (spring) 1993. In my study, the term "peasant" mainly functions as an analytical category.

25. Xiaorong Han, *The Chinese Discourses on the Peasant: 1900–1949* (Albany: State University of New York Press, 2005), 68.

26. Gellner, *Nations and Nationalism*, 11.

27. Yen, *China's New Scholar-Farmer*, 13.

28. Hsiao-t'ung Fei, *From the Soil, the Foundations of Chinese Society: A Translation of Fei Xiaotong's* Xiangtu Zhongguo (Berkeley: University of California Press, 1992), 45–46.

29. James Y. C. Yen (Yan Yangchu), *New Citizens for China* (Ting Hsien: Chinese National Association of the Mass Education Movement, 1929), 20. For the Chinese version, "Zhongguo de xinmin," see *Yan Yangchu quanji* (The Anthology of Yan Yangchu), vol. 1, 161–71.

30. Yan Yangchu, "Pingmin jiaoyu gailun" (An Introduction to the Commoners' Education), *Yan Yangchu quanji* (The Anthology of Yan Yangchu), vol. 1, 121–33, 122.

31. Jacques Rancière, "On Ignorant Schoolmasters," in *Jacques Rancière: Education, Truth, Emancipation*, ed. Charles Bingham and Gert J. J. Biesta (London: Continuum, 2010), 1–8.

32. Rancière, "On Ignorant Schoolmasters," 5.

33. Andrew Jones, *Developmental Fairy Tales: Evolutionary Thinking and Modern Chinese Culture* (Cambridge, MA: Harvard University Press, 2011), 6.

34. For a discussion of teacher-pupil relations, see Maurice Meisner, *Marxism, Maoism and Utopianism: Eight Essays* (Madison: University of Wisconsin Press, 1982), 105.

35. Joan Judge, "Reforming the Feminine: Female Literacy and the Legacy of 1898," in *Rethinking the 1898 Reform Period: Political and Cultural Change in Late Qing China*, ed. Rebecca E. Karl and Peter Zarrow (Cambridge, MA: Harvard University Asia Center, 2002), 159.

36. See Wu Xiangxiang, *Yan Yangchu zhuan: wei quanqiu xiangcun gaizao fendou liushinian* (James Yen and His Sixty Years of Struggle with Rural Reconstruction for the Peasant People of the World) (Taipei: Shibao wenhua chuban shiye youxian gongxi, 1981), 55.

37. For a thorough discussion, see Yang Ruisong, *Bingfu, huanghuo yu shuishi: xifang shiye de zhongguo xingxiang yu jinda zhongguo guozu lunshu xiangxiang* [Sick Man, Yellow Peril, and Sleeping Lion: The Image of China on the Western Horizon and the Chinese Imagination of the Nation] (Taipei: Zhengda chubanshe, 2010).

38. Ong, *Orality and Literacy*, 82.

39. Quote in Buck, *Tell the People*, 36.

40. For a brief discussion of the historical context in which the Chinese coolies worked in France, see Jonathan D. Spence, *The Search for Modern China* (New York: W. W. Norton, 1999), 283–89; Xu Guoqi, *Strangers on the Western Front: Chinese Workers in the Great War* (Cambridge, MA: Harvard University Press, 2011).

41. Buck, *Tell the People*, 15–16 (emphasis mine).

42. Buck, *Tell the People*, 21 (emphasis mine).
43. Yen, *Ting Hsien Experiment: 1930–1931*, 2.
44. Yen, *Ting Hsien Experiment: 1930–1931*, 12.
45. Buck, *Tell the People*, 22.
46. John Fitzgerald, *Awakening China: Politics, Culture and Class in the Nationalist Revolution* (Stanford: Stanford University Press, 1996).
47. Yan, "Pingmin de gongmin jiaoyu zhi wojian" [My View about the Commoners' Citizenship Education], a *Yan Yangchu quanji*, vol. 1, 63–67, 66.
48. See, for example, Laikwan Pang, *The Distorting Mirror: Visual Modernity in China* (Honolulu: University of Hawai'i Press, 2007); Jason C. Kuo, ed., *Visual Culture in Shanghai 1850s–1930s* (Washington, DC: New Academia Publications, 2007).
49. For a short history of the lantern slide in China, see Frank Dikotter, *Exotic Commodities: Modern Objects and Everyday Life in China* (New York: Columbia University Press, 2006), 251–52. Unfortunately, I could not find extant visual records of the lantern slides used in the Ding County experiment.
50. For a focused discussion, see Haiyan Lee, *Revolution of the Heart: A Genealogy of Love in China, 1900–1950* (Stanford: Stanford University Press, 2007), 224.
51. Rey Chow, *Primitive Passions: Visuality, Sexuality, Ethnography, and Contemporary Chinese Cinema* (New York: Columbia University Press, 1995), 5–18.
52. A major reason that Yen adopted lantern slides as a teaching instrument was that one teacher could use a single lantern slide machine in a large classroom to teach many students, saving the human resources of the teaching staff and helping cut the expenses of teaching facilities.
53. Yan, "Pingmin jiaoyu" (Commoners' Education), *Yan Yangchu quanji*, vol. 1, 47–51, 50.
54. Tom Gunning, "The Cinema of Attractions: Early Film, Its Spectator and the Avant-Garde," in *Early Cinema: Space, Frame, Narrative*, ed. Thomas Elsaesser and Adam Barker (London: British Film Institute, 1990), 59.
55. Walter Benjamin, *Illuminations: Essays and Reflections*, trans. Harry Zohn (New York: Schocken, 1968), 217–52.
56. Buck, *Tell the People*, 65.
57. Wu Xiangxiang, *Yan Yangchu zhuan*, 49–50.
58. See Benjamin, *Illuminations*, 83–110. See also Ong, *Orality and Literacy*, 69, who gives the following example about teaching: "A teacher speaking to a class which he feels and which feels itself as a close-knit group, finds that if the class is asked to pick up its textbooks and read a given passage, the unity of the group vanishes as each person enters into his or her private lifeworld."
59. Yan, "Chuji pingjiao jiaoxue de zhonglei ji zuzhi" (The Categories and Organization of the Elementary Commoners' Education), *Yan Yangchu quanji*, vol. 1, 94–96, 95.
60. Wu Xiangxiang, *Yan Yangchu zhuan*, 179–82.
61. See Buck, *Tell the People*, 68–69.
62. Yen, *China's New Scholar-Farmer*, 6. The literacy rate in Ding County rose to 60

percent between 1930 and 1934. For details, see Siyuan Liu, "A Mixed-Blooded Child," 277.

63. Yen, *China's New Scholar-Farmer*, 4.

64. The illustrated primer, *People's 1,000-Character Literacy Primer* [Pingmin qianzi ke], was the basis for Yen's mass education project. The first edition of this primer, edited by Fu Baochen, has four volumes and ninety-six lessons in total. The illustrations were by Li Guanlin (Wu Xiangxiang and Liu Shaotang, eds., Dingxian nongmin jiaoyu [The Education of the Peasants in Ding County], 2 vols. (Taipei: Zhuanji wenxue, 1971), 201. This series of primers was first published in 1922 by the Youth Association Press.

65. Zhonghua pingmin jiaoyu cujinhui pingmin wenxuebu, ed., *The Farmer's a Thousand Characters* [Nongmin qianzike], 4 vols. (Shanghai: Zhonghua pingmin jiaoyu cujinhui pingmin wenxuebu, 1930–1931). The following descriptions and discussions of the illustrations are all based on this edition. To avoid redundancy, I only provide the volume number and the lesson number for easy reference.

66. For a discussion of the use of the technique of lithography in illustrated books, see Pang, *Distorting Mirror*, 40.

67. The primer was originally edited by Fu Baochen, and its third edition was revised by Lin Dachun, Zheng Jin, and Wang Jianduo in 1931.

68. Pang, *Distorting Mirror*, 35–36. For a detailed discussion, see Robert Hegel, *Reading Illustrated Fiction in Late Imperial China* (Stanford: Stanford University Press, 1998).

69. Pang, *Distorting Mirror*, 34.

70. Pang, *Distorting Mirror*, 37.

71. For example, Tom Gunning, "Tracing the Individual Body: Photography, Detectives and Early Cinema," in *Cinema and the Invention of Modern Life*, ed. Leo Charney and Vanessa Schwartz (Berkeley: University of California Press, 1995), 15.

72. Yen, *Ting Hsien Experiment: 1930–1931*, 2.

73. Zhonghua pingmin jiaoyu cujinhui pingmin wenxuebu, ed., *The Farmer's A Thousand Characters*, vol. 2, 47.

74. Merkel-Hess, *The Rural Modern*, 23–54.

75. Benedict Anderson, *Imagined Communities: Reflections on the Origin and Spread of Nationalism* (London: Verso, 1983).

76. Zhonghua pingmin jiaoyu cujinhui pingmin wenxuebu, ed., *The Farmer's a Thousand Characters*, vol. 1, 21.

77. Zhonghua pingmin jiaoyu cujinhui pingmin wenxuebu, ed., *The Farmer's a Thousand Characters*, vol. 1, 52–53, 62.

78. Yen, *China's New Scholar-Farmer*, 3.

79. Zhonghua pingmin jiaoyu cujinhui pingmin wenxuebu, ed., *The Farmer's a Thousand Characters*, vol. 4, 37.

80. For a discussion of "hygienic modernity," see Ruth Rogaski, *Hygienic Modernity: Meanings of Health and Disease in Treaty-Port China* (Berkeley: University of California Press, 2004).

81. Zhonghua pingmin jiaoyu cujinhui pingmin wenxuebu, ed., *The Farmer's a Thousand Characters*, vol. 1, 17, 19.

82. Zhonghua pingmin jiaoyu cujinhui pingmin wenxuebu, ed., *The Farmer's a Thousand Characters*, vol. 4, 49.

83. Merkel-Hess, *The Rural Modern*, 26.

84. Yen, *New Citizens for China*, 20.

85. Xiong, *Xiong Foxi xiju wenji* [An Anthology of Xiong Foxi's Plays] (Shanghai: Shanghai wenyi chubanshe, 2000), 828.

86. Yen's experiment provided another counterexample to the "going to the people" trend in the May Fourth movement, in which young radicals went to small towns and villages outside of Beijing to give lectures in the hope of awakening the common people. Their lectures turned out to be very unattractive to their rural compatriots; see Vera Schwarcz, *The Chinese Enlightenment: Intellectuals and the Legacy of the May Fourth Movement of 1919* (Berkeley: University of California Press, 1986), 128–32.

87. Charles Taylor, *Sources of the Self: The Making of the Modern Identity* (Cambridge, MA: Harvard University Press, 1989); Robert C. Solomon, *A Passion for Justice: Emotions and the Origins of the Social Contract* (Reading, MA: Addison-Wesley, 1990); Martha C. Nussbaum, *Upheavals of Thought: The Intelligence of Emotions* (Cambridge: Cambridge University Press, 2001); Haiyan Lee, "All the Feelings That Are Fit to Print: The Community of Sentiment and the Literary Public Sphere in China, 1900–1918," *Modern China* 27, no. 3 (2001): 291–327. Eugenia Lean, *Public Passions: The Trial of Shi Jianqiao and the Rise of Popular Sympathy in Republican China* (Berkeley: University of California Press, 2007).

88. Nussbaum, *Upheavals of Thought*, 425–26.

89. Nussbaum, *Upheavals of Thought*, 426.

90. Haiyan Lee, "All the Feelings That Are Fit to Print"; Lean, *Public Passion*.

91. For example, Siyuan Liu, "A Mixed-Blooded Child."

92. Yan Yangchu, "Preface", in Xiong Foxi, *Xiju dazhonghua zhi shiyan* [Experiment in Theatrical Popularization] (Nanjing: Zhongzheng shuju, 1937).

93. Xiong Foxi, *Xiju dazhonghua zhi shiyan*, 101–2.

94. Jürgen Habermas, *The Philosophical Discourse of Modernity: Twelve Lectures*, trans. Frederick G. Lawrence (Cambridge, MA: MIT Press, 1995), 45.

95. Siyuan Liu, "A Mixed-Blooded Child," 276–77. For a detailed analysis of *yangge*, also see David Holm, *Art and Ideology in Revolutionary China* (Oxford: Oxford University Press, 1991), 118–22.

96. Xiong, *Xiju dazhonghua zhi shiyan*, 16–17.

97. David Johnson, *Spectacle and Sacrifice: The Ritual Foundations of Village Life in North China* (Cambridge, MA: Harvard University Asia Center, 2009), 4.

98. Li Jianghan and Zhang Shiwen, eds., *Dingxian yangge xuan* [Selected *Yangge* Plays from Ding County] (Beijing: Zhonghua pingmin jiaoyu cujinhui, 1933).

99. Yen, *China's New Scholar-Farmer*, 33.

100. Xiong, *Xiju dazhonghua zhi shiyan*, 25.

101. Xiong, *Xiju dazhonghua zhi shiyan*, 26–27.
102. Yang Cunbin, "Xu" [Preface], in *Guodu jiqi yanchu* [*Crossing the River* and Its Performance], ed. Xiong Foxi (Shanghai: Zhengzhong shuju, 1937), 9.
103. Xiong, *Xiju dazhonghua zhi shiyan*, 55–57.
104. Xiong, *Xiju dazhonghua zhi shiyan*, 21.
105. Xiong, *Xiju dazhonghua zhi shiyan*, 30.
106. For a discussion of Bertolt Brecht's epic theatre, see Walter Benjamin, *Illuminations*, 147–54.
107. Xiong Foxi, "Zhongguo xiju yundong de xintujing" (The new approach to Chinese theatrical movement), *Ziyou Pinglun* (Liberty Review, Nanjing), December 14, 1935.
108. Xiong, *Xiju dazhonghua zhi shiyan*, 25.
109. Solomon, *A Passion for Justice*, 198.
110. Xiong, *Xiju dazhonghua zhi shiyan*, 45.
111. Xiong, *Xiju dazhonghua zhi shiyan*, 45–46.
112. Xiong, *Xiju dazhonghua zhi shiyan*, 96–97.
113. Lean, *Public Passions*, 63.
114. Lean, *Public Passions*, 139–40. Although Lean's discussion of public sympathy was situated in the particular social context of the sensationalism of urban mass media, it is relevant to my discussion in terms of how the public was shaped by theatrical performances.
115. Lean, *Public Passions*, 12.
116. Nussbaum, *Upheavals of Thought*, 426.
117. Xiong, *Xiju dazhonghua zhi shiyan*, 40.
118. Xiong Foxi, "Guodu" [Cross the River], in *Zhongguo huaju bainian juzuo xuan* [Selection of Plays from the Past One Hundred Years of Chinese Spoken Drama], ed. Zhongguo huaju yishu yanjiu hui. 20 vols. (Beijing: Zhongguo duiwai fanyi chuban gongsi, 2007), vol. 2, 419–58.
119. Xiong, "Guodu," vol. 2, 427.
120. Xiong, "Guodu," vol. 2, 438.
121. Xiong, *Xiju dazhonghua zhi shiyan*, 46–53.
122. Xiong, "Guodu," vol. 2, 456 (emphasis mine).
123. Anderson, *Imagined Communities*, 80.
124. Yang, "Xu," 106.
125. Jacques Rancière, *The Politics of Aesthetics: The Distribution of the Sensible*, trans. Gabriel Rockhill (London: Continuum, 2004), 13, 9.
126. Dipesh Chakrabarty, *Provincializing Europe: Postcolonial Thought and Historical Difference* (Princeton: Princeton University Press, 2008), 7–10. Homi Bhabha characterizes the tension between two aspects of nationalism as "the continuist, accumulative temporality of the pedagogical" and "the repetitious, recursive strategy of the performative." On the one hand, peasants are "the historical 'objects' of a national pedagogy," and thus need to be educated to gain citizenship; on the other hand, they are also "the 'subject' of a process of signification" and can demonstrate

"the prodigious, living principles of the people as contemporaneity." Bhabha's dichotomy of pedagogy and performance is raised in the postcolonial context to foreground the agency of the colonized (through mimetic performances) to subvert the pedagogy of the colonizer. See Homi Bhabha, *The Location of Culture* (London: Routledge, 2004), 145. Bhabha recognizes the blurring of these polarized categories: "in place of the polarity of a pre-figurative self-generating nation 'in itself' and extrinsic to other nations, the performative introduces a temporality of the 'in-between'" (148). His emphasis on hybridity, in my view, reaffirms the dichotomy between the performative and the pedagogical.

127. Ma Ming, "Xiong Foxi 'Xiju dazhonghua shiyan' Xintan" (A New Study of "Xiong Foxi's Experiment on Theatrical Popularization"), Chen Duo, et al., *Xiandai xijujia Xiong Foxi* [Modern Dramatist Xiong Foxi] (Beijing: Zhongguo xiju, 1985), 138–74, 161.

128. Ma Ming, "Xiong Foxi 'Xiju dazhonghua shiyan' Xintan," 162.

129. Xiong, *Xiju dazhonghua zhi shiyan*, 72–84.

130. Xiong, *Xiju dazhonghua zhi shiyan*, 85–88.

131. Merkel-Hess, *The Rural Modern*.

132. For a detailed discussion, see Holm, *Art and Ideology in Revolutionary China*.

133. Hayford, *To the People*, 202–3.

134. See Wu Xiangxiang, *Yan Yangchu zhuan*, chapters 11–15. In 1950, after the victory of the Communist Revolution, Yen moved to the United States and relocated his mass-education movement to other parts of the world, such as the Philippines and Malaysia. His experience from the Ding County experiment took on global significance.

135. Nicole Sackley, "The Village as Cold War Site: Experts, Development, and the History of Rural Reconstruction," *Journal of Global History* 6, no. 3 (2011): 482, 484.

136. For details, see Tong Lam, *A Passion for Facts*, 155. Yan's contemporaries Liang Shuming and Tao Xingzhi shared the same belief that rural reconstruction should be locally anchored and closely related to the peasants' everyday life, which could help to form a cohesive rural community.

137. Edgar Snow, "Awakening the Masses in China," *New York Herald Tribune* (December 17, 1933).

138. Edgar Snow, "How Rural China Is Being Remade," *China Weekly Review* (December 16, 1933): 98–101; (December 30, 1933): 202.

139. Snow, "How Rural China Is Being Remade," 203. Though Snow also considers Yen's experiment a revolution, "it does not seem extravagant to say that the movement which he leads may in time become a revolution of far more puissant destiny than any march or counter-march of Chinese troops to which that term has been loosely applied in the past" (203).

140. Wu Jiliang, *Edgar Snow and China* [Sinuo yu zhongguo] (Beijing: Zhongguo shehui chubanshe, 2005), 116–17.

141. See Hayford, *To the People*, 111–12. For a discussion of the differences between the liberal reformers and the revolutionaries, see Xiaorong Han, *The Chinese Discourses on the Peasant: 1900–1949* (Albany: State University of New York Press, 2005), 171.

Chapter 3

1. Brantly Womack, *The Foundation of Mao Zedong's Political Thought, 1917–1935* (Honolulu: University Press of Hawaii, 1982), 195.

2. Bao'an served as the headquarters of the Chinese Communists between July 3, 1936 and January 10, 1937; afterward the headquarters moved to the town of Yan'an proper.

3. Edgar Snow, *Red Star Over China* (London: Victor Gollancz, 1937), 23.

4. *Red Star Over China* was first published by Gollancz, London, in October 1937 and was published in 1938 by Random House in the United States. For a detailed account of the translation and publication of *Red Star Over China* (under the title *Xixing manji*), see S. Bernard Thomas, *Season of High Adventure: Edgar Snow in China* (Berkeley: University of California Press, 1996), 157.

5. The Chinese translation was published by a nonprofit press, Fu She, in 1938. The book had gone through four printings by November 1938 and was widely circulated in China.

6. J. K. Fairbank, "Foreword," in Edgar Snow, *Random Notes on Red China, 1936–1945* (Cambridge, MA: East Asian Research Center, Harvard University, 1957).

7. "On the Way to Yan'an" [Qu Yan'an tuzhong], *Good Companion* (*Liangyou*) 147 (February 1939).

8. See Lu Ping, "Introduction" [Qian ji], in *Living in Yan'an* [Shenghuo zai Yan'an], ed. Lu Ping (Xi'an: Xinhua shushe, 1938), 1.

9. Maurice Meisner, *Mao's China and After: A History of the People's Republic* (New York: Free Press, 1986), 50.

10. Mark Selden, *The Yenan Way in Revolutionary China* (Cambridge, MA: Harvard University Press, 1971). Mark Selden, *China in Revolution: The Yenan Way Revisited* (New York: M. E. Sharpe, 1995).

11. David E. Apter and Tony Saich, *Revolutionary Discourse in Mao's Republic* (Cambridge, MA: Harvard University Press, 1994).

12. Chen Yongfa, *Yan'an Shadows* [Yan'an di yinying] (Taibei: Zhongyang yanjiuyuan jindaishi yanjiusuo, 1990). Gao Hua, *Hongtaiyang shi zenyang shengqide* [How Did the Red Sun Rise] (Hong Kong: Chinese University of Hong Kong, 2000).

13. Selden, *The Yenan Way in Revolutionary China*, 278.

14. For a comprehensive study, see Hung Changtai, *War and Popular Culture: Resistance in Modern China, 1937–1945* (Berkeley: University of California Press, 1994); David Holm, *Art and Ideology in Revolutionary China* (Oxford: Oxford University Press, 1991).

15. Richard Jean So, *Transpacific Community: America, China, and the Rise and Fall of a Cultural Network* (New York: Columbia University Press, 2016), 34. Also see Colleen Lye, *America's Asia: Racial Form and American Literature, 1893–1945* (Princeton: Princeton University Press, 2005), 204–54.

16. For other accounts about Red China by foreign writers, see Agnes Smedley, *China

Fights Back: An American Woman with the Eighth Route Army (London: V. Gollancz, 1938) and *Battle Hymn of China* (London: Gollancz, 1944); Helen Snow (under the name of Nym Wales), *Inside Red China* (New York: Doubleday, Doran, 1939); Robert Payne, *Journey to Red China* (London: Heinemann, 1947); Gunther Stein, *The Challenge of Red China* (London: Whittlesey house, 1945); Jack Belden, *China Shakes the World* (New York: Harpers, 1949); and Theodore White and Annalee Jacoby, *Thunder out of China* (New York: William Sloane Associates, 1946).

17. This chapter does not aim to offer a comprehensive discussion of *Red Star Over China*, which broadly covers many subjects—for example, the eve of the Xi'an Incident and Snow's meetings with Yang Hucheng and Zhang Xueliang. For details, see John Maxwell Hamilton, *Edgar Snow: A Biography* (Bloomington: Indiana University Press, 1988); Thomas, *Season of High Adventure*.

18. Snow, *Red Star Over China*, 21. John K. Fairbank describes Snow as "an activist, ready to encourage worthy causes rather than be a purely passive spectator" as well as "a zealous factual reporter, able to appraise the major trends of the day and describe them in vivid color for the American reading public." See "Introduction," in Snow, *Red Star Over China* (1968), 12.

19. William Stott, *Documentary Expression and Thirties America* (Chicago: University of Chicago Press, 1973).

20. Stott, *Documentary Expression and Thirties America*, 143.

21. Stott, *Documentary Expression and Thirties America*, 49.

22. Stott, *Documentary Expression and Thirties America*, 7.

23. Stott, *Documentary Expression and Thirties America*, x.

24. Stott, *Documentary Expression and Thirties America*, 14.

25. Stott, *Documentary Expression and Thirties America*, 26.

26. Stott, *Documentary Expression and Thirties America*, 49.

27. Stott, *Documentary Expression and Thirties America*, 8–9.

28. Charles Laughlin, *Chinese Reportage: The Aesthetics of Historical Experience* (Durham: Duke University Press, 2002), 13.

29. Laughlin, *Chinese Reportage*, 6–12.

30. Stott, *Documentary Expression and Thirties America*, 164, 178–79.

31. Stott, *Documentary Expression and Thirties America*, 61.

32. Stott, *Documentary Expression and Thirties America*, 188–89.

33. Snow, *Red Star Over China* (1968), 36.

34. Fairbank, "Introduction," 13.

35. Snow, *Red Star Over China*, 17.

36. This decline paradigm regarding the history of that region has been considered one-sided and misleading in the current rewriting of the local history of Guanzhong, which challenges the teleological assumption of the nation-centered narrative. See Ong Chang Woei, *Men of Letters within the Passes: Guanzhong Literati in Chinese History, 907–1911* (Cambridge, MA: Harvard University Press, 2008), 1–3.

37. For a detailed study of Fan Changjiang's work, see Hung Chang-tai, *War and Pop-*

ular Culture, 157; Laughlin, *Chinese Reportage*, 2–3, 7. Fan's writing was a representative case of the conspicuous presence of reportage literature in 1930s China.

38. Snow, *Red Star Over China*, 24.
39. Laughlin, *Chinese Reportage*, 208–9.
40. Laughlin, *Chinese Reportage*, 194.
41. Laughlin, *Chinese Reportage*, 12–13.
42. Snow, *Red Star Over China*, 39.
43. See Snow, *Red Star Over China*, 38. I noticed the difference between the Chinese version and the English version. The Chinese translation explicitly highlights that the site of the Han dynasty palace connects the past glory of the Han dynasty with the ongoing Chinese revolution, which legitimizes the revolution. See Dong Leshan, trans., *Xixing manji* (Beijing: Shenghuo, Dushu, Xinzhi Sanlian shudian, 1979), 24.
44. Snow, *Red Star Over China*, 71.
45. Snow, *Red Star Over China*, 40.
46. Snow, *Red Star Over China*, 44.
47. Snow, *Red Star Over China*, 73.
48. Snow, *Red Star Over China*, 114.
49. Snow, *Red Star Over China*, 114–16.
50. Snow, *Red Star Over China*, 114.
51. Patricia Bradley. *Making American Culture: A Social History, 1900–1920* (New York: Palgrave Macmillan, 2009), 13.
52. Bradley, *Making American Culture*, 13; Patricia McDonnell, *On the Edge of Your Seat: Popular Theater and Film in Early Twentieth-Century American Art* (New Haven: Yale University Press, 2002), 4.
53. McDonnell, *On the Edge of Your Seat*, 5.
54. Snow, *Red Star Over China*, 114.
55. Snow, *Red Star Over China*, 120.
56. Richard Jean So, *Transpacific Community: America, China, and the Rise and Fall of a Global Cultural Network* (New York: Columbia University Press, 2016), xx–xxii.
57. Selden, *China in Revolution*, 227.
58. Snow, *Red Star Over China*, 20.
59. Snow, *Red Star Over China*, 252.
60. Snow, *Red Star Over China*, 253–54.
61. Snow, *Red Star Over China*, 260.
62. Edgar Snow, "Preface to the 1938 edition of the Chinese translation," in Dong Leshan, trans., *Xixing manji* (Beijing: Shenghuo, Dushu, Xinzhi Sanlian shudian, 1979), 7.
63. Snow, "Preface," 7.
64. Snow, *Red Star Over China*, 79–80.
65. Xiaobing Tang, *Chinese Modern: The Heroic and the Quotidian* (Durham: Duke University Press, 2000), 182.

66. Colleen Lye, *America's Asia: Racial Form and American Literature, 1893–1945* (Princeton: Princeton University Press, 2006), 226.

67. Thomas, *Season of High Adventure*, 172. David Apter and Tony Saich question the authenticity of Mao's storytelling; see *Revolutionary Discourse in Mao's Republic*, 69–71.

68. Thomas, *Season of High Adventure*, 173. Thomas quotes Helen Foster Snow's words to explain *Red Star*'s appeal to Western readers: "it is a positive, happy book, telling of a wonderful new and happy experience" (189).

69. Hayden White, *Tropics of Discourse: Essays in Cultural Criticism* (Baltimore: Johns Hopkins University Press, 1986), 88.

70. Snow, *Red Star Over China*, 170. Mao's own storytelling constructed a fictional personality that paved the way for the subsequent cult of Mao, which begun in the Yan'an period and culminated during the Cultural Revolution. For a detailed study on this topic, see Daniel Leese, *Mao Cult: Rhetoric and Ritual in China's Cultural Revolution* (Cambridge: Cambridge University Press, 2011).

71. Thomas, *Season of High Adventure*, 109.

72. Snow, *Red Star Over China*, 126.

73. For details, see Lydia Liu, "Introduction," in *Tokens of Exchange: The Problem of Translation in Global Circulations* (Durham: Duke University Press, 1999), 1–12.

74. For details regarding the publication of Snow's writings and photos after his return from northwest China, see Thomas, *Season of High Adventure*, 151–52. For a detailed account of the reception of *Red Star in China* in the West, see chapter 10, "The Strange Life of a Classic," 169–89.

75. *China Weekly Review*, November 14, 1936.

76. Richard Jean So has pointed out that Chinese peasants were valorized as the ideal subject for left-wing political mobilizations. See *Transpacific Community*, 41–82. Colleen Lye has discussed the reception of Snow's *Red Star Over China* in conjunction with Pearl Buck's best-selling novel *The Good Earth* (1931) in the United States as evidence of a distinctly American version of Orientalism in the 1930s and 1940s. See Lye, *America's Asia*, 204–54.

77. Snow, "Preface to the 1968 Edition," 16. The West has a long tradition of blurring the boundaries between journalism and literature. For example, Walter Benjamin has discerned that "news stories were literary constructions; feuilleton novelists used news stories as content. The tendency of mass media is to render the distinction between art and politics meaningless." See Susan Buck-Morss, *The Dialectics of Seeing: Walter Benjamin and the Arcades Project* (Cambridge, MA: MIT Press, 1989), 140. Doug Underwood suggests that in England and America novelists with experience in journalism have used journalistic methods and adopted actual events in their dramatic narrative. Doug Underwood, *Journalism and the Novel: Truth and Fiction, 1700–2000* (Cambridge: Cambridge University Press, 2008), 3.

78. Snow, *Red Star Over China* (1968), 41.

79. Owen Lattimore, "Introduction," in Jack Belden, *China Shakes the World*, xii.

80. Zihui, "Huanghe dahechang de liangbu shougao dang'an" [The Archive of Two Manuscripts of the Chorus of the Yellow River], *Dangan chunqiu*, Issue 9 (2006), 2.

81. For example, Matei Calinescu, *Five Faces of Modernity: Modernism, Avant-garde, Decadence, Kitsch, Postmodernism* (Durham: Duke University Press, 1987), 21–22; Hannah Arendt, *On Revolution* (London: Penguin, 1963), 28–29.

82. Quoted in Rewi, *The Anna Louise Strong I Know: Her Life, Thought and Work* [Wo suo zhidao de sitelang: tade shenghuo, sixiang he zhuzuo], trans. Jiang Shanhui (Hong Kong: Xianggang chaoyang chubanshe, 1971).

83. Chen Xuezhao, *A Visit to Yan'an* [Yan'an fangwen ji] (Hong Kong: Beiji shudian, 1940), 232. The revolutionary culture in Yan'an also had the characteristics of the internationalists until the rectification movement in late 1941.

84. Joseph Levenson, *Revolution and Cosmopolitanism: The Western Stage and the Chinese Stages* (Berkeley: University of California Press, 1971), 7.

85. Shu-mei Shih, *The Lure of the Modern: Writing Modernism in Semicolonial China* (Berkeley: University of California Press, 2001), 49.

86. Norbert Elias, *Time: An Essay*, trans. Edmund Jephcott (Oxford: Blackwell, 1992), 11.

87. Wen-hsin Yeh, *Shanghai Splendor: Economic Sentiments and the Making of Modern China, 1843–1949* (Berkeley: University of California Press, 2007), 80–81.

88. Stephen Kern, *The Culture of Time and Space, 1880–1918* (Cambridge, MA: Harvard University Press, 1983), 111.

89. According to Zhu Hongzhao, even if some of the Communist leaders had watches sent from abroad, they tended to use different standards of time in their own administrative departments; for example, Mao followed his habit of working at night and sleeping during the day. Mao later set the standard time to accommodate the demands of building a radio station, but most communists and soldiers still did not have a consciousness of time. Zhu Hongzhao, *A History of the Everyday Life in Yan'an, 1937–1947* [Yan'an richang shenghuo zhong de lishi, 1937–1947] (Guilin: Guangxi shifan daxue chubanshe, 2007), 10–11.

90. Yan'an did not abolish time measurement based on the sundial until 1944.

91. Chen Xuezhao, *A Visit to Yan'an*, 200. For another interesting discussion of the sound culture in Yan'an, see Xiaobing Tang, "Listening to Yan'an: Illuminations from a Sonic Experience" [Lingting Yan'an: Yiduan tingjue jingyan de qishi], *Journal of Modern Chinese Studies* (Shanghai), January 2017.

92. Zhu Hongzhao, *A History of the Everyday Life in Yan'an*, 8.

93. Zhu Hongzhao, *A History of the Everyday Life in Yan'an*, 8.

94. Vanessa Ogle, *The Global Transformation of Time: 1870–1950* (Cambridge, MA: Harvard University Press, 2015), 8.

95. See Apter and Saich, *Revolutionary Discourse in Mao's Republic*.

96. Xiaobing Tang, *Chinese Modern: The Heroic and the Quotidian* (Durham: Duke University Press, 2000). 1.

97. Chen Xuezhao, *A Visit to Yan'an*, 63.
98. Chen Xuezhao, *A Visit to Yan'an*, 56.
99. Chen Xuezhao, *A Visit to Yan'an*, 86.
100. Ban Wang, *Illuminations from the Past: Trauma, Memory, and History in Modern China* (Stanford: Stanford University Press, 2004), 164–65.
101. Laughlin, *Chinese Reportage*, 7.
102. Snow, *Red Star Over China* (1937), 247.
103. Snow, *Red Star Over China* (1937), 56–57.
104. Snow, *Red Star Over China* (1937), 84.
105. Chen Xuezhao, *A Visit to Yan'an*, 117.
106. Chen Xuezhao, *A Visit to Yan'an*, 74.
107. Chen Xuezhao, *A Visit to Yan'an*, 215.
108. Chen Xuezhao, *A Visit to Yan'an*, 101.
109. Chen Xuezhao, *A Visit to Yan'an*, 137–39.
110. Chen Xuezhao, *A Visit to Yan'an*, 153.
111. Chen Xuezhao, *A Visit to Yan'an*, 218–19.
112. Chen Xuezhao, *A Visit to Yan'an*, 57, 306–7.
113. Rey Chow, *Woman and Chinese Modernity: The Politics of Reading Between West and East* (Minneapolis: University of Minnesota Press, 1991), 85.
114. Chen Xuezhao, *A Visit to Yan'an*, 221.
115. *A Visit to Yan'an* records Chen Xuezhao's first journey to Yan'an. Jeffrey Kinkley describes her next trip to Yan'an, in 1940, this way: "it was a time for 'study,' not individual creativity. [. . .] Chen attended Mao's famous May 1942 talks at the Yan'an forum on literature and art, and quite willingly underwent the great rectification campaign, yearning to rein in her 'immature' idealism and to learn to write for a different audience: workers, peasants, and soldiers, as specified by Mao Zedong" (Jeffrey Kinkley, "Introduction," in Chen Xuezhao, *Surviving the Storm: A Memoir* [Armonk, NY: M. E. Sharpe, 1990], xix–xxi).
116. Michael Dutton, "Passionately Governmental: Maoism and the Structured Intensities of Revolutionary Governmentality," in *China's Governmentalities: Governing Change, Changing Government*, ed. Elaine Jeffreys (London: Routledge, 2010), 24–37.
117. For a detailed account of Ding Ling's life experience in Yan'an, see Li Xiangdong and Wang Zengru, *Ding Ling Zhuan* [Ding Ling: The Biography], vol. 1 (Beijing: Zhongguo dabaike quanshu chubanshe, 2015), 137–347.
118. Ding Ling, "How I Came to Shanbei" [Wo shi zenyang lai shanbei de], in *The Collected Works of Ding Ling* (Ding Ling wenji) (Changsha: Hunan renmin chubanshe, 1983), 5: 305–11.
119. Holm, *Art and Ideology in Revolutionary China*, 46.
120. Tani Barlow, "Introduction," *I Myself Am a Woman: Selected Writings of Ding Ling*, ed. Tani E. Barlow and Gary J. Bjorge (Boston: Beacon Press, 1989), 30.
121. Huang Ziping, "The Metaphor of Sickness and Literary Production: Ding Ling's

'In the Hospital'" [Bing de yinyu yu wenxue shengchan: Ding Ling de "zai yiyuan zhong" ji qita], in *Rereading: Mass Literature and Ideology* [Zai jiedu: Dazhong wenyi yu yishi xingtai], ed. Tang Xiaobing (Beijing: Beijing daxue chubanshe, 2007), 19–33.

122. In regard to the image of the woman soldier, see Laughlin, *Chinese Reportage*, 200–201.

123. Haiyan Lee, *Revolution of the Heart: A Genealogy of Love in China, 1900–1950* (Stanford: Stanford University Press, 2007), 260.

124. Martha Nussbaum, *Love's Knowledge: Essays on Philosophy and Literature* (New York: Oxford University Press, 1990), 201.

125. Bonnie S. McDougall, *Mao Zedong's "Talks at the Yan'an Conference on Literature and Art": A Translation of the 1943 Text with Commentary* (Ann Arbor: Center for Chinese Studies, University of Michigan, 1980), 61.

126. The translation is from Gary Bjorge, in Ding Ling, "In the Hospital," *Modern Chinese Stories and Novellas, 1919–1949*, ed. Joseph S. M. Lau, C. T. Hsia, and Leo Ou-fan Lee (New York: Columbia University Press, 1981); Ding Ling, "In the Hospital" [Zai yiyuan Zhong], *Ding Ling Zuopin jingxuan* [A Selection of Ding Ling's Works], ed. Wu Lina and Wu Xuxi (Wuhan: Changjiang wenyi chubanshe, 2003), 280–99.

127. This episode illustrates the linking of the medical and the literary in modern literature: Lydia Liu suggests that the act of dissecting the human body is translated into the function of writing as a way of "dissecting the self." In *Translingual Practice: Literature, National Culture, and Translated Modernity—China, 1900–1937* (Stanford: Stanford University Press, 1995), 128.

128. Dutton, "Passionately Governmental," 24–37.

129. Translation by Bjorge, in Ding Ling, "In the Hospital," *Modern Chinese Stories and Novellas, 1919–1949*, 290; Ding Ling, "In the Hospital" [Zai yiyuan Zhong], *Ding Ling Zuopin jingxuan* [A Selection of Ding Ling's Works].

130. Wang Shiwei, "The Wild Lily," *Liberation Daily*, March 13, March 23, 1942.

131. Ding Ling, "In the Hospital," 285.

132. Wang Shiwei, "The Wild Lily."

133. Ding Ling, "In the Hospital," 290.

134. Ding Ling, "In the Hospital," 291.

135. Yi-tsi Mei Feuerwerker also points out that the narrative is written exclusively from Lu Ping's subjective point of view and therefore does not provide access to the external, objective reality of the hospital. This point of view evidently runs counter to revolutionary ideology. Yi-tsi Mei Feuerwerker, *Ding Ling's Fiction: Ideology and Narrative in Modern Chinese Literature* (Cambridge, MA: Harvard University Press, 1982), 110–11.

136. Ding Ling, "In the Hospital," 291.

137. See Kirk Denton, *The Problematic of Self in Modern Chinese Literature: Hu Feng and Lu Ling* (Stanford: Stanford University Press, 1998), 10, 23.

138. For details about rectification, see Kirk Denton, "Rectification: Party Discipline, Intellectual Remolding, and the Formation of a Political Community," in *Words and*

Their Stories: Essays on the Language of the Chinese Revolution, ed. Ban Wang (Leiden: Brill, 2010), 51–64.

139. For details about the criticism of Ding Ling in Yan'an and later in 1958, see Huang Ziping, "The Metaphor of Sickness and Literary Production," 19–33.

140. Liao Ying, "Person . . . Growing Up in the Hardship: A Review of Comrade Ding Ling's 'In the Hospital,'" [Ren . . . Zai jianku zhong chengzhang: ping Ding Ling tongzhi de 'zai yiyuan Zhong,'] in *The Research Materials of Ding Ling* [Ding Ling Yanjiu ziliao], ed. Yuan Liangjun (Tianjin: Tianjin renmin chubanshe, 1982), 278–81. The persecution of the literary dissident Wang Shiwei for his story "Wild Lily" was a great shock to the leftist writers who initially gathered in Yan'an with great enthusiasm. But fortunately Ding Ling was not purged from the Party, and she soon publicly apologized for what she called her incorrect portrayal of the physical and social scenes of Yan'an in "In the Hospital."

141. Mao Zedong, "Talks at the Yenan Forum on Literature and Art," https://www.marxists.org/reference/archive/mao/selected-works/volume-3/mswv3_08.htm (accessed November 4, 2019).

142. Mao Zedong, "The United Front in Cultural Work," https://www.marxists.org/reference/archive/mao/selected-works/volume-3/mswv3_21.htm (accessed November 4, 2019).

143. Leo Lee points out "the patriarchic manner" in Xiao Jun's way of unleashing his personal grudge due to his disappointment at the revolutionary reality. See Leo Lee, *The Romantic Generation of Modern Chinese Writers* (Cambridge, MA: Harvard University Press, 1973), 237.

144. Xiao Jun, *The Collective Work of Xiao Jun* [Xiao Jun Quanji] (Beijing: Huaxia chubanshe, 2008), vol. 11, 535–36.

145. Selden, *The Yenan Way in Revolutionary China*, 253.

146. See Tina Mai Chen's discussion of "a human-tool continuum": "Mao approached the interconnected levels of motion and existence and the ceaseless cycles of change through a notion of progress in which laboring human bodies were fused to the rudimentary tools and material conditions of work to produce a full consciousness." Tina Mai Chen, "The Human-Machine Continuum in Maoism: The Intersection of Soviet Socialist Realism, Japanese Theoretical Physics, and Chinese Revolutionary Theory," *Cultural Critique* 80 (Winter 2012): 158.

147. Ci Jiwei, *Dialectic of the Chinese Revolution: From Utopianism to Hedonism* (Stanford: Stanford University Press, 1994), 3–4.

Chapter 4

1. For a detailed discussion of the Talks at the Yan'an Forum on literature and art, see Richard King, *Milestones on a Golden Road: Writing for Chinese Socialism, 1945–80* (Vancouver: UBC Press, 2013), 18–29.

2. Brantly Womack, *The Foundation of Mao Zedong's Political Thought, 1917–1935* (Honolulu: University of Hawai'i Press, 1982), 84.

3. Hung Chang-tai, *War and Popular Culture: Resistance in Modern China, 1937–1945* (Berkeley: University of California Press, 1994), 14.

4. For example, Joseph W. Esherick, *The Origin of the Boxer Uprising* (Berkeley: University of California Press, 1987); Yue Meng. "'Baimaomv' yanbian de qishi: jianlun yan'an wenyi de lishi duozhixing" ("The Evolution of White-haired Girl and Its Inspiration: A Reflection on Literature and Art in Yan'an and Its Multiple Natures"), in *Zai Jiedu: Dazhong wenyi yu yishi xingtai* [Rereading: Mass Culture and Ideology], ed. Tang Xiaobing (Beijing: Beijing University Press), 48–69, 56–57; Cai Xiang, *Revolution/Narrative: Chinese Socialist Literary and Cultural Imagination, 1949-1966* [Geming/xushu: zhongguo shehui zhuyi wenxue wenhua xiangxiang] (Beijing: Peking University Press, 2010), 27.

5. See David Holm. "Folk Art as Propaganda: The Yangge Movement in Yan'an," in *Popular Chinese Literature and Performing Arts in the People's Republic of China, 1949-1979*, ed. Bonnie S. McDougall, 3–35 (Berkeley: University of California Press, 1984), 5; David Holm, *Art and Ideology in Revolutionary China* (Oxford: Oxford University Press. 1991), 20; Barbara Mittler, *A Continuous Revolution: Making Sense of Cultural Revolution Culture* (Cambridge, MA: Harvard University Press, 2012), 7, 12; Ban Wang, *The Sublime Figure of History: Aesthetics and Politics in Twentieth-Century China* (Stanford: Stanford University Press, 1997), 209–10; Hung Chang-tai, *War and Popular Culture: Resistance in Modern China, 1937-1945* (Berkeley: University of California Press, 1994), 221–69; Brian James DeMare, *Mao's Cultural Army: Drama Troupes in China's Rural Revolution* (Cambridge: Cambridge University Press, 2015).

6. Edgar Snow, *Red Star Over China* (New York: Grove Press, 1968), 16.

7. Cong, Xiaoping, *Marriage, Law, and Gender in Revolutionary China* (Cambridge: Cambridge University Press, 2016). For scholarship in Chinese, see Zhang Xipo, *Ma Xiwu and Ma Xiwu's Way of Adjudicating Cases* [Ma Xiwu yu Ma Xiwu shenpan fangshi] (Beijing: Falv chubanshe, 2013).

8. Cong, Xiaoping, *Marriage, Law, and Gender*, 4–7.

9. Althusser, Louis. *Lenin and Philosophy, and Other Essays*, trans. Ben Brewster (New York: Monthly Review Press, 1971), 143, 162.

10. Yi-Tsi Mei Feuerwerker, *Ideology, Power, Text: Self-Representation and the Peasant "Other" in Modern Chinese Literature* (Stanford: Stanford University Press, 1998), 102–3.

11. For details, see Feuerwerker, *Ideology, Power, and Text*, 118.

12. Feuerwerker, *Ideology, Power and Text*, 117–18.

13. For a discussion of the "the power of positive thinking" in China and its roots in the ordinary Chinese people's "attitudes towards the auspicious and inauspicious," see David Holm, *Art and Ideology in Revolutionary China* (Oxford: Oxford University Press, 1991), 8–9.

14. See Cai Xiang, *Revolution/Narrative: Chinese Socialist Literary and Cultural Imagination, 1949-1966* [Geming/xushu: zhongguo shehui zhuyi wenxue wenhua xiangxiang] (Beijing: Peking University Press, 2010), 174.

15. Hung Chang-tai, *War and Popular Culture: Resistance in Modern China, 1937-1945* (Berkeley: University of California Press, 1994), 249–50.

16. Cong Xiaoping, "From 'Freedom of Marriage' to 'Self-Determined Marriage'":

Recasting Marriage in the Shaan-Gan-Ning Border Region of the 1940s," *Twentieth-Century China* 38, no. 3 (October, 2013): 185.

17. Zhao Shuli, "The Marriage of Little Erhei" [Xiao Erhei jiehun], in *A Collection of Zhao Shuli's Work* [Zhao Shuli wenji], vol. 1 (Beijing: Gongren chubanshe, 1980), 9.

18. Arthur Smith, *Chinese Characteristics* (New York: Fleming H. Revell, 1894), 237.

19. Derk Bodde and Clarence Morris. *Law in Imperial China: Exemplified by 190 Ch'ing Dynasty Cases* (Cambridge, MA: Harvard University Press, 1967), 11–12.

20. Neil J. Diamant, *Revolutionizing the Family: Politics, Love, and Divorce in Urban and Rural China, 1949–1968* (Berkeley: University of California Press, 2000), 12.

21. For a detailed discussion of law and sentiment in the Republican period, see Eugenia Lean, *Public Passions: The Trial of Shi Jianqiao and the Rise of Popular Sympathy in Republican China* (Berkeley: University of California Press, 2007), 109–11.

22. For a detailed discussion of the difficulties and social barriers facing urban women in their pursuit of divorce, see Katheryn Bernhardt, "Women and the Law: Divorce in the Republican Period," in *Civil Law in Qing and Republican China*, ed. Kathryn Bernhardt and Philip Huang (Stanford: Stanford University Press, 1994).

23. See Leo Ou-fan Lee, *Shanghai Modern: The Flowering of a New Urban Culture in China, 1930–1945* (Cambridge, MA: Harvard University Press, 1999), 6.

24. Nancy Armstrong, *Desire and Domestic Fiction: A Political History of the Novel* (Oxford: Oxford University Press, 1987).

25. Moretti, Franco, *Signs Taken for Wonders: Essays in the Sociology of Literary Forms* (London: Verso, 1988), 111.

26. "Talks at the Yenan Forum on Literature and Art" (May 1942), *Selected Work of Mao Tse-tung*, transcription by the Maoist Documentation Project, https://www.marxists.org/reference/archive/mao/selected-works/volume-3/mswv3_08.htm (last access July 25, 2017).

27. This marriage dispute caused a sensation at the time, and other local newspapers in the border region also covered the legal case, such as *Longdong News* [Longdong bao] and *The Border Region Masses Weekly* [Bianqu qunzhong bao]. I was not able to gain access to these local newspapers. For details, see Xiaoping Cong, 2016, 175. On January 6, 1944, the party official Lin Boqu (1886–1960) in a speech first propagated "Ma Xiwu's Way of Adjudicating Cases"; see Zhang Xipo, *Ma Xiwu shenpan fangshi* [Ma Xiwu's Way of Adjudicating Cases] (Beijing: Falv chubanshe, 1983), 24.

28. "Bianqu tiaojie hunyin de yige shili," *Xinhua ribao*, October 22, 1944; "Yijian qianghun an," *Xinhua ribao*, April 11, 1945.

29. See Tong Lam, *A Passion for Facts: Social Surveys and the Construction of the Chinese Nation State, 1900–1949* (Berkeley: University of California Press, 2011).

30. Sun Xiaozhong and Gao Ming, eds., *A Collection of Materials on Rural Reconstruction in Yan'an* [Yan'an xiangcun jianshe ziliao], vol. 1 (Shanghai: Shanghai University Press, 2012), 218–21, 221.

31. Sun and Gao, eds., *A Collection of Materials*, vol. 1, 209–13.

32. Sun and Gao, eds., *A Collection of Materials*, vol. 1, 215.

33. Sun and Gao, eds., *A Collection of Materials*, vol. 1, 222.

34. Sun and Gao, eds., *A Collection of Materials*, vol. 1, 227, 199.

35. Hung Chang-tai, "Two Images of Socialism: Woodcuts in Chinese Communist Politics," *Comparative Studies in Society and History* 39, no. 1 (Jan., 1997): 34–60, 47, 50.

36. Quoted in Zhang Xipo. *Ma Xiwu shenpan fangshi* [Ma Xiwu's Way of Adjudging Cases] (Beijing: Falv chubanshe,1983), 31.

37. Xiaoping Cong, *Marriage, Law and Gender in Revolutionary China* (Cambridge: Cambridge University Press, 2016), 195–96.

38. According to Xiaoping Cong, the newspaper *Xinhua Daily* was based in the Nationalist wartime capital of Chongqing, and it reported the legal case to show the CCP's policies on women's emancipation; Cong, *Marriage, Law and Gender in Revolutionary China*, 3.

39. Li Pu, *Women de minzhu chuantong: kangri shiqi jiefangqu zhengzhi shenghuo fengmo* [Our Democratic Tradition: The Scene of Politics and Life in the Liberated Area during the Anti-Japanese War Period] (Chongqing: Xinhua chubanshe, 1980), 47.

40. Li Pu, *Women de minzhu chuantong*, 47–54.

41. Li Pu, *Women de minzhu chuantong*, 47–54.

42. Hung Chang-tai suggests that urban cultural forms and rural folk art were often interchangeable and distinctions between them were rendered ambiguous when both forms were introduced into the Chinese countryside. Hung Chang-tai, *War and Popular Culture: Resistance in Modern China, 1937–1945* (Berkeley: University of California Press, 1994), 11.

43. Regarding the term "cultural united line," see Mao Tse-tung, "The United Front in the Cultural Work," a talk given on October 30, 1944, *The Selected Works of Mao Tse-tung*, vol. 3 (Beijing: Renmin chubanshe, 1967), 961.

44. Imperial China also witnessed the entangled relation between law and literature: "the 'literary' permeated the processes of seeking and administering justice at all levels." In Daniel M. Youd, "Beyond Bao: Moral Ambiguity and the Law in Late Imperial Chinese Narrative Literature," in *Writing and Law in Late Imperial China: Crime, Conflict, and Judgment*, ed. Robert E. Hegel and Katherine Carlitz (Seattle: University of Washington Press, 2007), 215. Modern China also witnessed the simultaneous rise of new fiction and new legal discourse in 1902, and literature and law continued to be intertwined; see David Der-wei Wang, *The Monster That Is History: History, Violence, and Fictional Writing in Twentieth-Century China* (Berkeley: University of California Press, 2004), 41–42.

45. The movement from newspapers to the oral network also constituted "a chain of transmission through which events were both reported and interpreted in ways that reflected the outlook of the rural recipients as much as the ideologies of the urban modernizers who composed the newspapers." See Henrietta Harrison, "Newspapers and Nationalism in Rural China 1890–1929," *Past and Present* 166 (2000): 183.

46. For a detailed discussion about the storytelling in the border region, see Hung Chang-tai, "Reeducating a Blind Storyteller: Han Qixiang and the Chinese Communist Storytelling Campaign," *Modern China* 19, no. 4 (1993): 395–426.

47. Cong, *Marriage, Law and Gender in Revolutionary China*, 173, 271.

48. Prasenjit Duara, *Rescuing History from the Nation: Questioning Narratives of Modern China* (Chicago: University of Chicago Press, 1995), 31–32.

49. Haiyan Lee, "Tears that Crumbled the Great Wall: The Archaeology of Feeling in the May Fourth Folklore Movement," *Journal of Asian Studies* 64 (2005): 35–65.

50. Lydia Liu, "A Folksong Immortal and Official Popular Culture in Twentieth-Century China," *Writing and Materiality in China* (Cambridge, MA: Harvard University Asia Center, 2003), 554.

51. Quoted in Lydia Liu, "A Folksong Immortal," 554.

52. Leo Lee and Andrew Nathan, "The Beginnings of Mass Culture: Journalism and Fiction in the Late Ch'ing and Beyond," in *Popular Culture in Late Imperial China*, ed. David Johnson, Andrew Nathan, and Evelyn S, Rawski (Berkeley: University of California Press, 1985), 388.

53. Benedict Anderson, *Imagined Communities*, 34–35.

54. Walter Benjamin. *Illuminations*, trans. Harry Zohn (New York: Schocken Books. 1968), 158–59.

55. Regarding the invention of Aunt Li, see Cong, *Marriage, Law and Gender in Revolutionary China*, 224–25.

56. For details, see Su Li, *Law and Literature: A Case Study of Traditional Chinese Drama* [Falv yu wenxue: yi Zhongguo chuantong xiju wei cailiao] (Beijing: Shenghuo, dushu, xinzhi sanlian shudian, 2006), 95–99.

57. Sun Xiaozhong and Gao Ming eds., *A Collection of Materials on Rural Reconstruction in Yan'an* [Yan'an xiangcun jianshe ziliao], vol. 2 (Shanghai: Shanghai University Press, 2012), 385–86, 387–89.

58. Zhao Chaogou, *Yan'an in January* [Yan'an yiyue] (Nanjing: Xinmin baoshe, 1946), 206, 212. When a group of foreign journalists visited Yan'an in 1944, they were impressed by the broad mobilization in agricultural and handicraft production. Israel Epstein, "The Shaan-Gan-Ning Border Area I Saw" [Wo suo kandaode shanganning bianqu], in *Yan'an and the Liberation Area in the Eyes of the Foreign Journalists* [Waiguo jizhe yanzhong de Yan'an ji jiefangqu], ed. Qi Wen (Dalian: Dazhong Shudian, 1946), 5.

59. Sun Xiaozhong and Gao Ming, eds., *A Collection of Materials on Rural Reconstruction in Yan'an* (Yan'an xiangcun jianshe ziliao), vol. 2 (Shanghai: Shanghai University Press, 2012), 400–402, 413–14.

60. Xiaotong Fei, *From the Soil: The Foundations of Chinese Society*, trans. Gary G. Hamilton and Wang Zheng (Berkeley: University of California Press, 1992), 102.

61. Sun Xiaozhong and Gao Ming eds., *A Collection of Materials on Rural Reconstruction in Yan'an* (Yan'an xiangcun jianshe ziliao), vol. 1 (Shanghai: Shanghai University Press, 2012), 331–34, 338–44.

62. Roslyn Lee Hammers, *Pictures of Tilling and Weaving: Art, Labor, and Technology in Song and Yuan China* (Hong Kong: Hong Kong University Press, 2011), 1, 3.

63. Yuan Jing, *Liu Qiao'er Seeking Justice* [Liu Qiaoer Gaozhuang] (Harbin: Dongbei shudian, 1947), 44.

64. Jing, *Liu Qiao'er*, 54.
65. In Han Qixiang, *Liu Qiao Tuanyuan* [Liu Qiao's Reunion] (Wu'an: Xinhua shudian, 1949), 1.
66. Doris Sommer, "Irresistible Romance: The Foundational Fictions of Latin America," in *Nation and Narration*, ed. Homi K. Bhabha (London: Routledge, 1990), 71–98, 76.
67. For a discussion of the urban-based fictional genre "revolution plus romance" emerging in the late 1920s, see Jianmei Liu, *Revolution Plus Love: Literary History, Women's Bodies, and Thematic Repetition in Twentieth-Century Chinese Fiction* (Honolulu: University of Hawai'i Press, 2003); Haiyan Lee, *Revolution of the Heart: A Genealogy of Love in China, 1900–1950* (Stanford: Stanford University Press, 2007), 255–97.
68. Yuan Jing, *Liu Qiao'er gaozhuang* [Liu Qiao'er Seeking Justice] (Ha'erbin: Dongbei shudian, 1947), 43.
69. Sulamith Potter, "The Cultural Construction of Emotion in China," *Ethos* 16, no. 2 (June 1988): 199–206.
70. Sun Xiaozhong and Gao Ming, eds., *A Collection of Materials on Rural Reconstruction in Yan'an* (Yan'an xiangcun jianshe ziliao), vol. 1 (Shanghai: Shanghai University Press, 2012), 210.
71. Sun Xiaozhong and Gao Ming, eds., *A Collection of Materials on Rural Reconstruction in Yan'an* [Yan'an xiangcun jianshe ziliao], vol. 1 (Shanghai: Shanghai University Press, 2012), 227.
72. Xiaobing Tang, "Listening to Yan'an: Illumination from a Sonic Experience" (Lingting Yan'an: yiduan tingjue jingyan de qishi), *Journal of Modern Chinese Studies* [*Xiandai zhongwen xuekan*] (January 2017): 4–11.
73. Mao Zedong, "Oppose Book Worship," https://www.marxists.org/reference/archive/mao/selected-works/volume-6/mswv6_11.htm (accessed Nov. 4, 2019).
74. Yuan Jing, *Liu Qiao'er gaozhuang* [Liu Qiao Seeking Justice], 40–45.
75. For a detailed discussion of the culture of intimacy in Yan'an, see David Apter and Tony Saich. *Revolutionary Discourse in Mao's Republic* (Cambridge, MA: Harvard University Press, 1994), 87–88.
76. Quoted in Louise White, *Speaking with Vampires: Rumor and History in Colonial Africa* (Berkeley: University of California Press, 2000), 59–60; also Max Gluckman, "Gossip and Scandal," *Current Anthropology* 4, no. 3 (1963): 307–16, 312.
77. Tong Lam, *A Passion for Facts: Social Surveys and the Construction of the Chinese Nation-State, 1900–1949* (Berkeley: University of California Press, 2011), 94.
78. Wilt Idema, "Introduction," *Judge Bao and the Rule of Law: Eight Ballad-Stories from the Period 1250–1450*, trans. Wilt Idema (Singapore: World Scientific Publishing Co., 2010), ix–xxxiv.
79. Prasenjit Duara, "Superscribing Symbols: The Myth of Guandi, Chinese God of War," *Journal of Asian Studies* 47, no. 4 (1988): 778–95.
80. Yuan Jing, *Liu Qiao Seeking Justice*, 48–54.
81. James Scott, *Domination and the Arts of Resistance: Hidden Transcripts* (New Haven: Yale University Press, 1990).
82. Michael Warner, *Publics and Counterpublics* (Brooklyn: Zone Books, 2005), 78.

83. For a discussion about the party's carefully orchestrated public accusation meetings see Elizabeth Perry, "Moving the Masses: Emotion Work in the Chinese Revolution," *Mobilization: An International Journal* 7, no. 2 (2002): 116–17. For a discussion on how the investigation meetings resulted in ad hoc orthodoxies rather than a variety of opinions, see Thomas Mullaney, *Coming to Terms with the Nation: Ethnic Classification in Modern China* (Berkeley: University of California Press, 2011), 98.

84. Cai Xiang takes the rural masses' willingness to speak in collective meetings and public discussions about their ordinary concerns as a form of participation; Cai Xiang, *Revolution/Narrative: Chinese Socialist Literary and Cultural Imagination, 1949–1966* [Geming/xushu: zhongguo shehui zhuyi wenxue wenhua xiangxiang] (Beijing: Peking University Press, 2010), 354–62. For a detailed discussion of the fictional representation of the violence involved in the public trial, see David Der-wei Wang, *The Monster That Is History*, 70–73. Mühlhahn's characterization of "democratic terror" as a form of revolutionary-style justice took the form of terrorism legitimized by the masses, see *Criminal Justice in China*, 161.

85. Sun Xiaozhong and Gao Ming, eds., *A Collection of Materials on Rural Reconstruction in Yan'an* [Yan'an xiangcun jianshe ziliao], vol. 4 (Shanghai: Shanghai University Press, 2012), 142–51.

86. Sun and Gao, eds., *A Collection of Materials*, vol. 4, 140.

87. Sun and Gao, eds., *A Collection of Materials*, vol. 4, 142–51, 146–47.

88. Gao Minfu, "Introduction," in Han Qixiang, *Liu Qiao Tuanyuan*, 8.

89. Hung, Changtai, "Reeducating a Blind Storyteller: Han Qixiang and the Chinese Communist Storytelling Campaign," *Modern China* 19, no. 4 (Oct. 1993): 405–20.

90. Hung, Chang-tai, "Reeducating," 410, 418

91. For a detailed discussion of storytelling, see Walter Benjamin, "The Storyteller: Reflections on the Works of Nikolai Leskov" in *Illuminations: Essays and Reflections*, ed. Hannah Arendt (New York: Schocken Books, 1968), 83–109.

92. Sun and Gao, eds., *A Collection of Materials*, vol. 4, 142–51, 146–47.

93. Richard Jean So, *Transpacific Community*, 168–69. Hung Chang-tai also points out the effectiveness of the Communist propaganda as a political vehicle to create a new society that symbolizes the communist future and represents a new political culture. Hung Chang-tai, *War and Popular Culture: Resistance in Modern China, 1937–1945* (Berkeley: University of California Press, 1994), 221–69.

94. Richard Jean So, *Transpacific Community*, 172.

95. David Holm, *Art and Ideology in Revolutionary China* (New York: Oxford University Press, 1990), 20.

96. Walter J. Ong, *Orality and Literacy: The Technologizing of the Word* (London: Routledge, 1982), 45–46.

97. Ong, *Orality and Literacy*, 42.

98. Gao Minfu, "Introduction," 5–6.

99. For example, Cai Xiang, *Revolution/Narrative: Chinese Socialist Literary and Cultural Imagination, 1949–1966* [Geming/xushu: zhongguo shehui zhuyi wenxue wenhua xiangxiang] (Beijing: Peking University Press, 2010), 65.

100. Brian James DeMare, *Mao's Cultural Army: Drama Troupes in China's Rural Revolution*. (Cambridge: Cambridge University Press, 2015), 5–6.

101. Han Qixiang, *Liu Qiao Tuanyuan* [Liu Qiao Reunion] (Wu'an: Xinhua shudian, 1949), 36.

102. For a detailed discussion of "conscience" (*liangxin*) and its importance in rural society, see Ellen Oxfeld, *Drink Water, But Remember the Source: Moral Discourse in a Chinese Village* (Berkeley: University of California Press, 2010), 45–72.

103. Han Qixiang, *Liu Qiao Tuanyuan* [Liu Qiao Reunion] (Wu'an: Xinhua shudian, 1949).

104. For a detailed analysis of Han's narrative technique, see Hung Chang-tai 1993.

105. For a similar discussion, see Ong, *Orality and Literacy*, 33–36.

106. Han, *Liu Qiao Tuanyuan*, 56

107. Sun and Gao, eds., *A Collection of Materials*, vol. 1, 448.

108. Cong, Xiaoping, *Marriage, Law, and Gender in Revolutionary China* (Cambridge: Cambridge University Press, 2016), 243.

109. Ann Anagnost describes "speaking bitterness" narrative this way: "the speech of the subaltern subject is not the spontaneous flow of pent-up sorrow but the careful reworking of perception and experience into the narrative frame of Marxist class struggle as the specific lens that renders this vision." See *National Past-Times: Narrative, Representation, and Power in Modern China* (Durham: Duke University Press, 1997), 28

110. For details, see Cong, *Marriage, Law, and Gender in Revolutionary China*.

111. See Liu Chunhua, "Peasants Don't Like Some Rural Films" ("Nongmin buxihuan youxie nongyepian"), in *Popular Film* [Dazhong dianying] (October 1957): 17.

112. For a detailed discussion of the application of the marriage law after the founding of the P.R.C., see Neil Jeffrey Diamant, *Revolutionizing the Family: Politics, Love, and Divorce in Urban and Rural China, 1949–1968* (Berkeley: University of California, 2000); and for a discussion of the life of the rural women in rural Shanxi Province in the 1950s and 1960s, see Gail Hershatter, *The Gender of Memory: Rural Women and China's Collective Past* (Berkeley: University of California Press, 2011).

113. Now the residence of Feng Zhiqin (1924–2015) has been turned into an exhibition site for "Red Tourism," and Feng herself became a peasant entrepreneur in the late 1980s and 1990s. See http://culture.people.com.cn/BIG5/n/2015/0213/c172318-26562462.html, accessed on Nov. 14, 2917.

Chapter 5

1. "Return to Shaoshan" (Dao Shaoshan), in *Mao Zedong shici quanbian* [A Complete Collection of the Poems of Mao Zedong] (Wuhan: Hubei jiaoyu chubanshe, 1993), 203. The translation is from *The Poems of Mao Tse-Tung*, trans. Willis Barns Tone in collaboration with Ko Ching-Po (New York: Harper & Row, 1972), 94.

2. Zhonggong zhongyang bangongting, ed., "The Experience of Exercising the Cooperative Regulation in a County" [Zai yige xiangli jinxing hezuohua guihua de jingyan], *The High Tide of Socialism in the Chinese Countryside* [Zhongguo nongcunde shehuizhuyi gaochao] (Beijing: Renmin chubanshe, 1956), 320.

3. For details, see Mark Selden, "Mao Zedong and the Political Economy of Chinese Development," in *Marxism and the Chinese Experience: Issues in Contemporary Chinese Socialism*, ed. Arif Dirlik and Maurice Meisner (Armonk, NY: M. E. Sharpe, 1989), 43–58, 52; Maurice Meisner, *Mao's China and After: A History of the People's Republic* (New York: Free Press, 1986), 278–79.

4. In fact, when the rural industrialization started was still a controversial topic among China historians. Though rural industries like textile, food processing, and paper-making date back centuries, the modern state-led rural industrialization started in 1958 in China. Since the 1950s and 1960s, rural industrialization has become a worldwide phenomenon as both developing and developed countries sought to transform from agricultural to industrial countries; rural industrialization has been considered the key solution to development. In China this was no exception, and industrializing the countryside was part of the socialist blueprint for a promising future (see Zhu Daohua and Feng Meifa, *Nongcun gongyehua wenti tansuo* [*On Questions about Rural Industrialization*] (Beijing: Zhongguo nongye chubanshe, 1995, 1–2). For a thorough discussion of China's industrializing path in the second half of the twentieth century, see Carl Riskin, *China's Political Economy: The Quest for Development Since 1949* (Oxford: Oxford University Press, 1987).

5. See Van Fleit Hang, *Literature the People Love: Reading Literature in the Early Maoist Period (1949–1966)* (New York: Palgrave Macmillan, 2013); Christine I. Ho, "The People Eat for Free and the Art of Collective Production in Maoist China," *The Art Bulletin* 98, no. 3 (2016), 348–72; David Holm, *Art and Ideology in Revolutionary China* (Oxford: Oxford University Press, 1991); Richard King, *Milestones on a Golden Road: Writing for Chinese Socialism, 1945–80* (Vancouver: UBC Press, 2013); Jason McGrath, "Communists Have More Fun! The Dialectics of Fulfillment in Cinema of the People's Republic of China," *World Picture*, 3; Barbara Mittler, *A Continuous Revolution: Making Sense of Cultural Revolution Culture* (Cambridge, MA: Harvard Asia Center Publications, 2012); Laikwan Pang, *The Art of Cloning: Creative Production during China's Cultural Revolution* (London: Verso, 2017); Ban Wang, *The Sublime Figure of History: Aesthetics and Politics in Twentieth-Century China* (Stanford: Stanford University Press, 1997).

6. See Alexander Cook, ed., *Mao's Little Red Book: A Global History* (Cambridge: Cambridge University Press, 2014); Tina Mai Chen, "The Human-Machine Continuum in Maoism: The Intersection of Soviet Socialist Realism, Japanese Theoretical Physics, and Chinese Revolutionary Theory," *Cultural Critique* 80 (Winter 2012): 151–80; Nicolai Volland, *Socialist Cosmopolitanism: The Chinese Literary Universe, 1945–1965* (New York: Columbia University Press, 2017).

7. Benedict Anderson, *Imagined Communities: Reflections on the Origin and Spread of Nationalism* (London: Verso, 1983), 32.

8. A few exceptions are seen in the first modern Chinese spoken drama, *New Village*

Head [Xincun zheng, Zhang Pengchun, 1918], and the rural play *Cross the River* [*Guodu*] in chapter 2. In both plays, the urban-educated young men merge into the village life, contributing to the construction of their hometown.

9. Franco Marretti, *The Way of the World: The Bildungsroman in European Culture* (London: Verso, 2000), 5.

10. Marretti, *The Way of the World*, 5. The young people have not experienced the "lost illusion."

11. Cai Xiang, *Revolution/Narrative: Chinese Socialist Literary and Cultural Imagination, 1949–1966* [Geming/xushu: zhongguo shehui zhuyi wenxue wenhua xiangxiang] (Beijing: Peking University Press, 2010), 354–62.

12. Borge Bakken, *The Exemplary Society: Human Improvement, Social Control, and the Dangers of Modernity in China* (Oxford: Oxford University Press, 2000); Donald Munro, *The Concept of Man in Contemporary China* (Ann Arbor: University of Michigan Press, 1977), 135–57.

13. Maurice Meisner, *Marxism, Maoism, and Utopianism: Eight Essays* (Madison: University of Wisconsin Press, 1982), 71–72.

14. Jacob Eyferth, *Eating Rice from Bamboo Roots: The Social History of a Community of Handicraft Papermakers in Rural Sichuan, 1920–2000* (Cambridge, MA: Harvard University Press, 2009), 9.

15. This poster is from https://chineseposters.net/posters/pc-1958-014.php, in the website "chineseposters.net" maintained by Stefan R. Landsberger. There is no information regarding the identity of the author Zhang Yuqing, who designed this poster.

16. For a detailed discussion of mechanization in China's agricultural transformation, see Sigrid Schmalzer, *Red Revolution, Green Revolution: Scientific Farming in Socialist China* (Chicago: University of Chicago Press, 2016), 8–9.

17. For a detailed discussion on the impact of social change on rural women in 1950s and 1960s China, see Gail Hershatter, *The Gender of Memory: Rural Women and China's Collective Past* (Berkeley: University of California Press, 2011).

18. James Scott, *Seeing Like a State: How Certain Schemes to Improve the Human Condition Have Failed* (New Haven: Yale University Press, 1999), 254, 257.

19. Anonymous, "Two-Dragon Commune in Progress" [Qianjin Zhong de shuanglong gongshe], *China Pictorial* 15 (1960): 8–9.

20. Anonymous, "Two-Dragon Commune in Progress," 8.

21. Anonymous, "Small-Scale Reservoir Has Big Benefits" [Xiaoxing shuiku shouyi da], *China Pictorial*, April 16, 1960, 24–25.

22. For example, Anonymous, "The Scene of the Village" [Nongcun xiaojing], *China Pictorial* 13 (1960): 24–25.

23. Julian Wolfreys, *Introducing Criticism in the 21st Century* (Edinburgh: Edinburgh University Press, 2002), 157.

24. For details, see Tang Tsou, *The Cultural Revolution and Post-Mao Reform: A Historical Perspective*, (Chicago: University of Chicago Press, 1986), 260.

25. Raymond Williams, *Keywords: A Vocabulary of Culture and Society* (New York: Oxford University Press, 1985), 82.

26. Williams, *Keywords*, 84–86.

27. Laikwan Pang, *Creativity and Its Discontents: China's Creative Industries and Intellectual Property Rights Offenses* (Durham: Duke University Press, 2012), 30.

28. Pang, *Creativity and Its Discontents*, 31.

29. See Wolfreys, *Introducing Criticism in the 21st Century*, 151–78.

30. Judith Shapiro, *Mao's War Against Nature: Politics and the Environment in Revolutionary China*, Cambridge: Cambridge University Press (2001).

31. Sigrid Schmalzer, *Red Revolution, Green Revolution*, 4.

32. Mark Selden, *The Yenan Way in Revolutionary China* (Cambridge, MA: Harvard University Press, 1974), 210.

33. Richard King, *Milestones on a Golden Road: Writing for Chinese Socialism, 1945–80* (Vancouver: UBC Press, 2013), 71–74.

34. Sigrid Schmalzer, *The People's Peking Man: Popular Science and Human Identity in Twentieth-Century China* (Chicago: University of Chicago Press, 2008), 7.

35. Paola Iovene, *Tales of Futures Past: Literature and Anticipation in Contemporary China* (Stanford, CA: Stanford University Press, 2014), 32.

36. Matthew Johnson, "The Science Education Film: Cinematizing Technocracy and Internationalizing Development," *Journal of Chinese Cinemas* 5, no. 1 (2011): 31–53.

37. Regarding the self-made inventor as a phenomenon in colonial Korea, see Jung Lee, "Invention without Science: 'Korean Edisons' and the Changing Understanding of Technology in Colonial Korea," *Technology and Culture* 54, no. 4 (October 2013): 782–814.

38. Anonymous, "Advancing toward Irrigation" [Xiang shuilihua yuejin], *China Pictorial*, December 1959, 2–3.

39. Anonymous, "Advancing toward Irrigation," 2.

40. Anonymous, "Advancing toward Irrigation," 3.

41. Anonymous, "The Peasant Inventor" [Nongmin famingjia], *China Pictorial*, December 1959, 15.

42. According to Xia Yan, "China [had] already exported 297 long feature films by 1959, and 631 documentaries, science educational films, and animation films, and built a distribution and screening relationship with 80 countries and areas. The films had been much welcomed in Southeast Asia, West Asia, Africa, and Latin America." Xia Yan, "Let Three Flags Float on the Screen," in *Our Socialist Films in Development* [Zai fazhanzhong de woguo shehui zhuyi dianying], ed. Zhongguo dianying chuban she (Beijing: Zhongguo dianying chuban she, 1961), 2.

43. Matthew Johnson, "The Science Education Film: Cinematizing Technocracy and Internationalizing Development," *Journal of Chinese Cinemas* 5, no. 1 (2011): 49.

44. For a discussion of the social function of the films in the socialist period, see Ban Wang, *The Sublime Figure of History: Aesthetics and Politics in Twentieth-Century China* (Stanford, CA: Stanford University Press, 1997), 124. The rural-subject films could be classified into these categories: (1) rural revolutionary struggle, (2) rural production and construction, (3) rural life stories, and (4) the rural ethnic minority. See Li Huanzheng, *Rural China on the Silver Screen: A Study on the Customs and Everyday Lifestyle in*

Rural-Subject Films, 1949–1966 [Yinmushang de xiangtu zhongguo: shiqinian nongcun ticai dianying Zhong de minus yu richang shenghuo fangshi yanjiu] (Beijing: Zhongguo nongye daxue chubanshe, 2013).

45. See Li Xianyou, "Three Young People with Different Personalities: On the Film *The Young People in Our Village,*" *The Popular Cinema* [*Dazhong dianying*] 9 (1960): 15.

46. The TV documentary titled "New Legend of Cinema—*The Young People in Our Village*: Love is Like Water" [Xindianying chuanqi—*Women cunli de nianqingren*: aiqing ru shui], hosted by Cui Yongyuan, recalled the great influential power of the 1959 film at the time.

47. See the interview with Su Li, in another episode of the same TV documentary titled "Love Is Like Electricity" [Aiqing ru dian], hosted by Cui Yongyuan.

48. See Ban Wang, "Socialist Realism," in *Words and Its Stories, Words and Their Stories: Essays on the Language of the Chinese Revolution,* ed. Ban Wang (Leiden: Brill 2010), 101–18; Xudong Zhang, "The Power of Rewriting: Postrevolutionary Discourse on Chinese Socialist Realism," in *Socialist Realism without Shores,* ed. Thomas Lahusen and Evgeny Dobrenko (Durham: Duke University Press, 1997), 282–309.

49. Yomi Braester, *Painting the City Red: Chinese Cinema and the Urban Contract* (Durham: Duke University Press, 2010), 6.

50. Tina Mai Chen, "Propagating the Propaganda Film: The Meaning of Film in CCP Writings, 1949–1965," *Modern Chinese Literature and Culture* 15, no. 2 (Fall 2003): 154–93.

51. For details, see Judith Shapiro, *Mao's War Against Nature: Politics and the Environment in Revolutionary China* (Cambridge: Cambridge University Press, 2001).

52. Such playful scenes can be seen in films such as *Landmine Warfare* [*Dilei zhan,* Tang Yingqi, Xu Da, and Wu Jianhai dir., 1963], *Zhang Ga the Soldier Boy* [*Xiaobing Zhangga,* Cui Wei and Ouyang Hongying dir., 1964], and *Tunnel Warfare* (*Didao Zhan,* Ren Xudong dir., 1965). These films also represented warfare as a form of play. Many films with a playful spirit (including the two episodes of *The Young People in Our Village*) were produced between 1962 and 1964, one of the least controlled periods in the socialist era, after the end of the Great Leap Forward in 1960 and before the "Four Cleans [*siqing*]" purges between 1963 and 1966. For example, *Landmine Warfare,* about the Chinese people's fight against the Japanese invaders, contains a play element. With its association with resourcefulness and energy, being mischievous is considered a positive quality appreciated by the party and the people.

53. Zhen Zhang, *An Amorous History of the Silver Screen: Shanghai Cinema, 1896–1937* (Chicago: University of Chicago Press, 2005), 13.

54. Xinyu Dong, "The Laborer at Play: *Laborer's Love,* the Operational Aesthetic, and the Comedy of Inventions," *Modern Chinese Literature and Culture* (Fall 2008): 7.

55. Johan Huizinga, *Homo Ludens: A Study of the Play-Element in Culture* (Martino Centre, CT: Martino Publishing, 2014), 4.

56. Huizinga, *Homo Ludens,* 13.

57. Huizinga, *Homo Ludens,* 1.

58. Huizinga, *Homo Ludens,* 60.

59. Huizinga, *Homo Ludens*, 2–3.
60. Huizinga, *Homo Ludens*, 6.
61. Huizinga, *Homo Ludens*, 211.
62. Krista Van Fleit Hang briefly mentions that there was no distinction between leisure and labor in socialist China, which means labor was an ongoing activity, without stop or rest; see *Literature the People Love*, 152.
63. Karatani Kojin, *Origins of Modern Japanese Literature*, trans. Brett de Bary (Durham: Duke University Press, 1993), 121.
64. Elizabeth J. Perry, "Moving the Masses: Emotion Work in the Chinese Revolution," *Mobilization: An International Journal* 7, no. 2 (2002): 112.
65. Jason McGrath, "Communists Have More Fun! The Dialectics of Fulfillment in Cinema of the People's Republic of China," *World Picture* 3 (2009): 1.
66. Hang, *Literature the People Love: Reading Chinese Texts from the Early Maoist Period (1949–1966)* (New York: Palgrave Macmillan, 2013), 150; Iovene. *Tales of Futures*, 23.
67. Arif Dirlik, "The Politics of the Cultural Revolution in Historical Perspective," in *The Chinese Cultural Revolution Reconsidered: Beyond Purge and Holocaust*, ed. Kamyee Lam (New York: Palgrave Macmillan, 2003), 165.
68. Jiwei Ci, *Dialectic of the Chinese Revolution: From Utopianism to Hedonism* (Stanford: Stanford University Press, 1994), 168.
69. Christine I. Ho, "The People Eat for Free and the Art of Collective Production in Maoist China," *The Art Bulletin* 98, no. 3 (2016): 348.
70. Hang, *Literature the People Love*, 147–50; Iovene, *Tales of Futures Past*, 22.
71. Klaus Mühlhahn, *Criminal Justice in China: A History* (Cambridge, MA: Harvard University Press, 2009), 149.
72. See Mao Zedong, *Quotations from Chairman Mao Tsetung* (Peking: Foreign Language Press, 1972), 201–2. This fable is under the topic of "Self-Reliance and Arduous Struggle." The original written piece, "The Foolish Old Man Who Removed the Mountains," appears in *Selected Works of Mao* (June 11, 1945), vol. III, 322. For a detailed discussion of this fable, see chapter 4 in Barbara Mittler, *A Continuous Revolution: Making Sense of Cultural Revolution Culture* (Cambridge, MA: Harvard Asia Center Publications, 2012), 189–256. Barbara Mittler uses this fable as an example to show the power of Mao's words and their effectiveness and authority during the Cultural Revolution. The visual manifestations of the fable also exhibit the formation of the collective subjectivity and its power, which could transform the world (202).
73. For a discussion of the "malleability of man," see Munro, *The Concept of Man in Contemporary China*.
74. For a detailed analysis of socialist romanticism and socialist realism, see Pang Laikwan, *The Art of Cloning: Creative Production During China's Cultural Revolution* (London: Verso, 2017), 33.
75. Chen Mo, "A Symphony of Labor, Love, and Revolutionary Drive: On *The Young People in Our Village*," *Popular Cinema* 18 (1959): 25.

76. For a discussion of the Chinese way of representing the male-female interaction, see Chris Berry, "Sexual Difference and the Viewing Subject in Li Shuangshuang and The In-laws," in *Perspectives on Chinese Cinema*, ed. Chris Berry (London: BFI Publication, 1991).

77. Laura Mulvey, "Visual Pleasure and Narrative Cinema," in *Film Theory and Criticism: Introductory Readings*, ed. Leo Braudy and Marshall Cohen (New York: Oxford University Press, 1999), 833–44. Mulvey revised her argument in a later essay, "Changes: Thoughts on Myth, Narrative and Historical Experience," in *Visual and Other Pleasure*, ed. Laura Mulvey (Bloomington: Indiana University Press, 1989), 159–76.

78. Mao also indicates that "We are now carrying out a revolution not only in the social system, the change from private to public ownership, but also in technology, the change from handcraft to large-scale modern machine production, and the two revolutions are interconnected." See *Quotations from Chairman Mao Tse-Tung* (Peking: Foreign Language Press, 1967), 26.

79. Schmalzer, *The People's Peking Man*, 63.

80. Schmalzer, *The People's Peking Man*, 63.

81. Meisner, *Mao's China and After*, 270.

82. Schmalzer, *Red Revolution, Green Revolution*, 34–38.

83. Schmalzer, *Red Revolution, Green Revolution*, 36

84. Matei Calinescu, *Five Faces of Modernity: Modernism, Avant-garde, Decadence, Kitsch, Postmodernism* (Durham: Duke University Press, 1987), 48.

85. Xinyu Dong, "The Laborer at Play: *Laborer's Love*, the Operational Aesthetic, and the Comedy of Inventions," *Modern Chinese Literature and Culture* (Fall 2008): 7.

86. Zhen Zhang, *An Amorous History of the Silver Screen: Shanghai Cinema, 1896–1937* (Chicago: University of Chicago Press, 2005), 12–30.

87. Joseph Needham suggests that "the world owes far more to the relatively *silent craftsmen* of ancient and medieval China than to the Alexandrian mechanics, articulate theoreticians though they were" ("Science and China's Influence on the World," in *The Legacy of China*, ed. Raymond Dawson [Oxford: Clarendon Press, 1964], 238).

88. Quoted in Susan Buck-Morss, *The Dialectics of Seeing: Walter Benjamin and the Arcades Project* (Cambridge, MA: MIT Press, 1991), 125–26.

89. I thank Jacob Eyferth for pointing this out for me.

90. Eyferth, *Eating Rice from Bamboo Roots*, 44.

91. Scott, *Seeing Like a State*, 253.

92. Scott, *Seeing Like a State*, 224–25.

93. Scott, *Seeing Like a State*, 225.

94. Scott, *Seeling Like a State*, 253.

95. King, *Milestones on a Golden Road*, 94–96.

96. For example, the first episode of *The Young People in Our Village* was circulated in the Soviet Union, Great Britain, North Korea, North Vietnam, Hong Kong, and other countries. *A Compilation of the Statistics about the Distribution and Exhibition of the Chinese Film, 1958–1960* [Zhongguo dianying faxing fangying tongji ziliao huibian, 1958–1960, Zhongguo dianying faxing fangying gongsi, 1961].

97. See Schmalzer, *Red Revolution, Green Revolution*, 35. Wang Mingming, *Walking on the Countryside* [Zouzai xiangtu shang] (Beijing: Zhongguo renmin daxue chubanshe, 2009), 233–35.

98. Dai Jinhua, "Foreword," to Chen Xiaomei, *Occidentalism: A Theory of Counter-Discourse in Post-Mao China*, 2nd ed. (Lanham, MD: Roman & Littlefield, 2002), ix–xxiii, xiii–xiv. For a discussion of the uniqueness of Chinese socialism as an alternative to Soviet-style bureaucratic socialism and various forms of capitalism, see Lin Chun, *The Transformation of Chinese Socialism* (Durham, NC: Duke University Press, 2006).

99. Richard Wolin, *The Wind from the East: French Intellectuals, the Cultural Revolution, and the Legacy of the 1960s* (Princeton: Princeton University Press, 2010), 1–21.

100. Wolin, *The Wind from the East*, 11–12. For a discussion of the global circulation of Maoism, see Alexander C. Cook, ed., *Mao's Little Red Book: A Global History* (Cambridge: Cambridge University Press, 2014).

101. See Maurice Meisner, "Marx, Mao, and Deng on the Division of Labor in History," in *Marxism and the Chinese Experience: Issues in Contemporary Chinese Socialism*, ed. Arif Dirlik and Maurice Meisner (London: M. E. Sharpe, 1989), 79. Without reliable information about what was going on in China, in the world outside China, particularly in France in the 1960s, Maoism was widely regarded for presenting a genuinely humane version of socialism. See Wolin, *The Wind from the East*, 1–21.

102. Rhoads Murphey, *The Fading of the Maoist Vision: City and Country in China's Development* (New York: Methuen, 1980), 41–42. For a discussion of how Western scientists took China as "a model of sensible and sustainable environmental policy," see Schmalzer, *Red Revolution, Green Revolution*, 14, and chapter 2.

103. Eyferth, *Eating Rice from Bamboo Roots*, 10–11; Selden, "Mao Zedong and the Political Economy of Chinese Development," 53.

104. Arif Dirlik, "Revolutionary Hegemony and the Language of Revolution: Chinese Socialism between Present and Future," in *Marxism and the Chinese Experience: Issues in Contemporary Chinese Socialism*, ed. Arif Dirlik and Maurice Meisner (Armonk, NY: M. E. Sharpe, 1989), 27–42.

105. Films such as *Life* [*Rensheng*, dir. Wu Tianming, 1984], *Old Well* [*Laojing*, 1986], and *In the Wild Mountains* [*Yeshan*, 1986] show the dramatic psychological change of the young rural residents in the post-Mao reform and opening. Like *The Young People in Our Village*, these films feature the homecoming experience of educated rural youth.

106. Sheldon Lu, "Introduction: Cinema, Ecology, Modernity," in *Chinese Ecocinema in the Age of Environmental Challenge*, ed. Sheldon Lu and Jiayan Mi (Hong Kong: Hong Kong University Press, 2009), 5.

107. For a close reading of the film *Old Well*, see Rey Chow, *Primitive Passions: Visuality, Sexuality, Ethnography, and Contemporary Chinese Cinema* (New York: Columbia University Press, 1995), 65–66, 69–78.

Chapter 6

1. *Hushi riji* [The Nurse's Diary], directed by Tao Jin (Shanghai: Jiangnan Film Studio, 1957), film, 96 min.

2. Peter Watson, *The Modern Mind: An Intellectual History of the 20th Century* (New York: Harper Perennial, 2002), 186–205.

3. For a relevant discussion of the land-reclamation campaign, see Daisy Yan Du. "Socialist Modernity in the Wasteland: Changing Representations of the Female Tractor Driver in China, 1949–1964," *Modern Chinese Literature and Culture*, Spring 2017: 68–69.

4. Mao Zedong, *Quotations from Chairman Mao Tsetung* (Peking: Foreign Language Press, 1972), 36.

5. According to Anthony Giddens, disembedding refers to "the 'lifting out' of social relations from local contexts of interaction and their restructuring across indefinite spans of time-space." In Anthony Giddens, *The Consequences of Modernity* (Cambridge, UK: Polity Press, 1990), 21.

6. John Fitzgerald indicates that the "awakening" structure should be applied not only to the people, but to China's land: "While people were to be awakened through instruction, the landscape was to be awakened with saws and dredges, picks and hammers, road rollers and steam trains, to the rhythm of 'construction.' Sun Yatsen compiled elaborate plans to bring the country together by constructing tunnels and highways, huge canals and deep-sea ports." John Fitzgerald, *Awakening China: Politics, Culture, and Class in the Nationalist Revolution* (Stanford: Stanford University Press, 1996), 72.

7. Tina Mai Chen, "The Human-Machine Continuum in Maoism: The Intersection of Soviet Socialist Realism, Japanese Theoretical Physics, and Chinese Revolutionary Theory," *Cultural Critique* 80 (Winter 2012): 151–80.

8. These films are distinct from the socialist ethnic minority films that depict concrete frontier life, such as *Five Golden Flowers* (Wuduo jinhua, 1959).

9. For recent discussions of the socialist films and their propaganda function, see Yomi Braester, *Painting the City Red: Chinese Cinema and the Urban Contract* (Durham: Duke University Press, 2010), 13–15; Shouyi Wang, *Revolutionary Cycles in Chinese Cinema, 1951–1979* (New York: Palgrave Macmillan, 2014), 1–24.

10. Wolfgang Schivelbusch, *The Railway Journey: Trains and Travel in the Nineteenth Century* (New York: Urizen, 1979), 33–44.

11. Lynne Kirby, *Parallel Tracks: The Railroad and Silent Cinema* (Durham, NC: Duke University Press, 1997), 205.

12. *A Chinese History of Railway Construction* (Zhongguo Tielu jianshe she), ed. Zhongguo tielu jiansheshi bianweihui (Beijing: Zhongguo tiedao chubanshe, 2003), 37–39.

13. Paul Clark, *Chinese Cinema: Culture and Politics since 1949* (Cambridge: Cambridge University Press, 1987), 57–58.

14. For a detailed history of new Chinese cinema and its relationship to the nation-

state, see chapter 6 in Zhang Yingjin, *Chinese National Cinema* (New York: Routledge, 2004), 189–224. For a discussion of the political desire to incorporate the border areas into China in the Republican period, see Prasenjit Duara, *Sovereignty and Authenticity: Manchukuo and the East Asian Modern* (Lanham, MD: Rowman & Littlefield, 2004), 189–91.

15. Yomi Braester and Tina Mai Chen, "Introduction: Film in the People's Republic of China, 1949–1979: The Missing Years?" *Journal of Chinese Cinemas* 5, no. 1 (2011): 8. Railway travel is also one of the important subjects in the documentary films produced by the South Manchurian Railway Company (Mantetsu) in the Japanese puppet state of Manchuria. Many of the themes under discussion in this essay—movement, technological utopianism, railroads and machines as tools of nation-building, motorized passages from center to periphery—appeared in the Mantetsu documentaries. For details, see Li Jie, "Phantasmagoric Manchukuo: Documentaries Produced by the South Manchurian Railway Company, 1932–1940," *Position: East Asia Cultures Critique* 22, no. 2 (Spring 2014): 329–69. Regarding the image of the train in popular print, see James A. Flath, "The Chinese Railroad View: Transportation Themes in Popular Print, 1873–1915," *Cultural Critique* 58, no. 3 (2004), 168–90.

16. Jeffery Ruoff, "Introduction: The Filmic Fourth Dimension: Cinema as Audiovisual Vehicle," in *Virtual Voyages: Cinema and Travel*, ed. Jeffery Ruoff (Durham: Duke University Press, 2006), 1–24, 2.

17. Anne Friedberg, *Window Shopping: Cinema and the Postmodern* (Berkeley: University of California Press, 1993); Charles Musser, *Before the Nickelodeon: Edwin S. Porter and the Edison Manufacturing Company* (Berkeley: University of California Press, 1991), 260.

18. The film was officially produced by the Northeast Film Studio when the People's Liberation Army was marching to its national victory in October 1948 and was released in May 1949.

19. Weihong Bao, *Fiery Cinema: The Emergence of an Affective Medium in China, 1915–1945* (Minneapolis: University of Minnesota Press, 2015), 82–90.

20. Schivelbusch, *Railway Journey*, 80.

21. Marc Greuther, "Review of *Railways and the Victorian Imagination* by Michael Freeman," *Technology and Culture* 42, no. 3 (July 2001): 604–6.

22. For a discussion about the global cult of speed, see Stephen Kern, *The Culture of Time and Space, 1880–1918* (Cambridge, MA: Harvard University Press, 1983), 109–24.

23. Paola Iovene, *Tales of Futures Past: Anticipation and the Ends of Literature in Contemporary China* (Stanford: Stanford University Press, 2014), 3.

24. Zhang Henshui's novel *Beijing-Shanghai Express* describes the compartment where strangers from capitalist urban life are gathered in the 1930s. For details, see Rey Chow, *Woman and Chinese Modernity: The Politics of Reading between West and East* (Minneapolis: University of Minnesota Press, 1991), 76–82.

25. Elizabeth Perry, "Moving the Masses: Emotion Work in the Chinese Revolution," *Mobilization: An International Journal* 7, no. 2 (2002): 112.

26. Brian Curried, *A National Acoustics: Music and Mass Publicity in Weimar and Nazi Germany* (Minneapolis: University of Minnesota Press, 2006), 12.

27. Arif Dirlik, "Revolutionary Hegemony and the Language of Revolution: Chinese Socialism Between Present and Future," in *Marxism and the Chinese Experience: Issues in Contemporary Chinese Socialism*, ed. Arif Dirlik and Maurice Meisner (Armonk, NY: M. E. Sharpe, 1989), 27–42, 27–28.

28. For example, in his anthology *Rosy Clouds of Dawn Rise in the East* (Dongfang shengqi zhaoxia, 1959), dedicated to the tenth anniversary of the People's Republic of China, the poet Lu Mang (1920–1979) takes up the spatial image of "the construction site" and celebrates the spirit of rapid industrialization in Shanghai that had spread to every corner of the country. The anthology brims with images of factories, bulldozers, chimneys, blast furnaces, and other industrial objects.

29. Marshall Berman, *All That Is Solid Melts into Air: The Experience of Modernity* (New York: Penguin, 1988), 75.

30. Berman, *All That Is Solid*, 62.

31. Berman, *All That Is Solid*, 75

32. Benjamin I. Schwartz, *In Search of Wealth and Power: Yen Fu and the West* (Cambridge, MA: Harvard University Press, 1983), 238.

33. Schwartz, *In Search of Wealth and Power*, 242.

34. Tao Jin, "A Poetic Age—Random Thoughts from the Director of *A Nurse's Diary*," *Popular Cinema* (Dazhong dianying) 12 (1957): 27.

35. In the film, the name of the destination is unidentified (the shooting location was in fact a barren region of Inner Mongolia). The film did not reveal the name of a particular locality, but emphasized that it was a place that shared the universal identity of "wherever our motherland needs us to go."

36. Iovene, *Tales of Futures Past*, 29–30.

37. Sheila Fitzpatrick, *Everyday Stalinism: Ordinary Life in Extraordinary Times: Soviet Russia in the 1930s* (New York: Oxford University Press, 1999), 9. For an insightful discussion about the unreal qualities and anticipatory imagination of the construction site in the film, see Iovene, *Tales of Futures Past*, 29–30.

38. Stephanie Hemelryk Donald describes the "socialist-realist gaze" as a trope that "favors the romance of revolution and a heroic future over the intimacy of personal psychology." See Stephanie Donald, *Public Secrets, Public Spaces: Cinema and Civility in China* (Lanham, MD: Rowman & Littlefield, 2000), 62.

39. Maurice Meisner, *Mao's China and After: A History of the People's Republic* (New York: Free Press, 1986), 281.

40. Grace Yen Shen, *Unearthing the Nation: Modern Geology and Nationalism in Republican China* (Chicago: University of Chicago Press, 2014), 70, 177.

41. The slogan of "revolutionary successors" was officially brought up in 1964; nonetheless, the female protagonist Li Wanli in *A Blade of Grass* had already been transformed into a prototype of the revolutionary successor.

42. See Tang Xiaobing, *Chinese Modern: The Heroic and the Quotidian* (Durham: Duke University Press, 2000), 182.

43. My summary of these features defining geologists is based on Chen Xiaomei, "Playing in the Dirt: Plays about Geologists and the Memories of the Cultural Revolution and the Maoist Era," *China Review: A Special Issue on the Memory of the Cultural Revolution*, ed. Guobin Yang and Yue-ming Bao (2005): 86; Shen, *Unearthing the Nation*, 177; Charlotte Furth, *Ting Wen-chiang: Science and China's New Culture* (Cambridge, MA: Harvard University Press, 1970), 34–65; Tang Xiaobing, *Chinese Modern: The Heroic and the Quotidian* (Durham: Duke University Press, 2000), 182.

44. Shen, *Unearthing the Nation*, 178.

45. For details, see Wang Lingzhen, "Socialist Cinema and Female Authorship: Overdeterminatin and Subjective Revisions in Dong Kena's *A Blade of Grass on the Kunlun Mountain* (1962)," in *Chinese Women's Cinema: Transnational Contexts*, ed. Wang Lingzhen (New York: Columbia University Press, 2011), 47–65.

46. Lingzhen Wang suggests that the female characters Sister Hui and Wanli manage to overcome their disillusionment in their initial days and "negotiate a way of maintaining and renewing their previous visions of self and life" on the plateau. See Wang Lingzhen, "Socialist Cinema and Female Authorship," 59.

47. For details, see Elizabeth Perry, "Moving the Masses: Emotion Work in the Chinese Revolution," *Mobilization: An International Journal* 7, no. 2 (2002): 111–28.

48. Perry, "Moving the Masses," 114.

49. For details, see Yan Hairong, "Self-Development of Migrant Women and the Production of *Suzhi* [Quality] as Surplus Value," in *Everyday Modernity in China*, ed. Madeleine Yue Dong and Joshua L. Goldstein (Seattle: University of Washington Press, 2006), 227–58.

50. Moreover, in the socialist period, young people's adventurous spirit and longing for mobility was born out of the mythologized, revolutionary Long March, which marked a transition point for the Communist Revolution. As Mao Zedong put it on the eve of the Communist triumph, "our past work is only the first step in a long march of ten thousand *li*." A new Long March was soon to be launched. Therefore, mobility in the socialist context was not merely a geographical journey but a quality bound up with revolutionary tradition.

51. For a discussion of the use of ritualistic language during the socialist period, see Arif Dirlik, *Marxism and the Chinese Experience*, 32.

52. The final scene of the spoken drama version of *The Young Generation* also stages the scene of "trucks moving forward, passengers singing," which displays the fusion of the flow of emotion and motion; see Xiaobing Tang, "The Lyrical Age and Its Discontents: On the Staging of Socialist New China in the Young Generation," in *Chinese Modern: The Heroic and the Quotidian* (Durham: Duke University Press, 2000), 163–195, 191.

53. Xiaobing Tang, "The Historical Significance of the film *Never Forget*: Anxiety about Everyday Life and Modernity" (Qianwan buyao wangji de lishi—guanyu richang

shenghuo de jiaolv jiqi xiandaixing yiyi), in *Re-interpretation: Popular Culture and Ideology* (Zai Jiedu: Dazhong wenyi yu yishi xingtai) (Beijing: Beijing University Press, 2007), 233.

54. This is poster is copied from https://chineseposters.net/posters/e16-331.php, in the website "chineseposters.net" maintained by Stefan R. Landsberger. There is no information regarding the identity of the author Zhang Yuqing, who designed this poster.

55. Schivelbusch, *The Railway Journey*, xiii.

56. Cai Xiang, *Revolution/Narrative: Chinese Socialist Literary and Cultural Imagination, 1949–1966* (Geming/xushu: zhongguo shehui zhuyi wenxue wenhua xiangxiang) (Beijing: Peking University Press, 2010), 43, 73.

57. Xiaobing Tang, "The Lyrical Age and Its Discontents: On the Staging of Socialist New China in the Young Generation," in *Chinese Modern*, 163–95. 165.

58. Tang, "Lyrical Age," 171.

59. Ban Wang, *The Sublime Figure of History: Aesthetics and Politics in Twentieth-Century China* (Stanford: Stanford University Press, 1997), 123–54.

60. In his discussion of the imagery of the railway in 1980s literary works such as Wang Meng's "The Voice of the Spring" (*Chun zhi sheng*) and Tie Ning's "Oh, Xiangxue," Cai Xiang relates this imagery to fascination with speed and technology, the impulse to leave the homeland for a new destination, and a kind of new sense that there are signs of breaking with tradition. For details, see Cai Xiang, *The Book Series of Contemporary Literary and Cultural Criticism: Cai Xiang Volume* (Dangdai wenxue yu wenhua piping shuxi: Cai Xiang juan) (Beijing: Beijing shifan daxue chubanshe, 2010), 202–4.

61. Lu Xinhua, "Shanghen" (The Scar), *"Shanghen" ji qita: duanpian xiaoshuo he pinglunxuan* ("The Scar" and Others: Short Stories and a Selection of Reviews) (Beijing: Beijing chubanshe, 1978), 1–14.

62. If peasants were included in the community of the socialist builders during the early years of the PRC, "taking a look at the train" seems to suggest that the rural people were ignored, neglected, and isolated by the passing train in the reform era, which produced distinctions and differences.

63. Susan Buck-Morss, *The Dialectics of Seeing: Walter Benjamin and the Arcades Project* (Cambridge, MA: MIT Press, 1989), 92.

Conclusion

1. Martin King Whyte, "The Paradoxes of Rural-Urban Inequality in Contemporary China," *One Country, Two Societies: Rural-Urban Inequality in Contemporary China*, ed. Martin King Whyte (Cambridge, MA: Harvard University Press, 2010), 1–28, 5.

2. For example, He Xuefeng, ed., *Homecoming: The Rural China We Have Seen* (Huixiangji: women suo kanjian de xiangtu zhongguo) (Beijing: Dongfang chubanshe, 2014).

3. Yan Hairong, "Spectralization of the Rural: Reinterpreting the Labor Mobility of

Rural Young Women in Post-Mao China," *American Ethnologist* 30, no. 4 (November 2003): 578–96.

4. Wang Xiaoming, "L xian jianwen" [A Journey of L County], in *Xiangtu Zhongguo yu wenhua yanjiu* [Rural China and Cultural Studies], ed. Xue Yi (Shanghai: Shanghai shudian chubanshe, 2008), 338–55.

5. Arif Dirlik and Roxann Prazniak, "Introduction: The End of the Peasant? Global Capitalism and the Future of Agrarian Society," in *Global Capitalism and the Future of Agrarian Society*, ed. Arif Dirlik, Roxann Prazniak, and Alexander Woodside (London: Routledge, 2016), 4.

6. "Xi Jinping's Talks at the Beijing Forum on Literature and Art," October 16, 2014, https://chinacopyrightandmedia.wordpress.com/2014/10/16/xi-jinpings-talks-at-the-beijing-forum-on-literature-and-art/. The original Chinese version: http://news.xinhuanet.com/politics/2015-10/14/c_1116825558.htm, accessed October 23, 2017.

7. See the front-page feature story, "Local Worthies Returning to the Rural Home, Rebuilding Traditional Village Culture" (Xiangxian huixiang, chonggou chuantong xiangcun wenhua), *Guangming Daily* (July 2, 2014).

8. For example, Li Changping, *Wo xiang zongli shuoshihua* [I Told the Premier the Truth] (Beijing: Guangming ribao chubanshe, 2002). Li wrote a letter to the then-premier Zhu Rongji calling attention to "the three rural issues" in contemporary China. He Xuefeng, *Xin xiangtu zhongguo: zhuanxingqi xiangcun shehui diaocha biji* (New Rural China: Notes of Social Investigation on the Rural Society during the Transitional Period) (Nanjing: Guangxi shifan daxue chubanshe, 2003); Wen Tiejun, *Zhongguo nongcun jiben jingji zhidu yanjiu: "sannong" wenti de shiji fansi* [A Study of the Basic Economic System of the Chinese Rural Society: A Century's Reflection on the "Three Rural Issues"] (Beijing: Zhongguo jingji chubanshe, 2000). Both He and Wen have many other scholarly works on rural society from various perspectives. Cao Jinqing, *Huanghe bian de zhongguo: yige xuezhe dui xiangcun shehui de guancha yu sikao* (China along the Yellow River: A Scholar's Observations and Reflections on Rural Society) (Shanghai: Shanghai wenyi chubanshe, 2000). English translation: Cao Jinqing, *China along the Yellow River: Reflections on Rural Society*, trans. Nicky Harman and Ruhua Huang (London: Routledge, 2006). For a discussion of contemporary Chinese peasants in relation to the larger historical context, see Alexander Day, *The Peasant in Postsocialist China: History, Politics, and Capitalism* (Cambridge: Cambridge University Press, 2013).

9. For example, Liang Hong's *China in the Liang Village* [*Zhongguo zai Liangzhuang*] (Nanjing: Jiangsu renmin shubanshe, 2010) and Xiong Peiyun's *China in a Village* [*Yige cunzhuangli de Zhongguo*] (Beijing: Xinxing chubanshe, 2011).

10. For example, "Bishan Project" [Bishan jihua] launched by Ou Ning and Zuo Jing in 2011, "Xucun Project" initiated by Qu Yan in 2007, "Maogong Project" by Zuo Jin and Ren Hexin in 2015, and "Chaile Travel Agency" by Weng Fen in 2010.

11. Jia Ruiming, "Ziran nongren biji" [The Notes of the Natural Farmer], *Bi Shan* 3 (2013): 62–89.

12. Arif Dirlik and Roxann Prazniak, "Introduction: The End of the Peasant?"

13. Wen Tiejun, Qiu Jiansheng, and Che Haisheng, "'Sannong' wenti de yanjin yu xiangcun zhenxing zhanlue de tichu," (The Development of the 'Three Rural Problems' and the Proposal of the Strategy of Rural Vitalization," http://www.aisixiang.com/data/112750.html, last accessed on October 30, 2018.

14. Liu Shouying and Wang Yige, "From 'Rural China' to 'Urban-Rural China': The Perspective of the Village Change in China's Transformation" ["Cong xiangtu zhongguo dao chengxiang zhongguo: Zhongguo zhuanxing de xiangcun bianqian shijiao"], in *Guanli shijie*, issue 10 (2018): 128–46.

15. Han Shaogong, "Guancha Zhongguo xiangcun de liangge zuobiao" [Two Frames of Reference to Observe the Chinese Countryside"], http://www.cwzg.cn/politics/201801/40385.html, last accessed November 5, 2018.

16. Han, "Guancha Zhongguo xiangcun de liangge zuobiao" (Two Frames of Reference).

Bibliography

Alitto, Guy. *The Last Confucian: Liang Shu-ming and the Chinese Dilemma of Modernity*. Berkeley: University of California Press, 1986.
Althusser, Louis. *Lenin and Philosophy, and Other Essays*. Translated by Ben Brewster. New York: Monthly Review Press, 1971.
Anagnost, Ann. *National Past-Times: Narrative, Representation, and Power in Modern China*. Durham: Duke University Press, 1997.
Anderson, Benedict. *Imagined Communities: Reflections on the Origin and Spread of Nationalism*. London: Verso, 1983.
Anderson, Marston. *The Limits of Realism: Chinese Fiction in the Revolutionary Period*. Berkeley: University of California Press, 1990.
Anonymous. "Advancing toward Irrigation" [Xiang shuilihua yuejin]. *China Pictorial*, December 1959: 2–3.
Anonymous. "Bianqu tiaojie hunyin de yige shili." *Xinhua ribao* [Xinhua Daily]. October 22, 1944.
Anonymous. "On the Way to Yan'an" [Qu Yan'an tuzhong]. *Good Companion* [*Liangyou*], issue 147, March 1939.
Anonymous. "The Peasant Inventor" [Nongmin famingjia]. *China Pictorial*, December 1959, 15.
Anonymous. "Small-Scale Reservoir Has Big Benefits" [Xiaoxing shuiku shouyi da]. *China Pictorial*, April 16, 1960: 24–25.
Anonymous. "Two-Dragon Commune in Progress" [Qianjin Zhong de shuanglong gongshe]. *China Pictorial* [Renmin huabao] 15 (1960): 8–9.
Anonymous. "Yijian qianghun an." *Xinhua ribao* [Xinhua Daily]. April 11, 1945.
Apter, David, and Tony Saich. *Revolutionary Discourse in Mao's Republic*. Cambridge, MA: Harvard University Press, 1994.
Arendt, Hannah. *On Revolution*. London: Penguin, 1963.
Arkush, R. David. *Fei Xiaotong and Sociology in Revolutionary China*. Cambridge, MA: Harvard University Press, 1981.
Armstrong, Nancy. *Desire and Domestic Fiction: A Political History of the Novel*. Oxford: Oxford University Press, 1987.

Auerbach, Erich. *Mimesis: The Representation of Reality in Western Literature*. Princeton: Princeton University Press, 2003.
Bakken, Borge. *The Exemplary Society: Human Improvement, Social Control, and the Dangers of Modernity in China*. Oxford: Oxford University Press, 2000.
Bao, Weihong. *Fiery Cinema: The Emergence of an Affective Medium in China, 1915–1945*. Minneapolis: University of Minnesota Press, 2015.
Barlow, Tani. "Introduction." *I Myself Am a Woman: Selected Writings of Ding Ling*, edited by Tani E. Barlow and Gary J. Bjorge, 1–46. Boston: Beacon Press, 1989.
Beattie, Hilary J. *Land and Lineage in China: A Study of T'ung-ch'eng County, Anhwei, in the Ming and Ch'ing Dynasties*. Cambridge: Cambridge University Press, 1979.
Benjamin, Walter. *Illuminations: Essays and Reflections*. Translated by Harry Zohn. New York: Schocken, 1968.
Berman, Marshall. *All That Is Solid Melts into Air: The Experience of Modernity*. New York: Penguin, 1988.
Bernhardt, Kathryn. "Women and the Law: Divorce in the Republican Period." In *Civil Law in Qing and Republican China*, edited by Kathryn Bernhardt and Philip Huang, 187–214. Stanford: Stanford University Press, 1994.
Bernstein, Thomas P. *Up to the Mountains and Down to the Villages: The Transfer of Youth from Urban to Rural China*. New Haven: Yale University Press, 1977.
Bhabha, Homi. *The Location of Culture*. London: Routledge, 2004.
"Bianqu tiaojie hunyin de yige shili." *Xinhua ribao*, October 22, 1944.
Bodde, Derk, and Clarence Morris. *Law in Imperial China: Exemplified by 190 Ch'ing Dynasty Cases*. Cambridge, MA: Harvard University Press, 1967.
Bol, Peter K. "The Rise of Local History: History, Geography, and Culture in Southern Song and Yuan Wuzhou." *Harvard Journal of Asiatic Studies* 61, no. 1 (June 2001): 37–76.
Bonnin, Michel. *The Lost Generation: The Rustication of China's Educated Youth (1968–1980)*. Hong Kong: Chinese University Press, 2013.
Bradley, Patricia. *Making American Culture: A Social History, 1900–1920*. New York: Palgrave Macmillan, 2009.
Braester, Yomi. *Painting the City Red: Chinese Cinema and the Urban Contract*. Durham: Duke University Press, 2010.
Braester, Yomi, and Tina Mai Chen. "Introduction: Film in the People's Republic of China, 1949–1979: The Missing Years?" *Journal of Chinese Cinemas* 5, no. 1 (2011): 5–12.
Brian, Curried. *A National Acoustics: Music and Mass Publicity in Weimar and Nazi Germany*. Minneapolis: University of Minnesota Press, 2006.
Brown, Jeremy. *City Versus Countryside in Mao's China: Negotiating the Divide*. New York: Cambridge University Press, 2012.
Buck, Pearl. *Tell the People: Talks with James Yen about the Mass Education Movement*. New York: John Day Company, 1945.
Buck-Morss, Susan. *The Dialectics of Seeing: Walter Benjamin and the Arcades Project*. Cambridge, MA: MIT Press, 1989.

Cai Xiang. *The Book Series of Contemporary Literary and Cultural Criticism: The Work of Cai Xiang* [Dangdai wenxue yu wenhua piping shuxi: Cai Xiang juan]. Beijing: Beijing shifan daxue chubanshe, 2010.

Cai Xiang. *Revolution/Narrative: Chinese Socialist Literary and Cultural Imagination, 1949–1966* [Geming/xushu: zhongguo shehui zhuyi wenxue wenhua xiangxiang]. Beijing: Beijing University Press, 2010.

Calinescu, Matei. *Five Faces of Modernity: Modernism, Avant-garde, Decadence, Kitsch, Postmodernism*. Durham, NC: Duke University Press, 1987.

Cao Jinqing. *Huanghe bian de zhongguo: yige xuezhe dui xiangcun shehui de guancha yu sikao* [China along the Yellow River: A Scholar's Observations and Reflections on Rural Society] (Shanghai: Shanghai wenyi chubanshe, 2000). English translation: Cao Jinqing, *China Along the Yellow River: Reflections on Rural Society*. Translated by Nicky Harman and Ruhua Huang. London: Routledge, 2006.

Chakrabarty, Dipesh. *Provincializing Europe: Postcolonial Thought and Historical Difference*. Princeton: Princeton University Press, 2008.

Chanda, A. K. "The Young Man from the Provinces," *Comparative Literature* 33, no. 4 (Autumn 1981): 321–41.

Chang, Chung-li. *The Chinese Gentry: Studies on Their Role in Nineteenth-Century Chinese Society*. Seattle: University of Washington Press, 1955.

Chen Duo, et al. (The Study Group of Xiong Foxi Studies, Shanghai Drama College). *Xiandai xijujia Xiong Foxi* [Modern dramatist Xiong Foxi]. Beijing: Zhongguo xiju chubanshe, 1985.

Chen Mo. "A Symphony of Labor, Love, and Revolutionary Drive: On *The Young People in Our Village*." *Popular Cinema* 18 (1959): 25.

Chen, Tina Mai. "The Human-Machine Continuum in Maoism: The Intersection of Soviet Socialist Realism, Japanese Theoretical Physics, and Chinese Revolutionary Theory." *Cultural Critique* 80 (Winter 2012): 151–80.

Chen, Tina Mai. "Propagating the Propaganda Film: The Meaning of Film in CCP Writings, 1949–1965." *Modern Chinese Literature and Culture* 15, no. 2 (Fall 2003): 154–93.

Chen Xiaomei. "Playing in the Dirt: Plays about Geologists and the Memories of the Cultural Revolution and the Maoist Era." *China Review: A Special Issue on the Memory of the Cultural Revolution*, edited by Guobin Yang and Yue-ming Bao, 65–95, 2005.

Chen Xuezhao. *A Visit to Yan'an* [Yan'an fangwen ji]. Hong Kong: Beiji shudian, 1940.

Chen Yongfa. *Yan'an Shadows* [Yan'an di yinying]. Taibei: zhongyang yanjiuyuan jindaishi yanjiusuo, 1990.

Cheng, Yinghong. *Creating the New Man: From Enlightenment Ideals to Socialist Realities*. Honolulu: University of Hawai'i Press, 2008.

Chow, Rey. *Primitive Passions: Visuality, Sexuality, Ethnography, and Contemporary Chinese Cinema*. New York: Columbia University Press, 1995.

Chow, Rey. *Woman and Chinese Modernity: The Politics of Reading Between West and East*. Minneapolis: University of Minnesota Press, 1991.

Ci Jiwei. *Dialectic of the Chinese Revolution: From Utopianism to Hedonism*. Stanford: Stanford University Press, 1994.

Clark, Paul. *Chinese Cinema: Culture and Politics Since 1949*. Cambridge: Cambridge University Press, 1987.

Cohen, Myron. "Cultural and Political Inventions in Modern China: The Case of the Chinese 'Peasant.'" *Daedalus* 122, no. 2, China in Transformation (Spring 1993): 151–70.

Cong, Xiaoping. "From 'Freedom of Marriage' to 'Self-Determined Marriage': Recasting Marriage in the Shaan-Gan-Ning Border Region of the 1940s," *Twentieth-Century China* 38, no. 3 (October 2013): 184–209.

Cong, Xiaoping. *Marriage, Law and Gender in Revolutionary China*. Cambridge: Cambridge University Press, 2016.

Cook, Alexander, ed. *Mao's Little Red Book: A Global History*. Cambridge: Cambridge University Press, 2014.

Dai Jinhua. "Foreword." In *Occidentalism: A Theory of Counter-Discourse in Post-Mao China*. 2nd ed., edited by Chen Xiaomei, ix–xxiii. Lanham, MD: Rowman & Littlefield, 2002.

Daruvala, Susan. *Zhou Zuoren and an Alternative Chinese Response to Modernity*. Cambridge, MA: Harvard University Asia Center, 2000.

Day, Alexander. *The Peasant in Postsocialist China: History, Politics, and Capitalism*. Cambridge: Cambridge University Press, 2013.

DeMare, Brian James. *Mao's Cultural Army: Drama Troupes in China's Rural Revolution*. Cambridge: Cambridge University Press, 2015.

Dennerline, Jerry. *Qian Mu and the World of Seven Mansions*. New Haven: Yale University Press, 1988.

Denton, Kirk. *The Problematic of Self in Modern Chinese Literature: Hu Feng and Lu Ling*. Stanford: Stanford University Press, 1998.

Denton, Kirk. "Rectification: Party Discipline, Intellectual Remolding, and the Formation of a Political Community." In *Words and Their Stories: Essays on the Language of the Chinese Revolution*, edited by Ban Wang, 51–64. Leiden, the Netherlands: Brill, 2010.

Des Forges, Alexander. Book review, *Alternative Modernities* by Dilip Parameshwar Gaonkar. *Journal of Asian Studies* 61, no. 2 (May 2002): 670–72.

Diamant, Neil Jeffrey. *Revolutionizing the Family: Politics, Love, and Divorce in Urban and Rural China, 1949–1968*. Berkeley: University of California Press, 2000.

Dikotter, Frank. *Exotic Commodities: Modern Objects and Everyday Life in China*. New York: Columbia University Press, 2006.

Ding Fan. *A History of Chinese Native Soil Fiction* [Zhongguo xiangtu xiaoshuo shi]. Beijing: Beijing University Press, 2007.

Ding Ling. "How I Came to Shanbei" [Wo shi zenyang lai shanbei de]. In *The Collected Works of Ding Ling* [Ding Ling wenji]. Vol. 5, 305–11. Changsha: Hunan renmin chubanshe, 1983).

Ding Ling. "In the Hospital." In *Modern Chinese Stories and Novellas, 1919–1949*, edited by Joseph S. M. Lau, C. T. Hsia, and Leo Ou-fan Lee, translated by Gary Bjorge, 279–91. New York: Columbia University Press, 1981.

Ding Ling. "In the Hospital" [Zai yiyuan Zhong]. *Ding Ling Zuopin jingxuan* [A Selection of Ding Ling's Works], edited by Wu Lina and Wu Xuxi, 280–99. Wuhan: Changjiang wenyi chubanshe, 2003.
Dirlik, Arif. "The Politics of the Cultural Revolution in Historical Perspective." In *The Chinese Cultural Revolution Reconsidered: Beyond Purge and Holocaust*, edited by Kam-yee Lam, 158–83. New York: Palgrave Macmillan, 2003.
Dirlik, Arif. "Revolutionary Hegemony and the Language of Revolution: Chinese Socialism Between Present and Future." In *Marxism and the Chinese Experience: Issues in Contemporary Chinese Socialism*, edited by Arif Dirlik and Maurice Meisner, 27–42. Armonk, NY: M. E. Sharpe, 1989.
Dirlik, Arif, Roxann Prazniak, and Alexander Woodside, eds. *Global Capitalism and the Future of Agrarian Society*. London: Routledge, 2016.
Donald, Stephanie Hemelryk. *Public Secrets, Public Spaces: Cinema and Civility in China*. Lanham, MD: Rowman & Littlefield, 2000.
Dong, Xinyu. "The Laborer at Play: *Laborer's Love*, the Operational Aesthetic, and the Comedy of Inventions." *Modern Chinese Literature and Culture* (Fall 2008): 1–39.
Du, Daisy Yan. "Socialist Modernity in the Wasteland: Changing Representations of the Female Tractor Driver in China, 1949–1964." *Modern Chinese Literature and Culture* (Spring 2017): 55–94.
Duara, Prasenjit. "Local Worlds: The Poetics and Politics of the Native Place in Modern China." *South Atlantic Quarterly* 99, no. 1 (Winter 2000): 13–45.
Duara, Prasenjit. "The Regime of Authenticity: Timelessness, Gender, and National History in Modern China." *History and Theory* 37, no. 3 (Oct. 1998): 287–308.
Duara, Prasenjit. *Rescuing History from the Nation: Questioning Narratives of Modern China*. Chicago: University of Chicago Press, 1995.
Duara, Prasenjit. *Sovereignty and Authenticity: Manchukuo and the East Asian Modern*. Lanham, MD: Rowman & Littlefield, 2004.
Duara, Prasenjit. "Superscribing Symbols: The Myth of Guandi, Chinese God of War." *Journal of Asian Studies* 47, no. 4 (1988): 778–95.
Dutton, Michael. "Passionately Governmental: Maoism and the Structured Intensities of Revolutionary Governmentality." In *China's Governmentalities: Governing Change, Changing Government*, edited by Elaine Jeffreys, 24–37. London: Routledge, 2010.
Eastman, Lloyd E. *Family, Fields, and Ancestors: Constancy and Change in China's Social and Economic History, 1550–1949*. New York: Oxford University Press, 1988.
Egan, Charles. "Reconsidering the Role of Folk Songs in Pre-T'ang 'Yüeh-Fu' Development." *T'oung Pao*, Second Series. Vol. 86, fasc. 1/3 (2000): 47–99.
Egan, Michael. "Yu Dafu and the Transition to Modern Chinese Literature," in *Modern Chinese Literature in the May Fourth Era*, edited by Merle Goldman, 309–24. Cambridge, MA: Harvard University Press, 1977.
Elias, Norbert. *Time: An Essay*. Translated by Edmund Jephcott. Oxford: Blackwell, 1992.
Elman, Benjamin A. "Political, Social, and Cultural Reproduction via Civil Service Examination in Late Imperial China." *Journal of Asian Studies* 50, no. 1 (1991): 7–28.

Esherick, Joseph W. *The Origin of the Boxer Uprising*. Berkeley: University of California Press, 1987.

Eyferth, Jacob. *Eating Rice from Bamboo Roots: The Social History of a Community of Handicraft Papermakers in Rural Sichuan, 1920–2000*. Cambridge, MA: Harvard University Press, 2009.

Fairbank, J. K. "Foreword." In *Random Notes on Red China, 1936–1945*, edited by Edgar Snow, v–vi. Cambridge, MA: East Asian Research Center, Harvard University, 1957.

Fang, Ji. "The Power of the Loom" [*fangche de liliang*]. *Liberation Daily* [Jiefang ribao]. May 20 and 21, 1945.

Faure, David, and Tao Tao Liu. "Introduction." In *Town and Country in China: Identity and Perception*, edited by David Faure and Tao Tao Liu, 1–16. Oxford: Palgrave, 2002.

Fei Hsiao-tung (Fei Xiaotong). *China's Gentry: Essays in Rural-Urban Relations*. Chicago: University of Chicago Press, 1953.

Fei Hsiao-tung (Fei Xiaotong). *From the Soil: The Foundations of Chinese Society: A Translation of Fei Xiaotong's Xiangtu zhongguo*. Translated by Gary Hamilton and Wang Zheng. Berkeley: University of California Press, 1992.

Feng, Jin. *The New Woman in Early Twentieth-Century Chinese Fiction*. West Lafayette, IN: Purdue University Press, 2004.

Feng Yuanjun. *Feng Yuanjun xiaoshuo: Chunhen* [The Fiction of Feng Yuanjun: Spring Traces]. Shanghai: Shanghai guji chubanshe, 1997.

Feuerwerker, Yi-tsi Mei. *Ding Ling's Fiction: Ideology and Narrative in Modern Chinese Literature*. Cambridge, MA: Harvard University Press, 1982.

Fitzgerald, John. *Awakening China: Politics, Culture, and Class in the Nationalist Revolution*. Stanford: Stanford University Press, 1996.

Fitzpatrick, Sheila. *Everyday Stalinism: Ordinary Life in Extraordinary Times: Soviet Russia in the 1930s*. Oxford: Oxford University Press, 1999.

Flath, James A. "The Chinese Railroad View: Transportation Themes in Popular Print, 1873–1915." *Cultural Critique* 58, no. 3 (2004): 168–90.

Foucault, Michel. "Of Other Spaces." *Diacritics* 16 (Spring 1986): 22–27.

Friedberg, Anne. *Window Shopping: Cinema and the Postmodern*. Berkeley: University of California Press, 1993.

Frierson, Cathy A. *Peasant Icons: Representations of Rural People in Late Nineteenth-Century Russia*. Oxford: Oxford University Press, 1993.

Furth, Charlotte. *Ting Wen-chiang: Science and China's New Culture*. Cambridge, MA: Harvard University Press, 1970, 34–65.

Gamble, Sidney D. *Chinese Village Plays from the Ting Hsien Region* [*Yang Ke Hsüan*]; *A Collection of Forty-Eight Chinese Rural Plays as Staged by Villagers from Ting Hsien in Northern China*. Amsterdam: APA-Philo Press, 1970.

Gamble, Sidney D. *Ting Hsien, a North China Rural Community*. New York: International Secretariat Institute of Pacific Relations, 1954; reprint, Stanford University Press, 1968.

Gao Hua. *Hongtaiyang shi zenyang shengqide* [How Did the Red Sun Rise?]. Hong Kong: Chinese University of Hong Kong, 2000.

Gao Minfu. Introduction to Han Qixiang, *Liu Qiao Tuanyuan* [Liu Qiao Reunion]. Haerbin: Dongbei Shudian, 1947.

Gaonkar, Dilip Parameshwar, ed. *Alternative Modernities*. Durham: Duke University Press, 2001.

Gaonkar, Dilip Parameshwar. "Toward New Imaginaries: An Introduction." *Public Culture* 14, no. 1 (Winter 2002): 1–19.

Gellner, Ernest. *Nations and Nationalism*. Ithaca: Cornell University Press, 1983.

Giddens, Anthony. *The Consequences of Modernity*. Cambridge, UK: Polity Press, 1990.

Giddens, Anthony. *The Giddens Reader*, edited by Philip Cassel. Stanford: Stanford University Press, 1993.

Goodman, Bryna. *Native Place, City, and Nation: Regional Networks and Identities in Shanghai, 1853–1937*. Berkeley: University of California Press, 1995.

Goody, Jack, and Ian Watt. "The Consequences of Literacy." *Comparative Studies in Society and History* 5, no. 3 (1963): 304–45.

Greuther, Marc. Review of *Railways and the Victorian Imagination* by Michael Freeman. *Technology and Culture* 42, no. 3 (July 2001): 604–6.

Gu Yuan. "Ma Xiwu Mediating a Marriage Dispute Case." *Liberation Daily* (October 9, 1944).

Gunning, Tom. "The Cinema of Attractions: Early Film, Its Spectator and the Avant-Garde." In *Early Cinema: Space, Frame, Narrative*, edited by Thomas Elsaesser and Adam Barker, 56–63. London: British Film Institute, 1990.

Gunning, Tom. "Tracing the Individual Body: Photography, Detectives and Early Cinema." In *Cinema and the Invention of Modern Life*, edited by Leo Charney and Vanessa Schwartz, 15–45. Berkeley: University of California Press, 1995.

Habermas, Jürgen. *The Philosophical Discourse of Modernity: Twelve Lectures*, translated by Frederick G. Lawrence. Cambridge, MA: MIT Press, 1995.

Hamilton, John Maxwell. *Edgar Snow: A Biography*. Bloomington: Indiana University Press, 1988.

Hammers, Roslyn Lee. *Pictures of Tilling and Weaving: Art, Labor, and Technology in Song and Yuan China*. Hong Kong: Hong Kong University Press, 2011.

Han Qixiang. *Liu Qiao Tuanyuan* [Liu Qiao's Reunion]. Wu'an: Xinhua shudian, 1949.

Han Shaogong. "Guancha Zhongguo xiangcun de liangge zuobiao" [Two Frames of Reference to Observe the Chinese Countryside]. http://www.cwzg.cn/politics/201801/40385.html, last accessed on November 5, 2018.

Han Xiaorong. *The Chinese Discourses on the Peasant: 1900–1949*. New York: State University of New York Press, 2005.

Hang, Krista Van Fleit. *Literature the People Love: Reading Chinese Texts from the Early Maoist Period (1949–1966)*. New York: Palgrave Macmillan, 2013.

Hansen, Miriam. "Fallen Women, Rising Stars, New Horizons: Shanghai Silent Film as Vernacular Modernism." *Film Quarterly* 54, no. 1 (2000): 10–22.

Harrison, Henrietta. *The Man Awakened from Dreams: One Man's Life in a North China Village, 1857–1942*. Stanford: Stanford University Press, 2005.

Harrison, Henrietta. "Newspapers and Nationalism in Rural China 1890–1929." *Past and Present* 166 (2000): 181–204.

Hayford, Charles Wishart. *To the People: James Yen and Village China*. New York: Columbia University Press, 1990.
He Xuefeng. *Xin xiangtu zhongguo: zhuanxingqi xiangcun shehui diaocha biji* [New Rural China: Notes of Social Investigation on the Rural Society during the Transitional Period]. Nanjing: Guangxi shifan daxue chubanshe, 2003.
He Xuefeng, ed. *Homecoming: The Rural China We Have Seen* [Huixiangji: women suo kanjian de xiangtu zhongguo]. Beijing: Dongfang chubanshe, 2014.
Hershatter, Gail. *The Gender of Memory: Rural Women and China's Collective Past*. Berkeley: University of California Press, 2011.
Ho, Christine I. "The People Eat for Free and the Art of Collective Production in Maoist China." *The Art Bulletin* 98, no. 3 (2016): 348–72.
Ho, Christine I. *Drawing from Life: Socialist Realism and Socialist Painting in the People's Republic of China*, forthcoming from University of California Press, 2020.
Holm, David. *Art and Ideology in Revolutionary China*. Oxford: Oxford University Press, 1991.
Holm, David. "Folk Art as Propaganda: The Yangge Movement in Yan'an." In *Popular Chinese Literature and Performing Arts in the People's Republic of China, 1949–1979*, edited by Bonnie S. McDougall, 3–35. Berkeley: University of California Press, 1984.
Huang Ziping. "The Metaphor of Sickness and Literary Production: Ding Ling's 'In the Hospital'" [Bing de yinyu yu wenxue shengchan: Ding Ling de "zai yiyuan zhong" ji qita]. In *Rereading: Mass Literature and Ideology* [Zai jiedu: dazhong wenyi yu yishi xingtai], edited by Tang Xiaobing, 19–33. Beijing: Beijing daxue chubanshe, 2007.
Huizinga, Johan. *Homo Ludens: A Study of the Play-Element in Culture*. Martino Centre, CT: Martino Publishing, 2014.
Hung, Chang-tai. *Going to the People: Chinese Intellectuals and Folk Literature, 1918–1937*. Cambridge, MA: Harvard University Press, 1985.
Hung, Chang-tai. *Mao's New World: Political Culture in the Early People's Republic*. Ithaca: Cornell University Press, 2011.
Hung Chang-tai. "Reeducating a Blind Storyteller: Han Qixiang and the Chinese Communist Storytelling Campaign." *Modern China* 19, no. 4 (Oct. 1993): 395–426.
Hung Chang-tai. "Two Images of Socialism: Woodcuts in Chinese Communist Politics." *Comparative Studies in Society and History* 39, no. 1 (Jan, 1997): 34–60.
Hung Chang-tai. *War and Popular Culture: Resistance in Modern China, 1937–1945*. Berkeley: University of California Press, 1994.
Idema, Wilt. "Introduction." *Judge Bao and the Rule of Law: Eight Ballad-Stories from the Period 1250–1450*, translated by Wilt Idema, ix–xxxiv. Singapore: World Scientific Publishing Co., 2010.
Iovene, Paola. *Tales of Futures Past: Literature and Anticipation in Contemporary China*. Stanford: Stanford University Press, 2014.
Jia Ruiming. "Ziran nongren biji" [The Notes of the Natural Farmer]. *Bi Shan* 3 (2013): 62–89.
Johnson, David. *Spectacle and Sacrifice: The Ritual Foundations of Village Life in North China*. Cambridge, MA: Harvard University Asia Center, 2009.

Johnson, Matthew. "The Science Education Film: Cinematizing Technocracy and Internationalizing Development." *Journal of Chinese Cinemas* 5, no. 1 (2011): 31–53.

Jones, Andrew. *Developmental Fairy Tales: Evolutionary Thinking and Modern Chinese Culture*. Cambridge, MA: Harvard University Press, 2011.

Judge, Joan. "Reforming the Feminine: Female Literacy and the Legacy of 1898." In *Rethinking the 1898 Reform Period: Political and Cultural Change in Late Qing China*, edited by Rebecca E. Karl and Peter Zarrow, 158–79. Cambridge, MA: Harvard University Asia Center, 2002.

Keaveney, Christopher T. *Beyond Brushtalk: Sino-Japanese Literary Exchange in the Interwar Period*. Hong Kong: Hong Kong University Press, 2009.

Kern, Stephen. *The Culture of Time and Space, 1880–1918*. Cambridge, MA: Harvard University Press, 1983.

King, Richard. *Milestones on a Golden Road: Writing for Chinese Socialism, 1945–80*. Vancouver: UBC Press, 2013.

Kinkley, Jeffrey. Introduction to Chen Xuezhao, *Surviving the Storm: A Memoir*, vii–xxvi. Armonk, NY: M. E. Sharpe, 1990.

Kirby, Lynne. *Parallel Tracks: The Railroad and Silent Cinema*. Durham, NC: Duke University Press, 1997.

Kojin, Karatani. *Origins of Modern Japanese Literature*, translated by Brett de Bary. Durham, NC: Duke University Press, 1993.

Lam, Tong. *A Passion for Facts: Social Surveys and the Construction of the Chinese Nation State, 1900–1949*. Berkeley: University of California Press, 2011.

Landes, David S. *Revolution in Time: Clocks and the Making of the Modern World*. Cambridge, MA: Harvard University Press, 1983.

Lattimore, Owen. Introduction to Jack Belden, *China Shakes the World*, ix–xvi. New York: Harpers, 1949.

Laughlin, Charles. *Chinese Reportage: The Aesthetics of Historical Experience*. Durham, NC: Duke University Press, 2002.

Lean, Eugenia. *Public Passions: The Trial of Shi Jianqiao and the Rise of Popular Sympathy in Republican China*. Berkeley: University of California Press, 2007.

Lee, Haiyan. "The Other Chinese: Romancing the Folk in May Fourth Native Soil Fiction." *Concentric: Literary and Cultural Studies* 33, no. 2 (2007): 9–34.

Lee, Haiyan. *Revolution of the Heart: A Genealogy of Love in China, 1900–1950*. Stanford: Stanford University Press, 2007.

Lee, Haiyan. "Tears That Crumble the Great Wall: The Archeology of Feeling in the May Fourth Folklore Movement." *Journal of Asian Studies* 64, no. 1 (2005): 35–65.

Lee, Jung. "Invention without Science: 'Korean Edisons' and the Changing Understanding of Technology in Colonial Korea." *Technology and Culture* 54, no. 4 (October 2013): 782–814.

Lee, Leo Ou-fan. *The Romantic Generation of Modern Chinese Writers*. Cambridge, MA: Harvard University Press, 1973.

Lee, Leo Ou-fan. *Shanghai Modern: The Flowering of a New Urban Culture in China, 1930–1945*. Cambridge, MA: Harvard University Press, 1999.

Lee, Leo Ou-fan, and Andrew Nathan. "The Beginnings of Mass Culture: Journalism and Fiction in the Late Ch'ing and Beyond." In *Popular Culture in Late Imperial China*, edited by David Johnson, Andrew Nathan, and Evelyn S, Rawski, 360–95. Berkeley: University of California Press, 1985.

Leese, Daniel. *Mao Cult: Rhetoric and Ritual in China's Cultural Revolution*. Cambridge: Cambridge University Press, 2011.

Lepenies, Wolf. *Between Literature and Science: The Rise of Sociology*. Cambridge: Cambridge University Press, 1988.

Levenson, Joseph R. "The Province, the Nation, and the World: The Problem of Chinese Identity." In *Approaches to Modern Chinese History*, edited by Albert Feuerwerker, Rhoads Murphey, and Mary C. Wright, 268–88. Berkeley: University of California Press, 1967.

Levenson, Joseph. *Revolution and Cosmopolitanism: The Western Stage and the Chinese Stages*. Berkeley: University of California Press, 1971.

Li Changping. *Wo xiang zongli shuoshihua* [I Told the Premier the Truth]. Beijing: Guangming ribao chubanshe, 2002.

Li Dazhao. "Qingnian yu nongcun" [Youth and the Village]. In *Li Dazhao Quanji*, 565–68. Shijiazhuang Shi: Hebei jiao yu chubanshe, 1999.

Li Dazhao. "Stagnant Civilization and Dynamic Civilization" [Jing de wenming yu dong de wenming]. In *Li Dazhao Quanji*, 651–53. Shijiazhuang Shi: Hebei jiao yu chubanshe, 1999.

Li, Hsiao-t'i. "Making a Name and a Culture for the Masses in Modern China." *positions: east asia cultures critique* 9, no. 1 (Spring 2001): 29–68.

Li, Hsiao-t'i. *Opera, Society, and Politics in Modern China*. Cambridge, MA: Harvard University Asia Center, 2019.

Li, Hsiao-t'i. *Qingmo de xiaceng shehui qimeng yundong: 1901–1911* [Lower-Class Enlightenment in the Late Qing: 1901–1911]. Shijiazhuang: Hebei jiaoyu chubanshe, 2001.

Li Huanzheng. *Rural China on the Silver Screen: A Study on the Customs and Everyday Lifestyle in Rural-subject Films, 1949–1966* [Yinmushang de xiangtu zhongguo: shiqinian nongcun ticai dianying Zhong de minus yu richang shenghuo fangshi yanjiu]. Beijing: Zhongguo nongye daxue chubanshe, 2013.

Li Jie. "Phantasmagoric Manchukuo: Documentaries Produced by the South Manchurian Railway Company, 1932–1940." *Position: East Asia Cultures Critique* 22, no. 2 (Spring 2014): 329–69.

Li Jinghan. *Dingxian shehui gaikuang diaocha* [A Survey of Ding County Society]. Beiping: Zhongguo pingmin jiaoyu cujinhui, 1933.

Li Jinghan, and Zhang Shiwen, eds. *Dingxian yangge xuan* [Selected *Yangge* Plays from Ding County]. Beiping: Zhonghua pingmin jiaoyu cujinhui, 1933.

Li, Pu. *Women de minzhu chuantong: kangri shiqi jiefangqu zhengzhi shenghuo fengmo* [Our Democratic Tradition: The Scene of Politics and Life in the Liberated Area during the Anti-Japanese War Period]. Chongqing: Xinhua chubanshe, 1980.

Li, Su. *Law and Literature: A Case Study of Traditional Chinese Drama* [Falv yu wenxue:

yi Zhongguo chuantong xiju wei cailiao]. Beijing: Shenghuo, dushu, xinzhi sanlian shudian, 2006.

Li, Xianyou. "Three Young People with Different Personalities: On the Film *The Young People in Our Village*." *The Popular Cinema* [*Dazhong dianying*] 9 (1960): 15.

Li, Xiangdong, and Wang Zengru. *Ding Ling Zhuan* [Ding Ling: The Biography]. Vol. 1. Beijing: Zhongguo dabaike quanshu chubanshe, 2015.

Liang, Hong. *China in the Liang Village* [*Zhongguo zai Liangzhuang*]. Nanjing: Jiangsu renmin shubanshe, 2010.

Liang, Shuming. *The Collective Work of Liang Shuming* [*Liang Shuming Quanji*]. Vol. 5. Jinan: Shandong renmin chubanshe, 1989.

Liao, Ying. "Person . . . Growing Up in Hardship: A Review of Comrade Ding Ling's 'In the Hospital'" [Ren . . . Zai jianku zhong chengzhang: ping Ding Ling tongzhi de 'zai yiyuan Zhong]. In *The Research Materials of Ding Ling* [Ding Ling Yanjiu ziliao], edited by Yuan Liangjun, 278–81. Tianjin: Tianjin renmin chubanshe, 1982.

Lin Chun. *The Transformation of Chinese Socialism*. Durham: Duke University Press, 2006.

Liu, Jianmei. *Revolution Plus Love: Literary History, Women's Bodies, and Thematic Repetition in Twentieth-Century Chinese Fiction*. Honolulu: University of Hawai'i Press, 2003.

Liu, Lydia. "A Folksong Immortal and Official Popular Culture in Twentieth-Century China." *Writing and Materiality in China*, edited by Judith T. Zeitlin, Lydia H. Liu, and Ellen Widmer, 553–610. Cambridge, MA: Harvard University Asia Center, 2003.

Liu, Lydia H. "Narratives of Modern Selfhood: First-Person Fiction in May Fourth Literature." In *Politics, Ideology, and Literary Discourse in Modern China: Theoretical Interventions and Cultural Critique*, edited by Liu Kang and Xiaobing Tang. Durham: Duke University Press, 1993.

Liu, Lydia. *Tokens of Exchange: The Problem of Translation in Global Circulations*. Durham: Duke University Press, 1999.

Liu, Lydia H. *Translingual Practice: Literature, National Culture, and Translated Modernity—China, 1900–1937*. Stanford: Stanford University Press, 1995.

Liu Shouying, and Wang Yige. "From 'Rural China' to 'Urban-Rural China': The Perspective of the Village Change in China's Transformation" ["Cong xiangtu zhongguo dao chengxiang zhongguo: Zhongguo zhuanxing de xiangcun bianqian shijiao"]. *Guanli shijie*, issue 10 (2018): 128–46.

Liu, Siyuan "A Mixed-Blooded Child, Neither Western nor Eastern: Sinicization of Western-Style Theatre in Rural China in the 1930s." *Asian Theatre Journal* 25, no. 2 (Fall): 272–97.

"Local Worthies Returning to the Rural Home, Rebuilding Traditional Village Culture" [Xiangxian huixiang, chonggou chuantong xiangcun wenhua]. *Guangming Daily*, July 2, 2014.

Lu Ping, ed. *Living in Yan'an* [Shenghuo zai Yan'an]. Xi'an: Xinhua shushe, 1938.

Lu, Sheldon, and Jiayan Mi, eds. *Chinese Ecocinema in the Age of Environmental Challenge*. Hong Kong: Hong Kong University Press, 2009.

Lu Xinhua. "Shanghen" [The Scar]. *"Shanghen" ji qita: duanpian xiaoshuo he pinglunxuan* ["The Scar" and Others: Short Stories and a Selection of Reviews], 1–14. Beijing: Beijing chubanshe, 1978.

Lukacs, Georg. *The Theory of the Novel: A Historical-Philosophical Essay on the Forms of Great Epic Literature*. Cambridge, MA: MIT Press, 1971.

Lu Hsun. *Selected Stories of Lu Hsun: The True Stories of Ah-Q and Other Stories*. Translated by Gladys Yang and Yang Hsien-yi. Peking: Foreign Language Press, 1960.

Lu Xun. "My Old Home" [Guxiang]. In *Lu Xun Xuanji* [A Selection of Lu Xun's Work], 41–59. Beijing: Renmin wenxue chubanshe, 1959.

Lu Xun. "Xiaoshuo erji daoyan" [Introduction to *The Second Anthology of Fiction*]. In *Zhongguo xinwenxue daxi daoyan ji, 1917–1927* [A Collection of the Introductions to *A Compendium of Modern Chinese Literature, 1917–1927*], edited by Liu Yunfeng, 80–92. Tianjin: Tianjin renmin chubanshe, 2009.

Lye, Colleen. *America's Asia: Racial Form and American Literature, 1893–1945*. Princeton: Princeton University Press, 2005.

Ma Boyuan. "The Local Custom in Hubei and Henan" [Hubei Henan di fengsu]. *New Youth* 8, no. 1 (September 1, 1920): 1–11.

MacIntyre, Alasdair. *After Virtue: A Study in Moral Theory*. Notre Dame, IN: University of Notre Dame Press, 1984.

Mao Dun. "Xiaoshuo yiji daoyan" [Introduction to *The First Anthology of Modern Chinese Fiction*]. In *Zhongguo xinwenxue daxi daoyanji, 1917–1927* [A Collection of Introductions to *The Compendium of Modern Chinese Literature*], edited by Liu Yunfeng, 52–77. Tianjin: Tianjin renmin chubanshe, 2008.

Mao Tse-Tung. "The United Front in the Cultural Work" [Wenhua gongzuo zhong de tongyi zhanxian], a talk given on October 30, 1944. *The Selected Works of Mao Tse-Tung*. Vol. 3. Beijing: Renmin chubanshe, 1967.

Mao Zedong. *The Poems of Mao Tse-Tung*. Translated by Willis Barns Tone in collaboration with Ko Ching-Po. New York: Harper & Row, 1972.

Mao Zedong. *Quotations from Chairman Mao Tsetung*. Peking: Foreign Language Press, 1972.

Mao Zedong. "Talks at the Yenan Forum on Literature and Art" (May 1942). Selected Work of Mao Tse-tung. Transcription by the Maoist Documentation Project, https://www.marxists.org/reference/archive/mao/selected-works/volume-3/mswv3_08.htm (last access, July 25, 2017).

Marretti, Franco. *The Way of the World: The Bildungsroman in European Culture*. London: Verso, 2000.

McDonnell, Patricia. *On the Edge of Your Seat: Popular Theater and Film in Early Twentieth American Art*. New Haven: Yale University Press, 2002.

McDougall, Bonnie S. *Mao Zedong's "Talks at the Yan'an Conference on Literature and Art": A Translation of the 1943 Text with Commentary*. Ann Arbor: Center for Chinese Studies, University of Michigan, 1980.

McGrath, Jason. "Communists Have More Fun! The Dialectics of Fulfillment in Cinema of the People's Republic of China." *World Picture* 3 (2009). http://www.worldpicture journal.com/WP_3/McGrath.html. Accessed December 16, 2018.

Mei Feuerwerker, Yi-tsi. *Ideology, Power, Text: Self-Representation and the Peasant "Other" in Modern Chinese Literature*. Stanford: Stanford University Press, 1998.

Meisner, Maurice. *Mao's China and After: A History of the People's Republic*. New York: Free Press, 1986.

Meisner, Maurice. *Marxism, Maoism, and Utopianism: Eight Essays*. Madison: University of Wisconsin Press, 1982.

Meisner, Maurice. "Marx, Mao, and Deng on the Division of Labor in History." In *Marxism and the Chinese Experience: Issues in Contemporary Chinese Socialism*, edited by Arif Dirlik and Maurice Meisner, 79–116. London: M. E. Sharpe, 1989.

Meng, Yue. "'Baimaomv' yanbian de qishi: jianlun yan'an wenyi de lishi duozhixing" ["The Evolution of White-haired Girl and Its Inspiration: A Reflection on Literature and Art in Yan'an and Its Multiple Natures"]. In *Zai Jiedu: Dazhong wenyi yu yishi xingtai* [Rereading: Mass Culture and Ideology], edited by Tang Xiaobing, 48–69. Beijing: Beijing University Press.

Merkel-Hess, Kate. "Acting Out Reform: Theatre and Village in the Republican Rural Reconstruction Movement." *Twentieth-Century China* 37, no. 2 (2012): 161–80.

Merkel-Hess, Kate. *The Rural Modern: Reconstructing the Self and State in Republican China*. Chicago: University of Chicago Press, 2016.

Mittler, Barbara. *A Continuous Revolution: Making Sense of Cultural Revolution Culture*. Cambridge, MA: Harvard Asia Center Publications, 2012.

Moretti, Franco. *Signs Taken for Wonders: Essays in the Sociology of Literary Forms*. London: Verso, 1988.

Mote, Frederick W. "The Transformation of Nanking, 1350–1400." In *The City in Late Imperial China*, edited by G. William Skinner, 101–53. Stanford: Stanford University Press, 1977.

Mühlhahn, Klaus. *Criminal Justice in China: A History*. Cambridge, MA: Harvard University Press, 2009.

Mullaney, Thomas. *Coming to Terms with the Nation: Ethnic Classification in Modern China*. Berkeley: University of California Press, 2011.

Mulvey, Laura. "Visual Pleasure and Narrative Cinema." In *Film Theory and Criticism: Introductory Readings*, edited by Leo Braudy and Marshall Cohen, 833–44. New York: Oxford University Press, 1999.

Mulvey, Laura. "Changes: Thoughts on Myth, Narrative and Historical Experience." In *Visual and Other Pleasure*, 159–76. Bloomington: Indiana University Press, 1989.

Murphey, Rhoads. *The Fading of the Maoist Vision: City and Country in China's Development*. New York: Methuen, 1980.

Munro, Donald. *The Concept of Man in Contemporary China*. Ann Arbor: University of Michigan Press, 1977.

Musser, Charles. *Before the Nickelodeon: Edwin S. Porter and the Edison Manufacturing Company*. Berkeley: University of California Press, 1991.

Needham, Joseph. *The Legacy of China*, edited by Raymond Dawson. Oxford: Clarendon Press, 1964.
Nye, Joseph. *Soft Power: The Means to Success in World Politics*. New York: Public Affairs, 2004.
Nussbaum, Martha C. *Love's Knowledge: Essays on Philosophy and Literature*. New York: Oxford University Press, 1990.
Nussbaum, Martha C. *Upheavals of Thought: The Intelligence of Emotions*. Cambridge: Cambridge University Press, 2001.
Ong, Chang Woei. *Men of Letters within the Passes: Guanzhong Literati in Chinese History, 907–1911*. Cambridge, MA: Harvard University Press, 2008.
Ong, Walter J. *Orality and Literacy: The Technologizing of the Word*. London: Routledge, 1982.
Ogle, Vanessa. *The Global Transformation of Time: 1870–1950*. Cambridge, MA: Harvard University Press, 2015.
Owen, Stephen. "The Self's Perfect Mirror: Poetry as Autobiography." In *The Vitality of the Lyric Voice: Shih Poetry from the Late Han to the T'ang*, edited by Shuen-fu Lin and Stephen Owen, 71–102. Princeton: Princeton University Press, 1986.
Pang, Laikwan. *The Distorting Mirror: Visual Modernity in China*. Honolulu: University of Hawai'i Press, 2007.
Pang Laikwan. *The Art of Cloning: Creative Production during China's Cultural Revolution*. London: Verso, 2017.
Pang, Laikwan. *Creativity and Its Discontents: China's Creative Industries and Intellectual Property Rights Offenses*. Durham: Duke University Press, 2012.
Perry, Elizabeth. "Moving the Masses: Emotion Work in the Chinese Revolution." *Mobilization: An International Journal* 7, no. 2 (2002): 111–28.
Potter, Sulamith. "The Cultural Construction of Emotion in China." *Ethos* 16, no. 2 (June 1988): 199–206.
Qi, Wen, ed. *Yan'an and the Liberation Area in the Eyes of the Foreign Journalists* [Waiguo jizhe yanzhong de Yan'an ji jiefangqu]. Dalian: Dazhong Shudian, 1946.
Rancière, Jacques. "On Ignorant Schoolmasters." In *Jacques Rancière: Education, Truth, Emancipation*, edited by Charles Bingham and Gert J. J. Biesta, with Jacques Rancière, 1–24. London: Continuum, 2010.
Rancière, Jacques. *The Politics of Aesthetics: The Distribution of the Sensible*. Translated by Gabriel Rockhill. London: Continuum, 2004.
Rewi. *The Anna Louise Strong I Know: Her Life, Thought and Work* [Wo suo zhidao de sitelang: tade shenghuo, sixiang he zhuzuo]. Translated by Jiang Shanhui. Hong Kong: Xianggang chaoyang chubanshe, 1971.
Rogaski, Ruth. *Hygienic Modernity: Meanings of Health and Disease in Treaty-Port China*. Berkeley: University of California Press, 2004.
Ruoff, Jeffery. "Introduction: The Filmic Fourth Dimension: Cinema as Audiovisual Vehicle." In *Virtual Voyages: Cinema and Travel*, edited by Jeffery Ruoff, 1–24. Durham: Duke University Press, 2006.

Sackley, Nicole. "The Village as Cold War Site: Experts, Development, and the History of Rural Reconstruction." *Journal of Global History* 6, no. 3 (2011): 481–504.
Schivelbusch, Wolfgang. *The Railway Journey: Trains and Travel in the Nineteenth Century*. New York: Urizen Books, 1979.
Schmalzer, Sigrid. *The People's Peking Man: Popular Science and Human Identity in Twentieth-Century China*. Chicago: University of Chicago Press, 2008.
Schmalzer, Sigrid. *Red Revolution, Green Revolution: Scientific Farming in Socialist China*. Chicago: University of Chicago Press, 2016.
Schram, Stuart. *The Political Thought of Mao Tse-tung*. New York: Praeger, 1969.
Schwarcz, Vera. *The Chinese Enlightenment: Intellectuals and the Legacy of the May Fourth Movement of 1919*. Berkeley: University of California Press, 1986.
Schwartz, Benjamin I. *In Search of Wealth and Power: Yen Fu and the West*. Cambridge, MA: Harvard University Press, 1983.
Schwartz, Vanessa. *Spectacular Realities: Early Mass Culture in Fin-de-Siècle Paris*. Berkeley: University of California Press, 1998.
Schwartz, Vanessa, and Leo Charney. "Introduction." In *Cinema and the Invention of Modern Life*, edited by Leo Charney and Vanessa R. Schwartz. Berkeley: University of California Press, 1995.
Scott, James. *Domination and the Arts of Resistance: Hidden Transcripts*. New Haven, CT: Yale University Press, 1990.
Scott, James. *Seeing Like a State: How Certain Schemes to Improve the Human Condition Have Failed*. New Haven: Yale University Press, 1999.
Selden, Mark. *China in Revolution: The Yenan Way Revisited*. New York: M. E. Sharpe, 1995.
Selden, Mark. "Mao Zedong and the Political Economy of Chinese Development." In *Marxism and the Chinese Experience: Issues in Contemporary Chinese Socialism*, edited by Arif Dirlik and Maurice Meisner, 43–58. Armonk, NY: M. E. Sharpe, 1989.
Selden, Mark. *The Yenan Way in Revolutionary China*. Cambridge, MA: Harvard University Press, 1971.
Shapiro, Judith. *Mao's War Against Nature: Politics and the Environment in Revolutionary China*. Cambridge: Cambridge University Press, 2001.
Shen, Grace Yen. *Unearthing the Nation: Modern Geology and Nationalism in Republican China*. Chicago: University of Chicago Press, 2014.
Shih, Shu-mei, *The Lure of the Modern: Writing Modernism in Semicolonial China, 1917–1937*. Berkeley: University of California Press, 2001.
Smith, Arthur. *Chinese Characteristics*. New York: Fleming H. Revell, 1894.
Smith, Arthur. *Village Life in China; a Study in Sociology*. New York: F. H. Revell, 1899.
Snow, Edgar. "Awakening the Masses in China." *New York Herald Tribune*. December 17, 1933.
Snow, Edgar. "How Rural China Is Being Made." *China Weekly Review* (December 16, 1933): 98–101; (December 30, 1933): 202.
Snow, Edgar. "Preface to the 1938 edition of the Chinese translation." In *Xixing manji*, translated by Dong Leshan. Beijing: Shenghuo, Dushu, Xinzhi Sanlian shudian, 1979.

Snow, Edgar. *Red Star Over China*. London: Victor Gollancz, 1937.
Snow, Edgar. *Red Star Over China*. Rev. ed. New York: Grove Press, 1968.
Snow, Edgar. *Xixing manji*. Translated by Dong Leshan. Beijing: Shenghuo, Dushu, Xinzhi Sanlian shudian, 1979.
So, Richard Jean. *Transpacific Community: America, China, and the Rise and Fall of a Cultural Network*. New York: Columbia University Press, 2016.
Solomon, Robert C. *A Passion for Justice: Emotions and the Origins of the Social Contract*. Reading, MA: Addison-Wesley, 1990.
Sommer, Doris. "Irresistible Romance: The Foundational Fictions of Latin America." In *Nation and Narration*, edited by Homi K. Bhabha, 71–98. London: Routledge, 1990.
Song, Geng. *The Fragile Scholar: Power and Masculinity in Chinese Culture*. Hong Kong: Hong Kong University Press, 2004.
Spence, Jonathan D. *The Search for Modern China*. New York: W. W. Norton, 1999.
Stott, William. *Documentary Expression and Thirties America*. Chicago: University of Chicago Press, 1973.
Sun, Xiaozhong, and Gao Ming, eds. *A Collection of Materials on Rural Reconstruction in Yan'an* [Yan'an xiangcun jianshe ziliao]. Vols. 1, 2, and 4. Shanghai: Shanghai University Press, 2012.
Tang, Xiaobing. *Chinese Modern: The Heroic and the Quotidian*. Durham: Duke University Press, 2000.
Tang Xiaobing, "The Historical Significance of the film *Never Forget*: Anxiety about Everyday Life and Modernity" [Qianwan buyao wangji de lishi—guanyu richang shenghuo de jiaolv jiqi xiandaixing yiyi]. In *Re-interpretation: Popular Culture and Ideology* [Zai Jiedu: Dazhong wenyi yu yishi xingtai], 224–34. Beijing: Beijing University Press, 2007.
Tang, Xiaobing. "Listening to Yan'an: Illuminations from a Sonic Experience" [Lingting Yan'an: yiduan tingjue jingyan de qishi]. *Journal of Modern Chinese Studies* (Shanghai), January 2017: 4–11.
Tao Jin. "A Poetic Age—Random Thoughts from the Director of *A Nurse's Diary*." *Popular Cinema* [Dazhong dianying] 12 (1957).
Tao Lugong. "Introductory Remark." *New Youth* 4, no. 3 (March 3, 1917): 221–24.
Taylor, Charles. *Human Agency and Language: Philosophical Papers 1*. Cambridge: Cambridge University Press, 1985.
Taylor, Charles. "The Politics of Recognition." In *Multiculturalism: Examining the Politics of Recognition*, edited by Amy Gutmann, 25–74. Princeton: Princeton University Press, 1994.
Taylor, Charles. *Sources of the Self: The Making of the Modern Identity*. Cambridge, MA: Harvard University Press, 1989.
Thomas, S. Bernard. *Season of High Adventure: Edgar Snow in China*. Berkeley: University of California Press, 1996.
Tian Xiaofei. *Tao Yuanming & Manuscript Culture: The Record of a Dusty Table*. Seattle: University of Washington Press, 2005.

Trilling, Lionel. *Sincerity and Authenticity*. Cambridge, MA: Harvard University Press, 1971.
Tsou, Tang. *The Cultural Revolution and Post-Mao Reform: A Historical Perspective*. Chicago: University of Chicago Press, 1986.
Underwood, Doug. *Journalism and the Novel: Truth and Fiction, 1700–2000*. Cambridge: Cambridge University Press, 2008.
Visser, Robin. *Cities Surround the Countryside: Urban Aesthetics in Postsocialist China*. Durham: Duke University Press, 2010.
Volland, Nicolai. *Socialist Cosmopolitanism: The Chinese Literary Universe, 1945–1965*. New York: Columbia University Press, 2017.
Wang, Ban. *Illuminations from the Past: Trauma, Memory and History in Modern China*. Stanford: Stanford University Press, 2004.
Wang, Ban. "Socialist Realism." In *Words and Its Stories, Words and Their Stories: Essays on the Language of the Chinese Revolution*, edited by Ban Wang, 101–18. Leiden: Brill 2010.
Wang, Ban. *The Sublime Figure of History: Aesthetics and Politics in Twentieth-Century China*. Stanford: Stanford University Press, 1997.
Wang, David Der-wei. "Imaginary Nostalgia: Shen Congwen, Song Zelai, Mo Yan, and Li Yongping." In *From May Fourth to June Fourth: Fiction and Film in Twentieth-Century China*, edited by Ellen Widmer and David Der-wei Wang, 107–32. Cambridge, MA: Harvard University Press, 1993.
Wang, David Der-wei. *The Monster That Is History: History, Violence, and Fictional Writing in Twentieth-Century China*. Berkeley: University of California Press, 2004.
Wang, Lingzhen. *Personal Matters: Women's Autobiographical Practice in Twentieth-Century China*. Stanford: Stanford University Press, 2004.
Wang Lingzhen. "Socialist Cinema and Female Authorship: Overdetermination and Subjective Revisions in Dong Kena's *A Blade of Grass on the Kunlun Mountain* (1962)." In *Chinese Women's Cinema: Transnational Contexts*, edited by Wang Lingzhen, 47–65. New York: Columbia University Press, 2011.
Wang Mingming. *Walking on the Countryside* [Zouzai xiangtu shang]. Beijing: Zhongguo renmin daxue chubanshe, 2009.
Wang Shiwei. "The Wild Lily." *Liberation Daily*. March 13, March 23, 1942.
Wang Xiaoming. "L xian jianwen" [A Journey of L County]. In *Xiangtu Zhongguo yu wenhua yanjiu* [Rural China and Cultural Studies], edited by Xue Yi, 338–55. Shanghai: Shanghai shudian chubanshe, 2008.
Warner, Michael. *Publics and Counterpublics*. Brooklyn: Zone Books. 2005.
Watson, Peter. *The Modern Mind: An Intellectual History of the 20th Century*. New York: Harper Perennial, 2002.
Wen Tiejun. *Zhongguo nongcun jiben jingji zhidu yanjiu: "sannong" wenti de shiji fansi* [A Study of the Basic Economic System of Chinese Rural Society: A Century's Reflection upon the "Three Rural Issues"]. Beijing: Zhongguo jingji chubanshe, 2000.
Wen Tiejun, Qiu Jiansheng, and Che Haisheng. "'Sannong' wenti de yanjin yu xiangcun

zhenxing zhanlue de tichu" [The Development of the "Three Rural Problems" and the Proposal of the Strategy of the Rural Vitalization], http://www.aisixiang.com/data/112750.html. Last accessed on October 30, 2018.

White, Hayden. *Tropics of Discourse: Essays in Cultural Criticism*. Baltimore: Johns Hopkins University Press, 1986.

White, Louise. 2000. *Speaking with Vampires: Rumor and History in Colonial Africa*. Berkeley: University of California Press.

Whyte, Martin King. "The Paradoxes of Rural-Urban Inequality in Contemporary China." *One Country, Two Societies: Rural-Urban Inequality in Contemporary China*, edited by Martin King Whyte, 1–28. Cambridge, MA: Harvard University Press, 2010.

Williams, Raymond. *The Country and the City*. New York: Oxford University Press, 1973.

Williams, Raymond. *Keywords: A Vocabulary of Culture and Society*. New York: Oxford University Press, 1985.

Wolfreys, Julian. *Introducing the Criticism in the 21st Century*. Edinburgh: Edinburgh University Press, 2002.

Wolin, Richard. *The Wind from the East: French Intellectuals, the Cultural Revolution, and the Legacy of the 1960s*. Princeton: Princeton University Press, 2010.

Womack, Brantly. *The Foundation of Mao Zedong's Political Thought, 1917–1935*. Honolulu: University of Hawai'i Press, 1982.

Wu Jiliang. *Edgar Snow and China* [Sinuo yu zhongguo]. Beijing: Zhongguo shehui chubanshe, 2005.

Wu, Ka Ming. *Reinventing Chinese Tradition: The Cultural Politics of Late Socialism*. Champaign: University of Illinois Press. 2015.

Wu Xiangxiang. *Yan Yangchu zhuan: wei quanqiu xiangcun gaizao fendou liushinian* [James Yen and His Sixty Years of Struggle with Rural Reconstruction for the Peasant People of the World]. Taipei: Shibao wenhua chuban shiye youxian gongxi, 1981.

Wu, Xiangxiang. *Yan Yangchu zhuan—wei Quanqiu xiangcun gaizao fendou liushinian* [Biography of Yan Yangchu: Sixty Years' Rural Reform in the World]. Changsha: Yuelu shushe, 2001.

"Xi Jinping's Talks at the Beijing Forum on Literature and Art." October 16, 2014, https://chinacopyrightandmedia.wordpress.com/2014/10/16/xi-jinpings-talks-at-the-beijing-forum-on-literature-and-art/. The original Chinese version: http://news.xinhuanet.com/politics/2015-10/14/c_1116825558.htm, accessed October 23, 2017.

Xiao Jun. "On Love and Patience among Comrades" [Lun tongzhi zhi ai yu nai]. In *The Collective Work of Xiao Jun* [Xiao Jun Quanji]. Vol. 11, 542–45. Beijing: Huaxia chubanshe, 2008.

Xiong Foxi. "Guodu" [Cross the River]. In *Zhongguo huaju bainian juzuo xuan* [Selection of Plays from the Past One Hundred Years of Chinese Spoken Drama], edited by Zhongguo huaju yishu yanjiu hui. 20 vols. Vol. 2, 419–58. Beijing: Zhongguo duiwai fanyi chuban gongsi, 2007.

Xiong Foxi. *Xiandai xijujia Xiong Foxi* [Modern Playwright Xiong Foxi], edited by Xiong Foxi yanjiu xiaozu. Beijing: Zhongguo xiju,1985.

Xiong Foxi. *Xiju dazhonghua zhi shiyan* [Experiment in Theatrical Popularization]. Nanjing: Zhongzheng shuju, 1937.
Xiong Foxi. *Xiong Foxi xiju wenji* [An Anthology of Xiong Foxi's Plays]. Shanghai: Shanghai wenyi chubanshe, 2000.
Xiong Peiyun. *China in a Village* [*Yige cunzhuangli de Zhongguo*]. Beijing: Xinxing chubanshe, 2011.
Xu Jilin. "The Origin of Individualism: A Study of the View of the Self in the May Fourth Movement" [Geren zhuyi de qiyuan: Wusi shiqi de ziwoguan yanjiu]. *Social Science in Tianjin* [Tianjin shehui kexue] 6 (2008): 113–24.
Xu Qinwen. *Guxiang* [My Hometown]. Shanghai: Beixin shuju, 1926.
Yan Hairong. "Self-Development of Migrant Women and the Production of *Suzhi* [Quality] as Surplus Value." In *Everyday Modernity in China*, edited by Madeleine Yue Dong and Joshua L. Goldstein, 227–58. Seattle: University of Washington Press, 2006).
Yan Hairong. "Spectralization of the Rural: Reinterpreting the Labor Mobility of Rural Young Women in Post-Mao China." *American Ethnologist* 30, no. 4 (Nov. 2003): 578–96.
Yan, Jiayan. *Zhongguo xiandai xiaoshuo liupaishi* [A History of Schools of Chinese Fiction]. Beijing: Renmin wenxue chubanshe, 1989.
Yan, Yangchu. "Chuji pingjiao jiaoxue de zhonglei ji zuzhi" [The Categories and Organization of the Elementary Commoners' Education]. *Yan Yangchu quanji*. Vol. 1, 94–96.
Yan Yangchu. "Nongcun yundong de shiming" [The Mission of the Rural Movements]. In *Yan Yangchu quanji* [The Anthology of Yan Yangchu], edited by Song Enrong. Vol. 1, 293–304. Changsha: Hunan jiaoyu, 1989.
Yan, Yangchu. "Pingmin de gongmin jiaoyu zhi wojian" [My View about the Commoners' Citizenship Education]. *Yan Yangchu quanji* [The Anthology of Yan Yangchu], edited by Song Enrong. Vol. 1, 63–67. Changsha: Hunan jiaoyu, 1989.
Yan, Yangchu. "Pingmin jiaoyu" [Commoners' Education]. *Yan Yangchu quanji* [The Anthology of Yan Yangchu], edited by Song Enrong. Vol. 1, 47–51. Changsha: Hunan jiaoyu, 1989.
Yan Yangchu. "Pingmin jiaoyu gailun" [An Introduction to the Commoners' Education]. In *Yan Yangchu quanji* [The Anthology of Yan Yangchu], edited by Song Enrong. Vol. 1, 121–33. Changsha: Hunan jiaoyu, 1989.
Yan Yangchu. "You wenhua de zhongguo xinnongmin." In *Yan Yangchu quanji* [The Anthology of Yan Yangchu], edited by Song Enrong. Vol. 1, 141–60. Changsha: Hunan jiaoyu, 1989.
Yan Yangchu. "Zhongguo de xinmin." In *Yan Yangchu quanji* [The Anthology of Yan Yangchu], edited by Song Enrong. Vol. 1, 161–71. Changsha: Hunan jiaoyu, 1989.
Yan Yangchu. *See also* Yen, James Y. C.
Yan Yunxiang. *The Flow of Gifts: Reciprocity and Social Networks in a Chinese Village*. Stanford: Stanford University Press, 1996.
Yang Cunbin. "Xu" [Preface]. In *Guodu* jiqi yanchu [*Crossing the River* and Its Performance], edited by Xiong Foxi, 1–18. Shanghai: Zhengzhong shuju, 1937.

Yang, Mayfair Mei-hui. *Gifts, Favors and Banquets: The Art of Social Relationships in China*. Ithaca: Cornell University Press, 1994.

Ye Shengtao. *Ni Huanzhi*. Beijing: Renmin wenxue chubanshe, 1953.

Ye Yuan. "Social Investigation: The County of Cannei" [Shehui diaocha: Cannei xiang]. *New Youth* 4, no. 5 (May 15, 1918): 441–45.

Yeh, Wen-hsin. *The Alienated Academy: Culture and Politics in Republican China, 1919–1937*. Cambridge, MA: Council on East Asian Studies, Harvard University, 1990.

Yeh, Wen-hsin. *Shanghai Splendor: Economic Sentiments and the Making of Modern China, 1843–1949*. Berkeley: University of California Press, 2007.

Yen, James Y. C. (Yan Yangchu). *China's New Scholar-Farmer*. Ting Hsien: Chinese National Association of the Mass Education Movement, 1929.

Yen, James Y. C. (Yan Yangchu). *New Citizens for China*. Ting Hsien: Chinese National Association of the Mass Education Movement, 1929.

Yen, James Y. C. *Ting Hsien Experiment: 1930–1931*. Ting Hsien: Chinese National Association of the Mass Education Movements, 1931.

"Yijian qianghun an." *Xinhua ribao*, April 11, 1945.

Youd, Daniel M. "Beyond Bao: Moral Ambiguity and the Law in Late Imperial Chinese Narrative Literature." In *Writing and Law in Late Imperial China: Crime, Conflict, and Judgment*, edited by Robert E. Hegel and Katherine Carlitz, 215–233. Seattle: University of Washington Press, 2007.

Yu Dafu. "Wisteria and Dodder" [Niaoluo xing]. In *The Collected Works of Yu Dafu* [*Yu Dafu wenji*]. Vol. 1, 213–28. Hong Kong: Shenghuo, dushu, xinzhi sanlian shudian xianggang fendian and Huacheng chubanshe, 1982.

Yu Ronghu. *The Changing Theories on the Chinese Native Soil Fiction* [Zhongguo xian dai xiang tu wen xue li lun liu bian lun]. Beijing: Zhongguo shehui kexue chuban she, 2011.

Yuan Jing. *Liu Qiao'er gaozhuang* [Liu Qiao'er Seeking Justice]. Ha'erbin: Dongbei shudian, 1947.

Zhang Xipo. *Ma Xiwu and Ma Xiwu's Way of Adjudicating Cases* [Ma Xiwu yu Ma Xiwu shenpan fangshi]. Beijing: Falv chubanshe, 2013.

Zhang Xipo. *Ma Xiwu shenpan fangshi* [Ma Xiwu's Way of Adjudicating Cases]. Beijing: Falv chubanshe, 1983.

Zhang, Xudong. "The Power of Rewriting: Postrevolutionary Discourse on Chinese Socialist Realism." In *Socialist Realism Without Shores*, edited by Thomas Lahusen and Evgeny Dobrenko, 282–309. Durham: Duke University Press, 1997.

Zhang Yingjin. *Chinese National Cinema*. New York: Routledge, 2004.

Zhang Yingjin. *The City in Modern Chinese Literature and Film: Configurations of Space, Time, and Gender*. Stanford: Stanford University Press, 1996.

Zhang, Zhen. *An Amorous History of the Silver Screen: Shanghai Cinema, 1896–1937*. Chicago: University of Chicago Press, 2005.

Zhang Zuyin. "The Peasants in Zhenze," *New Youth* 4, no. 3 (March 3, 1917): 224–28.

Zhao Chaogou. *Yan'an in January* [Yan'an yiyue]. Nanjing: Xinmin baoshe, 1946.

Zhao, Henry Y. H. *The Uneasy Narrator: Chinese Fiction from the Traditional to the Modern*. Oxford: Oxford University Press, 1995.
Zhao Shuli. "The Marriage of Young Blacky" [Xiao Erhei jiehun]. In *A Collection of Zhao Shuli's Work* [Zhao Shuli wenji]. Vol. 1. (Beijing: Gongren chubanshe, 1980).
Zhao Yuan. *Di zhi zi* [The Son of the Earth]. Beijing: Beijing shiyue wenyi chubanshe, 1993.
Zhongguo dianying chuban she, ed. *Our Socialist Films in Development* [Zai fazhanzhong de woguo shehui zhuyi dianying]. Beijing: Zhongguo dianying chuban she, 1961.
Zhongguo tielu jiansheshi bianweihui, ed. *A Chinese History of Railway Construction* [*Zhongguo Tielu jianshe she*]. Beijing: Zhongguo tiedao chubanshe, 2003.
Zhonggong zhongyang bangongting, ed. *The High Tide of Socialism in the Chinese Countryside* [Zhongguo nongcunde shehuizhuyi gaochao]. Beijing: Renmin chubanshe, 1956.
Zhonghua pingmin jiaoyu cujinhui pingmin wenxuebu, ed. *The Farmer's a Thousand Characters* [Nongmin qianzike]. 4 vols. Shanghai: Zhonghua pingmin jiaoyu cujinhui pingmin wenxuebu, 1930-1931.
Zhu Daohua and Feng Meifa. *Nongcun gongyehua wenti tansuo* [*On Questions about Rural Industrialization*]. Beijing: Zhongguo nongye chubanshe, 1995.
Zhu Hongzhao. *A History of Everyday Life in Yan'an, 1937-1947* [Yan'an richang shenghuo zhong de lishi, 1937-1947]. Guilin: Guangxi shifan daxue chubanshe, 2007.
Zihui. "Huanghe dahechang de liangbu shougao dang'an" [The Archive of Two Manuscripts of the Chorus of The Yellow River]. *Dangan chunqiu*, issue 9, 2006: 2.

Films

Dong Kena, dir. *A Blade of Grass on the Kunlun Mountain* [*Kunlunshan shang yikecao*]. Beijing: Beijing Film Studio, 1962. 62 min.
Du Haibin, dir. *Along the Railway* [*Tielu yanxian*], 2000. Documentary film.
Li Yalin, dir. *A Love-Forsaken Corner* [*Bei aiqing yiwang de jiaoluo*]. Emei Film Studio, 1981.
Su Li, dir. *The Young People in Our Village* [*Women cunli de nianqingren*]. Changchun: Changchun Film Studio, 1959.
Su Li, dir. *The Young People in Our Village* [the sequel]. Changchun: Changchun Film Studio, 1963.
Tao Jin, dir. *The Nurse's Diary* [*Hushi riji*]. Shanghai: Jiangnan Film Studio, 1957.
Wang Bin, dir. *Bridge* [*Qiao*]. Changchun: Northeast Film Studio, 1949.
Wu Tianming, dir. *Life* [*Rensheng*]. Xi'an: Xian'an Film Studio, 1984.
Wu Tianming, dir. *Old Well* [*Laojing*]. Xi'an: Xian'an Film Studio, 1986.
Zhao Ming, dir. *The Young Generation* [*Nianqing de yidai*]. Shanghai: Shanghai Film Studio, 1965. 106 min.
Hu Bingliu, dir. *The Voice of the Village* [*Xiangyin*]. Zhujiang Film Studio, 1983.

Index

affect: communication and, 74–75, 135, 138; cultural productions and, 10–11; human-machine dynamic and, 185–86; in human relationships, 30–31, 34, 43 (*see also* interpersonal relationships); labor and, 164; in rural society, 24–26, 154; socialist industrialization and, 168–69, 177, 185–86, 193–97; value judgment and, 63, 66. *See also* emotion; sentiment
agency, 32, 74, 105, 140, 156, 163, 181, 229n126
agrarian time, 81, 93–94
agricultural field, 132–33
agricultural productivity, 148, 153, 241n58
alienated labor, 153, 185
Along the Railway (2000), 206
Althusser, Louis, 112
ambivalence, 29, 38
Anagnost, Ann, 244n109
Anderson, Benedict, 58, 72, 94, 127, 139
Anderson, Marston, 219n29
anticolonialism, 80
antifacism, 86–87, 90
Anti-Japanese Military and Political University, 95
Anti-Japanese War, 79, 110, 129. *See also* Japanese imperialism
arranged marriage. *See* marriage
"artisanal as industrial," 150, 170–78
attraction, 47, 48, 75; theatrical performances and, 63, 72–74; visual education and, 53–62

audience participation, 62–74, 85–87
authenticity, 27, 62; emotional, 126, 135
awakening, 53, 252n6

backwardness, 8, 11, 43, 59, 98, 148, 161, 185, 186, 217n51. *See also* underdevelopment
Bakken, Borge, 152
Bao, Judge, 135
Bao, Weihong, 188
Bao'an, 79, 90, 98, 230n2
Baudelaire, Charles, 170
Beijing, 44, 90, 209
Benjamin, Walter, 53–54, 127, 175, 206, 233n77
Bhabha, Homi, 228n126
bitterness, 53, 116; "eating bitterness," 97, 186, 197–203; "speaking bitterness," 143, 244n109
Blade of Grass on the Kunlun Mountain, A (1962), 186, 197–204, 254n41
Brecht, Bertolt, 66, 67
Bridge (1949), 188, 192
Buck, Pearl, 52–53, 89; *The Good Earth*, 82, 233n76

Cai Xiang, 151, 205, 243n84, 256n60
Cannei, Fujian Province, 23–24
cannibalistic views, 24
capitalist creativity, 156
capitalist industrialization, 87, 179
Castoriadis, Cornelius, 216n46
CCP. *See* Chinese Communist Party (CCP)

281

282 INDEX

Chakrabarty, Dipesh, 73
Chang, Eileen. *See* Zhang Ailing
Chang'an, 84
Changchun film Studio, 160
chatting, 122, 133–36
Chen, Tina Mai, 185, 237n146
Chen Duxiu, 39
Chen Mo, 168
Chen Tianhua, *The Roar of the Lion*, 61
Chen Xuezhao, 80, 81, 235n115; *A Visit to Yan'an*, 93, 94–98, 101
Chen Yun, 201
China: global system and, 92; "the other China"/"another China" discourse, 90–92, 94. *See also* national identity; nation-building; People's Republic of China (PRC)
China Pictorial, 152, 154–55, 158–59
China Weekly Review, 76, 90
Chinese classical literature, 46
Chinese Communist Party (CCP), 79; communication with villagers, 133–36; cultural policy, 110, 138; "explaining and persuading" communicative style, 113, 120–21, 125, 133, 138; headquarters, 230n2 (*see also* Yan'an); leaders of, 88 (*see also* Mao Zedong); marriage regulations, 114; newspaper of, 92; Red Army Long March, 82–85, 110. *See also* revolution
Chinese enlightenment. *See* enlightenment discourse
Chinese literary and cultural studies, 1–2; research methods, 7–8
Chinese writing system. *See* writing
Chow, Rey, 54
Ci Jiwei, 108, 166
cinema. *See* socialist cinema
cities. *See* Beijing; Shanghai; urban areas
citizenship training, 53, 228n126; emotion and, 63, 73, 87
Civil Rights Village, 61
civil-service examination, 49
Clark, Paul, 187
clocks, 93–94, 108
collective consciousness, 92, 105

collective creativity, 149
collective heroic personalities, 81, 90–91. *See also* labor heroes
collective labor, 13, 57, 71, 164, 166–67, 169, 175. *See also* labor
collective spectatorship, 54
collective subjectivity, 3, 64, 72, 192, 249n72
communal culture, 55
communication, 30–31, 42–43; affect and, 74–75, 135, 138; cultural forms and, 143; "explaining and persuading," 113, 120–21, 125, 133, 138; theatrical performance and, 64; village soundscape, 133–36; written, 57–58. *See also* interpersonal relationships
Communist movement: visibility of, 82. *See also* Chinese Communist Party (CCP); revolution
compassionate citizenship, 63, 70
Compendium of Modern Chinese Literature, 33
conciliation, 121, 133
Confucian system: breakdown of, 18–19; critiques of, 23; iconoclastic revolt against, 31; ideals of, 61; literati in, 21–22; rituals, 27
Cong, Xiaoping, 112, 114, 122, 126, 142, 240n38
conscience, 140
construction sites, 185, 186, 190, 193–99, 206
cosmopolitanism, 8, 11, 32, 47, 94, 98–99
countryside. *See* rural areas
courtship and dating, 168–69, 176–77. *See also* romantic love
craftsmanship, 170–78, 250n87
creativity: capitalist, 156; collective, 149, 157, 161; socialist, 149, 155–59. *See also* inventiveness
credibility, 83, 90
crudeness, rural, 81, 103. *See also* material scarcity
cultural elites, 47, 49
cultural imaginary, 216n46
cultural production: human subjec-

tivities and, 4, 10; and the rural, 3. *See also* documentary nonfiction; homecoming fiction; journalistic writings; native-soil fiction; newspapers; reportage literature; revolutionary literature; rural vernacular; socialist cinema; spoken drama; theatrical performance/education

Cultural Revolution, 9, 183, 206, 208. *See also* social engineering programs

current affairs, 111

Curried, Brian, 192

customs, local, 20–28, 42–43, 219n30, 219n33

Darwinism, Spencerian social, 194

decline, discourse of, 84, 91, 231n36

DeMare, Brian James, 139

democracy: antifascist, 86–87; in family relationships, 141–42; public trials and, 136; Yan'an and, 95

Deng Xiaoping, 209

Denton, Kirk, 105

development, 13, 148–49, 161, 205; modernity and, 73; rural industrialization and, 245n4. *See also* rural industrialization; socialist industrialization; urban development

developmentalism, 210–11

Diamant, Neil, 115

Ding County: literacy rate, 225n62; rural reconstruction movement, 11, 44–76

Ding Fan, 216n44

Ding Ling, 80, 109; "How I Came to Shanbei," 98; "In the Hospital," 82, 98–106, 237n140; "My Reflections on March 8," 99; "When I Was in the Xia Village," 99; "Yan'an in July," 98

Dirlik, Arif, 166, 193

disembedding, 184, 252n5

dissection, 236n127

documentary nonfiction, 82–83, 85

domestic labor, 153–54

domestic space, 59–60

Donald, Stephanie Hemelryk, 254n38

Dong Jiageng, 151–52

drama. *See* spoken drama; theatrical performance/education

Duara, Prasenjit, 34, 126, 135

Dutton, Michael, 98

Eastman, Lloyd E., 218n8

"eating bitterness," 97, 186, 197–203

ecocriticism, 155

education, 45; modern idea of, 64; scientific, 158. *See also* literacy campaigns; rural reconstruction movement

efficiency, 159, 185, 186, 206

Egan, Michael, 41

Eisenstein, Sergei, 54

electrification, 154–55, 158–78

Elias, Norbert, 92

Elman, Benjamin, 49

emotion: citizenship training and, 63, 73, 87; documentary nonfiction and, 83, 85; homecoming and, 42–43; motion and, 255n52; professionalism and, 102–3; railway travel and, 186–93, 203–4; revolutionary politics and, 85–87, 98–99, 103–4, 108; social justice and, 67–74; technology and, 177, 205; theatrical performances and, 48, 63–74. *See also* affect; sentiment

emotional authenticity, 126, 135

empathy, 47, 48, 75; theatrical performances and, 62–74

emplotment, 89

emptiness, 13–14, 184–85

enlightenment discourse, 11, 208; on characteristics of peasants, 47–48, 59; on countryside, 19–20; elites and, 46; individualism and, 32; rural-urban divisions and, 8; self-reflexivity, 75; spatial crossing and, 1

epic theater, 66

Equal People Village, 61

equality, 53

eroticism, 169

ethics, 18–19

exemplary society, 152

exploitative labor, 166–67

Express Train, An (1965), 189

Eyferth, Jacob, 175

Fairbank, John K., 80, 84, 231n18
family: democratic relationships within, 141–42; modern identity and, 32–36; obligations to, 32; social-survey essays on, 24–26. *See also* filial piety; marriage; patriarchal institutions
famine, 161, 171, 197–98
Fan Changjiang, *The Northwest Corner of China*, 84
Fang Ji, 80, 109; "The Power of the Loom," 82, 98, 106–8
farmers: characteristics of, 223n24; harmony between rulers and, 132. *See also* peasants; scholar-farmers
Farmer's A Thousand Character Primer, The, 56–62
Faust (Goethe), 193–94
Fei Xiaotong, 30, 50, 130
Feng, Jin, 221n63
Feng Yuanjun, 32, 41; "After My Mother Left," 38; "After Separation," 36–37; "My Loving Mother," 36–38; "Separation," 36–37; "The chaste woman," 38
Feuerwerker, Yi-tsi Mei, 236n135
fieldwork, 44–45, 186, 198. *See also* rural reconstruction
filial piety, 35–36, 57, 59, 65, 68, 139, 142, 204. *See also* family
films: circulation of, 187–88. *See also* socialist cinema
first-person narrative voice, 28
Fitzgerald, John, 7, 53, 252n6
folk entertainment, 137–42
folklore movement, 10, 18; emotional authenticity and, 126
folklore studies, 7–8
folk practices, 27
Foucault, Michel, 2, 201
France, 95, 251n101
free love, 38–39, 176
Friedberg, Anne, 188
frontier region, 182–207; construction sites in, 183, 193–97; hardship in, 198–99; human-land relationship and, 197–204; railway travel to, 182–93; remoteness and emptiness of, 13–14, 182–86
Fu Sinian, "A Sketch of the Peasants' Situation in Part of Shandong Province," 25

Gamble, Sidney, 45
Gao Mingfu, 137
Gaonkar, Dilip Parameshwar, 2
"gardens and fields," 4–5, 61
Gellner, Ernest, 50
gender, 60, 143; authorial voice and, 95–97. *See also* "man tilling, woman weaving"; women
gentry-scholars, 3–5, 17–18, 48–49. *See also* intellectuals
Geological Society, 199
geologists, 7–8, 198–99
Giddens, Anthony, 42, 252n5
gift-giving, 30–31
global capitalism, 210
global media, 149
Gluckman, Max, 134
Goethe, *Faust*, 193–94
"going to the city," 17, 36, 220n53. *See also* urban migration
"going to the countryside": as an unfamiliar place, 10–11; Chinese modernity and, 1–9, 208; as homecoming, 10–11; as "invitation card" to rural masses, 12–13, 72; as "returning to gardens and fields," 4–5, 61; socialist industrialization and, 13–14. *See also* rural areas; social engineering programs; urban-to-rural migration
"going to the people" movements, 5–6, 44–48, 227n86. *See also* rural reconstruction
Good Companion, The (periodical), 80
gossip, 122, 133–36, 140, 143
governance: multimedia regime of, 111, 126, 139; in villages, 133–36, 142–43
Great Leap Forward, 149, 154, 157, 170, 178; famine in, 161, 171
Guanzhong, 231n36
Gu Yuan, *Ma Xiwu Mediating a Marriage Dispute Case*, 122–23

Habermas, Jürgen, 63
handicraft production, 22, 87, 106–7, 175, 177, 241n58
Han dynasty, 85, 232n43
Hang, Krista Van Fleit, 249n62
Han Qixiang, *Liu Qiao's Reunion*, 125–33, 137–43
Han Shaogong, 211
hardship, 198–99, 208
Hayford, Charles W., 45, 75
historical progress, 81, 89, 108, 183, 206
historiography, 21, 46
homecoming: emotion and, 42–43; socialist discourse on, 147–50
homecoming fiction: human relationships and, 42–43; overview of, 17–20; in post-Mao era, 210; rural industrialization and, 13; sentimental, 10–11, 28–42
Huizinga, Johan, 163
human capacity, 156, 167, 177, 194
human-land relationship, 197–204
human-machine dynamic, 185, 196, 204–5
human-nature relationship, 155–56
human potential, 157, 166–67, 194
human subjectivities, 4, 10; collective, 3, 64, 72, 192, 249n72
human-tool continuum, 237n146
Hundred Flowers period, 189
Hung Chang-tai, 110, 114, 137, 240n42, 243n93
hydropower stations, 154–55, 158–78
hygiene movements, 45, 59–60, 97, 101–2

iconoclastic culture, 18–20, 31, 35
identity: family and, 32–36; peasants and, 75–76; rural-urban distinctions and, 4–5. *See also* national identity
illiteracy, 51–52, 67, 124, 127, 138
illness, metaphor of, 51–52, 99
illustrated primers, 11, 47, 53–54, 56–62, 75, 226n64
Imperial China, 240n44
individualism: confusion and, 19; morality and, 35; "problematic individual," 28; rights-based, 32, 39; romantic, 105
industrialization. *See* rural industrialization; socialist industrialization
inequality, 13–14, 22, 25, 31, 42, 209; social hierarchies and, 49–51 (*see also* social hierarchies); Yan'an approaches to, 80
Inner Mongolia, 194, 254n35
intellectuals, 1, 208; free love and, 39; handicraft production and, 106–7; homecoming narratives, 18; laborers and, 7; as public actors, 62–63; rural reconstruction and, 44–46 (*see also* rural reconstruction). *See also* gentry-scholars
intelligence, 50
intelligentsia, urban-based, 8, 11; communication with masses, 31; social Darwinism and, 194
Internationalists, 234n83
international socialism, 149
interpersonal relationships: in families, 41–43, 141–42; represented in illustrated primers, 57; revolutionaries and, 98, 103, 106; in rural society, 25–27, 29–32; social hierarchies and, 59 (*see also* social hierarchies); theatrical performance/education and, 64. *See also* communication; love
In the Wild Mountains (1986), 251n105
inventiveness: industrial-as-artisanal, 170–78; socialist creativity and, 155–59. *See also* creativity
Iovene, Paola, 190, 194
irrigation canals, 158–62, 169–70, 181

Japanese imperialism, 79–80, 86, 88, 90, 116, 248n52
Japanese New Village Movement, 6–7, 215n28
Johnson, David, 65
Johnson, Matthew, 160
Jones, Andrew, 51
journalistic writings, 1, 8, 81–91, 208, 233n77. *See also* reportage literature

Journey to the West, 25
Judge, Joan, 51
justice, 70. *See also* law; social justice

King, Richard, 157, 178
Kinkley, Jeffrey, 235n115
knowledge production, 42–43
Kojin, Karatani, 164
Kunlun Mountain, 199–200

labor: alienated, 153, 185; domestic, 153–54; exploitative, 166–67; leisure and, 249n62; love-labor conjunction, 112, 124–33, 168–69; nonalienated, 81, 87–88, 90, 108, 153, 178; as play, 150, 160–69, 178, 181; women and, 153–54. *See also* collective labor; handicraft production; manual labor
laborers: in France, 52–53; intellectuals and, 7; relationships with landlords, 25–26, 30
labor heroes, 129–30, 147–48, 152, 181. *See also* collective heroic personalities
Lam, Tong, 135
landlords: absentee, 5, 25–26; relationships with laborers, 25–26, 30
Landmine Warfare (1963), 248n52
landscape, 8, 13, 84–85, 167, 176–77; awakening of, 252n6; bleak, 100; in illustrated primers, 61; industrial, 159; leftist journalists on, 84–85, 87; militarized, 147; natural, 153; pastoral, 151; socialist national, 184–97, 200–207. *See also* nature
language: of law, 119 (*see also* law); limits of, 30–31; translation of, 89; westernization of, 46. *See also* communication; literacy campaigns; vernacular language; writing
Lanlan and Dongdong (1958), 189
lantern slides, 11, 47, 53–56, 75, 225n52
l'art pour l'art, 66
Last Train Home, 206
Lattimore, Owen, 90
Laughlin, Charles, 83
law, 69–71; literature and, 111, 240n44; love-law conjunction, 112–24, 132–33

Lean, Eugenia, 63, 69, 228n114
Lee, Haiyan, 63, 215n30
Lee, Leo, 237n143
leisure time: labor and, 249n62; in villages, 25, 102
Levenson, Joseph, 32, 92
Liang, Shuming, 5, 49, 229n136
Liang Qichao, 47
Liang Shuming, 229n136
Liberation Daily, 92, 102, 120–23
Li Changping, 257n8
Li Dazhao, "Youth and the Village," 6–7
Life (1984), 251n105
life-art boundary, 65–66
linear temporality, 92–94
Lin Shan, 137
Lintong County, Shaanxi Province, 155
listening, 133–36
literacy campaigns, 45, 47, 48–53, 75; illustrated primers used in, 11, 47, 53–54, 56–62, 75, 226n64; women and, 60. *See also* education
literati, self-identity of, 4–5
Little Inventors (1958), 158
Li Tuo, 126
Liu, Lydia, 19, 236n127
Liu Qiao'er, 53
Liu Qiao stories, 124–43
Liu Shaoqi, 148, 198
local customs, 20–28, 42–43, 219n30, 219n33
local gazetteers, 21–22, 27
locality, 94
Long March, 82–85, 110, 255n50
love: free love, 38–39, 176; love-labor conjunction, 112, 124–33, 168–69; love-law conjunction, 112–24, 132–33; marriage reform in May Fourth era, 36–39. *See also* courtship and dating; marriage; romantic love
Love-Forsaken Corner, A (1981), 206
love-law-labor conjunction, 112, 142–43
Lukacs, Georg, 28
Lu Mang, *Rosy Clouds of Dawn Rise in the East*, 254n28
Lu Xinhua, "The Scar," 206

Lu Xun, 26, 33, 38, 52, 101; "Diary of a Madman," 23–24; "My Old Home," 29–31; "Preface to Outcry," 54; "Regret for the Past," 31; "What Happens After Nora Leaves Home?," 31
Lye, Colleen, 233n76

Ma Boyuan, "Local Customs in Hubei and Henan," 26
MacIntyre, Alasdair, *After Virtue*, 19
Magnolia Flower in Blossom (1956), 189
male gaze, 169
Manchuria, 253n15
"man tilling, woman weaving," 126, 129–32, 139
manual labor: distinction between mental labor and, 7, 13, 149, 157, 159, 170, 198; patience and, 106; as suffering, 129. See also handicraft production; labor
Mao Dun, 19, 26–27, 217n5
Mao Zedong, 11–12, 51, 75; on "advantage of backwardness," 217n51; authority of, 249n72; global prestige, 251n101; human-tool continuum and, 237n146; industrialized countryside and, 152–53, 162, 168; on Long March, 255n50; "mass line" and, 136; "On the Mass Line," 105–6; "Oppose Book Worship," 134; personality, 88–90, 96, 233n70; "poor and blank" thesis, 184; "Return to Shaoshan," 147; on revolutionary successors, 197–98, 200–201, 204; socialist creativity and, 157; "Talks on Literature and Art in the Yan'an Forum," 102; on technology, 250n78; time consciousness, 234n89; Yan'an talks, 81, 102, 108–9, 110, 113, 116, 119, 124, 142, 168, 235n115
marriage: arranged, 34–38, 120–21, 128–29; disputes, 120–43, 239n27; national romance and, 143; regulations on, 36, 112–19, 143. See also courtship and dating; love
Marxism, 152–53, 155, 206

material prosperity, 5, 24, 81, 119, 159, 166, 210
material scarcity: patience and, 98; radical politics and, 81, 94–98; socialist labor and, 157, 159, 163, 167; water shortages in post-Mao era, 180–81. See also poverty
maternal love, 37–38
Ma Xiwu–Liu Qiao stories, 111, 125–43
Ma Xiwu Way of Adjudicating Cases, 113, 120–24
May Fourth new-culture movement, 8, 23–24, 50; antitraditionalism of, 21, 23; attacks on patriarchy, 37, 59 (see also patriarchal institutions); chaos of, 18–20; feminism and, 99; free love, 128; "going to the people," 227n86; homecoming fiction, 152; iconoclasm of, 35; individualism and, 31–32; intellectuals in, 50, 62–63; "man-eating ritual" slogan, 23, 27; romantic stories, 115; rural and, 11; vernacular, 46–47, 75 (see also rural vernacular); Yan'an popular culture and, 126. See also enlightenment discourse; Republican period
McGrath, Jason, 164
meaning, 138
mechanization, 151, 153–54, 159, 177, 196
media culture, 90. See also journalistic writings; print culture
Meisner, Maurice, 153
Mengzhen. See Fu Sinian
mental labor, distinction between manual labor and, 7, 13, 149, 157, 159, 170, 198. See also labor
Merkel-Hess, Kate, 45, 58, 61–62, 75
Merreti, Franco, 128
migration. See "going to the city"; "going to the countryside"; urban migration; urban-to-rural migration
Mittler, Barbara, 249n72
mobility: railway travel and, 189, 190–93; social, 28–29; upward, 151; of youth, 182–83, 255n50
mobilization, 178, 182–84, 186, 197, 205, 233n76, 241n58

modernity; creativity and, 155–56; development and, 1, 73; "going to the countryside" and, 1–9, 208; human-machine dynamic and, 185; industrial values and, 170; nature and, 155; rural and, 1–4, 208–11; sentiment and, 215n30

modernization, 3, 5, 147, 156, 160, 179, 183–84, 193, 206

morality, 18–19, 89, 157, 218n8

Moretti, Franco, 119, 150

Mote, F. W., 4

Muhlhahn, Klaus, 243n84

Mullaney, Thomas, 7

multimedia regime of governance, 111, 126, 139

Mulvey, Laura, 169

Murphey, Rhoads, 179

Musser, Charles, 188

narodnik movement (Russia), 6–7

national affairs, 151

national character, 223n17

national culture: print culture and, 58; and the rural, 4

national identity, 51–52, 206–7, 211; peasantry and, 6; rural industrial culture and, 14, 178–80

nationalism, 89; cities and, 29; citizenship training and, 228n126

Nationalist Party, 79

national-local duality, 20

national romance, 53

nation-building: communication and, 139; peasant political consciousness and, 62; railways and, 184, 187; socialist cinema and, 188; social-survey essays and, 23, 42; theatrical performances and, 72

native-place sentiment, 24, 29, 150, 154, 211, 217n7

native-soil fiction: emergence of, 8, 18; representations of folk in, 126, 219n30, 219n33; rural fiction and, 219n28; rural homecoming and, 20, 26–27, 29, 33; urban migration and, 220n53; vernacular fiction and, 216n44

nature: collective labor in, 167; human-nature relationship, 155–56. *See also* landscape

Needham, Joseph, 172, 250n87

neoliberalism, 209

New China Daily, 120, 123

New Culture Movement. *See* May Fourth new-culture movement

newspapers, 111–13, 126; Communist Party, 92; legal cases in, 239n27; love-law connection and, 120–24; national community and, 127–28; oral culture and, 240n45; storytelling and, 137–42

New Village Head (Zhang), 245n8

New Village Movement (Japan), 6–7, 215n28

New York Herald Tribune, 76

New Youth, 8, 11, 17–18, 20–27

nostalgia, 19–20, 29, 152, 208

Nurse's Diary, The, 186, 188–97, 204

Nussbaum, Martha C., 39, 63, 70

oath-taking, 197, 199, 203–4

Ogle, Vanessa, 93–94

Old House Association, 26

Old Well (1986), 180–81, 251n105

Ong, Walter, 52

opera, 64, 70, 74; local, 111, 126, 142–43; ritual and, 65

oral culture, 49, 54, 137–38, 143, 240n45

Orientalism, 233n76

"our young man" figure, 150

outdoor theater, 74, 86

Pang, Laikwan, 56

participant observation, 83, 85

participatory consciousness, 66–74

passion: collective labor and, 164, 169 (*see also* collective labor); revolution and, 98–99, 103–4, 108

pastoral life, 61, 98–99

paternalism, 24–26, 30

patience, 82, 98–109

patriarchal institutions: attacks on, 34, 37, 41–42, 59, 128; individualism and, 41; male gaze and, 169. *See also* family

patriotism, 8, 95, 198–99
peasants: as actors in spoken drama, 66; affective world of, 24–26 (*see also* affect; emotion); as backwards, 5, 8 (*see also* backwardness); characteristics of, 47–48, 50–53, 223n24; as collective national subject (*see* collective subjectivity); education and, 45; free love and, 39; morality and, 24–26; political consciousness, 62–74; poverty and, 21; in reform era, 256n62; revolution and, 7 (*see also* revolution and revolutionaries); as scholar-farmers, 48–53, 57, 75–76. *See also* farmers; villages
pedagogy, 74–75, 228n126
Peng Dehuai, 88
People's 1000-Character Literacy Primer, The, 75
People's Daily, The, 148, 155
People's Republic of China (PRC): accomplishments of, 159; film industry (*see* socialist cinema); internal colonization, 198; marriage laws in, 114–15, 143 (*see also* marriage); post-Mao era, 180–81, 187, 206, 209–11, 251n105; sovereignty, 180, 188. *See also* China; Mao Zedong; revolution; social engineering programs
Perry, Elizabeth, 201
physiognomy, 116, 127–28, 130, 168
play: functions of, 163–64; labor as, 150, 160–69, 178, 181; warfare as, 248n52
poetry, "gardens and fields," 61
political communities, 10
political consciousness, 62–74
political ideology, 138–39
political movements, 7
Popular Cinema, 168
popular culture, 110–11, 126
Popular Movies, 160
Popular Science, 158
poverty: rural, 60, 68, 184, 210; in Yan'an, 80, 95, 97. *See also* material scarcity
PRC. *See* People's Republic of China (PRC)

primers. *See* illustrated primers
primitiveness, 193
print culture, 58; revolution and, 90
productivity: creativity and, 159. *See also* agricultural productivity; efficiency; handicraft production
professionalism, 102–3
progress. *See* historical progress
propaganda: countryside and, 111; political culture and, 243n93; reportage literature and, 95; the rural and, 4, 86; socialist cinema and, 13, 188; socialist subjects and, 149
property rights, 67–68
Prospect and Future of the Village, The (Zhang), 153
public demonstrations, 140
public meetings, 133, 243n84
public trials, 121–23, 131, 136, 141
punctuality, 92–93

Qian Mu, 27
qiaogan (labor or work skillfully), 159, 171
Qing Empire, 61, 126, 187
quotidian details, 21, 57–58, 75, 200; communication and, 133, 135, 143; Mao and, 89; newspapers and, 125; revolution and, 101, 109; state-initiated homecoming and socialist industrialization, 151–52, 158, 186, 200, 206; in Yan'an, 81, 94–98

radical politics, 111; rural space and, 79–82. *See also* revolution
Railway Bodyguards (1960), 189
Railway Guerrilla (1956), 189
railway travel, 182–93, 203–7; awakening and, 252n6; documentary films on, 253n15; emotion and, 186–89, 203–4; geologists and, 198–99; global images of, 188; technology and, 256n60; in urban areas, 253n24; voluntary socialist subject and, 189–93
"raising standards," 110–11
Rancière, Jacques, 53, 73; *The Ignorant Schoolmaster*, 51

290 INDEX

reciprocity, 24
recognition, 33
Record of the Grand Historian, 21
Rectification campaign, 81, 105–6, 107, 234n83, 235n115
Red Army, 91, 96; Long March, 82–85, 110
Red Theater, 85–87
reformers, 1, 7, 10, 45, 208; national "illness" and, 51–52; theatrical performances and, 74 (*see also* theatrical performance/education). *See also* rural reconstruction
religion, 65
remoteness, 13–14, 182–86
renqing (human feeling), 30–31
reportage literature, 8, 83, 95, 112. *See also* journalistic writings
representation, 18; in documentary nonfiction, 83; history of, 10; reality and, 72
Republican period: chaos of, 11, 20; railway travel in, 192; vernacular and, 46. *See also* May Fourth new-culture movement
"return to the village" movement, 148
revolution and revolutionaries, 7, 79–109, 208; affect and, 98, 142–43 (*see also* affect); emotion and, 85–87, 98–99, 103–4, 108; local life and, 94–98; mobility and, 255n50; nonalienated rural industrialization and, 87–88 (*see also* labor); passion and, 98–99, 103–4, 108; patience and, 98–109; peasant political consciousness and, 62; rural space and, 11–12, 79–81; spatial crossing and, 1, 10 (*see also* "going to the countryside"); time consciousness and, 91–94; urban-to-rural transition, 12; utopianism in, 108–9; virtues of, 157. *See also* Yan'an
revolutionary literature, 12, 110–43; love-labor conjunction, 124–33; love-law conjunction, 112–24; point of view in, 236n135; popular propaganda culture, 111; storytelling and, 137–42; village soundscape and, 133–36
revolutionary successors, 197–99, 254n41
"revolution plus love," 101, 112
ritual, opera and, 65
"Robin Hood" narratives, 89
romantic love: agricultural field and, 126; labor and, 112; May Fourth movement and, 36–39; socialist industrial labor and, 162, 168–69, 172, 176–77. *See also* love
romantic stories, 114–15
rulers, harmony between farmers and, 132
rural areas: as aesthetic site, 3; approaches to, 9–14; modernity and, 1–9; modernized, 147–55 (*see also* rural industrialization); poverty in, 60, 68, 184, 210 (*see also* material scarcity); scholarship on, 2, 7–8; underemployment, 148. *See also* frontier region; "going to the countryside"; peasants; rural reconstruction movement; urban-to-rural migration; villages; wastelands; wilderness; Yan'an
rural fiction, 219n28. *See also* native-soil fiction
rural industrialization, 13; aesthetics, 147–50, 170–78; labor-as-play, 160–69; national identity and, 14, 178–80; nonalienated, 81, 87–88, 90, 108, 153, 178; socialist creativity and, 155–59; socialist homecoming and modernization, 147–55; start of, 245n4. *See also* development; socialist industrialization
rural reconstruction movement, 7, 10–11, 44–76, 215n37; global significance of, 76; literacy campaigns, 48–53; performative aspect of, 62; theatrical performances, 62–74; visual education and, 53–62
rural vernacular, 11; affective communication mode, 74–75 (*see also* affect); literacy campaigns and, 46–53; visual images and, 53–62, 72
Russia, *narodnik* (populist) movement, 6–7

Saneatsu Mushanokōji, 6
sanitary conditions, 97, 101–2. *See also* hygiene movements
Schiller, Friedrich, 64
Schivelbusch, Wolfgang, 187
scholar-farmers, 48–53, 57, 75–76
Schwarcz, Vera, 31
scientific dissemination, 158
scientific investigation, 198–99
Scott, James, 136, 154, 176
Selden, Mark, 156
self-reflexivity, 104–5
self-reliance and self-sufficiency, 149, 155, 158, 166, 170, 175, 177–78, 180
sensibility, 24
sentiment, 24; law and, 112, 143; limits of language and, 30–31; listening and, 135; modernity and, 215n30; native-place, 24, 29, 150, 154, 211, 217n7; railways and, 188; in rural reconstruction movement, 63; technology and, 177, 192–93. *See also* affect; emotion
Shaan-Gan-Ning border region, 79, 110, 113, 121, 129, 168
Shanghai, 87, 93, 182–83, 186, 209; industrialization in, 254n28; Japanese occupation of, 116; material culture, 117
Shanghai Girl, The (1957), 189
Shanghai Nursing School, 182, 189
Shaoshan, 147
Shen, Grace Yen, 199
Shih, Shu-mei, 46
short stories, 111
Shuanglong, 154
Sijiazhuang, 152
skilled crafts, 167–69
slideshows, 54. *See also* lantern slides
"small inventions," 158, 171–78
Smith, Arthur H., *Chinese Characteristics*, 115
Snow, Edgar, 112, 231n18; "Awakening the Masses in China," 76; "How Rural China Is Being Remade," 76, 229n139; *Red Star Over China*, 79–91, 94–98, 100–101, 108, 178, 231n17, 232n43
So, Richard Jean, 86, 138, 233n76

social anarchy, 18–19
social engineering programs, 8–10, 149–55; rural industrialization and, 13; urban-to-rural migration, 182–207
social hierarchies, 7; construction sites and, 206; interpersonal relationships and, 25–27, 29–32, 41–43, 59; May Fourth vernacular movement and, 46
social investigation, 44–45, 210; communication modes and, 121, 133–34; of legal cases, 111; in northwest China, 84. *See also* social-survey essays
socialist cinema, 149–51, 158, 160–69; international distribution, 247n42; nation-building and, 188; rural-subject films, categories of, 247n44; warfare as play in, 248n52
socialist industrialization, 10, 208; "artisanal as industrial," 150, 170–78; collective labor and, 13 (*see also* collective labor); in frontier regions, 14, 182–207; rural industry and, 87; spatial crossing and, 1 (*see also* "going to the countryside"). *See also* development; rural industrialization
socialist realism, 95, 160–61
socialist-realist gaze, 196, 254n38
social justice: Communist movement and, 88; emotion and, 67–74; theatrical performance/education and, 66–74
social mobility, 28–29
social movements, 7, 64
social science practitioners, 7
social-survey essays, 8, 11, 17–28, 42–43
sociology, 7–8, 18
Solomon, Richard, 67
Sommer, Doris, 132
Soviet Union, 197
spatial crossing. *See* "going to the countryside"
"speaking bitterness," 143, 244n109
spoken drama, 11, 47, 64–75, 127, 245n8. *See also* theatrical performance/education
stagnation, 80
Story of the Summer, The (1955), 151

storytelling, rural, 111, 126, 127, 137–43
street entertainment, 64
Strong, Anna Louise, 92
students: homecoming narratives and, 17–18, 29. *See also* youth
subaltern speech, 51–52, 89, 244n109
Su Li, 160
sundials, 93, 108, 234n90
Sun Yat-sen, 49, 60, 252n6
sympathy, 70. *See also* empathy

"taking root," 186, 197–204
Tang era, 84–85
Tang Xiaobing, 94, 133, 204, 205
Tao Jin, 194
Tao Lugong (Tao Menghe), 20–22, 28
Tao Xingzhi, 49, 229n136
Tao Yuanming, 5
Taylor, Charles, 32–33, 35, 216–17n46
teaching, 225n52, 225n58
technological "regression," 108
technologized visuality, 53–54, 72
technology: emotion and, 177, 205; in everyday life, 162–63; in frontier areas, 183; Mao on, 250n78; railways and, 256n60; sentiment and, 177, 192–93
theatrical performance/education, 45, 47; audience involvement, 62–74, 85–87; emotion and, 48, 63–74; empathy and, 62–74; outdoor stages, 74, 86; religion and, 65; vaudeville-style, 81, 86–87. *See also* spoken drama
Thousand Character Primer, The, 56
Tianjin, 152
Tibet, 199
Tie Ning, "Oh, Xiangxue," 256n60
time consciousness, 81, 91–94, 234nn89–90
Tolstoy, Leo, 7
Tong Lam, 23, 24, 222n4
traditional values, 57
Train No. 12 (1960), 189
translation, 89
transportation: awakening and, 252n6; modernization of, 13–14; rural, 108. *See also* railway travel; trucks

Trilling, Lionel, 34
triumphalist narrative, 192
trucks, 183, 196, 199–200, 205, 255n52
Tunnel Warfare (1965), 248n52

underdevelopment, 8, 148, 161, 183–86, 190. *See also* backwardness; development
Underwood, Doug, 233n77
unemployment, 36, 41–42, 148
united cultural line, 124–25
universality, 89–90, 94, 208
Universal Well-being Association, 26
"up to the mountains, down to the villages" movement, 183, 208
upward mobility, 151
urban areas: material culture of, 117; poverty in, 29, 36, 41–42; scholarship on, 2; unemployment in, 36, 41–42, 148
urban development and industrialization, 1, 5, 148–49, 209, 254n28
urban legends, 112
urban migration, 209, 220n53
urban-rural continuum, 4
urban-rural divide, 13, 148; hygiene and, 102; in post-Mao era, 209–11; railways and, 205; socialist homecoming and, 150
urban-rural integration, 211
urban-to-rural migration: by intellectuals, 44; patience and, 107–8; in post-Mao era, 209–11; by revolutionary youth, 99–101; time consciousness and, 90. *See also* rural reconstruction movement; social engineering programs
utopian-socialist communities, 6, 11, 108–9, 161; in frontier region, 186, 193–97. *See also* Yan'an

vaudeville, 81, 86–87
vernacular fiction, 216n44
vernacular language, 46. *See also* rural vernacular
victimhood, 20, 32
villages: backwardness and, 5, 8, 11 (*see*

also backwardness); culture in, 124–33 (*see also* revolutionary literature); governance, 133–36, 142–43; leisure time in, 25, 102; modernized model, 61; modern values and, 117; public trials in, 121–23, 131, 136, 141; rise of nation-state and, 3; social problems, 21; soundscape, 133–36; utopian, 60; youth and, 150–55. *See also* peasants
violence, 27, 161
visual education, 53–62
visual images, 47
visuality, technologized, 53–54, 72
vividness, 83, 90
Voice of the Village, The (1983), 206
voluntary socialist subjects, 189–93

waiting, 92
Wang, Ban, 95, 206
Wang, David Der-wei, 20
Wang Lingzhen, 38, 255n46
Wang Meng, "The Voice of the Spring," 256n60
Wang Shiwei, "The Wild Lily," 103, 105, 237n140
Wang Xiaoming, 209
Wang Zongyuan, "Sister Hui," 199
warfare as play, 248n52
wastelands, 183, 193
Water Margin, 25, 68, 70, 89, 141
water shortages, 180–81
weaving woman, 130
well digging, 180–81
Western journalism, 233n77
Western modernity, 18, 19, 179
West Jianyang, 74
White, Hayden, 89, 91
wilderness, 184–85, 194–97
Williams, Raymond, 2, 155–56
wives, rural, 39–42. *See also* marriage
Womack, Brantly, 79
women: abandoned rural wives, 39–42; authorial voice, 95–97; domestic labor and, 153–54; emancipation of, 112, 153, 240n38; literacy, 60; submissiveness, 40–41; victimization of, 27. *See also* "man tilling, woman weaving"; marriage
woodblock prints, 111, 122–23, 126
writing, 143; classical Chinese, 46, 54; instruction in, 57–58. *See also* literacy campaigns
Wu Liangping, 89
Wu Manyou, 129
Wuqi, 87

Xi'an, 84
Xian Xinghai, 92
Xiao Cheng, "The Social Situation in Part of Shanxi Province," 25–26, 30
Xiao Jun, "On Love and Patience among Comrades," 106
Xia Yan, 247n42
Xi Jinping, 209
Xing Yanzi, 151–52
Xinhua Daily, 240n38
Xinjiang, 182, 199
Xinyu Dong, 162–63
Xiong Foxi, 11, 45, 62–74, 87; *The Butcher*, 65–68; *Cross the River*, 67, 70–72, 246n8; *Driven to Revolt*, 67, 68–70
Xi River, 155
xuanchuan, 138, 141
Xu Qinwen, 31, 42; *My Old Home*, 33; "This Time's Leaving Home," 33–36

Yan'an, 79–143; Big Production Movement, 106, 129; communication modes in, 133–36; Communist base in, 10, 11–12, 79–91, 230n2; cultural policy, 110–43; foreign journalists in, 241n58; Forum on Literature and Art, 12, 105, 110; Internationalists, 234n83; journalistic writings on, 79–91, 94–98; literary writings on, 98–107; local life in, 94–98; time consciousness in, 91–94; time measurement, 234n90
Yan'an Peking Opera, 70
Yan Fu, 194
Yang, Mayfair, 31
Yang Cunbin, 72–73
yangge (folk dance), 64–65, 137

Yan Hairong, 209
Yan Yangchu. *See* Yen, James
Yan Yunxiang, 31
Yeh, Wen-hsin, 93
Yen, James (Yan Yangchu): on drama as educational tool, 64; educational background, 48; global mass-education movement, 229n134; illustrated primers and, 226n64; influence of, 76; lantern slides and, 225n52; Mao Zedong and, 75; May Fourth "going to the people" movement and, 227n86; rural reconstruction and literacy education, 11, 44–46, 48–57, 59–60, 62, 223n24, 229n139
"Yenan [Yan'an] Way," 156–57
Ye Shengtao, *School Master Ni Huanzhi*, 62–63
Ye Yuan, "Social Investigation," 23–25
Young Generation, The (1965), 186, 189, 197–204, 207, 255n52
Young People in Our Village, The (1959), 149–50, 160–79, 251n105; sequel (1963), 149–50, 170–78
youth: aspiring, 8, 12, 17, 99, 208; idealistic, 1, 190–93; mobility of, 182–83, 255n50; revolutionary, 88; socialist industrialization and, 13–14; village homecoming, 12, 150–55, 246n8, 251n105; as voluntary socialist subjects, 190–93

youxi (play or playfulness), 162–63
Yuan Jing: *Liu Qiao Seeking Justice*, 125–43; *The New Legend of Heroes and Heroines*, 125
Yu Dafu, 32; "A Supplement to Returning Home," 39; "Returning Home," 39; "Wisteria and Dodder," 39–42

Zhang, Zhen, 46–47
Zhang Ailing (Eileen Chang), 112, 116; *Floating Words*, 97; *The Golden Cangue*, 116; *Love in a Fallen City*, 116–18, 125
Zhang Ga the Soldier Boy (1964), 248n52
Zhang Guangyi, 159, 171
Zhang Henshui, *Beijing-Shanghai Express*, 253n24
Zhang Yuqing, 153
Zhang Zhen, 162, 171
Zhang Zuyin, "The Peasants in Zhenze," 21
Zhao Shuli, "The Marriage of Little Erhei," 111, 112–20, 125, 128, 132, 142
Zhou Enlai, 88
Zhou Yang, 168
Zhou Zuoren, "The Spirit of the New Village," 7
Zhu De, 88
Zhu Hongzhao, 92, 234n89
Zhu Rongji, 257n8